Sentence Skills
with Readings

Praise for *Sentence Skills with Readings*

"*Sentence Skills with Readings* is one of the most complete and thorough texts I've ever used in the basic writing classroom. The book works because it speaks to beginning students in a voice they understand with examples that have meaning in their lives."

Caryn L. Newburger, Austin Community College

"*Sentence Skills with Readings* connects with remedial students. . . . It is one of the most complete and thorough texts I've ever used in the basic writing classroom."

James De Ste Croix, Leeward Community College

"Here is the book you have been looking for to use with preparatory students. It is clear, complete, keeps its eye on writing as the ultimate goal and has provocative readings."

Dottie Burkhart, Davidson County Community College

"*Sentence Skills* is a down-to-earth, friendly text that doesn't intimidate developmental students yet gives them the essential grammar skills necessary to succeed in English 151."

Pam W. Feeney, Kellogg Community College

"After looking at all the texts that come across my desk for review, this is still the best one for our students."

Midge Shaw, Rogue Community College

"Strengths: thoroughness, completeness, versatility. Weaknesses: none. . . . Because it is so complete, it is perfect for the new teacher, or one who has just been assigned to a class. The seasoned teacher will enjoy the many features of the text and still have room to customize his/her class."

G. Jack Pond, Leeward Community College

Sentence Skills
with Readings
Third Edition

John Langan
Atlantic Cape Community College

Paul Langan

Boston   Burr Ridge, IL   Dubuque, IA   Madison, WI   New York   San Francisco   St. Louis
Bangkok   Bogotá   Caracas   Kuala Lumpur   Lisbon   London   Madrid   Mexico City
Milan   Montreal   New Delhi   Santiago   Seoul   Singapore   Sydney   Taipei   Toronto

The McGraw·Hill Companies

SENTENCE SKILLS WITH READINGS

2 3 4 5 6 7 8 9 0 FGR/FGR 0 9 8 7 6

ISBN-13: 978-0-07-301723-5 (student edition)
ISBN-10: 0-07-301723-X

ISBN-13: 978-0-07-301726-6 (annotated instructor's edition)
ISBN-10: 0-07-301726-4

Editor-in-chief: *Emily Barrosse*
Publisher: *Lisa Moore*
Senior sponsoring editor: *Alexis Walker*
Director of development: *Carla Samodulski*
Editorial assistant: *Jesse Hassenger*
Marketing manager: *Lori DeShazo*
Senior development editor, media: *Paul Banks*
Senior media producer: *Todd Vaccaro*
Project manager: *Leslie LaDow*
Lead production supervisor: *Randy Hurst*
Senior designer: *Cassandra Chu*
Cover and interior designer: *Glenda King*
Cover illustration: *Paul Turnbaugh*

This book was set in 11/13 Times Roman, PMS Color 286, by Electronic Publishing Services, Inc (TN), and printed on acid-free, 45# New Era Matte by Quebecor, Inc.

Library of Congress Cataloging-in-Publication Data

Langan, John, 1942–
    Sentence skills with readings / John Langan, Paul Langan.—3rd ed. Annotated instructor's ed.
        p.   cm. — (The Langan series)
    Includes index.
    ISBN 0-07-301723-X (soft cover : alk. paper)
    1. English language—Sentences—Problems, exercises, etc. 2. English language—Rhetoric—Problems, exercises, etc. 3. English language—Grammar—Problems, exercises, etc. 4. Report writing—Problems, exercises, etc. 5. College readers. I. Langan, Paul. II. Title.

PE1441.L356 2004
808'.0427—dc22   2004053071

www.mhhe.com

About the Authors

John Langan has taught reading and writing at Atlantic Cape Community College near Atlantic City, New Jersey, for over twenty-five years. The author of a popular series of college textbooks on both writing and reading, John enjoys the challenge of developing materials that teach skills in an especially clear and lively way. Before teaching, he earned advanced degrees in writing at Rutgers University and in reading at Rowan University. He also spent a year writing fiction that, he says, "is now at the back of a drawer waiting to be discovered and acclaimed posthumously." While in school, he supported himself by working as a truck driver, machinist, battery assembler, hospital attendant, and apple packer. John now lives with his wife, Judith Nadell, near Philadelphia. In addition to his wife and Philly sports teams, his passions include reading and turning on nonreaders to the pleasure and power of books. Through Townsend Press, his educational publishing company, he has developed the nonprofit "Townsend Library"—a collection of more than thirty new and classic stories that appeal to readers of all ages.

Paul Langan has tutored adult students in basic reading and writing skills since he was a college undergraduate. Beginning as a community college student, he went on to graduate with honors from La Salle University and later earned a Master's Degree in reading, writing, and literacy from the University of Pennsylvania. In addition to editing and authoring a popular series of young adult novels, Paul has taught composition at Camden County College. A new husband and father, he lives "a stone's throw" from Philadelphia and stubbornly clings to the hope that he will one day see a champion Philly sports team.

THE LANGAN SERIES

Essay-Level

College Writing Skills, Sixth Edition
ISBN: 0-07-287132-6 (Copyright © 2005)

College Writing Skills with Readings, Sixth Edition
ISBN: 0-07-287186-5 (Copyright © 2005)

College Writing Skills Online Edition
ISBN: 0-07-299417-7 (Copyright © 2005)

College Writing Skills with Readings Online Edition
ISBN: 0-07-299413-4 (Copyright © 2005)

Paragraph-Level

English Skills, Seventh Edition
ISBN: 0-07-238127-2 (Copyright © 2001)

English Skills with Readings, Fifth Edition
ISBN: 0-07-248003-3 (Copyright © 2002)

Sentence-Level

Sentence Skills: A Workbook for Writers, Form A, Seventh Edition
ISBN: 0-07-238132-9 (Copyright © 2003)

Sentence Skills: A Workbook for Writers, Form B, Seventh Edition
ISBN: 0-07-282087-X (Copyright © 2004)

Sentence Skills with Readings, Third Edition
ISBN: 0-07-301723-X (Copyright © 2005)

Grammar Review

English Brushup, Third Edition
ISBN: 0-07-281890-5 (Copyright © 2003)

Reading

Reading and Study Skills, Seventh Edition
ISBN: 0-07-244599-8 (Copyright © 2002)

Contents

Section 5: Word Use

Part Three: Reinforcement of the Skills   395

Appendixes

To the Instructor

Key Features of the Book

Sentence Skills with Readings will help students learn to write effectively. It is an all-in-one text that includes a basic rhetoric and compelling readings and gives full attention to grammar, punctuation, mechanics, and usage.

The book contains nine distinctive features to aid instructors and their students:

1 **Coverage of basic writing skills is exceptionally thorough.** The book pays special attention to fragments, run-ons, verbs, and other areas where students have serious problems. At the same time, a glance at the table of contents shows that the book treats skills (such as dictionary use and spelling improvement) not found in other texts. In addition, parts of the book are devoted to the basics of effective writing, to practice in editing and proofreading, and to achieving variety in sentences.

2 **The book has a clear and flexible format.** It is organized in four easy-to-use parts. Part One is a guide to the goals of effective writing followed by a series of activities to help students practice and master those goals. Part Two is a comprehensive treatment of the rules of grammar, mechanics, punctuation, and usage needed for clear writing. Part Three provides a series of mastery, editing, and proofreading tests to reinforce the sentence skills presented in Part Two. Finally, Part Four presents ten high-interest reading selections, followed by assignments that enable students to transfer the skills they have learned to realistic writing situations.

Since parts, sections, and chapters are self-contained, instructors can move easily from, for instance, a rhetorical principle in Part One to a grammar rule in Part Two to a mastery test in Part Three to a writing assignment in Part Four.

3 **Opening chapters deal with the writer's attitude, writing as a process, and the importance of specific details in writing.** In its opening pages, the book helps students recognize and deal with their attitude about writing—an

important part of learning to write well. In the pages that follow, students are encouraged to see writing as a multistage process that moves from prewriting to proofreading. Later, a series of activities helps students understand the nature of specific details and how to generate and use those details. As writing teachers well know, learning to write concretely is a key step for students to master in becoming effective writers.

4 **Practice exercises are numerous.** Most skills are reinforced by exercises, review tests, and mastery tests, as well as tests in the *Instructor's Manual.* For many of the skills in the book, there are over one hundred practice sentences.

5 **Practice materials are varied and lively.** In many basic writing texts, exercises are monotonous and dry, causing students to lose interest in the skills presented. In *Sentence Skills,* many exercises involve students in various ways. An inductive opening activity allows students to see what they already know about a given skill. Within chapters, students may be asked to underline answers, add words, generate their own sentences, or edit passages. The lively and engaging practice materials and readings in the book both maintain interest and help students appreciate the value of vigorous details in writing.

6 **Terminology is kept to a minimum.** In general, rules are explained using words students already know. A clause is a *word group;* a coordinating conjunction is a *joining word;* a nonrestrictive element is an *interrupter.* At the same time, traditional grammatical terms are mentioned briefly for students who learned them in the past and are comfortable seeing them again.

7 **Self-teaching is encouraged.** Students may check their answers to the introductory activities and the practice exercises in Part Two by referring to the answers in Appendix E. In this way, they are given the responsibility for teaching themselves. At the same time, to ensure that the answer key is used as a learning tool only, answers are not given for the review tests in Part Two or for any of the reinforcement tests in Part Three. These answers appear in the *Annotated Instructor's Edition* and the *Instructor's Manual;* they can be copied and handed out to students at the discretion of the instructor.

8 **Diagnostic and achievement tests are provided.** These tests appear in Appendixes C and D of the book. Each test may be given in two parts, the second of which provides instructors with a particularly detailed picture of a student's skill level.

9 **High-interest reading selections provide opportunities for writing.** The final part of the book contains ten high-interest readings followed by paragraph and essay assignments. These assignments allow students to explore interesting, relevant topics while practicing the basic writing principles learned in Part One and the sentence skills learned in Parts Two and Three.

Changes in the Third Edition

Here are the major changes in this new edition of *Sentence Skills with Readings*:

- Instructional hints have been added to the first item of nearly every practice activity in the book. These hints—set off in a second color—provide additional instructional support to students as they work to learn each sentence skill. Brief, practical, and specific, each hint serves as an instructional bridge, assisting students as they move from learning about a particular skill to applying it in an activity.

- The book features three new reading selections chosen for their wide appeal. In "The Most Hateful Words," the acclaimed author Amy Tan describes a healing event in her complex relationship with her mother. In an excerpt from his famous book, *The Road Less Traveled,* psychiatrist M. Scott Peck dramatizes one of his favorite themes: personal responsibility. And in "All the Good Things," a teacher tells a moving story about a special assignment she gave her students— one that forever changed their lives. Relevant and timeless, the three selections will engage students and provide a meaningful context for thinking, discussing, and learning.

- Five new "real-world" tests have been added to the Combined Editing Tests section of the book. These editing tests require students to apply their understanding of sentence skills to documents they will encounter—and need to write—outside the classroom: a job application form, two cover letters, and two résumés. By addressing sentence skills in a format that has direct relevance to students, these new tests underscore the importance of each lesson in the book.

- In addition to the five tests above, three other Combined Editing Tests have been added to the book, giving students ample practice in addressing some of the most common sentence-skills mistakes.

- Practice materials have been freshened throughout, with dozens of items added to ensure that the content is relevant to today's students.

Helpful Learning Aids Accompany the Book

Supplements for Instructors

- Access is provided to a toll-free support line dedicated to users and potential users of the Langan Series: 800-MCGRAWH (800-624-7294). E-mail inquiries may be sent to **langan@mcgraw-hill.com.**

- An *Annotated Instructor's Edition* (ISBN 0-07-301726-4) consists of the student text complete with answers to all activities and tests.

- The comprehensive *Instructor's Manual and Test Bank*, available online at **www.mhhe.com/langan** and on the *Instructor's Resource CD-ROM,* includes (1) a model syllabus along with suggestions for teaching the course, (2) an answer key, and (3) a complete set of additional mastery tests. The pages of the manual are 8½ × 11 inches, so that both the answer pages and the added mastery tests can be conveniently reproduced on copying machines.

- An *Online Learning Center* (**www.mhhe.com/langan**) offers a host of instructional aids and additional resources for instructors, including a comprehensive computerized test bank, the *Instructor's Manual and Test Bank,* online resources for writing instructors, and more.

- An *Instructor's CD-ROM* (ISBN 0-07-301724-8) offers all of the above supplements in a convenient offline format.

- *PageOut!* helps instructors create graphically pleasing and professional web pages for their courses, in addition to providing classroom management, collaborative learning, and content management tools. PageOut! is **FREE** to adopters of McGraw-Hill textbooks and learning materials. Learn more at **www.mhhe.com/pageout.**

Supplements for Students

- An *Online Learning Center* (**www.mhhe.com/langan**) offers a host of instructional aids and additional resources for students, including self-correcting exercises, writing activities for additional practice, a PowerPoint grammar tutorial, guides to doing research on the Internet and avoiding plagiarism, useful web links, and more.

- *AllWrite!* is an interactive, browser-based tutorial program that provides an online handbook, comprehensive diagnostic pre-tests and post-tests, plus extensive practice exercises in every area. Throughout the text, marginal icons, or Media Links, alert students to additional help in AllWrite.

- *Sentence Skills with Readings Virtual Workbook* (ISBN 0-07-312330-7) includes additional practices and tests. Icons in the margin let students know when they can find an additional activity in the *Virtual Workbook.*

You can contact your local McGraw-Hill representative or consult McGraw-Hill's website at **www.mhhe.com/english** for more information on the supplements that accompany *Sentence Skills with Readings,* Third Edition.

Dictionary and Vocabulary Resources

- *Random House Webster's College Dictionary* (ISBN 0-07-240011-0) This authoritative dictionary includes over 160,000 entries and 175,000 definitions. The most commonly used definitions are always listed first, so students can find what they need quickly.

- *The Merriam-Webster Dictionary* (ISBN 0-07-310057-9) Based on the best-selling *Merriam-Webster's Collegiate Dictionary,* this paperback version contains over 70,000 definitions.

- *The Merriam-Webster Thesaurus* (ISBN 0-07-310067-6) This handy paperback thesaurus contains over 157,000 synonyms, antonyms, related and contrasted words, and idioms.

- *Merriam-Webster's Vocabulary Builder* (ISBN 0-07-310069-2) This handy paperback introduces 3,000 words and includes quizzes to test progress.

- *Merriam-Webster's Notebook Dictionary* (ISBN 0-07-299091-0) An extremely concise reference to the words that form the core of English vocabulary, this popular dictionary, conveniently designed for 3-ring binders, provides words and information at students' fingertips.

- *Merriam-Webster's Notebook Thesaurus* (ISBN 0-07-310068-4) Conveniently designed for 3-ring binders, this thesaurus helps the student search for words they might need today. It provides concise, clear guidance for over 157,000 word choices.

- *Merriam-Webster's Collegiate Dictionary and Thesaurus,* Electronic Edition (ISBN 0-07-310070-6) Available on CD-ROM, this online dictionary contains thousands of new words and meanings from all areas of human endeavor, including electronic technology, the sciences, and popular culture.

Acknowledgments

Reviewers who have contributed to this edition through their helpful comments include

Tori Bula, Richland Community College

Dottie Burkhart, Davidson County Community College

James De Ste Croix, Leeward Community College

Pam Feeney, Kellogg Community College

Dawn Leonard, Charleston Southern University

Caryn Newburger, Austin Community College

G. Jack Pond, Leeward Community College

Midge Shaw, Rogue Community College

We owe thanks as well for the support provided by Carla Samodulski, Alexis Walker, and Paul Banks at McGraw-Hill. And we acknowledge people who have assisted in previous editions: Eliza Comodromos, Janet M. Goldstein, Beth Johnson, and Carole Mohr. With the help of others, *Sentence Skills with Readings* is a much better book than we could have managed by ourselves.

John Langan
Paul Langan

Sentence Skills
with Readings

Part One

Effective Writing

Introduction

Part One is a guide to the goals of effective writing followed by a series of activities to help you practice and master these goals. Begin with the introductory chapter, which makes clear the reasons for learning sentence skills. Then read the second chapter carefully; it presents all the essentials you need to know to become an effective writer. Finally, work through the series of activities in the third chapter. Your instructor may direct you to certain exercises, depending on your needs. After completing the activities, you'll be ready to take on the paragraph and essay writing assignments at the end of the chapter.

At the same time that you are writing papers, start working through the sentence skills in Parts Two and Three of the book. Practicing the sentence skills in the context of actual writing assignments is the surest way to master the rules of grammar, mechanics, punctuation, and usage.

Note: A writing progress chart on pages 704–705 (in Appendix F) will help you track your performance.

1 Learning Sentence Skills

Why Learn Sentence Skills?

Why should someone planning a career as a nurse have to learn sentence skills? Why should an accounting major have to pass a competency test in grammar as part of a college education? Why should a potential physical therapist or graphic artist or computer programmer have to spend hours on the rules of English? Perhaps you are asking questions like these after finding yourself in a class with this book. On the other hand, perhaps you *know* you need to strengthen basic writing skills, even though you may be unclear about the specific ways the skills will be of use to you. Whatever your views, you should understand why sentence skills—all the rules that make up standard English—are so important.

Clear Communication

Standard English, or "language by the book," is needed to communicate your thoughts to others with a minimal amount of distortion and misinterpretation. Knowing the traditional rules of grammar, punctuation, and usage will help you write clear sentences when communicating with others. You may have heard of the party game in which one person whispers a message to the next person; the message is passed, in turn, along a line of several other people. By the time the last person in line is asked to give the message aloud, it is usually so garbled and inaccurate that it barely resembles the original. Written communication in some form of English other than standard English carries the same potential for disaster.

To see how important standard English is to written communication, examine the pairs of sentences on the following pages and answer the questions in each case.

3

1. Which sentence indicates that there might be a plot against Ted?

   a. We should leave Ted. These fumes might be poisonous.

   b. We should leave, Ted. These fumes might be poisonous.

2. Which sentence encourages self-mutilation?

   a. Leave your paper and hand in the dissecting kit.

   b. Leave your paper, and hand in the dissecting kit.

3. Which sentence indicates that the writer has a weak grasp of geography?

   a. As a child, I lived in Lake Worth, which is close to Palm Beach and Alaska.

   b. As a child, I lived in Lake Worth, which is close to Palm Beach, and Alaska.

4. In which sentence does the dog warden seem dangerous?

   a. Foaming at the mouth, the dog warden picked up the stray.

   b. Foaming at the mouth, the stray was picked up by the dog warden.

5. Which announcer was probably fired from the job?

   a. Outside the Academy Awards theater, the announcer called the guests names as they arrived.

   b. Outside the Academy Awards theater, the announcer called the guests' names as they arrived.

6. Below are the opening lines of two students' exam essays. Which student seems likely to earn a higher grade?

   a. Defense mechanisms is the way people hides their inner feelings and deals with stress. There is several types that we use to be protecting our true feelings.

   b. Defense mechanisms are the methods people use to cope with stress. Using a defense mechanism allows a person to hide his or her real desires and goals.

7. The following lines are taken from two English papers. Which student seems likely to earn a higher grade?

   a. A big problem on this campus is apathy, students don't participate in college activities. Such as clubs, student government, and plays.

   b. The most pressing problem on campus is the disgraceful state of the student lounge area. The floor is dirty, the chairs are torn, and the ceiling leaks.

Continued

8. The following sentences are taken from reports by two employees. Which worker is more likely to be promoted?

   a. The spring line failed by 20 percent in the meeting of projected profit expectations. Which were issued in January of this year.

   b. Profits from our spring line were disappointing. They fell 20 percent short of January's predictions.

9. The following paragraphs are taken from two job application letters. Which applicant would you favor?

   a. Let me say in closing that their are an array of personal qualities I have presented in this letter, together, these make me hopeful of being interviewed for this attraktive position.

      sincerely yours'

      Brian Davis

   b. I feel I have the qualifications needed to do an excellent job as assistant manager of the jewelry department at Horton's. I look forward to discussing the position further at a personal interview.

      Sincerely yours,

      Richard O'Keeney

In each case, the first choice (*a*) contains sentence-skills mistakes. These mistakes range from missing or misplaced commas to misspellings to wordy or pretentious language. As a result of these mistakes, clear communication cannot occur—and misunderstandings, lower grades, and missed job opportunities are probable results. The point, then, is that all the rules that make up standard written English should be a priority if you want your writing to be clear and effective.

Success in College

Standard English is essential if you want to succeed in college. Any report, paper, review, essay exam, or assignment you are responsible for should be written in the best standard English you can produce. If you don't do this, it won't matter how fine your ideas are or how hard you worked—most likely, you will receive a lower grade than you would otherwise deserve. In addition, because standard English requires you to express your thoughts in precise, clear sentences, training yourself to follow the rules can help you think more logically. The basic logic you learn to practice at the sentence level will help as you work to produce well-reasoned papers in all your subjects.

Success at Work

Knowing standard English will also help you achieve success on the job. Studies have found repeatedly that skillful communication, more than any other factor, is the key to job satisfaction and steady career progress. A solid understanding of standard English is a basic part of this vital ability to communicate. Moreover, most experts agree that we are now living in an "age of information"—a time when people who use language skillfully have a great advantage over those who do not. Fewer of us will be working in factories or at other types of manual labor. Many more of us will be working with information in various forms—accumulating it, processing it, analyzing it. No matter what kind of job you are preparing yourself for, technical or not, you will need to know standard English to keep pace with this new age. Otherwise, you are likely to be left behind, limited to low-paying jobs that offer few opportunities or financial rewards.

Success in Everyday Life

Standard English will help you succeed not just at school and work but in everyday life as well. It will help you feel more comfortable, for example, in writing letters to friends and relatives. It will enable you to write effective notes to your children's schools. It will help you get action when you write a letter of complaint to a company about a product. It will allow you to write letters inquiring about bills—hospital, medical, utility, or legal—or about any kind of service. To put it simply, in our daily lives, those who can use and write standard English have more power than those who cannot.

How This Book Is Organized

- A good way to get a quick sense of any book is to turn to the table of contents. By referring to pages vii–xi, you will see that the book is organized into four basic parts. What are they?

  _____

  _____

  _____

  _____

- In Part One, the final section of Chapter 2 describes how a _____ can help in the writing process.

- Part Two deals with sentence skills. The first section is "Sentences." How many sections (skills areas) are covered in all? Count them. _____

- Part Three reinforces the skills presented in Part Two. What are the four kinds of reinforcement activities in Part Three?

  _____

  _____

  _____

  _____

- Turn to the introduction to Part Four to learn the purpose of that part of the book and write the purpose here: _____

  _____

  _____

- Helpful charts in the book include (*fill in the missing words*) the _____ _____ on the inside front cover, the _____ charts in Appendix F, and the _____ of sentence skills on the inside back cover.

- Finally, the six appendixes at the end of the book are:

  _____

  _____

  _____

How to Use This Book

Here is a way to use *Sentence Skills with Readings*. First, read and work through Part One, Effective Writing—a guide to the goals of effective writing followed by a series of activities to help you practice and master these goals. Your instructor may direct you to certain activities, depending on your needs.

Second, take the diagnostic test on pages 667–672. By analyzing which sections of the test give you trouble, you will discover which skills you need to concentrate on. When you turn to an individual skill in Part Two, begin by reading and thinking about the introductory activity. Often, you will be pleasantly surprised to find that you know more about this area of English than you thought you did. After all, you have probably been speaking English with fluency and ease for many years; you have an instinctive knowledge of how the language works. This knowledge gives you a solid base for refining your skills.

Your third step is to work on the skills in Part Two by reading the explanations and completing the practices. You can check your answers to each practice activity in this part by turning to the answer key at the back of the book (Appendix E). Try to figure out *why* you got some answers wrong—you want to uncover any weak spots in your understanding.

Your next step is to use the review tests at the ends of chapters in Part Two to evaluate your understanding of a skill in its entirety. Your instructor may also ask you to take the mastery tests or other reinforcement tests in Part Three of the book. To help ensure that you take the time needed to learn each skill thoroughly, the answers to these tests are *not* in the answer key.

Finally, the readings and writing assignments in Part Four are an important part of the book. The readings will motivate and inform you as well as give you practice in reading comprehension. The related writing assignments are crucial. To make standard English an everyday part of your writing, you must write not just single sentences but paragraphs and essays. The writing assignments will prove to you that clear, logical writing hinges on error-free sentences. You will see how the sentence skills you are practicing "fit in" and contribute to the construction of a sustained piece of writing. In the world of sports, athletes spend many days refining the small moves—serves, backhands, pitches, layups—so that they can reach their larger objective of winning the game. In the same way, you must work intently on writing clear sentences in order to produce effective papers.

The emphasis in this book is, nevertheless, on writing clear, error-free sentences as well as on composition. And the heart of the book is the practice material that helps reinforce the sentence skills you learn. A great deal of effort has been taken to make the practices lively and engaging and to avoid the dull, repetitive skills work that has given grammar books such a bad reputation. This text will help you stay interested as you work on the rules of English that you need to learn. The rest is a matter of your personal determination and hard work. If you decide—and only you can decide—that effective writing is important to your school and career goals and that you want to learn the basic skills needed to write clearly and effectively, this book will help you reach those goals.

2 A Brief Guide to Effective Writing

This chapter and Chapter 3 will show you how to write effective paragraphs and essays. The following questions will be answered in turn:

1 Why does your attitude toward writing matter?

2 What is a paragraph?

3 What are the goals of effective writing?

4 How do you reach the goals of effective writing?

5 What is an essay?

6 What are the parts of an essay?

7 How can a computer help?

Why Does Your Attitude toward Writing Matter?

Your attitude toward writing is an important part of learning to write well. To get a sense of just how you feel about writing, read the following statements. Put a check beside those statements with which you agree. (This activity is not a test, so try to be as honest as possible.)

_____   1. A good writer should be able to sit down and write a paper straight through without stopping.

_____   2. Writing is a skill that anyone can learn with practice.

_____   3. I'll never be good at writing because I make too many mistakes in spelling, grammar, and punctuation.

_____   4. Because I dislike writing, I always start a paper at the last possible minute.

_____   5. I've always done poorly in English, and I don't expect that to change.

Now read the following comments about these five statements. The comments will help you see if your attitude is hurting or helping your efforts to become a better writer.

1   *A good writer should be able to sit down and write a paper straight through without stopping.*

The statement is *false*. Writing is, in fact, a process. It is done not in one easy step but in a series of steps, and seldom at one sitting. If you cannot do a paper all at once, that simply means you are like most of the other people on the planet. It is harmful to carry around the false idea that writing should be an easy matter.

2   *Writing is a skill that anyone can learn with practice.*

This statement is *absolutely true*. Writing is a skill, like driving or word processing, that you can master with hard work. If you want to learn to write, you can. It is as simple as that. If you believe this, you are ready to learn how to become a competent writer.

Some people hold the false belief that writing is a natural gift which some have and others do not. Because of this belief, they never make a truly honest effort to learn to write—and so they never learn.

3   *I'll never be good at writing because I make too many mistakes in spelling, grammar, and punctuation.*

The first concern in good writing should be *content*—what you have to say. Your ideas and feelings are what matter most. You should not worry about spelling, grammar, and punctuation while working on content.

Unfortunately, some people are so self-conscious about making mistakes that they do not focus on what they want to say. They need to realize that a paper is best done in stages and that the rules can and should wait until a later stage in the writing process. Through review and practice, you will eventually learn how to follow the rules with confidence.

4   *Because I dislike writing, I always start a paper at the last possible minute.*

This is all too common. You feel you are *going to* do poorly, and then your behavior ensures that you *will* do poorly! Your attitude is so negative that you defeat yourself—not even allowing enough time to really try.

Again, what you need to realize is that writing is a process. Because it is done in steps, you don't have to get it right all at once. Just get started well in advance. If you allow yourself enough time, you'll find a way to make a paper come together.

5 *I've always done poorly in English, and I don't expect that to change.*

How you may have performed in the *past* does not control how you can perform in the *present*. Even if you did poorly in English in high school, it is in your power to make this one of your best subjects in college. If you believe writing can be learned, and if you work hard at it, you *will* become a better writer.

In brief, your attitude is crucial. If you believe you are a poor writer and always will be, chances are you will not improve. If you realize you can become a better writer, chances are you will improve. Depending on how you allow yourself to think, you can be your own best friend or your own worst enemy.

What Is a Paragraph?

A *paragraph* is a series of sentences about one main idea, or *point*. A paragraph typically starts with a point, and the rest of the paragraph provides specific details to support and develop that point.

Consider the following paragraph, written by a student named Gary Callahan.

Returning to School

Starting college at age twenty-nine was difficult. For one thing, I did not have much support from my parents and friends. My father asked, "Didn't you get dumped on enough in high school? Why go back for more?" My mother worried about where the money would come from. My friends seemed threatened. "Hey, there's the college man," they would say when they saw me. Another reason that starting college was hard was that I had bad memories of school. I had spent years of my life sitting in classrooms completely bored, watching clocks tick ever so slowly toward the final bell. When I was not bored, I was afraid of being embarrassed. Once a teacher called on me and then said, "Ah, forget it, Callahan," when he realized I did not know the answer. Finally, I soon learned that college would give me little time with my family. After work every day, I have just an hour and ten minutes to eat and spend time with my wife and daughter before going off to class. When I get back, my daughter is in bed, and my wife and I have only a little time together. Then the weekends go by quickly, with all the homework I have to do. But I am going to persist because I believe a better life awaits me with a college degree.

The preceding paragraph, like many effective paragraphs, starts by stating a main idea, or point. A *point* is a general idea that contains an opinion. In this case, the point is that starting college at age twenty-nine was not easy.

In our everyday lives, we constantly make points about all kinds of matters. We express all kinds of opinions: "That was a terrible movie." "My psychology instructor is the best teacher I have ever had." "My sister is a generous person." "Eating at that restaurant was a mistake." "That team should win the playoff game." "Waitressing is the worst job I ever had." "Our state should allow the death penalty." "Cigarette smoking should be banned everywhere." In *talking* to people, we don't always give the reasons for our opinions. But in *writing,* we *must* provide reasons to support our ideas. Only by supplying solid evidence for any point that we make can we communicate effectively with readers.

An effective paragraph, then, must not only make a point but support it with *specific evidence*—reasons, examples, and other details. Such specifics help prove to readers that the point is reasonable. Even if readers do not agree with the writer, at least they have in front of them the evidence on which the writer has based his or her opinion. Readers are like juries; they want to see the evidence so that they can make their own judgments.

Take a moment now to examine the evidence that Gary has provided to back up his point about starting college at twenty-nine. Complete the following outline of Gary's paragraph by summarizing in a few words his reasons and the details that develop them. The first reason and its supporting details are summarized for you as an example.

Point: Starting college at age twenty-nine was difficult.

Reason 1: Little support from parents and friends
Details that develop reason 1: Father asked why I wanted to be dumped on again, mother worried about tuition money, friends seemed threatened

Reason 2: _____

Details that develop reason 2: _____

_____

Reason 3: _____

Details that develop reason 3: _____

_____

As the outline makes clear, Gary provides three reasons to support his point about starting college at twenty-nine: (1) he had little support from his friends or parents, (2) he had bad memories of school, and (3) college left him little time with his family. Gary also provides vivid details to back up each of his three reasons. His reasons and descriptive details enable readers to see why he feels that starting college at twenty-nine was difficult.

To write an effective paragraph, then, aim to do what Gary has done: begin by making a point, and then go on to support that point with specific evidence. Finally, like Gary, end your paper with a sentence that rounds off the paragraph and provides a sense of completion.

What Are the Goals of Effective Writing?

Now that you have considered an effective student paragraph, it is time to look at four goals of effective writing:

Goal 1: Make a Point

It is often best to state your point in the first sentence of your paper, just as Gary does in his paragraph about returning to school. The sentence that expresses the main idea, or point, of a paragraph is called the *topic sentence.* Your paper will be unified if you make sure that all the details support the point in your topic sentence. Activities on pages 44–48 in Chapter 3 will help you learn how to write a topic sentence.

Goal 2: Support the Point

To support your point, you need to provide specific reasons, examples, and other details that explain and develop it. The more precise and particular your supporting details are, the better your readers can "see," "hear," and "feel" them. Activities on pages 39–44 and 48–60 in Chapter 3 will help you learn how to be specific in your writing.

Goal 3: Organize the Support

You will find it helpful to learn two common ways of organizing support in a paragraph—*listing order* and *time order.* You should also learn the signal words, known as *transitions,* that increase the effectiveness of each method.

Listing Order: The writer can organize supporting evidence in a paper by providing a list of two or more reasons, examples, or details. Often the most important or interesting item is saved for last because the reader is most likely to remember the last thing read.

Transition words that indicate listing order include the following:

one	second	also	next	last of all
for one thing	third	another	moreover	finally
first of all	next	in addition	furthermore	

The paragraph about starting college uses a listing order: it lists three reasons why starting college at twenty-nine is not easy, and each of those three reasons is introduced by one of the above transitions. In the spaces below, write in the three transitions:

_____   _____   _____

The first reason in the paragraph about starting college is introduced with *for one thing,* the second reason by *another,* and the third reason by *finally.*

Time Order: When a writer uses time order, supporting details are presented in the order in which they occurred. *First* this happened; *next* this; *after* that, this; and so on. Many paragraphs, especially paragraphs that tell a story or give a series of directions, are organized in a time order.
   Transition words that show time relationships include the following:

first	before	after	when	then
next	during	now	while	until
as	soon	later	often	finally

Read the paragraph below, which is organized in time order. See if you can underline the six transition words that show the time relationships.

Della had a sad experience while driving home last night. She traveled along the dark, winding road that led toward her home. She was only two miles from her house when she noticed a glimmer of light in the road. The next thing she knew, she heard a sickening thud and realized she had struck an animal. The light, she realized, had been its eyes reflected in her car's headlights. Della stopped the car and ran back to see what she had hit. It was a handsome cocker spaniel, with blond fur and long ears. As she bent over the still form, she realized there was nothing to be done. The dog was dead. Della searched the dog for a collar and tags. There was nothing. Before leaving, she walked to several nearby houses, asking if anyone knew who owned the dog. No one did. Finally Della gave up and drove on. She was sad to leave someone's pet lying there alone.

The main point of the paragraph is stated in its first sentence: "Della had a sad experience while driving home last night." The support for this point is all the details of Della's experience. Those details are presented in the order in which they occurred. The time relationships are highlighted by these transitions: *while, when, next, as, before,* and *finally.*

More about Transitions: Transitions are words and phrases that indicate relationships between ideas. They are like signposts that guide travelers, showing them how to move smoothly from one spot to the next. Be sure to take advantage of transitions. They will help organize and connect your ideas, and they will help your readers follow the direction of your thoughts.

To see how transitions help, put a check beside the item in each pair that is easier to read and understand.

Pair A

_____ One way to stay in shape is to eat low-calorie, low-fat foods. A good strategy is to walk or jog at least twenty minutes four times a week.

_____ One way to stay in shape is to eat low-calorie, low-fat foods. Another good strategy is to walk or jog at least twenty minutes four times a week.

Pair B

_____ I begin each study session by going to a quiet place and setting out my textbook, pen, and notebook. I check my assignment book to see what I have to read.

_____ I begin each study session by going to a quiet place and setting out my textbook, pen, and notebook. Then I check my assignment book to see what I have to read.

In each pair, the second item is easier to read and understand. In pair A, the listing word *another* makes it clear that the writer is going on to a second way to stay in shape. In pair B, the time word *then* makes the relationship between the sentences clear. The writer first sets out the textbook and a pen and notebook and *then* checks an assignment book to see what to do.

Activities on pages 61–65 will give you practice in the use of listing order and time order, as well as transitions, to organize the supporting details of a paragraph.

Goal 4: Write Error-Free Sentences

If you use correct spelling and follow the rules of grammar, punctuation, and usage, your sentences will be clear and well written. But by no means must you have all that information in your head. Even the best of writers need to use reference materials to be sure their writing is correct. So when you write your papers, keep a good dictionary and grammar handbook nearby.

In general, however, save them for after you've gotten your ideas firmly down in writing. You'll see in the next part of this guide that Gary made a number of sentence errors as he worked on his paragraph. But he simply ignored them until he got to a later draft of his paper, when there would be time enough to make the needed corrections.

How Do You Reach the Goals of Effective Writing?

Even professional writers do not sit down and write a paper automatically, in one draft. Instead, they have to work on it a step at a time. Writing a paper is a process that can be divided into the following steps:

- *Step 1:* Getting Started through Prewriting
- *Step 2:* Preparing a Scratch Outline
- *Step 3:* Writing the First Draft
- *Step 4:* Revising
- *Step 5:* Editing and Proofreading

These steps are described on the following pages.

Step 1: Getting Started through Prewriting

What you need to learn first are strategies for working on a paper. These strategies will help you do the thinking needed to figure out both the point you want to make and the support you have for that point.

There are several *prewriting strategies*—strategies you use before writing the first draft of your paper:

- Freewriting
- Questioning
- Clustering
- Making a list

Freewriting: *Freewriting* is just sitting down and writing whatever comes into your mind about a topic. Do this for ten minutes or so. Write without stopping and without worrying at all about spelling, grammar, or the like. Simply get down on paper all the information about the topic that occurs to you.

Here is the freewriting Gary did on his problems with returning to school. Gary had been given the assignment "Write about a problem you are facing at the present time." Gary felt right away that he could write about his college situation. He began prewriting as a way to explore and generate details on his topic.

Example of Freewriting

One thing I want to write about is going back to school. At age twenty-nine. A lot to deal with. I sometimes wonder if Im nuts to try to do this or just stupid. I had to deal with my folks when I decided. My dad hated school. He knew when to quit, I'll say that for him. But he doesn't understand Im different. I have a right to my own life. And I want to better myself. He teases me alot. Says things like didnt you get dumped on enough in high school, why go back for more. My mom doesnt understand either. Just keeps worring about where the money was coming from. Then my friends. They make fun of me. Also my wife has to do more of the heavy house stuff because I'm out so much. Getting back to my friends, they say dumb things to get my goat. Like calling me the college man or saying ooh, we'd better watch our grammer. Sometimes I think my dads right, school was no fun for me. Spent years just sitting in class waiting for final bell so I could escape. Teachers didnt help me or take an intrest, some of them made me feel like a real loser. Now things are different and I like most of my teachers. I can talk to the teacher after class or to ask questions if I'm confused. But I really need more time to spend with family, I hardly see them any more. What I am doing is hard all round for them and me.

Notice that there are problems with spelling, grammar, and punctuation in Gary's freewriting. Gary is not worried about such matters, nor should he be. He is just concentrating on getting ideas and details down on paper. He knows that it is best to focus on one thing at a time. At this stage, he just wants to write out thoughts as they come to him, to do some thinking on paper.

You should take the same approach when freewriting: explore your topic without worrying at all about being "correct." Figuring out what you want to say should have all your attention in this early stage of the writing process.

Questioning: *Questioning* means that you think about your topic by writing down a series of questions and answers about it. Your questions can start with words like *what, when, where, why,* and *how.*

Here are some questions that Gary might have asked while developing his paper, as well as some answers to those questions.

Example of Questioning

Why do I have a problem with returning to school? My parents and friends don't support me.

How do they not support me? Dad asks why I want to be dumped on more. Mom is upset because college costs lots of money. Friends tease me about being a college man.

When do they not support me? When I go to my parents' home for Friday night visits, when my friends see me walking toward them.

Where do I have this problem? At home, where I barely see my wife and daughter before having to go to class, and where I have to let my wife do house things on weekends while I'm studying.

Why else do I have this problem? High school was bad experience.

What details back up the idea that high school was bad experience? Sat in class bored, couldn't wait to get out, teachers didn't help me. One embarrassed me when I didn't know the answer.

ALLWRITE!

2.3e

Clustering: Clustering is another prewriting strategy that can be used to generate material for a paper. It is helpful for people who like to do their thinking in a visual way.

In *clustering*, you begin by stating your subject in a few words in the center of a blank sheet of paper. Then as ideas come to you, put them in ovals, boxes, or circles around the subject, and draw lines to connect them to the subject. Put minor ideas or details in smaller boxes or circles, and also use connecting lines to show how they relate.

Keep in mind that there is no right or wrong way of clustering. It is a way to think on paper about how various ideas and details relate to one another. Below is an example of clustering that Gary might have done to develop his idea.

Example of Clustering

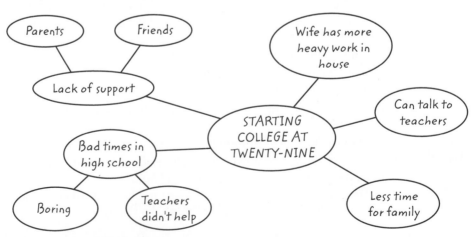

Making a List: In *making a list*—a prewriting strategy also known as *listing, list making,* and *brainstorming*—you make a list of ideas and details that could go into your paper. Simply pile these items up, one after another, without worrying about putting them in any special order. Try to accumulate as many details as you can think of.

After Gary did his freewriting about returning to school, he made up the list of details shown below.

Example of Listing

parents give me hard time when they see me

Dad hated school

Dad quit school after eighth grade

Dad says I was dumped on enough in high school

Dad asks why I want to go back for more

Mom also doesnt understand

keeps asking how Ill pay for it

friends give me a hard time too

friends call me college man

say they have to watch their grammar

my wife has more heavy work around the house

also high school had been no fun for me

just sat in class after class

couldnt wait for final bell to ring

wanted to escape

teachers didnt help me

teachers didnt take an interest in me

one called on me, then told me to forget it

I felt like a real loser

I didnt want to go back to his class

now I'm more sure of myself

OK not to know an answer

talk to teachers after class

job plus schoolwork take all my time

get home late, then rush through dinner

then spend evening studying

even have to do homework on weekends

One detail led to another as Gary expanded his list. Slowly but surely, more supporting material emerged that he could use in developing his paper. By the time he had finished his list, he was ready to plan an outline of his paragraph and to write his first draft.

Notice that in making a list, as in freewriting, details are included that will not actually end up in the final paragraph. Gary decided later not to develop the idea that his wife now has more heavy work to do in the house. And he realized that several of his details were about why school is easier in college ("now I'm more sure of myself," "OK not to know an answer," and "talk to teachers after class"); such details were not relevant to his point.

It is natural for a number of such extra or unrelated details to appear as part of the prewriting process. The goal of prewriting is to get a lot of information down on paper. You can then add to, shape, and subtract from your raw material as you take your paper through the series of writing drafts.

Important Points about Prewriting Strategies: Some writers may use only one of the prewriting strategies described here. Others may use bits and pieces of all four strategies. Any one strategy can lead to another. Freewriting may lead to questioning or clustering, which may then lead to a list. Or a writer may start with a list and then use freewriting or questioning to develop items on the list. During this early stage of the writing process, as you do your thinking on paper, anything goes. You should not expect a straight-line progression from the beginning to the end of your paper. Instead, there probably will be a constant moving back and forth as you work to discover your point and decide just how you will develop it.

Keep in mind that prewriting can also help you choose from among several topics. Gary might not have been so sure about which problem to write about. Then he could have made a list of possible topics—areas in his life in which he has had problems. After selecting two or three topics from the list, he could have done some prewriting on each to see which seemed most promising. After finding a likely topic, Gary would have continued with his prewriting activities until he had a solid main point and plenty of support.

Finally, remember that you are not ready to begin writing a paper until you know your main point and many of the details that can be used to support it. Don't rush through prewriting. It's better to spend more time on this stage than to waste time writing a paragraph for which you have no solid point and not enough interesting support.

Step 2: Preparing a Scratch Outline

A *scratch outline* is a brief plan for a paragraph. It shows at a glance the point of the paragraph and the main support for that point. It is the logical backbone on which the paper is built.

4.1

This rough outline often follows freewriting, questioning, clustering, or listing—or all four. Or it may gradually emerge in the midst of these strategies. In fact, trying to outline is a good way to see if you need to do more prewriting. If a solid outline does not emerge, then you know you need to do more prewriting to clarify your main point or its support. Once you have a workable outline, you may realize, for instance, that you want to do more listing to develop one of the supporting details in the outline.

In Gary's case, as he was working on his list of details, he suddenly discovered what the plan of his paragraph could be. He went back to the list, crossed out items that he now realized did not fit, and added the following comments.

Example of List with Comments

Starting college at twenty-nine isn't easy—three reasons

parents give me hard time when they see me
Dad hated school
Dad quit school after eighth grade
Dad says I was dumped on enough in high school
Dad asks why I want to go back for more *Parents and friends*
Mom also doesnt understand *don't support me*
keeps asking how Ill pay for it
friends give me a hard time too
friends call me college man
say they have to watch their grammar

~~my wife has more heavy work around the house~~
also high school had been no fun for me
just sat in class after class
couldnt wait for final bell to ring
wanted to escape
teachers didnt help me *Bad memories of school*
teachers didnt take an interest in me
one called on me, then told me to forget it
I felt like a real loser
I didnt want to go back to his class
~~now I'm more sure of myself~~
~~OK not to know an answer~~
~~talk to teachers after class~~
job plus schoolwork take all my time
get home late, then rush through dinner *Not enough time*
then spend evening studying *with family*
even have to do homework on weekends

Under the list, Gary was now able to prepare his scratch outline:

Example of Scratch Outline

Starting college at age twenty-nine isn't easy.
1. Little support from parents or friends
2. Bad memories of school
3. Not enough time to spend with family

After all his preliminary writing, Gary sat back, pleased. He knew he had a promising paper—one with a clear point and solid support. Gary was now ready to write the first draft of his paper, using his outline as a guide.

Step 3: Writing the First Draft

When you write your first draft, be prepared to put in additional thoughts and details that didn't emerge in your prewriting. And don't worry if you hit a snag. Just leave a blank space or add a comment such as "Do later" and press on to finish the paper. Also, don't worry yet about grammar, punctuation, or spelling. You don't want to take time correcting words or sentences that you may decide to remove later. Instead, make it your goal to develop the content of your paper with plenty of specific details.

Here is Gary's first draft:

First Draft

Last fall, I finaly realized that I was stuck in a dead-end job. I wasnt making enough money and I was bored to tears. I figured I had to get some new skills which meant going back to school. Beginning college at age twenty-nine turned out to be much tougher than I thought it would be. My father didnt understand, he hated school. That's why he quit after eighth grade. He would ask, Didnt you get dumped on enough in high school? Then wondered why I wanted to go back for more of the same thing. My mother was worried about where the money were coming from and said so. When my friends saw me coming down the st. They would make fun of me with remarks like Hey theres the college man. They may have a point. School never was much fun for me. I spent years just siting in class waiting for the bell to ring. So I could escape. The teachers werent much help to me. One time, a teacher called on me then told me to forget it. I felt like a real loser and didnt want to go back to his class. College takes time away from my family. ADD MORE DETAILS LATER. All this makes it very hard for me.

After Gary finished the draft, he was able to put it aside until the next day. You will benefit as well if you can allow some time between finishing a draft and starting to revise.

Step 4: Revising

Revising is as much a stage in the writing process as prewriting, outlining, and writing a first draft. *Revising* means rewriting a paper, building on what has been done, to make it stronger. One writer has said about revision, "It's like cleaning house—getting rid of all the junk and putting things in the right order." It is not just "straightening up"; instead, you must be ready to roll up your sleeves and do whatever is needed to create an effective paper. Too many students think that the first draft *is* the paper. They start to become writers when they realize that revising a rough draft three or four times is often at the heart of the writing process.

Here are some quick hints that can help make revision easier:

- Ideally, set your first draft aside for a while. A few hours is fine, but a day or two is best. You can then come back with a fresh, more objective point of view.

- Work from typed or printed text. You'll be able to see the paper more impartially in this way than if you were just looking at your own familiar handwriting.

- Read your draft aloud. Hearing how your writing sounds will help you pick up problems with meaning as well as style.

- As you do all these things, add your thoughts and changes above the lines or in the margins of your paper. Your written comments can serve as a guide when you work on the next draft.

Here is Gary's second draft.

Second Draft

Starting college at age twenty-nine turned out to be really tough. I did not have much support from my parents and friends. My father hated school, so he asked, Didnt you get dumped on enough in high school? Why go back for more? My mother asking about where the money were coming from. Friends would be making fun of me. Hey theres the college man they would say as soon as they saw me. Another factor was what happened to me in high school. I spent years just siting in class waiting for the bell to ring. I was really bored. Also the teachers liked to embaras me. One teacher called on me and then said forget it. He must of relized I didnt know the answer. I felt like a real loser and didnt want to go back in his class for weeks. Finally I've learned that college takes time away from my family. I have to go to work every day. I have a little over one hour to eat dinner and spend time with my wife and daughter. Then I have to go off to class and when I get back my daughter is in bed asleep. My wife and I have only a little time together. On weekends I have lots of homework to do, so the time goes by like a shot. College is hard for me, but I am going to stay there so I can have a better life.

Notice the improvements made in the second draft:

- Gary started by clearly stating the point of his paragraph. He remembered the first goal in effective writing: *Make a point.*
- He omitted the detail about his father quitting school to keep the focus on his own difficulties. He remembered that the first goal in effective writing is also to *stick to one point,* so the paper will have unity.
- He added more details so that he would have enough support for his reasons why college was hard. He remembered the second goal in effective writing: *Support the point.*
- He inserted transitions to set off the second reason ("Another factor") and third reason ("Finally") why starting college at twenty-nine was difficult for him. He remembered the third goal in effective writing: *Organize the support.*

Gary then went on to revise the second draft. Since he was doing the paper on a computer, he was able to print it out quickly. He double-spaced the lines, allowing room for revisions, which he added in longhand during his third draft. (Note that if you are not using a computer, you may want to do each draft on one side of a page, so that you see your entire paper at one time.) Shown below are some of the changes that Gary made in longhand as he worked on his third draft.

Part of Third Draft

Starting college at age twenty-nine turned out to be really tough.

I did not have much support from my parents and friends. My father hated

school, so he asked, Didnt you get dumped on enough in high school? Why

go back for more? My mother asking about where the money were coming

from. Friends would be making fun of me. Hey theres the college man they

would say as soon as they saw me. Another factor was what happened to

me in high school. I spent years just siting in class waiting for the bell to ring.

I was really bored. Also the teachers liked to embaras me. . . .

After writing these and other changes, Gary typed them into his computer file and printed out the almost-final draft of his paper. He knew he had come to the fourth goal in effective writing: *Write error-free sentences.*

Step 5: Editing and Proofreading

4.4

The next-to-last major stage in the writing process is *editing*—checking a paper for mistakes in grammar, punctuation, usage, and spelling. Students often find it hard to edit a paper carefully. They have put so much work into their writing, or so little, that it's almost painful for them to look at the paper one more time. You may simply have to *will* yourself to carry out this important closing step in the writing process. Remember that eliminating sentence-skills mistakes will improve an average paper and help ensure a strong grade on a good paper. Further, as you get into the habit of checking your papers, you will also get into the habit of using sentence skills consistently. They are an integral part of clear, effective writing.

The checklist of sentence skills on the inside back cover of the book will serve as a guide while you are editing your paper.

Here are hints that can help you edit the next-to-final draft of a paper for sentence-skills mistakes:

Editing Hints

1 Have at hand two essential tools: a good dictionary (see page 339) and a grammar handbook (you can use Part Two of this book).

2 Use a sheet of paper to cover your essay so that you can expose only one sentence at a time. Look for errors in grammar, spelling, and typing. It may help to read each sentence out loud. If the sentence does not read clearly and smoothly, chances are something is wrong.

3 Pay special attention to the kinds of errors you tend to make. For example, if you tend to write run-ons or fragments, be especially on the lookout for these errors.

4 Try to work on a typewritten or word-processed draft, where you'll be able to see your writing more objectively than you can on a handwritten page; use a pen with colored ink so that your corrections will stand out.

Shown below are some of the corrections in spelling, grammar, and punctuation that Gary made when editing his paper.

Part of Gary's Edited Draft

Starting college at age twenty-nine was difficult. For one thing I did not have much support from my parents and friends. My father asked Didn t you get dumped on enough in high school? Why go back for more? My mother woried about where the money were coming from. Friends would make fun of me. Hey there s the college man they would say as soon as they saw me. . . .

All that remained for Gary to do was to enter in his corrections, print out the final draft of the paper, and proofread it (see below for hints on proofreading) for any typos or other careless errors. He was then ready to hand the paper in to his instructor.

4.5

Proofreading, the final stage in the writing process, means checking a paper carefully for spelling, grammar, punctuation, and other errors. You are ready for this stage when you are satisfied with your choice of supporting details, the order in which they are presented, and the way they and your topic sentence are worded.

At this point in his work, Gary used his dictionary to do final checks on his spelling. He used a grammar handbook (such as the one in Part Two of this text) to be sure about grammar, punctuation, and usage. Gary also read through his paper carefully, looking for typing errors, omitted words, and any other errors he may have missed before. Proofreading is often hard to do—again, students have spent so much time with their work, or so little, that they want to avoid it. But if it is done carefully, this important final step will ensure that your paper looks as good as possible.

Proofreading Hints

1 One helpful trick at this stage is to read your paper out loud. You will probably hear awkward wordings and become aware of spots where the punctuation needs to be improved. Make the changes needed for your sentences to read smoothly and clearly.

2 Another helpful technique is to take a sheet of paper and cover your paragraph so that you can expose just one line at a time and check it carefully.

3 A third strategy is to read your paper backward, from the last sentence to the first. This helps keep you from getting caught up in the flow of the paper and missing small mistakes—which is easy to do, since you're so familiar with what you mean to say.

What Is an Essay?

An essay does the same thing a paragraph does: it starts with a point, and the rest of it provides specific details to support and develop that point. However, a paragraph is a series of *sentences* about one main idea or point, while an *essay* is a series of *paragraphs* about one main idea or point—called the *central idea*. Since an essay is much longer than one paragraph, it allows a writer to develop a topic in more detail. Despite the greater length of an essay, the process of writing it is the same as that for writing a paragraph: prewriting, preparing a scratch outline, writing and revising drafts, editing, and proofreading.

Here are the major differences between a paragraph and an essay:

Paragraph	*Essay*
Made up of sentences.	Made up of paragraphs.
Starts with a sentence containing the main point (topic sentence).	Starts with an introductory paragraph containing the central idea, expressed in a sentence called the *thesis statement* (or *thesis sentence*).
Body of paragraph contains specific details that support and develop the topic sentence.	Body of essay contains paragraphs that support and develop the central idea. Each of these paragraphs has its own main supporting point, stated in a topic sentence.
Paragraph often ends with a closing sentence that rounds it off.	Essay ends with a concluding paragraph that rounds it off.

Later in his writing course, Gary was asked to expand his paragraph into an essay. Here is the essay that resulted:

For a typical college freshman, entering college is fun, and an exciting time of life. It is a time not just to explore new ideas in classes but to lounge on the grass chatting with new friends, to sit having soda and pizza in the cafeteria, or to listen to music and play cards in the student lounge. I see the crowds of eighteen-year-olds enjoying all that college has to offer, and I sometimes envy them their freedom. Instead of being a typical freshman, I am twenty-nine years old, and beginning college has been a difficult experience for me. I have had to deal with lack of support, bad memories of past school experiences, and too little time for my family.

Few people in my life support my decision to enter college. My father is especially bewildered by the choice I have made. He himself quit school after finishing eighth grade, and he assumes that I should hate school as much as he did. "Didn't you get dumped on enough in high school?" he asks me. "Why go back for more?" My mother is a little more understanding of my desire for an education, but the cost of college terrifies her. She has always believed that college was a privilege only the rich could afford. "Where in the world will all that money come from?" she says. And my friends seem threatened by my decision. They make fun of me, suggesting that I'm going to think I'm too good to hang around with the likes of them. "Ooooh, here comes the college man," they say when they see me approach. "We'd better watch our grammar."

I have had to deal not only with family and friends but with unhappy memories of my earlier school career. I attended an enormous high school where I was just one more faceless kid in the crowd. My classes seemed meaningless to me. I can remember almost none of them in any detail. What I do remember about high school was just sitting, bored, until I felt nearly brain-dead, watching the clock hands move ever so slowly toward dismissal time. Such periods of boredom were occasionally interrupted by moments of acute embarrassment. Once an algebra teacher called on me and then said, "Oh, forget it, Callahan," in disgusted tones when he realized I didn't know the answer. My response, of course, was to shrink down in my chair and try to become invisible for the rest of the semester.

Furthermore, my decision to enter college has meant I have much less time to spend with my family. I work eight hours a day. Then I rush home and have all of an hour and ten minutes to eat dinner and spend time with my wife and daughter before I rush off again, this time to class. When I return from class, I am dead tired. My little girl is already asleep. My wife and I have only a little time to talk together before I collapse into bed. Weekends are a little better, but not much. That's when I try to get my papers written and catch up on a few chores around the house. My wife tries to be understanding, but it's hard on her to have so little support from me these days. And I'm missing out on a lot of special times in my daughter's life. For instance, I didn't realize she had begun to walk until three days after it happened.

So why do I put myself and my family through all these difficulties? Sometimes I'm not sure myself. But then I look at my little girl sleeping, and I think about the kind of life I am going to be able to give her. My college degree may make it possible for me to get a job that is more rewarding, both financially and emotionally. I believe I will be a better provider for my family, as well as a more well-rounded human being. I hope that the rewards of a college degree will eventually outweigh the problems I am experiencing now.

What Are the Parts of an Essay?

When Gary decided to expand his paragraph into an essay, he knew he would need to write an introductory paragraph, several supporting paragraphs, and a concluding paragraph.

Each of these parts of the essay is explained below.

Introductory Paragraph

ALLWRITE!
8.2

A well-written introductory paragraph will often do the following.

1 **Gain the reader's interest.**   On pages 29–31 are several time-tested methods used to draw the reader into an essay.

2 **Present the thesis statement.**   The thesis statement expresses the central idea of an essay, just as a topic sentence states the main idea of a paragraph. Here's an example of a thesis statement.

A vacation at home can be wonderful.

An essay with this thesis statement would go on to explain some positive things about vacationing at home.

What is the thesis statement in Gary's essay? Find that statement on page 27 and write it here:

_____

_____

You should have written down the next-to-the-last sentence in the introductory paragraph of Gary's essay.

3 **Lay out a plan of development.**   A *plan of development* is a brief statement of the main supporting details for the central idea. These supporting details should be presented in the order in which they will be discussed in the essay. The plan of development can be blended into the thesis statement or presented separately.

> *Blended into a thesis statement:*   A vacation at home can be wonderful because you can avoid the hassles of travel, make use of your knowledge of the area, and indulge in special activities.
>
> *Presented separately:*   A vacation at home can be wonderful. At home you can avoid the hassles of travel, make use of your knowledge of the area, and indulge in special activities.

Note that some essays lend themselves better to a plan of development than others do. At the least, your introductory paragraph should gain the reader's interest and present the thesis statement.

What is the plan of development in Gary's essay? Find the sentence on page 27 that states Gary's plan of development and write it here:

_____

_____

_____

You should have written down the last sentence in the introductory paragraph of Gary's essay.

Four Common Methods of Introduction

1 **Begin with a broad statement and narrow it down to your thesis statement.** A broad statement can capture your reader's interest while introducing your general topic. It may provide useful background material as well. The writer

of the introductory paragraph below begins with a broad statement about her possessions. She then narrows the focus down to the three possessions that are the specific topic of the paper.

> I have many possessions that I would be sad to lose. Because I love to cook, I would miss several kitchen appliances that provide me with so many happy cooking adventures. I would also miss the wonderful electronic equipment that entertains me every day, including my large-screen television set and my VCR. I would miss the two telephones on which I have spent many interesting hours chatting in every part of my apartment, including the bathtub. But if my apartment were burning down, I would most want to rescue three things that are irreplaceable and hold great meaning for me— the silverware set that belonged to my grandmother, my mother's wedding gown, and my giant photo album.

2 **Present an idea or situation that is the opposite of what you will be writing about.**   One way to gain the reader's interest is to show the difference between your opening idea or situation and the one to be discussed in the essay.

> The role of computers in schools is constantly growing. Such growth is based on a widespread faith that computers can answer many of the learning needs of our students. Many people believe that it is just a matter of time before computers do all but take the place of human teachers. However, educators should be cautious about introducing computers into curriculums. Computers may interfere with the learning of critical language skills, they may move too fast for students to digest new concepts, and they are poor substitutes for certain real-world experiences.

3 **Tell a brief story.**   An interesting incident or anecdote is hard for a reader to resist. In an introduction, a story should be no more than a few sentences, and it should relate meaningfully to—and so lead the reader toward—your central idea. The story you tell can be an experience of your own, of someone you know, or of someone you have read about. For instance, in the following introduction, the author tells a simple personal story that serves as background for his central idea.

> I remember the September morning that I first laid eyes on Jill. I'd been calling clients at my desk at work when I heard a warm, musical laugh. There was something so attractive about the sound that I got up to get a cup of coffee and to find the source of that laugh. I discovered the voice to be that of a young, auburn-haired woman we had just hired from a temporary agency. Soon after that, Jill and I began going out, and we spent the next two years together. Only recently have we decided to break up because of disagreements about finances, about children, and about our relationship with her family.

4 Ask one or more questions. The questions may be those you intend to answer in your essay, or they may show that your topic relates directly to readers. In the following example, the questions are designed to gain readers' interest and convince them that the essay applies to them.

> Does your will to study collapse when someone suggests getting a pizza? Does your social life compete with your class attendance? Is there a huge gap between your intentions and your actions? If the answers to these questions are yes, yes, and yes, read on. You can benefit from some powerful ways to motivate yourself: setting goals and consciously working to reach them, using rational thinking, and developing a positive personality.

Which of these four methods of introduction does Gary use in his essay?

_____

Gary begins with an idea that is the opposite of what he is writing about. His essay is about his difficulties with college life, but he begins with the idea that college "is fun, and an exciting time" for some students.

Supporting Paragraphs

The traditional college essay has three supporting paragraphs. But some essays will have two supporting paragraphs, and others will have four or more. Each supporting paragraph should have its own topic sentence, stating the point to be developed in that paragraph.

   Notice that each of the supporting paragraphs in Gary's essay has its own topic sentence. For example, the topic sentence of his first supporting paragraph is "Few people in my life support my decision to enter college."

   What is the topic sentence of Gary's second supporting paragraph?

_____

   What is the topic sentence of Gary's third supporting paragraph?

_____

In each case, Gary's topic sentence is the first sentence of the paragraph.

Concluding Paragraph

An essay that ended with its final supporting paragraph would probably leave the reader wondering if the author was really done. A concluding paragraph is needed for a sense of completion. Here are two common methods of conclusion.

Two Common Methods of Conclusion

1 Provide a summary and a final thought.   Using wording different from your introduction, restate your thesis and main supporting points. This review gives readers an overview of your essay and helps them remember what they've read. A final thought signals the end of the paper, as in the following concluding paragraph from an essay about personal possessions.

> If my home ever really did burn down, I would hope to be able to rescue some of the physical things that so meaningfully represent my past. My grandmother's silver set is a reminder of the grandparents who enriched my childhood, my mother's wedding gown is a glamorous souvenir of two important weddings, and my photo album is a rich storage bin of family and personal history. I would hate to lose them. However, if I did, I would take comfort in the fact that the most important storage place for family and personal memories is my own mind.

2 Focus on the future.   Focusing on the future often involves making a prediction or a recommendation. This method of conclusion may refer in a general way to the central idea, or it may include a summary. The following conclusion from an essay about self-motivation combines a summary with a prediction. The prediction adds further support for the central idea.

> So get your willpower in gear, and use the three keys to self-motivation— set goals and work to reach them, think rationally, and develop a positive personality. You will find that a firm commitment to this approach becomes easier and easier. Progress will come more often and more readily, strengthening your resolve even further.

What kind of conclusion does Gary use in his essay?

_____

In his conclusion, Gary refers to his central idea in the context of the future. He makes hopeful points about what his and his family's life will be like after he gets a college degree.

How Can a Computer Help?

If you don't yet write on a computer, it's time to start. In today's world, word processing is an essential mechanical skill, just as effective writing is a vital communication skill.

The computer can be a real aid in the writing process. You can quickly add or delete anything, from a word to an entire section. You can "cut" material and "paste" it elsewhere in seconds. A word-processing program makes it easy to set margins, space lines, and number pages. It can also help you check your spelling, your grammar, and to some extent your style. And at any point during your work, you can print out one or more copies of your text.

Word processing is not hard to learn. Just as you don't need to know how a car works to drive one, you don't need to understand how a computer functions to use it. Once you have learned a few simple keystrokes, you can begin. You do not even need to own your own computer. Nearly every college has at least one computer center, complete with rows of computers and staff members to provide assistance. Free classes in word processing may be available as well.

Tips on Using a Computer

- If you are using your school's computer center, allow enough time. You may have to wait for a computer or printer to be free. In addition, you may need several sessions at the computer and printer to complete your paper.

- Every word-processing program allows you to "save" your writing by hitting one or more keys. Save your work file frequently as you write your draft. A saved file is stored safely on the computer. A file that is not saved will be lost if the computer crashes or if the power is turned off.

- Keep your work in two places—the hard drive or disk you are working on and a backup disk. At the end of each session with the computer, copy your work onto the backup disk. Then if the hard drive or working disk becomes damaged, you'll have the backup copy.

- Print out your work at least at the end of every session. Then not only will you have your most recent draft to work on away from the computer; you'll also have a copy in case something should happen to your disks.

- Work in single spacing so that you can see as much of your writing on the screen at one time as possible. Just before you print out your work, change to double spacing.

- Before making major changes in a paper, create a copy of your file. For example, if your file is titled "Worst Job," create a file called "Worst Job 2." Then make all your changes in that new file. If the changes don't work out, you can always go back to the original file.

Using a Computer at Each Stage of the Writing Process

Following are some ways to make word processing a part of your writing.

Prewriting

If you're a fast typist, many kinds of prewriting will go well on the computer. With freewriting in particular, you can get ideas onto the screen almost as quickly as they occur to you. A passing thought that could be productive is not likely to get lost. You may even find it helpful, when freewriting, to dim the screen of your monitor so that you can't see what you're typing. If you temporarily can't see the screen, you won't have to worry about grammar or spelling or typing errors (all of which do not matter in prewriting); instead, you can concentrate on getting down as many ideas and details as possible about your subject.

After any initial freewriting, questioning, and list-making on a computer, it's often very helpful to print out a hard copy of what you've done. With a clean print-out in front of you, you'll be able to see everything at once and revise and expand your work with handwritten comments in the margins of the paper.

Word processing also makes it easy for you to experiment with the wording of the point of your paper. You can try a number of versions in a short time. After you have decided on the version that works best, you can easily delete the other versions—or simply move them to a temporary "leftover" section at the end of the paper.

Preparing a Scratch Outline

If you have prepared a list of items during prewriting, you may be able to turn that list into an outline right on the screen. Delete the ideas you feel should not be in your paper (saving them at the end of the file in case you change your mind), and add any new ideas that occur to you. Then use the cut and paste functions to shuffle the supporting ideas around until you find the best order for your paper.

Writing Your First Draft

Like many writers, you may want to write out your first draft by hand and then type it into the computer for revision. Even as you type your handwritten draft, you may find yourself making some changes and improvements. And once you have a draft on the screen, or printed out, you will find it much easier to revise than a handwritten one.

If you feel comfortable composing directly on the screen, you can benefit from the computer's special features. For example, if you have written an anecdote in your freewriting that you plan to use in your paper, simply copy the story from your freewriting file and insert it where it fits in your paper. You can refine it then or later. Or if you discover while typing that a sentence is out of place, cut it out from where it is and paste it wherever you wish. And if while writing you realize that an earlier sentence can be expanded, just move your cursor back to that point and type in the added material.

Revising

It is during revision that the virtues of word processing really shine. All substituting, adding, deleting, and rearranging can be done easily within an existing file. All changes instantly take their proper places within the paper, not scribbled above the line or squeezed into the margin. You can concentrate on each change you want to make, because you never have to type from scratch or work on a messy draft. You can carefully go through your paper to check that all your supporting evidence is relevant and to add new support as needed here and there. Anything you decide to eliminate can be deleted in a keystroke. Anything you add can be inserted precisely where you choose. If you change your mind, all you have to do is delete or cut and paste. Then you can sweep through the paper, focusing on other changes, such as improving word choice, increasing sentence variety, eliminating wordiness, and so on.

If you are like many students, you will find it convenient to print out a hard copy of your file at various points throughout the revision. You can then revise in longhand—adding, crossing out, and indicating changes—and later quickly make these changes in the document.

Editing and Proofreading

Editing and proofreading also benefit richly from word processing. Instead of crossing or whiting out mistakes, or rewriting an entire paper to correct numerous errors, you can make all necessary changes within the most recent draft. If you find editing or proofreading on the screen hard on your eyes, print out a copy. Mark any corrections on that copy, and then transfer them to the final draft.

If the word-processing package you're using includes spelling and grammar checks, by all means use them. The spell-check function tells you when a word is not in the computer's dictionary. Keep in mind, however, that the spell-check cannot tell you how to spell a name correctly or when you have mistakenly used, for example, *their* instead of *there*. To a spell-check, *Thank ewe four the complement* is as correct as *Thank you for the compliment*. Also, use the grammar check with caution. Any errors it doesn't uncover are still your responsibility.

A word-processed paper, with its clean look and handsome formatting, looks so good that you may feel it is in better shape than it really is. Do not be fooled by your paper's appearance. Take sufficient time to review your grammar, punctuation, and spelling carefully.

Even after you hand in your paper, save the computer file. Your instructor may ask you to do some revising, and then the file will save you from having to type the paper from scratch.

Chapter Review

Answer each of the following questions by filling in the blank or circling the answer you think is correct.

1. *True or false?* _____ Writing is a skill that anyone can learn with practice.
2. An effective paragraph or essay is one that
   a. makes a point.
   b. provides specific support.
   c. makes a point and provides specific support.
   d. none of the above.
3. The sentence that states the main idea of a paragraph is known as the _____ sentence; the sentence that states the central idea of an essay is known as the _____ statement.
4. Prewriting can help a writer find
   a. a good topic to write about.
   b. a good main point to make about the topic.
   c. enough details to support the main point.
   d. all of the above.
5. One step that everyone should use at some stage of the writing process is to prepare a plan for the paragraph or essay known as a(n) _____ _____.
6. When you start writing, your first concern should be
   a. spelling.
   b. content.
   c. grammar.
   d. punctuation.
7. Two common ways of organizing a paragraph are _____ order and _____ order.

8. A thesis statement
   a.   is generally part of an essay's introduction.
   b.   states the central idea of the essay.
   c.   can be followed by the essay's plan of development.
   d.   all of the above.

9. The words *first, next, then, also, another,* and *finally* are examples of signal

   words, commonly known as _____ .

10. A computer can help a writer
    a.   turn a list into an outline.
    b.   find just the right words to express a point.
    c.   add and delete supporting evidence.
    d.   all of the above.

Preview: A Look Ahead

Chapter 3 provides a series of activities to help you master three of the four goals of effective writing: (1) making a point, (2) supporting the point with specific details, and (3) organizing the support. Part Two of this book and a dictionary will help you with the fourth goal—writing error-free sentences. Part Three provides various tests to reinforce the sentence skills studied in Part Two. Part Four of the book presents ten reading selections that will develop both your reading and writing skills.

3 Practice in Effective Writing

The following series of activities will strengthen your understanding of the writing guidelines presented in Chapter 2. Through practice, you will gain a better sense of the goals of effective writing and how to reach those goals. You will also help prepare yourself for the writing assignments that follow the activities.

Your instructor may ask you to do the entire series of activities or may select the activities that are most suited to your particular needs.

1 Understanding General versus Specific Ideas

A paragraph is made up of a main idea, which is general, and the specific ideas that support it. So to write well, you must understand the difference between general and specific ideas.

It is helpful to realize that you use general and specific ideas all the time in your everyday life. For example, in choosing a video to rent, you may think, "Which should I rent, an action movie, a comedy, or a romance?" In such a case, *video* is the general idea, and *action movie, comedy,* and *romance* are the specific ideas.

Or you may decide to begin an exercise program. In that case, you might consider walking, jumping rope, or lifting weights. In this case, *exercise* is the general idea, and *walking, jumping rope,* and *lifting weights* are the specific ideas.

Or if you are talking to a friend about a date that didn't work out well, you may say, "The dinner was terrible, the car broke down, and we had little to say to each other." In this case, the general idea is *the date didn't work out well,* and the specific ideas are the three reasons you named.

The four activities here will give you experience in recognizing the relationship between general and specific. They will also provide a helpful background for all the information and activities that follow.

Activity 1

Each group of words consists of one general idea and four specific ideas. The general idea includes all the specific ideas. Underline the general idea in each group.

Example   jeep   van   truck   vehicle   sedan

1. salty   bitter   flavor   sweet   sour
2. jewelry   necklace   ring   earrings   bracelet
3. dime   nickel   coin   quarter   half-dollar
4. fax machine   copier   computer   calculator   office machine
5. theft   murder   rape   crime   holdup
6. cracker   snack   carrot stick   cookie   popcorn
7. mascara   cosmetic   foundation   lipstick   eyeshadow
8. yes   no   I don't know   answer   maybe
9. yard work   mowing   planting   trimming hedges   feeding plants
10. job interviews   weddings   car accidents   being fired   stressful times

Activity 2

In each item below, one idea is general and the others are specific. The general idea includes the specific ones. In the spaces provided, write in two more specific ideas that are covered by the general idea.

Example   *General:* exercises
           Specific: chin-ups, jumping jacks, _____ , _____

1. *General:* pizza toppings
   Specific: sausage, mushrooms,   _____ , _____
2. *General:* furniture
   Specific: rocking chair, coffee table,   _____ , _____
3. *General:* magazines
   Specific: Reader's Digest, Newsweek,   _____ , _____
4. *General:* birds
   Specific: eagle, pigeon,   _____ , _____
5. *General:* types of music
   Specific: jazz, classical,   _____ , _____

6. *General:* cold symptoms

  Specific: aching muscles, watery eyes, _____ , _____

7. *General:* children's games

  Specific: hopscotch, dodgeball, _____ , _____

8. *General:* transportation

  Specific: plane, motorcycle, _____ , _____

9. *General:* city problems

  Specific: overcrowding, pollution, _____ , _____

10. *General:* types of TV shows

  Specific: cartoons, situation comedies, _____ , _____

Activity 3

Read each group of specific ideas below. Then circle the letter of the general idea that tells what the specific ideas have in common. Note that the general idea should not be too broad or too narrow. Begin by trying the example item, and then read the explanation that follows.

Example   *Specific ideas:* peeling potatoes, washing dishes, cracking eggs, cleaning out refrigerator

  The general idea is

  a.   household jobs.

  b.   kitchen tasks.

  c.   steps in making dinner.

Explanation: It is true that the specific ideas are all household jobs, but they have in common something even more specific—they are all tasks done in the kitchen. Therefore answer *a* is too broad, and the correct answer is *b*. Answer *c* is too narrow because it doesn't cover all the specific ideas. While two of them could be steps in making a dinner ("peeling potatoes" and "cracking eggs"), two have nothing to do with making dinner.

1. *Specific ideas:* crowded office, rude co-workers, demanding boss, unreasonable deadlines

  The general idea is:

  a.   problems.

  b.   work problems.

  c.   problems with work schedules.

2. *Specific ideas:* cactus, rosebush, fern, daisy

   The general idea is:

   a. plants.

   b. plants that have thorns.

   c. plants that grow in the desert.

3. *Specific ideas:* Band-Aids, gauze, smelling salts, aspirin

   The general idea is:

   a. supplies.

   b. first-aid supplies.

   c. supplies for treating a headache.

4. *Specific ideas:* trout, whales, salmon, frogs

   The general idea is:

   a. animals.

   b. fish.

   c. animals living in water.

5. *Specific ideas:* Hershey bar, lollipop, mints, fudge

   The general idea is:

   a. food.

   b. candy.

   c. chocolate.

6. *Specific ideas:* "Go to bed," "Pick up that trash," "Run twenty laps," "Type this letter."

   The general idea is:

   a. remarks.

   b. orders.

   c. the boss's orders.

7. *Specific ideas:* "I had no time to study," "The questions were unfair," "I had a headache," "The instructor didn't give us enough time."

   The general idea is:

   a. statements.

   b. excuses for being late.

   c. excuses for not doing well on a test.

8. *Specific ideas:* candle, sun, headlight, flashlight

   The general idea is:

   a.   things that are very hot.

   b.   light sources for a home.

   c.   sources of light.

9. *Specific ideas:* driving with expired license plates, driving over the speed limit, parking without putting money in the meter, driving without a license

   The general idea is:

   a.   ways to cause a traffic accident.

   b.   traffic problems.

   c.   ways to get a ticket.

10. *Specific ideas:* "Are we there yet?" "Where do people come from?" "Can I have that toy?" "Do I have to go to bed now?"

   The general idea is:

   a.   Things adults say to one another.

   b.   Things children ask adults.

   c.   Things children ask at school.

Activity 4

In the following items, the specific ideas are given but the general ideas are unstated. Fill in the blanks with the unstated general ideas.

Example   *General idea:*   _____car problems_____

           Specific ideas: flat tire   dented bumper
                           cracked windshield   dirty oil filter

1. *General idea:*   _____
   Specific ideas: nephew   grandmother
                   aunt   cousin

2. *General idea:*   _____
   Specific ideas: boots   sneakers
                   moccasins   slippers

3. *General idea:*   _____
   Specific ideas: camping   hiking
                   fishing   hunting

4. *General idea:* _____
   Specific ideas: broom   sponge
                      mop   glass cleaner

5. *General idea:* _____
   Specific ideas: cloudy   sunny
                      snowy   rainy

6. *General idea:* _____
   Specific ideas: Spread mustard on slice of bread
                      Add turkey and cheese
                      Put lettuce on top of cheese
                      Cover with another slice of bread

7. *General idea:* _____
   Specific ideas: thermos of lemonade   insect repellent
                      basket of food   blanket

8. *General idea:* _____
   Specific ideas: fleas in carpeting   loud barking
                      tangled fur   veterinary bills

9. *General idea:* _____
   Specific ideas: diabetes   cancer
                      appendicitis   broken leg

10. *General idea:* _____
    Specific ideas: flooded basements   wet streets
                       rainbow   overflowing rivers

2 Understanding the Paragraph

A *paragraph* is made up of a main idea and a group of related sentences developing the main idea. The main idea often appears in a sentence known as the *topic sentence.*

It is helpful to remember that a topic sentence is a *general* statement. The other sentences provide specific support for the general statement.

Activity

Each group of sentences below could be written as a short paragraph. Circle the letter of the topic sentence in each case. To find the topic sentence, ask yourself, "Which is a general statement supported by the specific details in the other three statements?"

Begin by trying the example item below. First circle the letter of the sentence you think expresses the main idea. Then read the explanation.

Example   a.   Newspapers are a good source of local, national, and world news.

b.   The cartoons and crossword puzzles in newspapers are entertaining.

c.   Newspapers have a lot to offer.

d.   Newspapers often include coupons worth far more than the cost of the paper.

Explanation: Sentence *a* explains one important benefit of newspapers. Sentences *b* and *d* provide other specific advantages of newspapers. In sentence *c,* however, no one specific benefit is explained. Instead, the words "a lot to offer" refer only generally to such benefits. Therefore sentence *c* is the topic sentence; it expresses the main idea. The other sentences support that idea by providing examples.

1. a.   Even when Food City is crowded, there are only two cash registers open.

   b.   The frozen foods are often partially thawed.

   c.   I will never shop at Food City again.

   d.   The market is usually out of sale items within a few hours.

2. a.   Buy only clothes that will match what's already in your closet.

   b.   To be sure you're getting the best price, shop in a number of stores before buying.

   c.   Avoid trendy clothes; buy basic pieces that never go out of style.

   d.   By following a few simple rules, you can have nice clothes without spending a fortune.

3. a.   Once my son said a vase jumped off the shelf by itself.

   b.   When my son breaks something, he always has an excuse.

   c.   He claimed that my three-month-old daughter climbed out of her crib and knocked a glass over.

   d.   Another time, he said an earthquake must have caused a mirror to crack.

4. a.   Mars should be the first planet explored by astronauts.

   b.   Astronauts could mine Mars for aluminum, magnesium, and iron.

   c.   The huge volcano on Mars would be fascinating to study.

   d.   Since Mars is close to Earth, we might want to have colonies there one day.

5. a. Instead of talking on the telephone, we leave messages on answering machines.

    b. People rarely talk to one another these days.

    c. Rather than talking with family members, we sit silently in front of our TV sets all evening.

    d. In cars, we ignore our traveling companions to listen to the radio.

3 Understanding the Topic Sentence

ALLWRITE!
3.2

As already explained, most paragraphs center on a main idea, which is often expressed in a topic sentence. An effective topic sentence does two things. First, it presents the topic of the paragraph. Second, it expresses the writer's attitude or opinion or idea about the topic. For example, look at the following topic sentence:

Professional athletes are overpaid.

In the topic sentence, the topic is *professional athletes;* the writer's idea about the topic is that professional athletes *are overpaid.*

Activity

For each topic sentence below, underline the topic and double-underline the point of view that the writer takes toward the topic.

Examples   Living in a small town has many advantages.

Cell phones should be banned in schools.

1. The apartments on Walnut Avenue are a fire hazard.

2. Losing my job turned out to have benefits.

3. Blues is the most interesting form of American music.

4. Our neighbor's backyard is a dangerous place.

5. Paula and Jeff are a stingy couple.

6. Snakes do not deserve their bad reputation.

7. Pollution causes many problems in American cities.

8. New fathers should receive "paternity leave."

9. People with low self-esteem often need to criticize others.

10. Learning to write effectively is largely a matter of practice.

4 Identifying Topics, Topic Sentences, and Support

The following activity will sharpen your sense of the differences between topics, topic sentences, and supporting sentences.

Activity

Each group of items below includes one topic, one main idea (expressed in a topic sentence), and two supporting details for that idea. In the space provided, label each item with one of the following:

> *T* — topic
> *MI* — main idea
> *SD* — supporting details

1. _____ a. The weather in the summer is often hot and sticky.

   _____ b. Summer can be an unpleasant time of year.

   _____ c. Summer.

   _____ d. Bug bites, poison ivy, and allergies are a big part of summertime.

2. _____ a. The new Ultimate sports car is bound to be very popular.

   _____ b. The company has promised to provide any repairs needed during the first three years at no charge.

   _____ c. Because it gets thirty miles per gallon of gas, it offers real savings on fuel costs.

   _____ d. The new Ultimate sports car.

3. _____ a. Decorating an apartment doesn't need to be expensive.

   _____ b. A few plants add a touch of color without costing a lot of money.

   _____ c. Inexpensive braided rugs can be bought to match nearly any furniture.

   _____ d. Decorating an apartment.

4. _____ a. Long practice sessions and busy game schedules take too much time away from schoolwork.

_____ b. High school sports.

_____ c. The competition between schools may become so intense that, depending on the outcome of one game, athletes are either adored or scorned.

_____ d. High school sports put too much pressure on young athletes.

5. _____ a. After mapping out the best route to your destination, phone ahead for motel reservations.

_____ b. A long car trip.

_____ c. Following a few guidelines before a long car trip can help you avoid potential problems.

_____ d. Have your car's engine tuned as well, and have the tires, brakes, and exhaust system inspected.

5 Recognizing Specific Details I

Specific details are examples, reasons, particulars, and facts. Such details are needed to support and explain a topic sentence effectively. They provide the evidence needed for us to understand, as well as to feel and experience, a writer's point.

Below is a topic sentence followed by two sets of supporting sentences. Write a check mark next to the set that provides sharp, specific details.

Topic sentence: Ticket sales for a recent Rolling Stones concert proved that the classic rock band is still very popular.

_____ a. Fans came from everywhere to buy tickets to the concert. People wanted good seats and were willing to endure a great deal of various kinds of discomfort as they waited in line for many hours. Some people actually waited for days, sleeping at night in uncomfortable circumstances. Good tickets were sold out extremely quickly.

_____ b. The first person in the long ticket line spent three days standing in the hot sun and three nights sleeping on the concrete without even a pillow. The man behind her waited equally long in his wheelchair. The ticket window opened at 10:00 A.M., and the tickets for the good seats—those in front of the stage—were sold out an hour later.

Explanation: The second set (*b*) provides specific details. Instead of a vague statement about fans who were "willing to endure a great deal of various kinds of discomfort," we get vivid details we can see and picture clearly: "three days standing in the hot sun," "three nights sleeping on the concrete without even a pillow," "The man behind her waited equally long in his wheelchair."

Instead of a vague statement that tickets were "sold out extremely quickly," we get exact and vivid details: "The ticket window opened at 10:00 A.M., and the tickets for the good seats—those in front of the stage—were sold out an hour later."

Specific details are often like a movie script. They provide us with such clear pictures that we could make a film of them if we wanted to. You would know just how to film the information given in the second set of sentences. You would show the fans in line under a hot sun and, later, sleeping on the concrete. The first person in line would be shown sleeping without a pillow under her head. You would show tickets finally going on sale, and after an hour you could show the ticket seller explaining that all of the seats in front of the stage were sold out.

In contrast, the writer of the first set of sentences (*a*) fails to provide the specific information needed. If you were asked to make a film based on set *a,* you would have to figure out on your own just what particulars to show.

When you are working to provide specific supporting information in a paper, it might help to ask yourself, "Could someone easily film this information?" If the answer is yes, your supporting details are specific enough for your readers to visualize.

Activity

Each topic sentence below is followed by two sets of supporting details. Write *S* (for *specific*) in the space next to the set that provides specific support for the point. Write *G* (for *general*) next to the set that offers only vague, general support.

1. *Topic sentence:* The West Side shopping mall is an unpleasant place.

    _____ a.   The floors are covered with cigarette butts, dirty paper plates, and spilled food. The stores are so crowded I had to wait twenty minutes just to get a dressing room to try on a shirt.

    _____ b.   It's very dirty, and not enough places are provided for trash. The stores are not equipped to handle the large number of shoppers that often show up.

    Hint: Which set of supporting details could you more readily use in a film?

2. *Topic sentence:* Our golden retriever is a wonderful pet for children.

    _____ a.   He is gentle, patient, eager to please, and affectionate. Capable of following orders, he is also ready to think for himself and find solutions to a problem. He senses children's moods and goes along with their wishes.

_____ b. He doesn't bite, even when children pull his tail. After learning to catch a ball, he will bring it back again and again, seemingly always ready to play. If the children don't want to play anymore, he will just sit by their side, gazing at them with his faithful eyes.

3. *Topic sentence:* My two-year-old daughter's fearlessness is a constant source of danger to her.

_____ a. She doesn't realize that certain activities are dangerous. Even when I warn her, she will go ahead and do something that could hurt her. I have to constantly be on the lookout for dangerous situations and try to protect her from them.

_____ b. For instance, she loves going to the swimming pool. That's great. But she will jump into water that is way over her head. She likes animals and will run to pet any dog that wanders by, no matter how unfriendly.

4. *Topic sentence:* People's views of scientists are often more fiction than fact.

_____ a. Scientists are portrayed in movies as crazy guys with long hair, thick glasses, and shabby clothes. Incapable of remembering the time of day, these imaginary scientists skip meals and prefer the company of laboratory animals to that of their own children. In reality, scientists get hungry at mealtime, love their children, and go to work in suits.

_____ b. People don't know exactly what scientists do and fantasize a lot about their work. Instead of thinking of scientists as real people who do a particular type of work, people think of them as weird, antisocial geniuses whom one could spot a mile away. In reality, most scientists look and act much like their neighbors.

5. *Topic sentence:* Early theories of child raising were very different from today's theories.

_____ a. The first books on child raising came out hundreds of years ago. The advice they contained was based almost entirely on superstitions and other untrue beliefs. Some of the advice was harmless, but some could lead to long-term effects. They told parents to do things to their children that seem to us to make no sense at all.

_____ b. One early book, for example, advised mothers not to breast-feed their babies right after feeling anger because the anger would go into the milk and injure the child. Another told parents to begin toilet-training their children at the age of three weeks and to tie their babies' arms down for several months to prevent thumb sucking.

7 Providing Specific Details

Activity

Each of the following sentences contains a general word or words, set off in *italic* type. Substitute sharp, specific words in each case.

Example   After the parade, the city street was littered with *garbage.*
           After the parade, the city street was littered with multicolored

           confetti, dirty popcorn, and lifeless balloons.

1. If I had enough money, I'd visit *several places.*

   _____

   _____

2. It took her *a long time* to get home.

   _____

   _____

3. Ron is often stared at because of his *unusual hair color and hairstyle.*

   _____

   _____

4. After you pass *two buildings,* you'll see my house on the left.

   _____

   _____

5. Nia's purse is crammed with *lots of stuff.*

   _____

   _____

6. I bought *some junk food* for the long car trip.

   _____

   _____

7. The floor in the front of my car is covered with *things.*

   _____

   _____

8. When his mother said no to his request for a toy, the child *reacted strongly.*

   _____

   _____

9. Devan gave his girlfriend a *surprise present* for Valentine's Day.

_____

_____

10. My cat can *do a wonderful trick.*

_____

_____

8 Selecting Details That Fit

5

The details in your paper must all clearly relate to and support your opening point. If a detail does not support your point, leave it out. Otherwise, your paper will lack unity. For example, see if you can circle the letter of the two sentences that do *not* support the topic sentence below.

Topic sentence: Mario is a very talented person.

a.   Mario is always courteous to his professors.

b.   He has created beautiful paintings in his art course.

c.   Mario is the lead singer in a local band.

d.   He won an award in a photography contest.

e.   He is hoping to become a professional photographer.

Explanation: Being courteous may be a virtue, but it is not a talent, so sentence *a* does not support the topic sentence. Also, Mario's desire to become a professional photographer tells us nothing about his talent; thus sentence *e* does not support the topic sentence either. The other three statements all clearly back up the topic sentence. Each in some way supports the idea that Mario is talented—in art, as a singer, or as a photographer.

Activity

In each group below, circle the two items that do *not* support the topic sentence.

1. *Topic sentence:* Carla seems attracted only to men who are unavailable.

a.   She once fell in love with a man serving a life sentence in prison.

b.   Her parents worry about her inability to connect with a nice single man.

c.   She wants to get married and have kids before she is thirty.

d.   Her current boyfriend is married.

e.   Recently she had a huge crush on a Catholic priest.

2. *Topic sentence:* Some dog owners have little consideration for other people.

   a. Obedience lessons can be a good experience for both the dog and the owner.

   b. Some dog owners let their dogs leave droppings on the sidewalk or in other people's yards.

   c. They leave the dog home alone for hours, barking and howling and waking the neighbors.

   d. Some people keep very large dogs in small apartments.

   e. Even when small children are playing nearby, they let their bad-tempered dogs run loose.

3. *Topic sentence:* Dr. Eliot is a very poor teacher.

   a. He cancels class frequently with no explanation.

   b. When a student asks a question that he can't answer, he becomes irritated with the student.

   c. He got his Ph.D at a university in another country.

   d. He's taught at the college for many years and is on a number of faculty committees.

   e. He puts off grading papers until the end of the semester, and then returns them all at once.

4. *Topic sentence:* Some doctors seem to think it is all right to keep patients waiting.

   a. Pharmaceutical sales representatives sometimes must wait hours to see a doctor.

   b. The doctors stand in the hallway chatting with nurses and secretaries even when they have a waiting room full of patients.

   c. Patients sometimes travel long distances to consult with a particular doctor.

   d. When a patient calls before an appointment to see if the doctor is on time, the answer is often yes even when the doctor is two hours behind schedule.

   e. Some doctors schedule appointments in a way that ensures long lines, to make it appear that they are especially skillful.

5. *Topic sentence:* Several factors were responsible for the staggering loss of lives when the *Titanic* sank.

   a. Over 1,500 people died in the *Titanic* disaster; only 711 survived.

   b. Despite warnings about the presence of icebergs, the captain allowed the *Titanic* to continue at high speed.

c. If the ship had hit the iceberg head on, its watertight compartments might have kept it from sinking; however, it hit on the side, resulting in a long, jagged gash through which water poured in.

d. The *Titanic*, equipped with the very best communication systems available in 1912, sent out SOS messages.

e. When the captain gave orders to abandon the *Titanic,* many passengers refused because they believed the ship was unsinkable, so many lifeboats were only partly filled.

9 Providing Details That Fit

Activity 1

Each topic sentence below is followed by one supporting detail. See if you can add a second detail in each case. Make sure your detail supports the topic sentence.

1. *Topic sentence:* There are good reasons why the video store is losing so many customers.

   a. The store stocks only one copy of every movie, even the most popular titles.

   b. _____

2. *Topic sentence:* The little boy did some dangerous stunts on his bicycle.

   a. He rode down a flight of steps at top speed.

   b. _____

3. *Topic sentence:* Craig has awful table manners.

   a. He stuffs his mouth with food and then begins a conversation.

   b. _____

4. *Topic sentence:* There are many advantages to living in the city.

   a. One can meet many new people with interesting backgrounds.

   b. _____

5. *Topic sentence:* All high school students should have summer jobs.

   a. Summer jobs help teens learn to handle a budget.

   b. _____

Activity 2

See if you can add *two* supporting details for each of the topic sentences below.

1. *Topic sentence:* The managers of this apartment building don't care about their renters.

   a. Mrs. Harris has been asking them to fix her leaky faucet for two months.

   b. _____

   c. _____

2. *Topic sentence:* None of the shirts for sale were satisfactory.

   a. Some were attractive but too expensive.

   b. _____

   c. _____

3. *Topic sentence:* After being married for forty years, Mr. and Mrs. Lambert have grown similar in odd ways.

   a. They both love to have a cup of warm apple juice just before bed.

   b. _____

   c. _____

4. *Topic sentence:* It is a special time for me when my brother is in town.

   a. We always go bowling together and then stop for pizza.

   b. _____

   c. _____

5. *Topic sentence:* Our neighbor's daughter is very spoiled.

   a. When anyone else in the family has a birthday, she gets several presents too.

   b. _____

   c. _____

10 Providing Details in a Paragraph

Activity

The following paragraph needs specific details to back up its three supporting points. In the spaces provided, write two or three sentences of convincing details for each supporting point.

A Disappointing Concert

Although I had looked forward to seeing my favorite musical group in concert, the experience was disappointing. For one thing, our seats were terrible, in two ways. _____

_____

_____

_____

In addition, the crowd made it hard to enjoy the music. _____

_____

_____

_____

_____

And finally, the band members acted as if they didn't want to be there. _____

_____

_____

_____

_____

11 Omitting and Grouping Details in Planning a Paper

One common way to develop material for a paper involves three steps: (1) First, make up a list of details about your point. (2) Then omit details that don't truly support your point. (3) Finally, group remaining details together in logical ways. Omitting details that don't fit and grouping related details together are part of learning how to write effectively.

See if you can figure out a way to put the following details into three groups. Write *A* in front of the details that go with one group, *B* in front of the details that go with a second group, and *C* in front of the details that make up a third group. Cross out the four details that do not relate to the topic sentence.

Topic sentence: My brother Sean caused our parents lots of headaches when he was a teenager.

_____   In constant trouble at school

_____   While playing a joke on his lab partner, nearly blew up the chemistry lab

_____   Girlfriend was eight years older than he and had been married twice

_____   Girlfriend had a very sweet four-year-old son

_____   Parents worried about people Sean spent his time with

_____   Several signs that he was using drugs

_____   Failed so many courses that he had to go to summer school in order to graduate

_____   Was suspended twice for getting into fights between classes

_____   Our father taught math at the high school we attended

_____   His money just disappeared, and he never had anything to show for it

_____   His best pal had been arrested for armed robbery

_____   Often looked glassy-eyed

_____   Hung around with older kids who had dropped out of school

_____   Until he was in eighth grade, he had always been on the honor roll

_____   No one was allowed in his room, which he kept locked whenever he was away from home

_____   Has managed to turn his life around now that he's in college

Explanation: After thinking about the list for a while, you probably realized that the details about Sean's trouble at school form one group. He got in trouble at school for nearly blowing up the chemistry lab, failing courses, and fighting between classes. Another group of details has to do with his parents' worrying about the people he spent time with. His parents were worried because he had an older girlfriend, a best friend who was arrested for armed robbery, and older friends who were school dropouts. Finally, there are the details about signs that he was using drugs: his money disappearing, his glassy-eyed appearance, and not allowing others in his room.

The main idea—that as a teenager, the writer's brother caused their parents lots of headaches—can be supported with three kinds of evidence: the trouble he got into at school, his friends, and the signs indicating he was on drugs. The other four items in the list do not logically go with any of these three types of evidence and so should be omitted.

Activity

This activity will give you practice in omitting and grouping details. See if you can figure out a way to put the following details into three groups. Write *A* in front of the details that go with one group, *B* in front of the details that go with a second group, and *C* in front of the details that make up a third group. Cross out the four details that do not relate to the topic sentence.

Topic sentence: There are interesting and enjoyable ways for children to keep their classroom skills strong over summer vacation.

_____ Kids can help figure out how big a tip to leave in a restaurant.

_____ They can keep their reading skills sharp in various ways.

_____ Summer is a good time for learning to swim.

_____ Reading the newspaper with Mom or Dad will keep kids in touch with challenging reading.

_____ Adults can ask a child to do such tasks as count their change.

_____ Kids can have fun improving their writing skills.

_____ A child might enjoy writing a diary of his or her summer activities.

_____ Weekly visits to the library will keep them in touch with good books.

_____ After returning to school, children can write about their summer vacation.

_____ Kids should also have plenty of physical exercise over the summer.

_____ Arithmetic skills can be polished over the summer.

_____ Parents can encourage kids to write letters to relatives.

_____ Parents should take children to the library during the school year too.

_____ In the grocery store, a child can compare prices and choose the best bargains.

_____ Even the comic strips provide reading practice for a young child.

_____ Getting a pen-pal in another state can give a child an enjoyable reason to write over the summer.

12 Using Transitions

6.1

As already stated, transitions are signal words that help readers follow the direction of the writer's thought. To see the value of transitions, look at the two versions of the short paragraph below. Check the version that is easier to read and understand.

_____ a.   Where will you get the material for your writing assignments? There are several good sources. Your own experience is a major resource. For an assignment about childhood, for instance, you can draw on your own numerous memories of childhood. Other people's experience is extremely useful. You may have heard people you know or even people on TV or radio talking about their childhood. Or you can interview people with a specific writing assignment in mind. Books and magazines are a good source of material for assignments. Many experts, for example, have written about various aspects of childhood.

_____ b.   Where will you get the material for your writing assignments? There are several good sources. First of all, your own experience is a major resource. For an assignment about childhood, for instance, you can draw on your own numerous memories of childhood. In addition, other people's experiences are extremely useful. You may have heard people you know or even people on TV or radio talking about their childhood. Or you can interview people with a specific writing assignment in mind. Finally, books and magazines are a good source of material for assignments. Many experts, for example, have written about various aspects of childhood.

Explanation: You no doubt chose the second version, _b._ The listing transitions—_first of all, in addition,_ and _finally_—make it clear when the author is introducing a new supporting point. The reader of paragraph _b_ is better able to follow the author's line of thinking and to note that three main sources of material for assignments are being listed: your own experience, other people's experience, and books and magazines.

Activity

The following paragraphs use listing order or time order. In each case, fill in the blanks with appropriate transitions from the box above the paragraph. Use each transition once.

1.

after	now	first	soon	while

My husband has developed an involving hobby, in which I, unfortunately, am unable to share. He _____ enrolled in ground flight instruction classes at the local community college. The lessons were all about air safety regulations and procedures. _____ passing a difficult exam, he decided to take flying lessons at the city airport. Every Monday he would wake at six o'clock in the morning and drive happily to the airport, eager to see his instructor. _____ he was taking lessons, he started to buy airplane magazines and talk about them constantly. "Look at that Cessna 150," he would say. "Isn't she a beauty?" _____, after many lessons, he is flying by himself. _____ he will be able to carry passengers. That is my biggest nightmare. I know he will want me to fly with him, but I am not a lover of heights. I can't understand why someone would leave the safety of the ground to be in the sky, defenseless as a kite.

2.

finally	for one thing	second

The karate class I took last week convinced me that martial arts may never be my strong point. _____, there is the issue of balance. The instructor asked everyone in class to stand on one foot to practice kicking. Each time I tried, I wobbled and had to spread my arms out wide to avoid falling. I even stumbled into Mr. Kim, my instructor, who glared at me.

_____, there was the issue of flexibility. Mr. Kim asked us to stretch and touch our toes. Everyone did this without a problem—except me. I could barely reach my knees before pain raced up and down my back.

_____, there was my lack of coordination. When everyone started practicing blocks, I got confused. I couldn't figure out where to move my arms and legs. By the time I got the first move right, the whole group had finished three more. By the end of my first lesson, I was completely lost.

3.

later	soon	when	then

At the age of thirty-one I finally had the opportunity to see snow for the first time in my life. It was in New York City on a cloudy afternoon in November.

My daughter and I had gone to the American Museum of Natural History.

_____ we left the museum, snow was falling gently. I thought that it was so beautiful! It made me remember movies I had seen countless times in my native Brazil. We decided to find a taxi.

_____ we were crossing Central Park, snuggled in the cozy cab, watching the snow cover trees, bushes, branches, and grass. We were amazed to see the landscape quickly change from fall to winter.

_____ we arrived in front of our hotel, and I still remember stepping on the crisp snow and laughing like a child who is touched by magic.

_____ that day, I heard on the radio that another snowstorm was coming. I was naive enough to wait for thunder and the other sounds of a rainstorm. I did not know yet that snow, even a snowstorm, is silent and soft.

4.

| last of all | another | first of all | in addition |

Public school students who expect to attend school from September to June, and then have a long summer vacation, may be in for a big surprise before long. For a number of reasons, many schools are switching to a year-round calendar. _____ , many educators point out that the traditional school calendar was established years ago when young people had to be available during the summer months to work on farms, but this necessity has long since passed. _____ reason is that a longer school year accommodates individual learning rates more effectively. That is, fast learners can go into more depth about a subject that interests them, while those who learn at a slower pace have more time to master the essential material.

_____ , many communities have gone to year-round school to relieve overcrowding, since students can be put on different schedules throughout the year. _____ , and perhaps most important, educators feel that year-round schools eliminate the loss of learning that many students experience over a long summer break.

13 Organizing Details in a Paragraph

The supporting details in a paragraph must be organized in a meaningful way. The two most common methods of organizing details are listing order and time order. The activities that follow will give you practice in both methods of organization.

Activity 1

Use *listing order* to arrange the scrambled list of sentences below. Number each supporting sentence 1, 2, 3, . . . so that you go from the least important item to what is presented as the most important item.

Note that transitions will help by making clear the relationships between some of the sentences.

Topic sentence: I am no longer a big fan of professional sports, for a number of reasons.

_____   Basketball and hockey continue well into the baseball season, and football doesn't have its Super Bowl until the middle of winter, when basketball should be at center stage.

_____   In addition, I detest the high fives, taunting, and trash talk that so many professional athletes now indulge in during games.

_____   Second, I am bothered by the length of professional sports seasons.

_____   Also, professional athletes have no loyalty to a team or city as they greedily sell their abilities to the highest bidder.

_____   For one thing, greed is the engine running professional sports.

_____   There are numerous news stories of professional athletes in trouble with the law because of drugs, guns, fights, traffic accidents, or domestic violence.

_____   After a good year, athletes making millions become unhappy if they aren't rewarded with a new contract calling for even more millions.

_____   But the main reason I've become disenchanted with professional sports is the disgusting behavior of so many of its performers.

Activity 2

Use *time order* to arrange the scrambled sentences below. Number the supporting sentences in the order in which they occur in time (1, 2, 3, . . .).

Note that transitions will help by making clear the relationships between sentences.

Topic sentence: If you are a smoker, the following steps should help you quit.

_____   Before your "quit day" arrives, have a medical checkup to make sure it will be all right for you to begin an exercise program.

_____   You should then write down on a card your decision to quit and the date of your "quit day."

_____ When your "quit day" arrives, stop smoking and start your exercise program.

_____ Finally, remind yourself repeatedly how good you will feel when you can confidently tell yourself and others that you are a non-smoker.

_____ Place the card in a location where you will be sure to see it every day.

_____ When you begin this exercise program, be sure to drink plenty of water every day and to follow a sensible diet.

_____ After making a definite decision to stop smoking, select a specific "quit day."

_____ Eventually, your exercise program should include activities strenuous enough to strengthen your lung capacity and your overall stamina.

14 Understanding the Plan of Development in an Essay

Activity

Complete each thesis statement below by adding a third supporting idea. Use wording that is parallel to the two supporting ideas already provided.

1. The people who have given me the best advice are my father, my grand-mother, and my _____.

2. The qualities I most admire in my best friend are her sense of humor, her loyalty, and her _____.

3. Reading a novel, taking a warm bath, and _____ are excellent ways to relax at the end of a long day.

4. Fights with my wife usually stem from disagreements about money, child raising, and _____.

5. Sticking to a diet, keeping a schedule, and _____ are the most difficult challenges I face.

6. My three favorite possessions are my photograph albums, my letters from friends, and my _____.

7. To find work in a day care center satisfying, a person should enjoy teaching, have lots of patience, and _____.

8. My neighbors are most annoying when they play music late at night, borrow items and never return them, and _____.

9. New college students need advice on managing their time, communicating with their instructors, and _____.

10. Three weeks of vacation, an exercise center, and _____ are among the great benefits I receive at work.

15 Recognizing Specific Details in an Essay

Activity

For each supporting paragraph in the essay below, there are two sets of supporting details. Write *S* (for *specific*) in the blank next to the set that provides specific support for the topic sentence. Write *G* (for *general*) in the blank next to the set with only vague, general support.

Introduction

What would you do if one of your friends—a terrific guy who is good-natured, generous, and outgoing—invited you over for dinner? You're probably thinking, "I'd certainly go. Why not?" Would you still go if your friend, a prince of a fellow, was a lousy host? Well, that's the dilemma my old college friend Ben presents. Everybody likes Ben, but nobody wants to be invited to his place for the evening because he doesn't manage his time well, he's an awful cook, and he's messy.

Supporting Paragraph 1

The first problem is that Ben has no sense of how to plan a schedule.

_____ a. He doesn't seem to think ahead when he invites people over for the evening. When you show up at the time he invited you, you find that he isn't ready for you at all. In fact, he hasn't even begun to prepare dinner. Because he's so busy preparing dinner, he is unable to give his attention to his guests. He expects his guests to take care of themselves or follow him around the kitchen while he prepares dinner. His inability to manage his time can cause his guests a lot of inconvenience and result in a pretty boring evening.

_____ b. For example, say he invites you over for dinner at six. When you show up at that hour, you will probably meet him just getting home from work. Then you will watch him wander around his kitchen for a while, wondering aloud what to make for dinner. Likely as not, he'll decide to try something that takes a great deal of time, like eggplant Parmesan, leaving you to entertain yourself either watching him prepare dinner or watching TV. By nine o'clock, you'll be begging him for a few carrot sticks, an apple—anything.

Supporting Paragraph 2

Second, Ben is a truly awful cook.

_____ a. If he does manage to come up with something to eat before you die of hunger, it will probably be so terrible it'll make your tongue curl. He has dreamed up such creative dishes as pork chops with lime sauce and potatoes mashed with sardines. After the first bite, most guests try to find a way to hide the rest under their napkins. Once he stood in front of the cupboard for twenty minutes, muttering, "Well, now let's see what we've got here." Then he fussed like a mad scientist over ingredients he found and came up with something he called "cereal burgers."

_____ b. Although it doesn't seem that hard to find some tasty-sounding recipes and follow them, Ben doesn't seem capable of doing that. In fact, he prefers not to use recipes at all. He likes to make up his own food combinations. This sounds like a good idea, but it rarely turns out well when Ben does it. The main reasons are that he has such bad taste and also he often has very few ingredients in the apartment. He considers it a challenge to come up with an edible meal based on whatever happens to remain on his cupboard shelves. The idea of shopping with guests in mind never enters his mind.

Supporting Paragraph 3

Finally, Ben's apartment is so messy it's unpleasant to spend time there.

_____ a. It is challenging to find a place to sit in his apartment, and you may have something on the floor get on your shoes. Ben doesn't seem to notice that he can't find anything and doesn't have any room to sit down. The truth is, it doesn't bother him to be surrounded by all types of things that most people would have thrown in the garbage can or recycled ages ago. Even people who are not terribly neat themselves are shocked by the jumbled environment in Ben's apartment.

_____ b. When you cross his living room floor, a half-eaten lollipop may stick to the soles of your shoes. When you sit on the sofa, you hear the crunch of hidden crackers. You'd like to move, but all the other seats are buried under mountains of papers, laundry, and pizza boxes. One measure of Ben's messiness is the reaction of our friend Cruz. Cruz's bedroom floor is covered with underwear and empty Chinese food containers. His living room rug, once green, is gray with dust. Last time I spoke to Cruz, he observed, "I had dinner at Ben's last night. Boy, is his apartment a mess."

Conclusion

As I said, Ben is a heck of a guy. He is kind to old people and children. He doesn't have a bad thing to say about anyone. In December, he collects toys for the poor. He tells wonderful jokes and is extremely well read. His friends can't say enough good things about him. They love to spend time with him—anywhere except at his place.

16 Providing Details in an Essay

Activity

The supporting paragraphs of the following essay need more specific details. In the spaces provided, add a sentence or two of convincing details for each idea.

Introduction

I remember the September morning that I first laid eyes on Jill. I'd been calling clients at my desk at work when I heard a warm, musical laugh. There was something so attractive about the sound that I got up to get a cup of coffee and to find the source of that laugh. I discovered the voice to be that of a young, auburn-haired woman we had just hired from a temporary agency. Soon after, Jill and I began going out, and we spent the next two years together. Only recently have we decided to break up because of disagreements about finances, about children, and about our relationship with her family.

Supporting Paragraph 1

First of all, Jill and I have very different ideas about how to handle money. She likes to spend a lot of money on entertainment, and I don't. _____

_____

_____

_____

_____

_____

In addition, while I think saving for the future is essential, she thinks it's silly.

_____

_____

_____

_____

_____

Also, I feel she uses credit cards too freely. _____

_____

_____

_____

_____

_____

Supporting Paragraph 2

Second, our thoughts about children are quite different. One conflict we had was over whether or not we should have any children. _____

_____

_____

_____

_____

_____

If we did have children, her ideas about how they should be cared for are different from mine. _____

_____

_____

_____

_____

Her ideas about how children should be educated also differ greatly from my own. _____

_____

_____

_____

_____

Supporting Paragraph 3

Finally, we disagreed about how to deal with her family. Jill expected us to spend a lot of time with her parents, a prospect that horrifies me. _____

_____

_____

_____

_____

She also expected us to consult her parents before we made any major decisions; I haven't found their advice all that wise. _____

_____

_____

_____

_____

Conclusion

I care a lot about Jill, and I miss having her in my life. But I am convinced that our marriage would have been a mistake because of our conflicting views on finances, children, and family. I have no regrets about the decision to break off our relationship.

17 Providing Transitions in an Essay

ALLWRITE!
6.1

Activity 1

The following essay uses time order. Fill in the blanks with appropriate transitions from the box. Use every transition once. You will probably find it helpful to check off (✓) each transition as you use it.

then	finally	first	as
before	often	soon	when
until	while	next	after

Most mornings at my office pass in a rather typical—and peaceful—fashion. _____ , I go over the calendar and write reminders to myself about my day's schedule. I also go through the list of orders that were taken the day before, checking to be sure everything is clear. Other tasks follow _____ it's time for lunch. However, life at my office was not so typical this morning because of a black cloud, a loud alarm, and a visitor wearing a mask.

The surprises began with a mistake made by our office boy. _____ I was working at my computer, I suddenly heard cursing behind me.

_____ trying to replace the toner cartridge in our copying machine, Greg, the office boy, had dropped the cartridge, and a cloud of black toner dust was rising in the air above the copier. _____ the dust could begin to subside, it started to go into an air conditioning duct nearby. Someone ran to turn off the air conditioning, but some dust still got into the duct system. We all became aware of a fine black powder on our bodies and all the surfaces in the office.

The _____ episode of the morning was equally upsetting. Suddenly a very loud clanging filled the offices, as if a giant telephone were ringing. It took us a few seconds to realize that it was the fire alarm.

Everyone _____ herded quickly down the stairs. In short order, there were around two hundred people on the front sidewalk wondering where the smoke and hot flames were. As it turned out, there were none. Someone on another floor had burned some toast in a toaster that he had, against the rules, brought into the building. As a result, he triggered the alarm system. We all returned to our desks, hoping to get some work done.

_____ we had to deal with a third unexpected event: a visitor wearing a mask. Our office is in the same building as a veterinarian. We

_____ hear the yipping of dogs and the yowling of cats as they are carried in to see the doctor. However, we had never actually had a visitor from the vet's office. But _____ a secretary heard some scratching and opened the office door to check, something large and furry dashed past her. It hid under a desk where we couldn't really get a good look at it, but we could hear it snarling and spitting at us. Fortunately, it was _____ followed by its owner, who told us the angry animal was a raccoon. "Don't worry," he assured us. "We're almost sure it doesn't have rabies, but we're just having it tested to be certain."

_____ his announcement, the office once again cleared out very quickly.

After the black cloud, the false alarm, and the surprise visitor, I decided I had had enough for one day. I've been home all afternoon with a cold cloth on my forehead, and I'm hoping for a boring day tomorrow.

Activity 2

The following essay uses listing order. Fill in the blanks with appropriate transitions from the box. Use every transition once. You will probably find it helpful to check off (✓) each transition as you use it.

other	another	one	also
furthermore	third	moreover	

Does your will to study collapse when someone suggests getting a pizza? Does your social life compete with your class attendance? Is there a huge gap between your intentions and your actions? If the answers to these questions are yes, yes, and yes, read on. You can benefit from three powerful ways to motivate yourself: setting goals and working consciously to reach them, using rational thinking, and developing a positive personality.

_____ key to self-motivation is deciding on your goals—both long- and short-term—and then really working to reach them. Do you want to be an accountant or a nurse in a few years? Do you want to raise your grade point average this semester? Do you want to get at least a B on a paper this week? Whatever your goal, keep it in mind; it is the future you're working toward. _____ keep in mind that the great majority of students who can be classified as failures have no goals. Once you've got some goals firmly in mind, decide how to reach them. Perhaps you'll need to study for at least two hours a day. Then think about the reward you'll give yourself for reaching a goal. Maybe for every hour of study, you'll eat a special snack or listen to your favorite music.

_____ rewards for achieving short-term goals might be going to the park, seeing a movie, calling a friend on the phone, and taking a nap.

Along with setting goals, _____ key to self-motivation is learning to think rationally. Instead of seeking shortcuts, do things right. If you're not sure about an important point on an assignment, ask instead of guessing. Don't rationalize about why you don't need to study for a math quiz. Instead, remind yourself that you need a passing grade in math to graduate. Also, rationally examine the benefits of good study habits. When you develop good study habits, studying takes less time and you get more out of it. _____ , as your studying becomes more and more productive, your self-image improves.

A _____ key to self-motivation is developing a positive personality. A positive personality includes attitudes that bring success. For instance, a positive person is enthusiastic, dependable, and supportive of others. _____ , a positive student has an upbeat, can-do self-image. "I can't," "It's too tough," and "Why bother?" aren't in this student's vocabulary.

So get your willpower in gear and use the three keys to self-motivation—set goals and work to reach them, think rationally, and develop a positive personality. You will find that a firm commitment to this approach becomes easier and easier. Progress will come more often and more readily, strengthening your resolve even further.

18 Introductory and Concluding Paragraphs

8.1

Activity 1

Four common methods of introducing an essay are as follows:

a Begin with a broad statement and narrow it down to your thesis statement.
b Present an idea or situation that is the opposite of the one you will develop.
c Tell a brief story.
d Ask one or more questions.

Following are four introductions. In the space provided, write the letter of the method of introduction used in each case.

_____ 1. One morning twenty-nine years ago, my father backed out of his parking space, smashed into the Cadillac parked across the street, put the car into drive, and kept going. "Take it easy, Floyd," yelled Mom. "Better to be late than to die!" But that didn't keep him from accelerating, weaving in and out of traffic, and running into a telephone booth. As a result, I was born in my parents' old green-and-white Chevy instead of at Bradley Hospital. Perhaps it's no surprise, then, that my own car was the location of other key events in my life—an accident that almost killed me, the place where I made a crucial job decision, and my proposal to my wife.

2. I have had a lot of interesting teachers through the years. Some have taught me useful and interesting facts. Even better, some have shown me how to learn. Some have even inspired me. But of all the wonderful teachers I've had, my favorite is Mrs. Rogers, who taught me how to write, showed me the pleasures of reading, and most important, helped me realize I could do just about anything I put my mind to.

3. Most mornings at my office pass in a rather typical—and peaceful—fashion. First, I go over the calendar and write reminders to myself about my day's schedule. I also go through the list of orders that were taken the day before, checking to be sure everything is clear. Other tasks follow until it's time for lunch. However, life at my office was not so typical this morning because of a black cloud, a loud alarm, and a visitor wearing a mask.

4. Does your will to study collapse when someone suggests getting a pizza? Does your social life compete with your class attendance? Is there a huge gap between your intentions and your actions? If the answers to these questions are yes, yes, and yes, read on. You can benefit from three powerful ways to motivate yourself: setting goals and working consciously to reach them, using rational thinking, and developing a positive personality.

Activity 2

Two common methods of concluding an essay are as follows:

a   Provide a summary and a final thought.

b   Focus on the future.

Following are two conclusions. In the space provided, write the letter of the method of conclusion used in each case.

1. I care a lot about Jill, and I miss having her in my life. But I am convinced that our marriage would have been a mistake because of our conflicting views on finances, children, and family. I have no regrets about the decision to break off our relationship.

2. So get your willpower in gear and use the three keys to self-motivation— set goals and work to reach them, think rationally, and develop a positive

personality. You will find that a firm commitment to this approach becomes easier and easier. Progress will come more often and more readily, strengthening your resolve even further.

19 Prewriting

These activities will give you practice in some of the prewriting strategies you can use to generate material for a paper. While the focus here is on writing a paragraph, the strategies apply to writing an essay as well. See if you can do two or more of these prewriting activities.

Activity 1: Freewriting

On a sheet of paper, freewrite for several minutes about the best or most disappointing friend you ever had. Don't worry about grammar, punctuation, or spelling. Try to write, without stopping, about whatever comes into your head concerning your best or most disappointing friend.

Activity 2: Questioning

On another sheet of paper, answer the following questions about the friend you've started to write about.

1. When did this friendship take place?
2. Where did it take place?
3. What is one reason you liked or were disappointed in this friend? Give one quality, action, comment, etc. Also, give some details to illustrate this quality.
4. What is another reason that you liked or were disappointed in your friend? What are some details that support the second reason?
5. Can you think of a third thing about your friend that you liked or were disappointed in? What are some details that support the third reason?

Activity 3: Clustering

In the center of a blank sheet of paper, write and circle the words *best friend* or *most disappointing friend.* Then, around the circle, add reasons and details about the friend. Use a series of boxes, circles, or other shapes, along with connecting lines, to set off the reasons and details. In other words, try to think about and explore your topic in a very visual way.

Activity 4: Making a List

On separate paper, make a list of details about the friend. Don't worry about putting them in a certain order. Just get down as many details about the friend as occur to you. The list can include specific reasons you liked or were disappointed in the person and specific details supporting those reasons.

20 Outlining, Drafting, and Revising

4

Here you will get practice in the writing steps that follow prewriting: outlining, drafting, revising, editing, and proofreading.

Activity 1: Scratch Outline

On the basis of your prewriting, see if you can prepare a scratch outline made up of your main idea and the three main reasons you liked or were disappointed in your friend. Use the form below:

_____ was my best *or* most disappointing friend.

Reason 1: _____

Reason 2: _____

Reason 3: _____

Activity 2: First Draft

Now write a first draft of your paper. Begin with your topic sentence, stating that a certain friend was the best or most disappointing one you ever had. Then state the first reason to support your main idea, followed by specific details supporting that reason. Next, state the second reason, followed by specific details supporting that reason. Finally, state the third reason, followed by support.

Don't worry about grammar, punctuation, or spelling. Just concentrate on getting down on paper the details about your friend.

Activity 3: Revising the Draft

Ideally, you will have a chance to put your paper aside for a while before writing the second draft. In your second draft, try to do all of the following:

1. Add transition words such as *first of all, another,* and *finally* to introduce each of the three reasons you liked or were disappointed in the friend you're writing about.

2. Omit any details that do not truly support your topic sentence.

3. Add more details as needed, making sure you have plenty of support for each of your three reasons.

4. Check to see that your details are vivid and specific. Can you make a supporting detail more concrete? Are there any persuasive, colorful specifics you can add?

5. Try to eliminate wordiness (see page 391) and clichés (see page 388).

6. In general, improve the flow of your writing.

7. Be sure to include a final sentence that rounds off the paper, bringing it to a close.

Activity 4: Editing and Proofreading

When you have your almost-final draft of the paper, proofread it as follows:

1. Using your dictionary, check any words that you think might be misspelled. Or use a spell-check program on your computer.

2. Using Part Two of this book, check your paper for mistakes in grammar, punctuation, and usage.

3. Read the paper aloud, listening for awkward or unclear spots. Make the changes needed for the paragraph to read smoothly and clearly. Even better, see if you can get another person to read the draft aloud to you. The spots that this person has trouble reading are spots where you may have to do some rewriting.

4. Take a sheet of paper and cover your writing so that you can expose and carefully check one line at a time. Or read your writing backward, from the end of the paragraph to the beginning. Look for typing errors, omitted words, and other remaining errors.

Don't fail to edit and proofread carefully. You may be tired of working on your paper at this point, but you want to give the extra effort needed to make it as good as possible. A final push can mean the difference between a higher and a lower grade.

21 Paragraph and Essay Writing Assignments

Your instructor may ask you to do some of the following paragraph and essay writing assignments. Be sure to refer to the activities above as you write. Also, check the rules for paper format on page 266.

Five Paragraph Assignments

■ Paragraph Assignment 1: A Sharp Memory of Your Mother or Father

Think of a particularly clear memory you have of your mother or father. It might be a happy memory that warms your heart. Or it could be humorous, frightening, or enraging. The important thing is that it is a sharp, specific recollection that produces a strong emotional response in you. Then write a paragraph about your memory.

Your goal will be to let the reader see exactly what happened and understand what you felt. To accomplish this, you must provide very specific details. Remember that your reader will have no prior knowledge of your mother or father. You are responsible for painting a "word picture" that will let your reader see your parent the way you saw him or her.

Before you begin writing the paragraph itself, do some prewriting. You might jot down answers to the kind of questions a curious reader would have about your memory. Here are a few such questions: Where did this event take place? When? Who was present? How old was your parent when this occurred? How old were you? What did your parent look like? What did he or she say? How did he or she say it? Why is this memory so vivid for you? The answers to questions like these will provide the kind of concrete detail that will make your paragraph come alive.

Begin your paragraph with a summary statement, such as these:

One of my family's most amusing experiences took place when I found my father sleepwalking in the kitchen.

Seeing my mother trip on the sidewalk was the beginning of a difficult morning for me.

Your paragraph will probably be organized in time order, describing the events that occurred from beginning to end. You can help your reader understand the sequence of events if you use time transitions such as *first, next, then, later,* and *finally.*

If you prefer, write instead about a memory of another relative.

■ Paragraph Assignment 2: A Disagreeable Characteristic

Even the most saintly person has one or more unpleasant traits. Write a paragraph about a particularly disagreeable characteristic of someone you know. Your topic sentence will be a general statement about that person and the quality you've chosen to write about. For example, if you decide to write about your own extreme impatience, your topic sentence might be:

When I let my impatience get out of hand, I often damage my relationships with others.

A paragraph with this topic sentence might list two or three experiences supporting that main idea. Here are two other examples of topic sentences for this paper:

Our neighbor Mr. Nagle is a cruel person.

While my minister is basically a kind man, he much prefers hearing his own voice to anyone else's.

■ Paragraph Assignment 3: A Special Goal

We all have goals, long-term and short-term. Write a paragraph about one of your important goals. It might be something you hope to achieve over the next few months or the next few years.

Perhaps you plan to overcome a bad habit or get a better job. Begin your paragraph with a topic sentence that clearly states the goal and when you expect to reach it, such as "I hope to have quit smoking by the end of this year" or "After I graduate, I hope to get a nursing job at a local hospital." Then go on to list and explain two or three reasons you wish to reach the goal. To generate some reasons, make a list, and then choose the three you feel are the strongest. Save the most important reason for last.

■ Paragraph Assignment 4: In Praise of Something

We all are fans of something that we feel greatly enriches our life, such as a pet, basketball, or chocolate. Write a paragraph in which your supporting details show the benefits or virtues of something you adore. For instance, you could write about the advantages of having a dog around the house. Use whatever prewriting strategy you choose to help you come up with more benefits or virtues than you need. Then choose two or three you feel you can explain in colorful detail.

One benefit you might list, for instance, is that a dog makes one feel loved. You could illustrate this benefit by describing an experience such as the following:

A week ago, I spilled hot coffee on a customer's lap. He was not amused. After the customer left—without leaving a tip, of course—the manager walked past me and said quietly, "Strike one!" When I got home that day and collapsed on a chair, my friend Goldie, a cocker spaniel, hopped onto my lap and licked my face with his broad, warm tongue. I could feel the knot in my stomach loosening.

Here's a sample scratch outline for this assignment.

Topic sentence: Having a dog around the house is one of life's rich pleasures.

(1) A dog is entertaining.

(2) A dog brings out the best in a person.

(3) A dog makes a person feel loved.

■ Paragraph Assignment 5: A Popular Saying

It seems there are sayings to cover every type of experience, from our sleeping habits ("Early to bed, early to rise, makes a man healthy, wealthy and wise") to our expectations ("Hope for the best but expect the worst"). Write a paragraph in which you demonstrate through an experience you have had that a particular saying is either true or false.

Begin your paragraph with a clear statement supporting or opposing the saying, such as "When I painted my house last summer, I learned the truth of the saying 'Haste makes waste'" or "When it comes to escaping a fire, the saying 'Haste makes waste' doesn't apply." Then go on to tell your experience in vivid detail. To help your reader follow the sequence of events involved, use a few time transitions (*before, then, during, now,* and so on). Below are some other popular sayings you might wish to consider using in your paper—or use some other popular saying.

Here today, gone tomorrow.

If you don't help yourself, nobody will.

A penny saved is a penny earned.

The early bird catches the worm.

Curiosity killed the cat.

You get what you pay for.

A rolling stone gathers no moss.

Don't count your chickens before they're hatched.

An ounce of prevention is worth a pound of cure.

A journey of a thousand miles must begin with a single step.

Whatever can go wrong will go wrong.

Don't judge someone until you've walked a mile in his shoes.

Five Essay Assignments

■ Essay Assignment 1: The Place Where You Live

Write an essay about the best or worst features of your apartment or house. In your introduction, you might begin with a general description of where you live. Then end the paragraph with your thesis statement and plan of development.

Here are some thesis statements that may help you think about and develop your own paper.

Thesis statement: I love my apartment because of its wonderful location, its great kitchen, and my terrific neighbors.

(A supporting paragraph on the apartment's location, for example, might focus on the fact that it's in the middle of a lively, interesting neighborhood with a good supermarket, a drugstore, a variety of restaurants, and so on.)

Thesis statement: My house has three key advantages: a wonderful landlord, a beautiful yard, and housemates that are like family.

(A supporting paragraph about the landlord might explain how he or she fixes things promptly and once, in a special circumstance, allowed you to pay your rent late.)

Thesis statement: A tiny kitchen, dismal decor, and noisy neighbors are the three main disadvantages of my apartment.

(A supporting paragraph on the apartment's dismal decor could begin with this topic sentence: "The dark and poorly kept walls and floorings are ugly and, even worse, gloomy." Such a sentence might then be followed by some very carefully worded, concrete specifics and perhaps a revealing anecdote.)

Note that listing transitions such as *first of all, second, another, also, in addition, finally,* and so on may help you introduce your supporting paragraphs as well as set off different supporting details within those paragraphs.

■ Essay Assignment 2: What Children Really Need

There are many theories about what children need from the adults in their lives. Give some thought to your own childhood, your own children, or your observations of children you know. Decide on three things that *you* believe are essential to a child's growth and development. Then write a five-paragraph essay on those three qualities.

Your introductory paragraph should arouse your readers' interest. For instance, you might explain how important a person's childhood is to the rest of his or her life. The introductory paragraph should also include a thesis statement made up of your central idea and the three necessities you think are so important. For instance, one student's thesis was this: "I feel that three things all children need are love, approval, and a sense of belonging."

Devote each of the following three supporting paragraphs to one of these important things. Begin each paragraph with a clearly stated topic sentence, and use concrete examples to show how adults can provide each quality to children.

Be equally specific in showing what you believe happens when children are not provided with these things. To help your reader make the transition from paragraph to paragraph, use such words as *another thing, in addition,* and *a final quality.* You may wish to consider writing about some of the following things many people feel children need for healthy growth and development:

Unconditional love

Approval

Sense of belonging

Opportunities to experiment

Feeling of safety

Clearly defined limits to behavior

Sense of responsibility

In a concluding paragraph, provide a summary of the points in your paper as well as a final thought to round off your discussion.

■ Essay Assignment 3: Something Special

Imagine that your apartment or house is burning down. Of course, the best strategy would be to get yourself and others out of the building as quickly as possible. But suppose you knew for sure that you had time to rescue three of your possessions. Which three would you choose? Write an essay in which you discuss the three things in your home that you would most want to save from a fire.

Begin by doing some prewriting to find the items you want to write about. You could, for instance, try making a list and then choosing several of the most likely candidates. Then you could freewrite about each of those candidates. In this way, you are likely to find three possessions that will make strong subjects for this essay. Each will be the basis of a supporting paragraph. Each supporting paragraph will focus on why the object being discussed is so important to you. Make your support as specific and colorful as possible, perhaps using detailed descriptions, anecdotes, or quotations to reveal the importance of each object.

In planning your introduction, consider beginning with a broad, general idea and then narrowing it down to your thesis statement. Here, for example, is one such introduction for this paper:

I have many possessions that I would be sad to lose. Because I love to cook, I would miss various kitchen appliances that provide me with so many happy cooking adventures. I would also miss the wonderful electronic equipment that entertains me every day, including my large-screen television set and my VCR. I would miss the various telephones on which I have spent many interesting hours chatting in every part of my apartment, including the bathtub. But if my apartment were burning down, I would most want to rescue three things that are irreplaceable and hold great meaning for me—the silverware set that belonged to my grandmother, my mother's wedding gown, and my giant photo album.

■ Essay Assignment 4: Teaching the Basics

What are you experienced in? Fixing cars? Growing flowers? Baking? Waiting on customers? Giving children's birthday parties? Write an essay teaching readers the basics of an activity in which you have some experience. If you're not sure about which activity to choose, use prewriting to help you find a topic you can support strongly. Once you've chosen your topic, continue to prewrite as a way to find your key points and organize them into three supporting paragraphs. The key details of waiting on customers in a diner, for instance, might be divided according to time order, as seen in the following topic sentences:

Topic sentence for supporting paragraph 1: Greeting customers and taking their orders should not be done carelessly.

Topic sentence for supporting paragraph 2: There are right and wrong ways to bring customers their food and to keep track of them during their meal.

Topic sentence for supporting paragraph 3: The final interaction with customers may be brief, but it is important.

To make your points clear, be sure to use detailed descriptions and concrete examples throughout your essay. Also, you may want to use transitional words such as *first, then, also, another, when, after, while,* and *finally* to help organize your details.

■ Essay Assignment 5: Advantages or Disadvantages of Single Life

More and more people are remaining single longer, and almost half of the people who marry eventually divorce and become single again. Write an essay on the advantages or disadvantages of single life. Each of your three supporting paragraphs will focus on one advantage or one disadvantage. To decide which approach to take, begin by making two lists. A list of advantages might include:

More freedom of choice

Lower expenses

Fewer responsibilities

Dating opportunities

A list of disadvantages could include:

> Loneliness
>
> Depression on holidays
>
> Lack of support in everyday decisions
>
> Disapproval of parents and family

Go on to list as many specific details as you can think of to support your advantages and disadvantages. Those details will help you decide whether you want your thesis to focus on benefits or drawbacks. Then create a scratch outline made up of your thesis statement and each of your main supporting points. Put the most important or most dramatic supporting point last.

In your introduction, you might gain your reader's interest by asking several questions or by telling a brief, revealing story about single life. As you develop your supporting paragraphs, make sure that each paragraph begins with a topic sentence and focuses on one advantage or disadvantage of single life. While writing the essay, continue developing details that vividly support each of your points.

In a concluding paragraph, provide a summary of the points in your paper as well as a final thought to round off your discussion. Your final thought might be in the form of a prediction or a recommendation.

Additional Writing Assignments

Detailed writing assignments follow each of the ten readings in Part Four. As you work on these assignments, you will find it helpful to turn back to the writing activities on pages 75–77.

Part Two

Sentence Skills

Introduction

Part Two explains the basic skills needed to write clear, error-free sentences. While the skills are presented within five traditional categories (sentences; verbs, pronouns, and agreement; modifiers and parallelism; punctuation and mechanics; word use), each section is self-contained so that you can go directly to the skills you need to work on. Note, however, that you may find it helpful to cover "Subjects and Verbs" before turning to other skills. Typically, the main features of a skill are presented on the first pages of a section; secondary points are developed later. Numerous activities are provided so that you can practice skills enough to make them habits. The activities are varied and range from underlining answers to writing complete sentences involving the skill in question. One or more review tests at the end of each section offer additional practice activities.

4 Subjects and Verbs

Introductory Activity

Understanding subjects and verbs is a big step toward mastering many sentence skills. As a speaker of English, you already have an instinctive feel for these basic building blocks of English sentences. See if you can insert an appropriate word in each space below. The answer will be a subject.

1. The _____ will soon be over.

2. _____ cannot be trusted.

3. A strange _____ appeared in my backyard.

4. _____ is one of my favorite activities.

Now insert an appropriate word in the following spaces. Each answer will be a verb.

5. The prisoner _____ at the judge.

6. My sister _____ much harder than I do.

7. The players _____ in the locker room.

8. Rob and Marilyn _____ with the teacher.

Finally, insert appropriate words in the following spaces. Each answer will be a subject in the first space and a verb in the second.

9. The __Cat__ almost __fell__ out of the tree.

10. Many __people__ _Sub_ today __read what__ _predict verb_ sex and violence.

11. The __Doctor__ _Sub_ carefully __Observe__ _predict verb_ the patient.

12. A _____ quickly _____ the ball.

87

The basic building blocks of English sentences are subjects and verbs. Understanding them is an important first step toward mastering a number of sentence skills.

Every sentence has a subject and a verb. Who or what the sentence speaks about is called the *subject;* what the sentence says about the subject is called the *verb*. In the following sentences, the subject is underlined once and the verb twice:

People gossip.

The truck belched fumes.

He waved at me.

Alaska contains the largest wilderness area in the United States.

That woman is a millionaire.

The pants feel itchy.

A Simple Way to Find a Subject

To find a subject, ask *who* or *what* the sentence is about. As shown below, your answer is the subject.

Who is the first sentence about? People

What is the second sentence about? The truck

Who is the third sentence about? He

What is the fourth sentence about? Alaska

Who is the fifth sentence about? That woman

What is the sixth sentence about? The pants

It helps to remember that the subject of a sentence is always a *noun* (any person, place, or thing) or a pronoun. A *pronoun* is simply a word like *he, she, it, you,* or *they* used in place of a noun. In the preceding sentences, the subjects are persons (*People, He, woman*), a place (*Alaska*), and things (*truck, pants*). And note that one pronoun (*He*) is used as a subject.

A Simple Way to Find a Verb

ALLWRITE!

14.1c

To find a verb, ask what the sentence *says about* the subject. As shown below, your answer is the verb.

What does the first sentence *say about* people? They <u>gossip</u>.

What does the second sentence *say about* the truck? It <u>belched</u> (fumes).

What does the third sentence *say about* him? He <u>waved</u> (at me).

What does the fourth sentence *say about* Alaska? It <u>contains</u> (the largest wilderness area in the United States).

What does the fifth sentence *say about* that woman? She <u>is</u> (a millionaire).

What does the sixth sentence *say about* the pants? They <u>feel</u> (itchy).

A second way to find the verb is to put *I, you, he, she, it,* or *they* in front of the word you think is a verb. If the result makes sense, you have a verb. For example, you could put *they* in front of *gossip* in the first sentence above, with the result, *they gossip,* making sense. Therefore, you know that *gossip* is a verb. You could use the same test with the other verbs as well.

Finally, it helps to remember that most verbs show action. In "People gossip," the action is gossiping. In "The truck belched fumes," the action is belching. In "He waved at me," the action is waving. In "Alaska contains the largest wilderness area in the United States," the action is containing.

Certain other verbs, known as *linking verbs,* do not show action. They do, however, give information about the subject of the sentence. In "That woman is a millionaire," the linking verb *is* tells us that the woman is a millionaire. In "The pants feel itchy," the linking verb *feel* gives us the information that the pants are itchy.

Practice 1

In each of the following sentences, draw one line under the subject and two lines under the verb.

To find the subject, ask *who* or *what* the sentence is about. Then to find the verb, ask what the sentence *says about* the subject.

1. Carl spilled cocoa on the pale carpet.

   Who is the sentence about? What does the sentence say about him?

2. A ladybug landed on my shoulder.

3. Nick eats cold pizza for breakfast.

4. The waitress brought someone else's meal by mistake.

5. I found a blue egg under the tree in my backyard.

6. Diane stapled her papers together.

7. The audience applauded before the song was finished.

8. My boss has a lot of patience.

9. I tasted poached eggs today for the first time.

10. The new paperboy threw our newspaper under the car.

Practice 2

Follow the directions given for Practice 1. Note that all the verbs here are linking verbs.

1. My parents are not very sociable.

   Who is the sentence about? What linking verb gives us information about them?

2. I am always nervous on the first day of classes.

3. Tri Lee was the first person to finish the exam.

4. Our dog becomes friendly after a few minutes of growling.

5. Estelle seems ready for a nervous breakdown.

6. That plastic hot dog looks good enough to eat.

7. Most people appear slimmer in clothes with vertical stripes.

8. Many students felt exhausted after finishing the placement exam.

9. A cheeseburger has more than seven times as much sodium as French fries.

10. Yesterday, my telephone seemed to be ringing constantly.

Practice 3

Follow the directions given for Practice 1.

1. The rabbits ate more than their share of my garden.

   What is the sentence about? What did they do?

2. My father prefers his well-worn jeans to new ones.

3. A local restaurant donated food for the homeless.

4. Stanley always looks ready for a fight.

5. An elderly couple relaxed on a bench in the shopping mall.

6. Lightning brightened the dark sky for a few seconds.

7. Our town council voted for a curfew on Halloween.

8. Lola's sore throat kept her home from work today.

9. Surprisingly, Vonda's little sister decided not to go to the circus.

10. As usual, I chose the slowest checkout line in the supermarket.

(handwritten: "Noun clauses?, 10/11/06", "Subject 3x4")

More about Subjects and Verbs

Distinguishing Subjects from Prepositional Phrases

The subject of a sentence never appears within a prepositional phrase. A *prepositional phrase* is simply a group of words beginning with a preposition and ending with the answer to the question *what, when,* or *where.* Here is a list of common prepositions.

Common Prepositions

about	before	by	inside	over
above	behind	during	into	through
across	below	except	of	to
among	beneath	for	off	toward
around	beside	from	on	under
at	between	in	onto	with

When you are looking for the subject of a sentence, it is helpful to cross out prepositional phrases.

In the middle of the night, we heard footsteps on the roof.

The magazines on the table belong in the garage.

Before the opening kickoff, a brass band marched onto the field.

The hardware store across the street went out of business.

In spite of our advice, Sally quit her job at Burger King.

Practice

Cross out prepositional phrases. Then draw a single line under subjects and a double line under verbs.

1. By accident, Anita dropped her folder into the mailbox.

   What are the two prepositional phrases? What is the subject? What does the sentence say about her?

(handwritten in left margin: "If subject is plural, the verb is plural")

skeleton of the sentence

2. Before the test, I glanced through my notes.
3. My car stalled on the bridge at rush hour.
4. I hung a photo of Whitney Houston above my bed.
5. On weekends, we visit my grandmother at a nursing home.
6. During the movie, some teenagers giggled at the love scenes.
7. A pedestrian tunnel runs beneath the street to the train station.
8. The parents hid their daughter's Christmas gifts in the garage.
9. All the teachers, except Mr. Blake, wear ties to school.
10. The strawberry jam in my brother's sandwich dripped onto his lap.

Verbs of More Than One Word

Many verbs consist of more than one word. Here, for example, are some of the many forms of the verb *help:*

Some Forms of the Verb Help		
helps	should have been helping	will have helped
helping	can help	would have been helped
is helping	would have been helping	has been helped
was helping	will be helping	had been helped
may help	had been helping	must have helped
should help	helped	having helped
will help	have helped	should have been helped
does help	has helped	had helped

Below are sentences that contain verbs of more than one word:

Yolanda is working overtime this week.
Another book has been written about the Kennedy family.
We should have stopped for gas at the last station.
The game has just been canceled.

Notes

1 Words like *not, just, never, only,* and *always* are not part of the verb although they may appear within the verb.

Yolanda is not working overtime next week.

The boys should just not have stayed out so late.

The game has always been played regardless of the weather.

2 No verb preceded by *to* is ever the verb of a sentence.

Sue wants to go with us.

The newly married couple decided to rent a house for a year.

The store needs extra people to help out at Christmas.

3 No *-ing* word by itself is ever the verb of a sentence. (It may be part of the verb, but it must have a helping verb in front of it.)

We planning the trip for months. (This is not a sentence, because the verb is not complete.)

We were planning the trip for months. (This is a complete sentence.)

Practice

Draw a single line under subjects and a double line under verbs. Be sure to include all parts of the verb.

1. Ellen has chosen blue dresses for her bridesmaids.

   Who is the sentence about? What does it say about her? What two words make up the verb?

2. You should plan your weekly budget more carefully.

3. Felix has been waiting in line for tickets all morning.

4. We should have invited Terri to the party.

5. I would have preferred a movie with a happy ending.

6. Classes were interrupted three times today by a faulty fire alarm.

7. Sam can touch his nose with his tongue.

8. I have been encouraging my mother to quit smoking.

9. Tony has just agreed to feed his neighbor's fish over the holiday.

10. Many students have not been giving much thought to selecting a major.

Compound Subjects and Verbs

A sentence may have more than one verb:

The dancer stumbled and fell.
Lola washed her hair, blew it dry, and parted it in the middle.

A sentence may have more than one subject:

Cats and dogs are sometimes the best of friends.
The striking workers and their bosses could not come to an agreement.

A sentence may have several subjects and several verbs:

Holly and I read the book and reported on it to the class.
Pete, Nick, and Fran caught the fish in the morning, cleaned them in the afternoon, and ate them that night.

Practice

Draw a single line under subjects and a double line under verbs. Be sure to mark
all the subjects and verbs.

1. Boards and bricks make a nice bookcase.
   What two things are the sentence about? What does it say about them?
2. We bought a big bag of peanuts and finished it by the movie's end.
3. A fly and a bee hung lifelessly in the spider's web.
4. The twins look alike but think, act, and dress quite differently.
5. Canned salmon and tuna contain significant amounts of calcium.
6. I waited for the bubble bath to foam and then slipped into the warm tub.
7. The little girl in the next car waved and smiled at me.
8. The bird actually dived under the water and reappeared with a fish.
9. Singers, dancers, and actors performed at the heart-association benefit.
10. The magician and his assistant bowed and disappeared in a cloud of smoke.

■ Review Test 1

Draw one line under the subjects and two lines under the verbs. To help find subjects, cross out prepositional phrases as necessary. Underline all the parts of a verb. You may find more than one subject and verb in a sentence.

1. Most breakfast cereals contain sugar.
2. The drawer of the bureau sticks on rainy days.
3. Our local bus company offers special rates for senior citizens.
4. Drunk drivers in Norway must spend three weeks in jail at hard labor.
5. On weekends, the campus bookstore closes at five o'clock.
6. We wrapped and labeled all the Christmas gifts over the weekend.
7. Motorcycles have been banned from the expressway.
8. Episodes of this old television series are in black and white.
9. The computer sorted, counted, and recorded the ballots within minutes after the closing of the polls.
10. Eddie stepped to the foul line and calmly sank both free throws to win the basketball game.

■ Review Test 2

Follow the directions given for Review Test 1.

1. Gasoline from the broken fuel line dripped onto the floor of the garage.
2. All the carrot tops in the garden had been eaten by rabbits.
3. An old man with a plastic trash bag collected aluminum cans along the road.
4. The majority of people wait until April 15 to file their income tax.
5. My mother became a college freshman at the age of forty-two.
6. At the delicatessen, Linda and Paul ate corned beef sandwiches and drank root beer.
7. The window fan made a clanking sound during the night and kept us from sleeping.
8. An umbrella tumbled across the street in the gusty wind and landed between two cars.
9. Telephones in the mayor's office rang continuously with calls from angry citizens about the city tax increase.
10. A teenager pushed a woman, grabbed her purse, and ran off through the crowd.

5 Fragments

Introductory Activity

Every sentence must have a subject and a verb and must express a complete thought. A word group that lacks a subject or a verb and does not express a complete thought is a *fragment*.

   Listed below are a number of fragments and sentences. See if you can complete the statement that explains each fragment.

1. Telephones.   *Fragment*
   Telephones ring.   *Sentence*

"Telephones" is a fragment because, while it has a subject (*Telephones*), it lacks a __verb__ (*ring*) and so does not express a complete thought.

2. Explains.   *Fragment*
   Darrell explains.   *Sentence*

"Explains" is a fragment because, while it has a verb (*Explains*), it lacks a __subject__ (*Darrell*) and does not express a complete thought.

3. Scribbling notes in class.   *Fragment*
   Jayne was scribbling notes in class.   *Sentence*

"Scribbling notes in class" is a fragment because it lacks a __subj__ (*Jayne*) and also part of the __verb__ (*was*). As a result, it does not express a complete thought.

4. When the dentist began drilling.   *Fragment*
   When the dentist began drilling, I closed my eyes.   *Sentence*

"When the dentist began drilling" is a fragment because we want to know *what happened when* the dentist began drilling. The word group does not follow through and __express a complete thought__

Answers are on page 680.

What Fragments Are

15.2

Every sentence must have a subject and a verb and must express a complete thought. A word group that lacks a subject or a verb and does not express a complete thought is a *fragment*. Following are the most common types of fragments that people write:

1 Dependent-word fragments
2 *-ing* and *to* fragments
3 Added-detail fragments
4 Missing-subject fragments

Once you understand the specific kind or kinds of fragments that you might write, you should be able to eliminate them from your writing. The following pages explain all four types of fragments.

Look up-complex sentences

1 Dependent-Word Fragments

Some word groups that begin with a dependent word are fragments. Here is a list of common dependent words:

Common Dependent Words	
after	unless
although, though	until
as	what, whatever
because	when, whenever
before	where, wherever
even though	whether
how	which, whichever
if, even if	while
in order that	who
since	whose
that, so that	

Whenever you start a sentence with one of these dependent words, you must be careful that a dependent-word fragment does not result. The word group beginning with the dependent word *After* in the selection below is a fragment.

> After I stopped drinking coffee. I began sleeping better at night.

A *dependent statement*—one starting with a dependent word like *After*—cannot stand alone. It depends on another statement to complete the thought. "After I stopped drinking coffee" is a dependent statement. It leaves us hanging. We expect in the same sentence to find out *what happened after* the writer stopped drinking coffee. When a writer does not follow through and complete a thought, a fragment results.

To correct the fragment, simply follow through and complete the thought:

> After I stopped drinking coffee, I began sleeping better at night.

Remember, then, that *dependent statements by themselves* are fragments. They must be attached to a statement that makes sense standing alone.*

Here are two other examples of dependent-word fragments.

> Brian sat nervously in the dental clinic. While waiting to have his wisdom tooth pulled.
>
> Maria decided to throw away the boxes. That had accumulated for years in the basement.

"While waiting to have his wisdom tooth pulled" is a fragment; it does not make sense standing by itself. We want to know in the same statement *what Brian did* while waiting to have his tooth pulled. The writer must complete the thought. Likewise, "That had accumulated for years in the basement" is not in itself a complete thought. We want to know in the same statement what *that* refers to.

How to Correct Dependent-Word Fragments

In most cases, you can correct a dependent-word fragment by attaching it to the sentence that comes after it or to the sentence that comes before it:

> After I stopped drinking coffee, I began sleeping better at night.
>
> (The fragment has been attached to the sentence that comes after it.)

---

*Some instructors refer to a dependent-word fragment as a *dependent clause*. A *clause* is simply a group of words having a subject and a verb. A clause may be *independent* (expressing a complete thought and able to stand alone) or *dependent* (not expressing a complete thought and not able to stand alone). A dependent clause by itself is a fragment. It can be corrected simply by adding an independent clause.

Brian sat nervously in the dental clinic while waiting to have his wisdom tooth pulled.

(The fragment has been attached to the sentence that comes before it.)

Maria decided to throw away the boxes that had accumulated for years in the basement.

(The fragment has been attached to the sentence that comes before it.)

Another way of correcting a dependent-word fragment is to eliminate the dependent word and make a new sentence:

I stopped drinking coffee.

He was waiting to have his wisdom tooth pulled.

They had accumulated for years in the basement.

Do not use this second method of correction too frequently, however, for it may cut down on interest and variety in your writing style.

Notes

1 Use a comma if a dependent-word group comes at the *beginning* of a sentence (see also page 321):

After I stopped drinking coffee, I began sleeping better at night.

However, do not generally use a comma if the dependent-word group comes at the end of a sentence:

Brian sat nervously in the dental clinic while waiting to have his wisdom tooth pulled.

Maria decided to throw away the boxes that had accumulated for years in the basement.

2 Sometimes the dependent words *who, that, which,* or *where* appear not at the very start but *near* the start of a word group. A fragment often results.

Today I visited Hilda Cooper. A friend who is in the hospital.

"A friend who is in the hospital" is not in itself a complete thought. We want to know in the same statement *who* the friend is. The fragment can be corrected by attaching it to the sentence that comes before it:

Today I visited Hilda Cooper, a friend who is in the hospital.

(Here a comma is used to set off "a friend who is in the hospital," which is extra material placed at the end of the sentence.)

Practice 1

Turn each of the dependent-word groups into a sentence by adding a complete thought. Put a comma after the dependent-word group if a dependent word starts the sentence.

Examples   After I got out of high school
After I got out of high school, I spent a year traveling.

The watch that I got fixed
The watch that I got fixed has just stopped working again.

1. Before I go to work
   Describe something you do before you go to work.

   _____

   _____

2. Because I have a test tomorrow

   _____

   _____

3. Since it was such a hot day

   _____

   _____

4. The sandwich that I bought

   _____

   _____

5. When the department store closed

   _____

   _____

Practice 2

Underline the dependent-word fragment (or fragments) in each selection. Then correct each fragment by attaching it to the sentence that comes before or the sentence that comes after—whichever sounds more natural. Put a comma after the dependent-word group if it starts the sentence.

10-16-06

1. When the waitress coughed in his food, Frank lost his appetite. He didn't even take home a doggy bag.
   Which word group begins with a dependent word?

   The waitre _____

   or   *Pata connon before Front* _____

2. Our power went out During a thunderstorm. I lost the paper I was writing on the computer.

   _____

   _____

3. Tony doesn't like going to the ballpark. If he misses an exciting play, There's no instant replay.

   _____

   _____

4. After the mail carrier comes, I run to our mailbox. I love to get mail. Even if it is only junk mail.

   _____

   _____

5. Even though she can't read, My little daughter likes to go to the library. She chooses books with pretty covers. While I look at the latest magazines.

   _____

   _____

2 *-ing* and *to* Fragments

When a word ending in *-ing* or the word *to* appears at or near the start of a word group, a fragment may result. Such fragments often lack a subject and part of the verb.

Underline the word groups in the examples below that contain *-ing* words. Each is an *-ing* fragment.

Example 1

I spent all day in the employment office. Trying to find a job that suited me. *participal phrase* The prospects looked bleak. *I tried applying sub & pred.*

Example 2

Lola surprised Tony on the nature hike. Picking blobs of resin off pine trees. Then she chewed them like bubble gum. *missing a subject*

Example 3

Mel took an aisle seat on the bus, His reason being that he had more legroom.

[handwritten annotations: "was", "fms (or)", "Run-on Sentence"]

People sometimes write *-ing* fragments because they think the subject in one sentence will work for the next word group as well. In the first selection above, they might think the subject *I* in the opening sentence will also serve as the subject for "Trying to find a job that suited me." But the subject must actually be *in* the sentence.

How to Correct *-ing* Fragments

1 Attach the fragment to the sentence that comes before it or the sentence that comes after it, whichever makes sense. Example 1 above could read, "I spent all day in the employment office, trying to find a job that suited me." (Note that here a comma is used to set off "trying to find a job that suited me," which is extra material placed at the end of the sentence.)

2 Add a subject and change the *-ing* verb part to the correct form of the verb. Example 2 could read, "She picked blobs of resin off pine trees."

3 Change *being* to the correct form of the verb *be* (*am, are, is, was, were*). Example 3 could read, "His reason was that he had more legroom."

How to Correct *to* Fragments

As noted above, when *to* appears at or near the start of a word group, a fragment sometimes results.

> To remind people of their selfishness. Otis leaves handwritten notes on cars that take up two parking spaces.

The first word group in the example above is a *to* fragment. It can be corrected by adding it to the sentence that comes after it.

> To remind people of their selfishness, Otis leaves handwritten notes on cars that take up two parking spaces.

(Note that here a comma is used to set off "To remind people of their selfishness," which is introductory material in the sentence.)

Practice 1

Underline the *-ing* fragment in each of the three items below. Then make the fragment a sentence by rewriting it, using the method described in parentheses.

Example   The dog eyed me with suspicion. <u>Not knowing whether its master was at home.</u> I hesitated to open the gate.
(Add the fragment to the sentence that comes after it.)

Not knowing whether its master was at home, I hesitated to open the gate.

Comma here or here

1. Vince sat nervously in the dentist's chair. Waiting for his x-rays to be developed. He prayed there would be no cavities.
   Add the *-ing* fragment to the preceding sentence.

   _____

   _____

2. Looking through the movie ads for twenty minutes, Lew and Marian tried to find a film they both wanted to see.
   Add fragment to the sentence that comes after it.

   _____

   _____

3. The jeep went too fast around the sharp curve. As a result, tipping over.
   Add the subject *It* and change the verb *tipping* to the correct form, *tipped.*

   _____

   As a result it tipped over.

   _____

Practice 2

Underline the *-ing* or *to* fragment in each selection. Then rewrite each selection correctly, using one of the methods of correction described on page 103.

1. Some workers dug up the street near our house. Causing frequent vibrations inside. By evening, all the pictures on our walls were crooked.
   Add the *-ing* fragment to the preceding sentence.

   _____

   _____

2. I had heard about the surprise party for me. I therefore walked slowly into the darkened living room. Preparing to look shocked.

_____

_____

3. Dribbling skillfully up the court, Luis looked for a teammate who was open. Then he passed the ball.

_____

_____

4. As I was dreaming of a sunny day at the beach, the alarm clock rang. Wanting to finish the dream. I pushed the snooze button.

_____

_____

5. To get back my term paper, I went to see my English instructor from last semester. I also wanted some career advice.

_____

_____

3 Added-Detail Fragments

Added-detail fragments lack a subject and a verb. They often begin with one of the following words.

also	except	including
especially	for example	such as

See if you can underline the one added-detail fragment in each of these examples:

Example 1

Tony has trouble accepting criticism, Except from Lola. She has a knack for tact.

Example 2

My apartment has its drawbacks, For example, no hot water in the morning.

Example 3

I had many jobs while in school. <u>Among them, busboy, painter, and security guard.</u>

People often write added-detail fragments for much the same reason they write *-ing* fragments. They think the subject and verb in one sentence will serve for the next word group as well. But the subject and verb must be in *each* word group.

How to Correct Added-Detail Fragments

1 Attach the fragment to the complete thought that precedes it. Example 1 could read: "Tony has trouble accepting criticism, except from Lola." (Note that here a comma is used to set off "except from Lola," which is extra material placed at the end of the sentence.)

2 Add a subject and a verb to the fragment to make it a complete sentence. Example 2 could read: "My apartment has its drawbacks. For example, there is no hot water in the morning."

3 Change words as necessary to make the fragment part of the preceding sentence. Example 3 could read: "Among the many jobs I had while in school have been busboy, painter, and security guard."

Practice 1

Underline the fragment in each selection below. Then make it a sentence by rewriting it, using the method described in parentheses.

Example   My husband and I share the household chores. <u>Including meals.</u> I do the cooking and he does the eating.

Add the fragment to the preceding sentence.

My husband and I share the household chores, including meals.

comma or what's

1. Denise puts things off until the last minute. For example, waiting until the night before a test to begin studying.

   Correct the fragment by adding the subject *she* and changing *waiting* to the proper form of the verb, *waits*.

   _____

   _____

2. My eleventh-grade English teacher picked on everybody. Except the athletes. They could do no wrong.

Add the fragment to the preceding sentence.

_____

_____

3. Bernardo always buys things out of season. For example, an air conditioner in December. He saves a lot of money this way.

Correct the fragment by adding the subject and verb *he bought.*

_____

_____

Practice 2

Underline the added-detail fragment in each selection. Then rewrite that part of the selection needed to correct the fragment. Use one of the three methods of correction described on page 106.

1. I find all sorts of things in my little boy's pockets. Including crayons, stones, and melted chocolate. Luckily, I haven't found anything alive there yet.

   Attach the added-detail fragment to the preceding sentence.

   _____

2. There are certain chores I hate to do. Especially cleaning windows. So I clean only the windows I look out of.

   _____

   _____

3. Some of the foods in our school cafeteria should not be eaten. The meat loaf, for instance. It is as tender and tasty as shoe leather.

   _____

   _____

4. By midnight, the party looked like the scene of an accident. With people stretched out on the floor.

   _____

   _____

5. Some people on television really annoy me. For example, game show hosts. Their smiles look pasted on their faces.

   _____

   _____

4 Missing-Subject Fragments

In each example below, underline the word group in which the subject is missing.

Example 1

One example of my father's generosity is that he visits sick friends in the hospital. And takes along get-well cards with a few dollars folded in them.

Example 2

The weight lifter grunted as he heaved the barbells into the air. Then, with a loud groan, dropped them.

People write missing-subject fragments because they think the subject in one sentence will apply to the next word group as well. But the subject, as well as the verb, must be in *each* word group to make it a sentence.

How to Correct Missing-Subject Fragments

1   Attach the fragment to the preceding sentence. Example 1 could read: "One example of my father's generosity is that he visits sick friends in the hospital and takes along get-well cards with a few dollars folded in them."

2   Add a subject (which can often be a pronoun standing for the subject in the preceding sentence). Example 2 could read: "Then, with a loud groan, he dropped them."

Practice

Underline the missing-subject fragment in each selection. Then rewrite that part of the selection needed to correct the fragment. Use one of the two methods of correction described above.

1. Artie tripped on his shoelace. Then looked around to see if anyone had noticed.
   The missing subject is *he.*

   _____

   _____

2. I started the car. And quickly turned down the blaring radio.

   _____

   _____

3. The fire in the fireplace crackled merrily. Its orange-red flames shot high in the air, And made strange shadows all around the dark room.

_____ *, or they* _____

_____

4. The receptionist at that office is not very well trained. She was chewing gum and talking with a co-worker at the same time she took my call, And forgot to take my name.

_____

_____

5. My elderly aunt never stands for long on a bus ride. She places herself in front of a seated young man, And stands on his feet until he gets up.

_____ *remove* _____

_____

A Review: How to Check for Fragments

1   Read your paper aloud from the *last* sentence to the *first*. You will be better able to see and hear whether each word group you read is a complete thought.

2   If you think any word group is a fragment, ask yourself: Does this contain a subject and a verb and express a complete thought?

3   More specifically, be on the lookout for the most common fragments.

- Dependent-word fragments (starting with words like *after, because, since, when,* and *before*)

- *-ing* and *to* fragments (*-ing* or *to* at or near the start of a word group)

- Added-detail fragments (starting with words like *for example, such as, also,* and *especially*)

- Missing-subject fragments (a verb is present but not the subject)

Collaborative Activity

Part A: Editing and Rewriting

Working with a partner, read the short paragraph below and underline the five fragments. Then use the space provided to correct the fragments. Feel free to discuss the rewrite quietly with your partner and refer back to the chapter when necessary.

1I can't remember a time when my sister didn't love to write. 2In school, when teachers assigned a composition or essay. 3Her classmates often groaned. 4She would join them in their protests. 5Because she didn't want to seem different. 6Secretly, though, her spirit would dance. 7Words were special to her. 8I remember an incident when she was in third grade. 9She wrote a funny story. 10About the time my dog made a mess of our kitchen. 11The teacher made my sister stand in front of the class and read it aloud. 12By the time she finished. 13The classroom was bedlam. 14Even the teacher wiped away tears of laughter. 15It was a magic moment. 16Which made my sister more in love with writing than ever.

_____

_____

_____

_____

_____

_____

_____

_____

Part B: Creating Sentences

Working with a partner, make up your own short fragments test as directed.

Continued

1. Write a dependent-word fragment in the space below. Then correct the fragment by making it into a complete sentence. You may want to begin your fragment with the word *before*, *after*, *when*, *because*, or *if*.

Fragment _____

Sentence _____

_____

2. In the space below, write a fragment that begins with a word that has an *-ing* ending. Then correct the fragment by making it into a complete sentence. You may want to begin your fragment with the word *laughing*, *walking*, *shopping*, or *talking*.

Fragment _____

Sentence _____

_____

3. Write an added-detail fragment in the space below. Then correct the fragment by making it into a complete sentence. You may want to begin your fragment with the word *also*, *especially*, *except*, or *including*.

Fragment _____

Sentence _____

_____

Reflective Activity

1. Look at the paragraph that you revised above. How has removing fragments affected the paragraph? Explain.

2. Explain what it is about fragments that you find most difficult to remember and apply. Use an example to make your point clear. Feel free to refer to anything in this chapter.

■ Review Test 1

Turn each of the following word groups into a complete sentence. Use the space provided.

Examples   Feeling very confident
   Feeling very confident, I began my speech.

   Until the rain started
   We played softball until the rain started.

1. After we ate dinner

2. Whenever the instructor is late

3. Under the bed

4. If the weather is bad

5. Dave, who is not very organized

6. To get to know each other better

7. Which was annoying

8. Will meet me later

9. Staring at the computer screen

10. Waiting in the long line

■ Review Test 2

Underline the fragment in each item below. Then correct the fragment in the space provided.

Example   Sam received all kinds of junk mail. Then complained to the post office. Eventually, some of the mail stopped coming.
   Then he complained to the post office.

1. Fascinated, Nina stared at the stranger. Who was standing in the doorway. She wondered if she could convince him they had met before.

   _____

   _____

2. Trees can survive on a steep mountain slope if they obey two rules. They must grow low to the ground. And bend with the wind.

   _____

   _____

3. While waiting in line at the supermarket. I look in people's baskets. Their food choices give hints about their personalities.

   _____

   _____

4. I saw spectacular twin rainbows through the kitchen window. So I rushed to get my camera. To take a picture before they vanished.

   _____

   _____

5. Whenever you buy cotton clothes, get them one size too large. By allowing for shrinkage. You will get a longer life out of them.

   _____

   _____

6. My nutty cousin cuts the address labels off his magazines. Then pastes them on envelopes. This way, he doesn't have to write his return address.

   _____

   _____

7. Marian never has to buy ketchup or mustard. Because she saves the extra packets that come with fast-food orders.

   _____

   _____

8. The soccer players were amazing. Using their feet as well as most people use their hands.

   _____

   _____

9. My husband climbed his first mountain yesterday. Now he's calling all our friends. To tell them about his peak experience.

_____

_____

10. The trivia book listed some interesting facts about Babe Ruth. For instance, he spoke German fluently. Also, kept cool on hot days by putting wet cabbage leaves under his cap.

_____

_____

■ Review Test 3

Dne 10-16-06

In the space provided, write *C* if a word group is a complete sentence; write *frag* if it is a fragment. The first two are done for you.

frag   1. When the bus drivers went on strike.

C   2. I saw many people giving rides to strangers.

C   3. Some even drove out of their way for others.

F   4. Especially when the weather was bad.

C   5. One rainy day, I saw an elderly woman pull her cab over to the curb.

F   6. Yelling and waving for five shivering students to get into her car.

F   7. Until the strike finally ended.

C   8. Scenes like that were not uncommon.

C   9. It seems that community problems bring people together.

F   10. By weakening the feeling that we live very separate lives.

Now correct the *fragments* you have found. Attach each fragment to the sentence that comes before or after it, or make whatever other change is needed to turn the fragment into a sentence. Use the space provided. The first one is corrected for you.

1. *When the bus drivers went on strike, I saw many people giving rides to strangers.*

2. _____

    _____

3. _____

    _____

4. _____

_____

5. _____

_____

■ **Review Test 4**

Write quickly for five minutes about the house or apartment where you live. Don't worry about spelling, punctuation, finding exact words, or organizing your thoughts. Just focus on writing as many words as you can without stopping.

After you have finished, go back and make whatever changes are needed to correct any fragments in your writing.

[Handwritten notes:]

Wednesday test is on 10/18/06

(All)

1) Fragments

2) Added – Detail

3)

4)

Rules 2 joins independent clause w/coordination conjunction

I ran and I fell, — Compound Sentence con 10-25-06
sub verb   sub verb — (contrary sentence)
joins — I ran but I fell,

I ran ; I fell, — Independent clauses
Sentence   Sentence

I ran then I fell / I RAN before I fell
Complex sentence

Only
coordinate
Conjunction   6) Nor
1) And   7) yet
2) but   8) (;)
3) for
4) or   SEMI colon
5) so

10-35-06

If there's no (,) commas
or semi colon (;) - It is a (Run-on)

2 clause that are independent
w/ semi colon semi-color

① words that joins ② clauses (contrary
                                    conjunctions)

1) And
2) but   (A comma has to come before
3) for   One of these words)
4) or
5) nor
6) so
7) yet

Addition
(;) - semi + colon

However — contrary transition join ideals

but

. However - (doesn't join the sentence
                        because it becomes a run on)

then - (watch for) - It is a transition

Don't join a corrordant and a semi color

Parrell Structure

Veni Vici Vinci
    I come, I see, I conquer

6 Run-Ons

study page (405)

Introductory Activity

A run-on occurs when two sentences are run together with no adequate sign given to mark the break between them. Shown below are four run-on sentences, each followed by a correct sentence. See if you can complete the statement that explains how each run-on is corrected.

1. A man coughed in the movie theater the result was a chain reaction of copycat coughing.

   A man coughed in the movie theater. The result was a chain reaction of copycat coughing.

The run-on has been corrected by using a __period & capital letter__ and a capital letter to separate the two complete thoughts.

2. I heard laughter inside the house, no one answered the bell.

   I heard laughter inside the house, but no one answered the bell.

The run-on has been corrected by using a joining word, __but__, to connect the two complete thoughts. proceeded by a comma

3. A car sped around the corner, it sprayed slush all over the pedestrians.

   A car sped around the corner; it sprayed slush all over the pedestrians.

The run-on has been corrected by using a __semi-colon__ to connect the two closely related thoughts.

4. I had a campus map, I still could not find my classroom building.

   Although I had a campus map, I still could not find my classroom building. alt

The run-on has been corrected by using the subordinating word __Although__ to connect the two closely related thoughts. complex sentence

Answers are on page 681.

What Are Run-Ons?

A *run-on* is two complete thoughts that are run together with no adequate sign given to mark the break between them. As a result of the run-on, the reader is confused, unsure of where one thought ends and the next one begins. Two types of run-ons are fused sentences and comma splices.

Some run-ons have no punctuation at all to mark the break between the thoughts. Such run-ons are known as *fused sentences:* they are fused or joined together as if they were only one thought.

Fused Sentence

Rita decided to stop smoking she didn't want to die of lung cancer.

Fused Sentence

The exam was postponed the class was canceled as well.

In other run-ons, known as *comma splices,* a comma is used to connect or "splice" together the two complete thoughts.* However, a comma alone is *not enough* to connect two complete thoughts. Some connection stronger than a comma alone is needed.

Comma Splice

Rita decided to stop smoking, she didn't want to die of lung cancer.

Comma Splice

The exam was postponed, the class was canceled as well.

Comma splices are the most common kind of run-on. Students sense that some kind of connection is needed between thoughts, and so they put a comma at the dividing point. But the comma alone is *not sufficient.* A stronger, clearer mark is needed between the two thoughts.

---

*Notes:
1. Some instructors feel that the term *run-ons* should be applied only to fused sentences, not to comma splices. But for many other instructors, and for our purposes in this book, the term *run-on* applies equally to fused sentences and comma splices. The bottom line is that you do not want either fused sentences or comma splices in your writing.
2. Some instructors refer to each complete thought in a run-on as an *independent clause.* A *clause* is simply a group of words having a subject and a verb. A clause may be *independent* (expressing a complete thought and able to stand alone) or *dependent* (not expressing a complete thought and not able to stand alone). A run-on is two independent clauses that are run together with no adequate sign given to mark the break between them.

10-30/06

A Warning: Words That Can Lead to Run-Ons

People often write run-ons when the second complete thought begins with one of the following words. Be on the alert for run-ons whenever you use these words:

I	we	there	now
you	they	this	then
he, she, it		that	next

Correcting Run-Ons

Here are four common methods of correcting a run-on:

1 Use a period and a capital letter to separate the two complete thoughts. (In other words, make two separate sentences of the two complete thoughts.)

Rita decided to stop smoking. She didn't want to die of lung cancer.
The exam was postponed. The class was canceled as well.

2 Use a comma plus a joining word (*and, but, for, or, nor, so, yet*) to connect the two complete thoughts.

Rita decided to stop smoking, for she didn't want to die of lung cancer.
The exam was postponed, and the class was canceled as well.

3 Use a semicolon to connect the two complete thoughts.

Rita decided to stop smoking; she didn't want to die of lung cancer.
The exam was postponed; the class was canceled as well.

4 Use subordination.

Because Rita didn't want to die of lung cancer, she decided to stop smoking.
When the exam was postponed, the class was canceled as well.

Watch not to over use (semi-colons)

The following pages will give you practice in all four methods of correcting run-ons. The use of subordination will be explained further on page 143, in a chapter that deals with sentence variety.

Method 1: Period and a Capital Letter

One way of correcting a run-on is to use a period and a capital letter at the break between the two complete thoughts. Use this method especially if the thoughts are not closely related or if another method would make the sentence too long.

Practice 1

Locate the split in each of the following run-ons. Each is a *fused sentence*—that is, each consists of two sentences fused or joined together with no punctuation at all between them. Reading each sentence aloud will help you "hear" where a major break or split in the thought occurs. At such a point, your voice will probably drop and pause.

Correct the run-on by putting a period at the end of the first thought and a capital letter at the start of the second thought.

Example   Gary was not a success at his job. his mouth moved faster than his hands.

1. The fern hadn't been watered in a month its leaves looked like frayed brown shoelaces.
    The fern hadn't been watered in a month is a complete thought. *Its leaves looked like frayed brown shoelaces* is also a complete thought.

2. Newspapers are piled up on the neighbors' porch they must be out of town.

3. Joyce's recipe for chocolate fudge is very easy to make it is also very expensive.

4. Watching television gave the old man something to do he didn't have many visitors anymore.

5. Jon accidentally ruined his favorite black shirt a few drops of bleach spilled onto it in the laundry room.

6. The first Olympic Games were held in 776 B.C. the only event was a footrace.

7. Gloria decorated her apartment creatively and cheaply she papered her bedroom walls with magazine covers.

8. There were papers scattered all over Lena's desk she spent twenty minutes looking for a missing receipt.

9. Spring rain dripped into the fireplace the room smelled like last winter's fires.

10. The car swerved dangerously through traffic its rear bumper sticker read, "School's Out—Drive Carefully."

Practice 2

Locate the split in each of the following run-ons. Some of the run-ons are fused sentences, and some of them are *comma splices*—run-ons spliced or joined together only with a comma. Correct each run-on by putting a period at the end of the first thought and a capital letter at the start of the next thought.

1. My father is a very sentimental man he still has my kindergarten drawings.
   My father is the subject of the first complete thought. *He* is the subject of the second one.

2. Sue dropped the letter into the mailbox then she regretted mailing it.

3. Certain street names are very common the most common is "Park."

4. Bacteria are incredibly tiny, a drop of liquid may contain fifty million of them.

5. The fastest dog in the world is the greyhound, it can run over forty-one miles an hour.

6. Mandy's parents speak only Chinese, she speaks Chinese, English, and French.

7. My portable CD player stopped working, its batteries were worn out.

8. A shadow on the kitchen wall was lovely, it had the shape of a plant on the windowsill.

9. The little girl hated seeing her father drink one day, she poured all his liquor down the kitchen drain.

10. Children have been born at odd times for instance, one child was born during his mother's funeral.

Practice 3

Write a second sentence to go with each sentence below. Start the second sentence with the word given at the left.

Example   He   My dog's ears snapped up. <u>He had heard a wolf howling on</u>
                                          <u>television.</u>

He   1. Carlos likes going to the mall.

_____

_____

They   2. Ants marched across our kitchen floor.

_____

_____

Now   3. Our car just broke down.

_____

_____

There   4. Raccoons knocked over our garbage cans.

_____

_____

Then   5. First I stopped at the bakery.

_____

_____

Method 2: Comma and a Joining Word

Another way of correcting a run-on is to use a comma plus a joining word to connect the two complete thoughts. Joining words (also called *coordinating conjunctions*) include *and, but, for, or, nor, so,* and *yet.* Here is what the four most common joining words mean:

and   in addition, along with

> Lola was watching Monday night football, and she was doing her homework as well.

(*And* means *in addition:* Lola was watching Monday night football; *in addition,* she was doing her homework as well.)

but   however, except, on the other hand, just the opposite

> I voted for the president two years ago, but I would not vote for him today.

(*But* means *however:* I voted for the president two years ago; *however,* I would not vote for him today.)

for   because, the reason why, the cause for something

Saturday is the worst day to shop, for people jam the stores.

(*For* means *because:* Saturday is the worst day to shop *because* people jam the stores.) If you are not comfortable using *for,* you may want to use *because* instead of *for* in the activities that follow. If you do use *because,* omit the comma before it.

SO   as a result, therefore

Our son misbehaved again, so he was sent upstairs without dessert.

(*So* means *as a result*: Our son misbehaved again; *as a result,* he was sent upstairs without dessert.)

Practice 1   10-30-06

shows Results

Insert the comma and the joining word (*and, but, for, so*) that logically connects the two thoughts in each sentence.

Example   A trip to the zoo always depresses me, *for* I hate to see animals in cages.

1. I want to stop smoking *but* I don't want to gain weight.
   Both complete thoughts begin with "I."

2. Packages are flown to distant cities during the night *and* vans deliver them the next morning.

3. The grass turned brown in the summer's heat *and* the grapes shriveled and died on the vine.

4. Woody wanted to buy his girlfriend a ring *so* he began saving ten dollars a week.

5. I enjoy watching television *but* I feel guilty about spending so much time in front of the tube.

6. It was too hot indoors to study *so* I decided to go down to the shopping center for ice cream.

7. I don't like to go to the doctor's office *for* I'm afraid one of the other patients will make me really sick.

8. This world map was published only three years ago *but* the names of some countries are already out of date. *opposite*

9. Nate is color-blind *so* his wife lays out his clothes every morning.

10. We knew there had been a power failure *for* all our digital clocks were blinking "12:00."

Practice 2

Add a complete, closely related thought to each of the following statements. When you write the second thought, use a comma plus the joining word shown at the left.

Example   but   I was sick with the flu, _*but I still had to study for the test.*_

but   1. We have the same taste in clothes

_____

_____

so   2. Keisha needed a little break from studying

_____

_____

and   3. I hammered two nails into the wall

_____

_____

for   4. The house was unusually quiet

_____

_____

but   5. Harry meant to stick to his diet

_____

_____

Method 3: Semicolon

A third method of correcting a run-on is to use a semicolon to mark the break between two thoughts. A *semicolon* (;) is made up of a period above a comma and is sometimes called a *strong comma*. The semicolon signals more of a pause than a comma alone but not quite the full pause of a period.

Occasional use of semicolons can add variety to sentences. For some people, however, the semicolon is a confusing mark of punctuation. Keep in mind that if you are not comfortable using it, you can and should use one of the first two methods of correcting a run-on sentence.

10-30-06

Semicolon Alone

Here are some earlier sentences that were connected with a comma plus a joining word. Now they are connected with a semicolon. Notice that a semicolon, unlike a comma, can be used alone to connect the two complete thoughts in each sentence.

Lola was watching Monday night football; she was doing her homework as well.

I voted for the president two years ago; I would not vote for him today.

Saturday is the worst day to shop; people jam the stores.

Practice

Insert a semicolon where the break occurs between the two complete thoughts in each of the following sentences.

Example   She had a wig on; it looked more like a hat than a wig.

1. I eat pound cake a lot for dessert; I seem to gain a pound each time.
   Both complete thoughts begin with "I."
2. The puppy quickly ate; the baby watched with interest.   *Run-on sentence*
3. The elderly woman smiled at me; her face broke into a thousand wrinkles.
4. The park has become a dumping ground; old freezers and washing machines are abandoned there.
5. The first birthday parties in history were for kings and queens; birth records were not yet kept for common people.

Semicolon with a Transition

A semicolon is sometimes used with a transitional word and a comma to join two complete thoughts:

transitional word

I figured that the ball game would cost me about twenty dollars; however, I didn't consider the high price of food and drinks.

Fred and Martha have a low-interest mortgage on their house; otherwise, they would move to another neighborhood.

Sharon didn't understand the instructor's point; therefore, she asked him to repeat it.

Note   Sometimes transitional words do not join complete thoughts but are merely interrupters in a sentence (see page 322):

My parents, moreover, plan to go on the trip.

I believe, however, that they'll change their minds.

Transitional Words   *10 - 30-06*

Here is a list of common transitional words (also known as *adverbial conjunctions*).

Common Transitional Words

however	moreover	therefore
on the other hand	in addition	as a result
nevertheless	also	consequently
instead	furthermore	otherwise

Practice 1

For each item, choose a logical transitional word from the box above and write it in the space provided. In addition, put a semicolon *before* the transition and a comma *after* it.

Example   It was raining harder than ever ___; however,___ Bobby was determined to go to the amusement park.

1. A new car is always fun to drive *; On the other hand* the payments are never fun to make.
    "Car" and "payments" are the subjects of the two complete thoughts.

2. The fork that fell into our garbage disposal looks like a piece of modern art *therefore* it is useless.

3. Auto races no longer use gasoline *; as a result* spectators have nothing to fear from exhaust fumes.

4. We got to the stadium two hours before the game started *nevertheless* all the parking spaces were already taken.

5. Mice use their sensitive whiskers as feelers *; Consequently* they scurry along close to walls.

Practice 2

Punctuate each sentence by using a semicolon and a comma.

Example   Our tap water has a funny taste; consequently, we buy bottled water to drink.

1. Nora lives two blocks from the grocery store; nevertheless, she always drives there.
   To correctly punctuate this sentence, first locate the transitional word that joins the two complete thoughts.

2. The little boy ate too much Halloween candy; as a result, he got a stomachache.

3. Our dog protects us by barking at strangers; however, he also barks at our friends.

4. Jeff cut back a few hours on his work schedule; otherwise, he would have had very little time for studying.

5. My sister invited her ex-husband over to celebrate the holiday with the children; furthermore, she bought a gift for him from the children.

Method 4: Subordination

A fourth method of joining related thoughts is to use subordination. *Subordination* is a way of showing that one thought in a sentence is not as important as another thought. Here are three sentences where one idea is subordinated to (made less emphatic than) the other idea:

Because Rita didn't want to die of lung cancer, she decided to stop smoking.

The wedding reception began to get out of hand when the guests started to throw food at each other.

Although my brothers wanted to watch a *Law and Order* rerun, the rest of the family insisted on turning to the network news.

Dependent Words

Notice that when we subordinate, we use dependent words like *because, when,* and *although.* Following is a brief list of common dependent words (see also the list on page 98). Subordination is explained in full on page 143.

10-30-06

Common Dependent Words

after	before	unless
although	even though	until
as	if	when
because	since	while

Practice 1

Choose a logical dependent word from the box above and write it in the space provided.

Example   _____Until_____ I was six, I thought chocolate milk came from brown cows.

1. Will hasn't had a cigarette ___Since___ July 4, 2000.
   Which dependent word best signals that something extends from the past (July 4, 2000) to the present?

2. ___Unless___ you're willing to work hard, don't sign up for Professor Dunn's class.

3. The lines at that supermarket are so long ___because___ there are too few cashiers.

4. ___After___ reading the scary novel, my sister had nightmares for days.

5. My boss gave me smoked salmon for my birthday ___although___ he knows I'm a vegetarian.
   even though

Practice 2

Rewrite the five sentences below (all taken from this chapter) so that one idea is subordinate to the other. Use one of the dependent words from the box above.

Example   Auto races no longer use gasoline; spectators have nothing to fear from exhaust fumes.

Since auto races no longer use gasoline, spectators have nothing to

fear from exhaust fumes.

1. I want to stop smoking; I don't want to gain weight.
   Select a dependent word that logically connects the two ideas (a wish to stop smoking and a wish not to gain weight).

   _____

   _____

2. It was too hot indoors to study; I decided to go down to the shopping center for ice cream.

_____

_____

3. The puppy quickly ate; the baby watched with interest.

_____

_____

4. The elderly woman smiled at me; her face broke into a thousand wrinkles.

_____

_____

5. This world map was published only three years ago; the names of some countries are already out of date.

_____

_____

Collaborative Activity

Part A: Editing and Rewriting

Working with a partner, read carefully the short paragraph below and underline the five run-ons. Then use the space provided to correct the five run-ons. Feel free to discuss the rewrite quietly with your partner and refer back to the chapter when necessary.

[1] When Mark began his first full-time job, he immediately got a credit card, a used sports car was his first purchase. [2] Then he began to buy expensive clothes that he could not afford he also bought impressive gifts for his parents and his girlfriend. [3] Several months passed before Mark realized that he owed an enormous amount of money. [4] To make matters worse, his car broke down, a stack of bills suddenly seemed to be due at once. [5] Mark tried to cut back on his purchases, he soon realized he had to cut up his credit card to prevent himself from using it. [6] He also began keeping a careful record of his spending he had no idea where his money had gone till then. [7] He hated to admit to his family and friends that he

Continued

had to get his budget under control. [8]However, his girlfriend said she did not mind inexpensive dates, and his parents were proud of his growing maturity.

_____

_____

_____

_____

_____

_____

_____

_____

_____

Part B: Creating Sentences

Working with a partner, make up your own short run-ons test as directed.

1. Write a run-on sentence. Then rewrite it, using a period and capital letter to separate the thoughts into two sentences.

   Run-on

   _____

   Rewrite

   _____

2. Write a sentence that has two complete thoughts. Then rewrite it, using a comma and a joining word to correctly join the complete thoughts.

   Two complete thoughts

   _____

   Rewrite

   _____

   Continued

3. Write a sentence that has two complete thoughts. Then rewrite it, using a semicolon to correctly join the complete thoughts.

Two complete thoughts

_____

Rewrite

_____

Reflective Activity

1. Look at the paragraph that you revised above. Explain how run-ons affect the paragraph.

2. In your own written work, which type of run-on are you most likely to write: comma splices or fused sentences? Why do you tend to make this kind of mistake?

3. Which method for correcting run-ons are you most likely to use in your own writing? Which are you least likely to use? Why?

■ Review Test 1

Correct the following run-ons by using either (1) a period and a capital letter or (2) a comma and the joining word *and, but, for,* or *so.* Do not use the same method of correction for each sentence.

Example   Fred pulled the cellophane off the cake, the icing came along with it.

1. I put a dollar in the soda machine all I got was an empty can.

2. I tore open a ketchup packet a bright red streak flew across the front of my new white shirt.

3. Yolanda wanted to sleep late her dog woke her up at dawn.

4. The theater's parking lot was full we missed the first ten minutes of the movie.

5. Helen bites her nails she tries to keep her hands hidden.

10-30-06

6. The waiter cheerfully filled our coffee cups three times ,we left him a generous tip.

7. I love to wander through old cemeteries,I enjoy reading the gravestones and taking pictures of them.

8. Travel to distant planets has long been a dream of humanity,the technology to achieve that dream will soon be available.

9. Gordon no longer has to worry about missing the bus,he rides to work in a car pool.

10. The baby wouldn't stop crying,all the passengers on the bus gave the mother dirty looks.

■ Review Test 2

Correct each run-on by using subordination. Choose from among the following dependent words.

after	before	unless
although	even though	until
as	if	when
because	since	while

Example   Tony hated going to a new barber, he was afraid of butchered hair.

Because Tony was afraid of butchered hair, he hated going to a

new barber.

1. Mom was frying potatoes, the heat set off the smoke alarm.

_____

_____

2. I love animals I'm not ready to take on the responsibility of a pet.

_____

_____

3. Lani leaves a lecture class, she reviews and clarifies her notes.

_____

_____

4. Matthew jogs, he thinks over his day's activities.

_____

_____

5. My mother puts apples in the fruit bowl she first washes the wax off them.

_____

_____

6. I began to shake on the examining table the nurse reached out and held my hand.

_____

_____

7. Some pets are easy to care for, others require patience and lots of hard work.

_____

_____

8. Molly forgot to turn the oven off her homemade bread looked like burned toast.

_____

_____

9. A wheel hit a crack in the sidewalk the skateboard shot out from under Danny.

_____

_____

10. John Grisham and Stephen King make huge fortunes with their novels most writers barely make a living.

_____

_____

■ Review Test 3

On separate paper, write six sentences, each of which has two complete thoughts. In two of the sentences, use a period and a capital letter between the thoughts. In another two sentences, use a comma and a joining word (*and, but, or, nor, for, so, yet*) to join the thoughts. In the final two sentences, use a semicolon to join the thoughts.

■ Review Test 4

Write for five minutes about something that makes you angry. Don't worry about spelling, punctuation, finding exact words, or organizing your thoughts. Just focus on writing as many words as you can without stopping.

After you have finished, go back and make whatever changes are needed to correct any run-on sentences in your writing.

7 Sentence Variety I

This chapter will show you how to write effective and varied sentences. You'll learn more about two techniques—subordination and coordination—you can use to expand simple sentences, making them more interesting and expressive. You'll also reinforce what you have learned in Chapters 5 and 6 about how subordination and coordination can help you correct fragments and run-ons in your writing.

Four Traditional Sentence Patterns

Sentences in English are traditionally described as *simple, compound, complex,* or *compound-complex.* Each is explained below.

The Simple Sentence

A simple sentence has a single <u>subject</u>-<u>verb</u> combination.

<u>Children</u> <u>play</u>.
The <u>game</u> <u>ended</u> early.
My <u>car</u> <u>stalled</u> three times last week.
The <u>lake</u> <u>has been polluted</u> by several neighboring streams.

A simple sentence may have more than one subject:

<u>Lola</u> and <u>Tony</u> <u>drove</u> home.
The <u>wind</u> and <u>water</u> <u>dried</u> my hair.

135

or more than one verb:

> The children smiled and waved at us.
> The lawn mower smoked and sputtered.

or several subjects and verbs:

> Manny, Moe, and Jack lubricated my car, replaced the oil filter, and cleaned the spark plugs.

Practice

On separate paper, write:

> Three sentences, each with a single subject and verb
> Three sentences, each with a single subject and a double verb
> Three sentences, each with a double subject and a single verb

In each case, underline the subject once and the verb twice. (See pages 88–89 if necessary for more information on subjects and verbs.)

The Compound Sentence

A compound, or "double," sentence is made up of two (or more) simple sentences. The two complete statements in a compound sentence are usually connected by a comma plus a joining word (*and, but, for, or, nor, so, yet*).

A compound sentence is used when you want to give equal weight to two closely related ideas. The technique of showing that ideas have equal importance is called *coordination*.

Following are some compound sentences. Each sentence contains two ideas that the writer considers equal in importance.

> The rain increased, so the officials canceled the game.
> Martha wanted to go shopping, but Fred refused to drive her.
> Hollis was watching television in the family room, and April was upstairs on the phone.
> I had to give up wood carving, for my arthritis had become very painful.

Practice 1

Combine the following pairs of simple sentences into compound sentences. Use a comma and a logical joining word (*and, but, for, so*) to connect each pair.

Note   If you are not sure what *and, but, for,* and *so* mean, review pages 122–123.

Example   • We hung up the print.
          • The wall still looked bare.

We hung up the print, but the wall still looked bare.

1. • Cass tied the turkey carcass to a tree.
     • She watched the birds pick at bits of meat and skin.
     Use *and* to connect the two thoughts of equal importance.

_____

_____

2. • I ran the hot water faucet for two minutes.
     • Only cold water came out.

_____

_____

3. • Nathan orders all his Christmas gifts through the Internet.
     • He dislikes shopping in crowded stores.

_____

_____

4. • I need to buy a new set of tires.
     • I will read *Consumer Reports* to learn about various brands.

_____

_____

5. • I asked Cecilia to go out with me on Saturday night.
     • She told me she'd rather stay home and watch TV.

_____

_____

Practice 2

On separate paper, write five compound sentences of your own. Use a different joining word (*and, but, for, or, nor, so, yet*) to connect the two complete ideas in each sentence.

The Complex Sentence

A complex sentence is made up of a simple sentence (a complete statement) and a statement that begins with a dependent word.* Here is a list of common dependent words:

Dependent Words		
after	if, even if	when, whenever
although, though	in order that	where, wherever
as	since	whether
because	that, so that	which, whichever
before	unless	while
even though	until	who
how	what, whatever	whose

A complex sentence is used when you want to emphasize one idea over another in a sentence. Look at the following complex sentence:

Because I forgot the time, I missed the final exam.

The idea that the writer wants to emphasize here—*I missed the final exam*—is expressed as a complete thought. The less important idea—*Because I forgot the time*—is subordinated to the complete thought. The technique of giving one idea less emphasis than another is called *subordination*.

Following are other examples of complex sentences. In each case, the part starting with the dependent word is the less emphasized part of the sentence.

While Aisha was eating breakfast, she began to feel sick.

I checked my money *before* I invited Pedro for lunch.

When Jerry lost his temper, he also lost his job.

Although I practiced for three months, I failed my driving test.

---

*The two parts of a complex sentence are sometimes called an independent clause and a dependent clause. A *clause* is simply a word group that contains a subject and a verb. An *independent clause* expresses a complete thought and can stand alone. A *dependent clause* does not express a complete thought in itself and "depends on" the independent clause to complete its meaning. Dependent clauses always begin with a dependent or subordinating word.

Practice 1

Use logical dependent words to combine the following pairs of simple sentences into complex sentences. Place a comma after a dependent statement when it starts the sentence.

Example
- I obtained a credit card.
- I began spending money recklessly.

When I obtained a credit card, I began spending money recklessly.

_____

- Alan dressed the turkey.
- His brother greased the roasting pan.

Alan dressed the turkey while his brother greased the roasting pan.

_____

1. • Cindy opened the cutlery drawer.
   • A bee flew out.

   Use the dependent word *when.*

   _____

   _____

2. • I washed the windows thoroughly.
   • They still looked dirty.

   _____

   _____

3. • I never opened a book all semester.
   • I guess I deserved to flunk.

   _____

   _____

4. • Manny gets up in the morning.
   • He does stretching exercises for five minutes.

   _____

   _____

5. • My son spilled the pickle jar at dinner.
   • I had to wash the kitchen floor.

   _____

   _____

Practice 2

Rewrite the following sentences, using subordination rather than coordination. Include a comma when a dependent statement starts a sentence.

Example   The hair dryer was not working right, so I returned it to the store.

Because the hair dryer was not working right, I returned it to

the store.

1. Carlo set the table, and his wife finished cooking dinner.
   Use the dependent word *as.*

   _____

   _____

2. Maggie could have gotten good grades, but she did not study enough.

   _____

   _____

3. I watered my drooping African violets, and they perked right up.

   _____

   _____

4. The little boy kept pushing the down button, but the elevator didn't come any more quickly.

   _____

   _____

5. I never really knew what pain is, and then I had four impacted wisdom teeth pulled at once.

   _____

   _____

Practice 3

Combine the following simple sentences into complex sentences. Omit repeated words. Use the dependent words *who, which,* or *that.*

Notes

a   The word *who* refers to persons.

b   The word *which* refers to things.

c   The word *that* refers to persons or things.

Use commas around the dependent statement only if it seems to interrupt the flow of thought in the sentence. (See pages 322–323.)

Examples
- Clyde picked up a hitchhiker.
  - The hitchhiker was traveling around the world.

  Clyde picked up a hitchhiker who was traveling around the world.

  _____

  - Larry is a sleepwalker.
  - Larry is my brother.

  Larry, who is my brother, is a sleepwalker.

  _____

1.
- Karen just gave birth to twins.
  - Karen is an old friend of mine.
  Use commas and *who*.

  _____

  _____

2.
- The tea burned the roof of my mouth.
  - The tea was hotter than I expected.

  _____

  _____

3.
- I dropped the camera.
  - My sister had just bought the camera.

  _____

  _____

4.
- Ernie brought us some enormous oranges.
  - Ernie is visiting from California.

  _____

  _____

5.
- Liz used a steam cleaner to shampoo her rugs.
  - The rugs were dirtier than she realized.

  _____

  _____

Practice 4

On separate paper, write eight complex sentences, using, in turn, the dependent words *unless, if, after, because, when, who, which,* and *that.*

The Compound-Complex Sentence

A compound-complex sentence is made up of two (or more) simple sentences and one or more dependent statements. In the following examples, there is a solid line under the simple sentences and a dotted line under the dependent statements.

> When the power line snapped, Jack was listening to the stereo, and Linda was reading in bed.
>
> After I returned to school following a long illness, the math teacher gave me makeup work, but the history teacher made me drop her course.

Practice 1

Read through each sentence to get a sense of its overall meaning. Then insert a logical joining word (*and, or, but, for,* or *so*) and a logical dependent word (*because, since, when,* or *although*).

1. _____ you paint the closet, remember to open a window,

   _____ you might get a headache from the smell.
   Use *after* and *for.*

2. _____ I get into bed at night, I try to read a book, _____ I always fall asleep within minutes.

3. Russell ate less butter _____ he learned that his cholesterol level

   was a little too high, _____ he also included some bran in his diet.

4. _____ she made the honor roll, Molly received a library pass from

   the principal, _____ she didn't have to sit in study hall the whole semester.

5. We planned to go to a rock concert tonight, _____ it was canceled

   _____ the lead singer was arrested.

Practice 2

On separate paper, write five compound-complex sentences.

Review of Subordination and Coordination

ALLWRITE!

15.5

Subordination and coordination are ways of showing the exact relationship of ideas within a sentence. Through **subordination** we show that one idea is less important than another. When we subordinate, we use dependent words like *when, although, while, because,* and *after.* (A list of common dependent words has been given on page 138.) Through **coordination** we show that ideas are of equal importance. When we coordinate, we use the words *and, but, for, or, nor, so, yet.*

Practice

Use subordination or coordination to combine the following groups of simple sentences into one or more longer sentences. Be sure to omit repeated words. Since various combinations are possible, you might want to jot down several combinations on separate paper. Then read them aloud to find the combination that sounds best.

Keep in mind that, very often, the relationship among ideas in a sentence will be clearer when subordination rather than coordination is used.

Example
- My car does not start on cold mornings.
- I think the battery needs to be replaced.
- I already had it recharged once.
- I don't think charging it again would help.

Because my car does not start on cold mornings, I think the battery needs to be replaced. I already had it recharged once, so I don't think charging it again would help.

Comma Hints

a Use a comma at the end of a word group that starts with a dependent word (as in "Because my car does not start on cold mornings, . . .").

b Use a comma between independent word groups connected by *and, but, for, or, nor, so, yet* (as in "I already had it recharged once, so . . .").

1. • Sidney likes loud music.
    • His parents can't stand it.
    • He wears earphones.
    Use *although,* two commas, and the joining word *so.*

_____

_____

2. • The volcano erupted.
   • The sky turned black with smoke.
   • Nearby villagers were frightened.
   • They clogged the roads leading to safety.

   _____

   _____

   _____

   _____

3. • Glenda had a haircut today.
   • She came home and looked in the mirror.
   • She decided to wear a hat for a few days.
   • She thought she looked like a bald eagle.

   _____

   _____

   _____

   _____

4. • I ran out of gas on the way to work.
   • I discovered how helpful strangers can be.
   • A passing driver saw I was stuck.
   • He drove me to the gas station and back to my car.

   _____

   _____

   _____

   _____

5. • Our dog often rests on the floor in the sunshine.
   • He waits for the children to get home from school.
   • The sunlight moves along the floor.
   • He moves with it.

   _____

   _____

   _____

   _____

6. • My father was going to be late from work.
   • We planned to have a late dinner.
   • I was hungry before dinner.
   • I ate a salami and cheese sandwich.
   • I did this secretly.

   _____

   _____

   _____

   _____

7. • A baseball game was scheduled for early afternoon.
   • It looked like rain.
   • A crew rolled huge tarps to cover the field.
   • Then the sun reappeared.

   _____

   _____

   _____

   _____

8. • Cassy worries about the pesticides used on fruit.
   • She washes apples, pears, and plums in soap and water.
   • She doesn't rinse them well.
   • They have a soapy flavor.

   _____

   _____

   _____

   _____

9. • Charlene needed to buy stamps.
   • She went to the post office during her lunch hour.
   • The line was long.
   • She waited there for half an hour.
   • She had to go back to work without stamps.

   _____

   _____

   _____

   _____

10. • The weather suddenly became frigid.

  • Almost everyone at work caught a cold.

  • Someone brought a big batch of chicken soup.

  • She poured it into one of the office coffeepots.

  • The pot was empty by noon.

_____

_____

_____

_____

■ Review Test 1

Combine each group of short sentences into one sentence. Various combinations are possible. Choose the combination that reads most smoothly and clearly and that sounds most appropriate in the context of surrounding sentences.

  Here is an example of a group of sentences and some possible combinations:

Example • Martha moved in the desk chair.
  • Her moving was uneasy.
  • The chair was hard.
  • She worked at the assignment.
  • The assignment was for her English class.

  Martha moved uneasily in the hard desk chair, working at the assignment for her English class.

  Moving uneasily in the hard desk chair, Martha worked at the assignment for her English class.

  Martha moved uneasily in the hard desk chair as she worked at the assignment for her English class.

  While she worked at the assignment for her English class, Martha moved uneasily in the hard desk chair.

Note   In combining short sentences into one sentence, omit repeated words where necessary. Use separate paper.

Doctor's Waiting Room

- People visit the doctor.
- Their ordeal begins.

- A patient has an appointment for 2:00.
- He is told he will have to wait.
- The wait will be at least one hour.

- Other people arrive.
- Everyone takes a seat.
- Soon the room becomes crowded.

- Some people read old magazines.
- Others count the stripes.
- The stripes are in the wallpaper.

- Some people look at each other.
- Some people may smile.
- No one talks to anyone else.

- Some people are very sick.
- They cough a lot.
- They hold tissues to their noses.

- The people around them turn away.
- They hold their breath.
- They are afraid of becoming infected.

- Time passes.
- It passes slowly.
- All the people count.
- They count the number of people ahead of them.

- The long-awaited moment finally arrives.
- The receptionist comes into the waiting area.

- She looks at the patient.
- She says the magic words.
- "The doctor will see you now."

■ Review Test 2

Combine each group of short sentences into one sentence. Various combinations are possible. Choose the combination that reads most smoothly and clearly and that sounds most appropriate in the context of surrounding sentences.

Notes   In combining short sentences into one sentence, omit repeated words where necessary. Use separate paper.

A Remedy for Shyness

- Linda Nelson was shy.
- She seldom met new people.
- She spent a lot of time alone.

- Too often Linda avoided speaking.
- She did not want to take a risk.
- The risk was embarrassing herself.

- Luckily, Linda got some advice.
- The advice was good.
- She got the advice from her cousin Rose.
- Linda decided to try to change.
- She would change her behavior.

- Rose told Linda not to blame herself for being shy.
- She told her the shyness made her seem attractive.
- She told her the shyness made her seem modest.

- Rose encouraged her to talk to others.
- Linda began to join conversations at school.
- Linda began to join conversations at work.

- Gradually, Linda learned something.
- She could start conversations.
- She could start them herself.
- She could do this even though her heart pounded.
- She could do this even though her stomach churned.

- Linda still feels uncomfortable sometimes.
- She is doing things that once seemed impossible.

- Linda joined a bowling league.
- She did this recently.
- Some of her new friends invited her to join.
- The friends were from work.

- She is not the best bowler on the team.
- She is winning a victory over shyness.
- She is winning, thanks to her cousin's help.
- She is winning, thanks to her own determination.

- Linda is a happier person today.
- She has taken charge of her life.
- She has made herself a more interesting person.

8 Standard English Verbs

Introductory Activity

Underline what you think is the correct form of the verb in each pair of sentences below.

That radio station once (play, played) top-forty hits.
It now (play, plays) classical music.

When Jean was a little girl, she (hope, hoped) to become a movie star.
Now she (hope, hopes) to be accepted at law school.

At first, my father (juggle, juggled) with balls of yarn.
Now that he is an expert, he (juggle, juggles) raw eggs.

On the basis of the above examples, see if you can complete the following statements.

1. The first sentence in each pair refers to an action in the (past time, present time), and the regular verb has an _____ ending.
2. The second sentence in each pair refers to an action in the (past time, present time), and the regular verb has an _____ ending.

Answers are on page 683.

151

Many people have grown up in communities where nonstandard verb forms are used in everyday life. Such nonstandard forms include *they be, it done, we has, you was, she don't,* and *it ain't.* Community dialects have richness and power but are a drawback in college and the world at large, where standard English verb forms must be used. Standard English helps ensure clear communication among English-speaking people everywhere, and it is especially important in the world of work.

This chapter compares the community dialect and the standard English forms of a regular verb and three common irregular verbs.

Regular Verbs: Dialect and Standard Forms

The chart below compares community dialect (nonstandard) and standard English forms of the regular verb *talk.*

TALK

Community Dialect		Standard English	
(Do not use in your writing)		(Use for clear communication)	
Present Tense			
I talks	we talks	I talk	we talk
you talks	you talks	you talk	you talk
he, she, it talk	they talks	he, she, it talks	they talk
Past Tense			
I talk	we talk	I talked	we talked
you talk	you talk	you talked	you talked
he, she, it talk	they talk	he, she, it talked	they talked

One of the most common nonstandard forms results from dropping the endings of regular verbs. For example, people might say "Rose work until ten o'clock tonight" instead of "Rose work*s* until ten o'clock tonight." Or they'll say "I work overtime yesterday" instead of "I work*ed* overtime yesterday." To avoid such nonstandard usage, memorize the forms shown above for the regular verb *talk.* Then do the activities that follow. These activities will help you make it a habit to include verb endings in your writing.

Present Tense Endings

18.2a

The verb ending -s or -es is needed with a regular verb in the present tense when the subject is *he, she, it,* or any one person or thing.

He	He lifts weights.
She	She runs.
It	It amazes me.
One person	Their son Ted swims.
One person	Their daughter Terry dances.
One thing	Their house jumps at night with all the exercise.

Practice 1

All but one of the ten sentences that follow need -s or -es endings. Cross out the nonstandard verb forms and write the standard forms in the spaces provided. Mark the one sentence that needs no change with a *C*.

_____*ends*_____   Example   The sale ~~end~~ tomorrow.

_____   1. Tim drive too fast for me.
        Add *s* to *drive.*

_____   2. Our washing machine always get stuck at the rinse cycle.

_____   3. Roberto practice his saxophone two hours each day.

_____   4. Whenever I serve meat loaf, my daughter make a peanut butter sandwich.

_____   5. My grandfather brush his teeth with baking soda.

_____   6. While watching television in the evening, Kitty usually fall asleep.

_____   7. Mom always wakes me by saying, "Get up, the day is growing older."

_____   8. On my old car radio, a static sound come from every station but one.

_____   9. My little sister watch fireworks with her hands over her ears.

_____   10. The broken computer buzz like an angry wasp.

Practice 2

Rewrite the short selection below, adding present tense -s verb endings in the ten places where they are needed.

My little sister want to be a singer when she grow up. She constantly hum and sing around the house. Sometimes she make quite a racket. When she listen to music on the radio, for example, she sing very loudly in order to hear herself over the radio. And when she take a shower, her voice ring through the whole house because she think nobody can hear her from there.

_____

_____

_____

_____

_____

_____

_____

_____

_____

_____

Past Tense Endings

The verb ending *-d* or *-ed* is needed with a regular verb in the past tense.

Yesterday we finished painting the house.

I completed the paper an hour before class.

Fred's car stalled on his way to work this morning.

Practice 1

All but one of the ten sentences that follow need *-d* or *-ed* endings. Cross out the nonstandard verb forms and write the standard forms in the spaces provided. Mark the one sentence that needs no change with a *C*.

jumped   Example   The cat ~~jump~~ onto my lap when I sat down.

_____   1. A waiter at the new restaurant accidentally spill ice water into Phil's lap. Add *ed* to *spill*.

_____   2. In a prim Indiana town, a couple was actually jail for kissing in public.

_____   3. While ironing my new shirt this morning, I burn a hole right through it.

_____   4. Fran wrapped the gag gift in waxed paper and tie it with dental floss.

_____   5. Pencil marks dotted Matt's bedroom wall where he measure his height each month.

_____   6. My brother was eating too fast and almost choked on a piece of bread.

_____   7. Last summer, a burglar smash my car window and stole my jacket.

_____   8. The kids construct an obstacle course in the basement out of boxes and toys.

_____   9. The rain came down so hard it level the young cornstalks in our garden.

_____   10. As Alfonso pulled up to the red light, he suddenly realize his brakes were not working.

Practice 2

Rewrite this selection, adding past tense -*d* or -*ed* verb endings in the fifteen places where they are needed.

My cousin Joel complete a course in home repairs and offer one day to fix several things in my house. He repair a screen door that squeak, a dining room chair that wobble a bit, and a faulty electrical outlet. That night when I open the screen door, it loosen from its hinges. When I seat myself in the chair Joel had fix, one of its legs crack off. Remembering that Joel had also fool around with the electrical outlet, I quickly call an electrician and ask him to stop by the next day. Then I pray the house would not burn down before he arrive.

_____

_____

_____

_____

_____

_____

_____

_____

_____

Three Common Irregular Verbs: Dialect and Standard Forms

The following charts compare the community dialect (nonstandard) and standard English forms of the common irregular verbs *be, have,* and *do.* (For more on irregular verbs, see Chapter 9, beginning on page 161.)

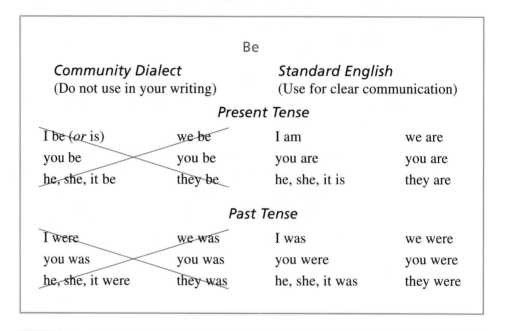

Be

Community Dialect (Do not use in your writing)		*Standard English* (Use for clear communication)	
Present Tense			
I be (*or* is)	we be	I am	we are
you be	you be	you are	you are
he, she, it be	they be	he, she, it is	they are
Past Tense			
I were	we was	I was	we were
you was	you was	you were	you were
he, she, it were	they was	he, she, it was	they were

Have

Community Dialect (Do not use in your writing)		*Standard English* (Use for clear communication)	
Present Tense			
I has	we has	I have	we have
you has	you has	you have	you have
he, she, it have	they has	he, she, it has	they have
Past Tense			
I has	we has	I had	we had
you has	you has	you had	you had
he, she, it have	they has	he, she, it had	they had

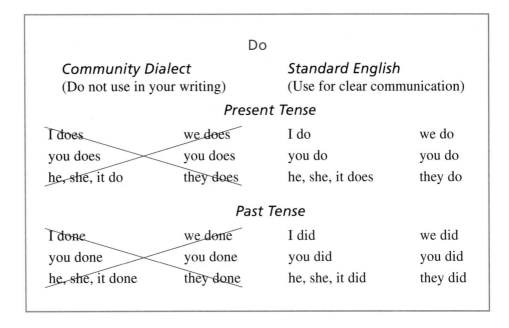

Do

Community Dialect (Do not use in your writing)		Standard English (Use for clear communication)	
Present Tense			
~~I does~~	~~we does~~	I do	we do
you does	you does	you do	you do
~~he, she~~, it do	~~they does~~	he, she, it does	they do
Past Tense			
~~I done~~	~~we done~~	I did	we did
you done	you done	you did	you did
~~he, she~~, it done	~~they done~~	he, she, it did	they did

Note   Many people have trouble with one negative form of *do.* They will say, for example, "She don't listen" instead of "She doesn't listen," or they will say "This pen don't work" instead of "This pen doesn't work." Be careful to avoid the common mistake of using *don't* instead of *doesn't.*

Practice 1

Underline the standard form of the irregular verbs *be, have,* or *do.*

1. The piranha (be, is) a fish that lives in South American rivers.
   Be is never a verb by itself.

2. Only eight to twelve inches long, piranhas (do, does) not look very frightening.

3. But the smell of blood in the water (have, has) the effect of driving piranhas crazy with excitement.

4. Even the tiny drop of blood produced by a single mosquito bite (be, is) enough to attract the vicious fish.

5. Piranhas (has, have) double rows of teeth which make them dangerous hunters.

6. Those teeth (be, are) so sharp that some Indian tribes use them as arrowheads.

7. A single piranha's bite (has, have) the potential to cause severe injury, such as the loss of a finger or toe.

8. However, piranhas (does, do) their greatest damage when they attack in large numbers.

9. Some travelers (was, were) boating on the Amazon when they saw a school of piranhas strip a four-hundred pound hog to a skeleton in minutes.

10. "What the piranha (does, do) is believable only if you see it," reported one witness.

Practice 2

Cross out the nonstandard verb form in each sentence. Then write the standard form of *be, have,* or *do* in the space provided.

_____ 1. If you does your assignments on time, you may not understand my friend Albert.
You does is never a correct form.

_____ 2. Albert be the world's worst procrastinator.

_____ 3. Procrastinators be people who always put things off.

_____ 4. They has problems with deadlines of all kinds.

_____ 5. Albert were a procrastinator at the age of six.

_____ 6. The boy next door have a few friends over for lunch one day.

_____ 7. Albert's parents was upset when they learned Albert got there three hours late.

_____ 8. They done the neighbors a favor by taking Albert home at once.

_____ 9. Today, Albert still do everything at the last minute or even later.

_____ 10. He have plans to join Procrastinators Anonymous—when he gets around to it.

Practice 3

Fill in each blank with the standard form of *be, have,* or *do.*

My cousin Rita _____ decided to lose thirty pounds, so she

_____ put herself on a rigid diet that _____ not allow her to eat

anything that she enjoys. Last weekend, while the family _____ at Aunt

Jenny's house for dinner, all Rita _____ to eat _____ a can of Diet

Delight peaches. We _____ convinced that Rita meant business when

she joined an exercise club whose members _____ to work out on

enormous machines and _____ twenty sit-ups just to get started. If Rita

_____ reach her goal, we _____ all going to be very proud of her.

But I would not be surprised if she _____ not succeed, because this

_____ her fourth diet this year.

■ Review Test 1

Underline the standard verb form.

1. A cake in the oven (make, makes) the whole house smell good.

2. My brother deliberately (wear, wears) socks that clash with his clothes.

3. Our boss (don't, doesn't) want us to take any extra coffee breaks.

4. After I got home from the movie theater, I (realize, realized) I had lost my wallet.

5. The cheap ballpoint pen (leak, leaked) ink on my favorite shirt.

6. If they (was, were) my children, I wouldn't let them play near that creek.

7. We have to be quiet, because my sister (is, be) studying for her sociology test.

8. A neighbor (watch, watched) our house while we were away on vacation.

9. When the sculptor (unveil, unveiled) his work, no one could figure out what it was.

10. *Consumer Reports* (did, done) a report last month on cars, and mine was the lowest-rated model on the list.

■ Review Test 2

Cross out the nonstandard verb form in each of the sentences that follow. Then write the standard English verb form in the space at the left, as shown.

__played__   Example   Yesterday morning, the children ~~play~~ quietly in the sandbox.

_____   1. Making promises be easier than keeping them.

_____   2. Baked potatoes doesn't have as many calories as I thought.

_____   3. The game were lost when the other team scored a fourth-quarter touchdown.

_____   4. Our psychology professor ride a motorcycle to school.

_____   5. The mayor cover his face from photographers as he was escorted to jail.

_____   6. The large dog growl fiercely when I approached my neighbor's house.

_____   7. Lightning struck a nearby building last night and cause a major fire.

_____   8. Many childhood diseases, such as scarlet fever and whooping cough, has almost vanished in the United States.

_____   9. Stanley turned the television on during the day because the house sound too quiet without it.

_____   10. That restaurant offers free nonalcoholic drinks to the person who be the driver for a group.

9 Irregular Verbs

Introductory Activity

You may already have a sense of which common English verbs are regular and which are not. To test yourself, fill in the past tense and past participle of the verbs below. Five are regular verbs and so take *-d* or *-ed* in the past tense and past participle. For these verbs, write *R* under *Verb Type* and then write their past tense and past participle verb forms. Five are irregular verbs and will probably not sound right when you try to add *-d* or *-ed*. For these verbs, write *I* under *Verb Type*. Also, see if you can write in their irregular verb forms.

Present	Verb Type	Past	Past Participle
fall	I	fell	fallen
1. scream			
2. write			
3. steal			
4. ask			
5. kiss			
6. choose			
7. ride			
8. chew			
9. think			
10. dance			

Answers are on page 684.

A Brief Review of Regular Verbs

Every verb has four principal parts: present, past, past participle, and present participle. These parts can be used to build all the verb tenses (the times shown by a verb).

Most verbs in English are regular. The past and past participle of a regular verb are formed by adding *-d* or *-ed* to the present. The *past participle* is the form of the verb used with the helping verbs *have, has,* or *had* (or some form of *be* with passive verbs, which are explained on page 192). The *present participle* is formed by adding *-ing* to the present.

Here are the principal forms of some regular verbs:

Present	*Past*	*Past Participle*	*Present Participle*
laugh	laughed	laughed	laughing
ask	asked	asked	asking
touch	touched	touched	touching
decide	decided	decided	deciding
explode	exploded	exploded	exploding

List of Irregular Verbs

Irregular verbs have irregular forms in the past tense and past participle. For example, the past tense of the irregular verb *grow* is *grew;* the past participle is *grown.*

Almost everyone has some degree of trouble with irregular verbs. When you are unsure about the form of a verb, you can check the following list of irregular verbs. (The present participle is not shown on this list, because it is formed simply by adding *-ing* to the base form of the verb.) Or you can check a dictionary, which gives the principal parts of irregular verbs.

Present	Past	Past Participle
arise	arose	arisen
awake	awoke *or* awaked	awoke *or* awaked
be (am, are, is)	was (were)	been
become	became	become
begin	began	begun
bend	bent	bent
bite	bit	bitten
blow	blew	blown
break	broke	broken
bring	brought	brought
build	built	built
burst	burst	burst
buy	bought	bought
catch	caught	caught
choose	chose	chosen
come	came	come
cost	cost	cost
cut	cut	cut
do (does)	did	done
draw	drew	drawn
drink	drank	drunk
drive	drove	driven
eat	ate	eaten
fall	fell	fallen
feed	fed	fed
feel	felt	felt
fight	fought	fought
find	found	found
fly	flew	flown
freeze	froze	frozen
get	got	got *or* gotten
give	gave	given
go (goes)	went	gone
grow	grew	grown
have (has)	had	had
hear	heard	heard
hide	hid	hidden
hold	held	held
hurt	hurt	hurt
keep	kept	kept
know	knew	known

Present	Past	Past Participle
lay	laid	laid
lead	led	led
leave	left	left
lend	lent	lent
let	let	let
lie	lay	lain
light	lit	lit
lose	lost	lost
make	made	made
meet	met	met
pay	paid	paid
ride	rode	ridden
ring	rang	rung
rise	rose	risen
run	ran	run
say	said	said
see	saw	seen
sell	sold	sold
send	sent	sent
shake	shook	shaken
shrink	shrank	shrunk
shut	shut	shut
sing	sang	sung
sit	sat	sat
sleep	slept	slept
speak	spoke	spoken
spend	spent	spent
stand	stood	stood
steal	stole	stolen
stick	stuck	stuck
sting	stung	stung
swear	swore	sworn
swim	swam	swum
take	took	taken
teach	taught	taught
tear	tore	torn
tell	told	told
think	thought	thought
wake	woke *or* waked	woken *or* waked
wear	wore	worn
win	won	won
write	wrote	written

Practice 1

Cross out the incorrect verb form in the following sentences. Then write the correct form of the verb in the space provided.

began   Example   When the mud slide started, the whole neighborhood ~~begun~~ going downhill.

_____   1. The coach caught Otto when he come in two hours after curfew.
Use the past tense of *come.*

_____   2. We standed out in the rain all night to buy tickets to the concert.

_____   3. The Romans had builded a network of roads so the army could travel more quickly from place to place.

_____   4. Our championship team has swam in every important meet this year.

_____   5. The nervous mother holded her child's hand tightly as they crossed the busy street.

_____   6. Hakeem drived in circles for an hour before he admitted that he was lost.

_____   7. He had wrote the answers to all the questions before anyone else had finished the first page.

_____   8. The tornado blowed the sign from the top of the bank, and it landed five blocks away in the motel swimming pool.

_____   9. Kathy buyed school clothes with the money she earned from her summer job.

_____   10. The poker players knowed they were in trouble when the stranger shuffled the cards with one hand.

Practice 2

For each of the italicized verbs in the following sentences, fill in the three missing forms in the order shown in the box:

> a. Present tense, which takes an *-s* ending when the subject is *he, she, it,* or any *one person* or *thing* (see page 153)
>
> b. Past tense
>
> c. Past participle—the form that goes with the helping verb *have, has,* or *had*

Example   My little nephew loves to *break* things. Every Christmas he (a)
_____breaks_____ his new toys the minute they're unwrapped. Last year he
(b) _____broke_____ five toys in seven minutes and then went on to smash
his family's new china platter. His mother says he won't be happy until
he has (c) _____broken_____ their hearts.

1. Did you ever go to *sleep* on a water bed? My cousin Nancy (a) _____
   on one. Last year I spent the weekend at Nancy's apartment, and I (b)
   _____ on it. Since then I have (c) _____ on it several more
   times, without once getting seasick.
   Add an *s* to *sleep* in choice a. Use the past tense of *sleep* for b and c.

2. A dreadful little boy in my neighborhood loves to *ring* my doorbell and run
   away. Sometimes he (a) _____ it several times a day. The last time it
   (b) _____ over and over, I finally refused to answer the door. Then I
   found out that the mail carrier had (c) _____ the doorbell to deliver a
   gift from my boyfriend.

3. Why does every teacher ask us to *write* about our summer vacations? Most
   students (a) _____ about what really happened, but that is usually too
   dull. I (b) _____ an essay about being taken aboard an alien spacecraft.
   I bet it was the most interesting essay anybody has ever (c) _____ for
   my teacher's English class.

4. My sister never has to *stand* in line for a movie very long. She always (a)
   _____ for a few minutes and then walks straight to the entrance. "I (b)
   _____ in line as long as I could," she tells the ticket taker. "In fact,"
   she continues in a weak voice, "I have (c) _____ in line too long
   already. I feel faint." She is always ushered inside immediately.

5. As usual, Ron planned to *swim* at least a hundred laps before breakfast. He
   knew that an Olympic hopeful (a) _____ while others sleep. That
   morning he (b) _____ with a deliberate stroke, counting the rhythm
   silently. He had (c) _____ this way daily for the last two years. It was
   a price he was willing to pay to be one of the best.

6. I know a woman who likes to *buy* things and return them after she uses them.
   For example, she always (a) _____ new shoes to wear for special occa-
   sions. Then she wears them for the event and returns them the next day. Once

she (b) _____ a complete outfit, wore it twice, and returned it a week later. Whenever I shop, I worry that I have (c) _____ something that she has used and returned.

7. Craig sat in his car at the rural crossroads and wondered which direction to *choose*. Should he (a) _____ left or right? He sighed and turned right, knowing that if he (b) _____ the wrong way, he would run out of gas before finding his way back to the highway. After several anxious minutes, he spotted an Exxon sign. He pulled into the service station, grateful that he had (c) _____ the right direction after all.

8. My friend Alice loves to *eat*. But no matter how much she (a) _____, she stays thin. Her husband, on the other hand, is fat. "Why?" he jokingly complains. "I (b) _____ very little today. In fact," he adds with a grin, "all my life I have (c) _____ just one meal a day. Of course, it usually lasts from morning till night."

9. All the kids in the neighborhood waited each winter for Mahoney's pond to *freeze*. They knew that a sudden cold snap (a) _____ only the surface. It took at least a week of low temperatures before the pond (b) _____ more than a few inches deep. Mr. Mahoney checked the ice each day. When it had finally (c) _____ to a depth of six inches, he gave his permission for the children to skate on it.

10. It is important for people to *give* blood. A healthy person can (a) _____ a pint of blood in less than fifteen minutes with little or no discomfort. The first time I (b) _____ blood, I was afraid the needle would hurt, but all I felt was a slight pinch. I have (c) _____ blood many times since then. Each time I do, I feel good, knowing that my gift will help other people.

Troublesome Irregular Verbs

Three common irregular verbs that often give people trouble are *be, have,* and *do*. See pages 156–157 for a discussion of these verbs. Three sets of other irregular verbs that can lead to difficulties are *lie-lay, sit-set,* and *rise-raise*.

Lie-Lay

The principal parts of *lie* and *lay* are as follows:

Present	Past	Past Participle
lie	lay	lain
lay	laid	laid

To lie means *to rest* or *recline. To lay* means *to put something down.*

To Lie	To Lay
Tony *lies* on the couch.	I *lay* the mail on the table.
This morning he *lay* in the tub.	Yesterday I *laid* the mail on the counter.
He has *lain* in bed all week with the flu.	I have *laid* the mail where everyone will see it.

Practice

Underline the correct verb. Use a form of *lie* if you can substitute *recline.* Use a form of *lay* if you can substitute *place.*

1. On warm sunny days, Serena's kitten often (lies, lays) on the bedroom windowsill.
    Since the kitten is resting, what is the correct answer?
2. (Lying, Laying) too long in bed in the morning can give me a headache.
3. The Magna Carta (lay, laid) the foundation for the establishment of the English Parliament.
4. He was certain he had (lain, laid) the tiles in a straight line until he stepped back to look.
5. I (lay, laid) down on the couch and pressed my face into the pillow.

Sit-Set

The principal parts of *sit* and *set* are as follows:

Present	Past	Past Participle
sit	sat	sat
set	set	set

To sit means *to take a seat* or *to rest. To set* means *to put* or *to place.*

To Sit	To Set
I *sit* down during work breaks.	Tony *sets* out the knives, forks, and spoons.
I *sat* in the doctor's office for three hours.	His sister already *set* out the dishes.
I have always *sat* in the last desk.	They have just *set* out the dinnerware.

Practice

Underline the correct form of the verb. Use a form of *sit* if you can substitute *rest.* Use a form of *set* if you can substitute *place.*

1. The movers have (sat, set) all the smaller boxes on the kitchen table.
   Since the movers placed the boxes, what is the correct verb?
2. When I'm on a bus, I like (sitting, setting) in front.
3. The aircraft carrier (sat, set) five miles offshore as helicopters shuttled to and from the island.
4. (Sit, Set) the plant on the windowsill so it will get the morning sun.
5. Lupe helped decorate for the party by (sitting, setting) vases of fresh flowers on each of the tables.

Rise-Raise

The principal parts of *rise* and *raise* are as follows:

Present	*Past*	*Past Participle*
rise	rose	risen
raise	raised	raised

To rise means *to get up* or *to move up*. *To raise* (which is a regular verb with simple *-ed* endings) means *to lift up* or *to increase in amount*.

To Rise	*To Raise*
The soldiers *rise* at dawn.	I'm going to *raise* the stakes in the card game.
The crowd *rose* to applaud the batter.	I *raised* the shades to let in the sun.
Dracula has *risen* from the grave.	I would have quit if the company had not *raised* my salary.

Practice

Underline the correct verb. Use a form of *rise* if you can substitute *get up* or *move up*. Use a form of *raise* if you can substitute *lift up* or *increase*.

1. It is usually warmer upstairs because heat (rises, raises).

   Since heat moves upward, what is the correct verb?
2. The new owner (rose, raised) the rent, so now I will have to look for another apartment.
3. We (rose, raised) at three o'clock in the morning to watch the meteor shower.
4. After four days of rain, the river had (risen, raised) over its banks and threatened to flood the highway.
5. A single sailboat made them (rise, raise) the drawbridge, stopping traffic in both directions for fifteen minutes.

■ **Review Test 1**

Cross out the incorrect verb form. Then write the correct form of the verb in the space provided.

_____ 1. The spare key under the mat falled through a crack in the porch floor.

_____ 2. When he blowed out the dozens of candles on his cake, the old man used a hair dryer.

_____ 3. Many residents fighted the city's plan to build a new stadium in their neighborhood.

_____ 4. Oscar said he could have swam ten more laps if he hadn't gotten leg cramps.

_____ 5. After he had broke the vase, the little boy hid the pieces under the sofa.

_____ 6. People looked away from the homeless man who was laying on the sidewalk.

_____ 7. You should have saw Ann's face when she passed her driving test.

_____ 8. After I lended Dave money, I remembered that he seldom pays people back.

_____ 9. My grandmother has growed tomatoes and peppers in her backyard for many years.

_____ 10. The health inspector come into the kitchen as the cook picked up a hamburger from the floor.

■ **Review Test 2**

Write short sentences using the form noted for the following irregular verbs.

Example   Past of *ride* *The Lone Ranger rode into the sunset.*

1. Present of *shake* _____

2. Past participle of *write* _____

3. Past participle of *begin* _____

4. Past of *go* _____

5. Past participle of *grow* _____

6. Present of *speak* _____

7. Past of *bring* _____

8. Present of *do* _____

9. Past participle of *give* _____

10. Past of *drink* _____

10 Subject-Verb Agreement

Introductory Activity

As you read each pair of sentences below, write a check mark beside the sentence that you think uses the underlined word correctly.

The pictures in that magazine <u>is</u> very controversial. _____

The pictures in that magazine <u>are</u> very controversial. _____

There <u>was</u> many applicants for the job. _____

There <u>were</u> many applicants for the job. _____

Everybody usually <u>watch</u> the lighted numbers in an elevator. _____

Everybody usually <u>watches</u> the lighted numbers in an elevator. _____

On the basis of the above examples, see if you can complete the following statements.

1. In the first two pairs of sentences, the subjects are _____ and _____. Since both these subjects are plural, the verb must be plural.

2. In the last pair of sentences, the subject, *Everybody,* is a word that is always (singular, plural), and so its accompanying verb must be (singular, plural).

Answers are on page 684.

A verb must agree with its subject in number. A *singular subject* (one person or thing) takes a singular verb. A *plural subject* (more than one person or thing) takes a plural verb. Mistakes in subject-verb agreement are sometimes made in the following situations:

1   When words come between the subject and the verb
2   When a verb comes before the subject
3   With indefinite pronouns
4   With compound subjects
5   With *who, which,* and *that*

Each situation is explained on the following pages.

Words between the Subject and the Verb

Words that come between the subject and the verb do not change subject-verb agreement. In the following sentence,

The breakfast cereals in the pantry are made mostly of sugar.

the subject (*cereals*) is plural, and so the verb (*are*) is plural. The words *in the pantry* that come between the subject and the verb do not affect subject-verb agreement. To help find the subject of certain sentences, you should cross out prepositional phrases (explained on page 91):

One ~~of the crooked politicians~~ was jailed for a month.
The boxes ~~in my grandmother's attic~~ contained old family photos and long forgotten toys.

Following is a list of common prepositions.

Common Prepositions

about	before	by	inside	over
above	behind	during	into	through
across	below	except	of	to
among	beneath	for	off	toward
around	beside	from	on	under
at	between	in	onto	with

Practice

Draw one line under the subject. Then lightly cross out any words that come between the subject and the verb. Finally, draw two lines under the correct verb in parentheses.

Example   The price of the stereo speakers (is, are) too high for my wallet.

1. A trail of bloodstains (leads, lead) to the spot where the murder was committed.
   Cross out the preposition between the subject and verb.

2. The winter clothes in the hall closet (takes, take) up too much room.

3. A basket of fancy fruit and nuts (was, were) delivered to my house.

4. The garbled instructions for assembling the bicycle (was, were) almost impossible to follow.

5. Smoke from the distant forest fires (is, are) visible from many miles away.

6. Workers at that automobile plant (begins, begin) each day with a period of exercise.

7. The earliest date on any of the cemetery gravestones (appears, appear) to be 1804.

8. The line of cars in the traffic jam (seems, seem) to extend for miles.

9. Several boxes in the corner of the attic (contains, contain) old family pictures.

10. Sleeping bags with the new insulation material (protects, protect) campers even in subzero temperatures.

Verb before the Subject

ALLWRITE!

17.3c, d

A verb agrees with its subject even when the verb comes *before* the subject. Words that may precede the subject include *there, here,* and, in questions, *who, which, what,* and *where.*

Inside the storage shed <u>are</u> the garden <u>tools.</u>

At the street corner <u>were</u> two <u>panhandlers.</u>

There <u>are</u> <u>times</u> when I'm ready to quit my job.

Where <u>are</u> the <u>instructions</u> for the DVD player?

If you are unsure about the subject, ask *who* or *what* of the verb. With the first sentence above, you might ask, "What is inside the storage shed?" The answer, garden *tools,* is the subject.

Practice

Draw one line under the subject. Then draw two lines under the correct verb in parentheses.

1. There (is, are) a scratching <u>noise</u> coming from behind this wall.

   To find the subject, ask "What is coming from behind the wall?"

2. On the bottom of the <u>jar of preserves</u> (is, are) the berries.

3. Floating near the base of the dock (was, were) several discarded aluminum cans.

4. In the middle of the woods behind our home (sits, sit) an abandoned cabin.

5. There (was, were) so many <u>students</u> talking at once that the instructor shouted for quiet.

6. Outside the novelty shop at the mall (stands, stand) a life-size cutout of W. C. Fields.

7. Coming out of the fog toward the frightened <u>boys</u> (was, were) the menacing shape of a large dog.

8. In the rear of the closet (was, were) the basketball <u>sneakers</u> that I thought I had lost.

9. On the table in the doctor's office (is, are) some magazines that are five years old.

10. Lining one wall of the gym (was, were) a row of <u>lockers</u> for the team members.

Indefinite Pronouns

17.5

The following words, known as *indefinite pronouns,* always take singular verbs.

Indefinite Pronouns			
(-one words)	*(-body* words)	*(-thing* words)	
one	nobody	nothing	each
anyone	anybody	anything	either
everyone	everybody	everything	neither
someone	somebody	something	

Note   *Both* always takes a plural verb.

Practice

Write the correct form of the verb in the space provided.

keeps,
keep

1. Something always _____ me from getting to bed on time.
   The indefinite pronoun *something* requires a singular verb.

works,
work

2. Nobody that I know _____ as hard as Manuel.

pays,
pay

3. Neither of the jobs offered to me _____ more than six dollars an hour.

has,
have

4. Both of the speakers _____ told us more than we care to know about the dangers of water pollution.

slips,
slip

5. Someone in Inez's apartment house _____ an unsigned valentine under her door every year.

leans,
lean

6. Anything sitting on the old wooden floor _____ to one side.

expects,
expect

7. Each of my friends _____ to be invited to my new backyard pool.

was,
were

8. Not one of the three smoke detectors in the house _____ working properly.

stops,
stop

9. Only one of all the brands of waxes _____ the rust on my car from spreading.

has,
have

10. Just about everybody who hates getting up early for work _____ jumped out of bed at 6 A.M. to go on vacation.

Compound Subjects

ALLWRITE!
17.2

Subjects joined by *and* generally take a plural verb.

<u>Yoga</u> and <u>biking</u> <u>are</u> Lola's ways of staying in shape.
<u>Ambition</u> and <u>good luck</u> <u>are</u> the keys to his success.

When subjects are joined by *either . . . or, neither . . . nor, not only . . . but also,* the verb agrees with the subject closer to the verb.

Either the <u>restaurant manager</u> or his <u>assistants</u> <u>deserve</u> to be fired for the spoiled meat used in the stew.

The nearer subject, *assistants,* is plural, and so the verb is plural.

Practice

Write the correct form of the verb in the space provided.

saddens,
sadden

1. The shivering and crying of animals in pet stores _____ me very much.
   The compound subject *shivering and crying* requires a plural verb.

needs,
need

2. The floor and cabinets in the kitchen _____ to be cleaned.

has,
have

3. Her best friend and her coach _____ more influence on Sally than her parents do.

continues,
continue

4. Crabgrass and dandelions _____ to spread across the lawn despite my efforts to wipe them out.

tears,
tear

5. Either the neighborhood kids or an automatic car-wash machine always _____ the antenna off my car.

Who, Which, and *That*

ALLWRITE!
17.3a

When *who, which,* and *that* are used as subjects of verbs, they take singular verbs if the word they stand for is singular and plural verbs if the word they stand for is plural. For example, in the sentence

Gary is one of those people <u>who</u> <u>are</u> very private.

the verb is plural because *who* stands for *people,* which is plural. On the other hand, in the sentence

Gary is a person <u>who</u> <u>is</u> very private.

the verb is singular because *who* stands for *person,* which is singular.

Practice

Write the correct form of the verb in the space provided.

has,
have

1. The young man who _____ mowed my grass for years just left for college.
   Who stands for a singular subject and requires a singular verb.

goes,
go

2. The jacket that _____ with those pants is at the cleaners.

becomes,
become

3. Women who _____ police officers often have to prove themselves more capable than their male coworkers.

tastes,
taste

4. The restaurant serves hamburgers which _____ like dry cereal.

is,
are

5. The ceiling in Kevin's bedroom is covered with stars that _____ arranged in the shape of the constellations.

Collaborative Activity

Part A: Editing and Rewriting

Working with a partner, read the short paragraph below and see if you can underline the five mistakes in subject-verb agreement. Then use the space provided to correct these five errors. Feel free to discuss the rewrite quietly with your partner and refer back to the chapter when necessary.

When most people think about cities, they do not thinks about wild animals. But in my city apartment, there is enough creatures to fill a small forest. In the daytime, I must contend with the pigeons. These unwanted guests at my apartment makes a loud feathery mess on my bedroom windowsill. In the evening, my apartment is visited by roaches. These large insects creep onto my kitchen floor and walls after dark and frighten me with their shiny glistening bodies. Later at night, my apartment is invaded by mice. Waking from sleep, I can hear their little feet tapping as they

Continued

scurry behind walls and above my ceiling. Everybody I know think I should move into a new apartment. What I really need is to go somewhere that have less wild creatures—maybe a forest!

_____

_____

_____

_____

_____

Part B: Creating Sentences

Working with a partner, write sentences as directed. Use separate paper. For each item, pay special attention to subject-verb agreement.

1. Write a sentence in which the words *in the cafeteria* or *on the table* come between the subject and verb. Underline the subject of your sentence and circle the verb.

2. Write a sentence that begins with the words *There is* or *There are*. Underline the subject of your sentence and circle the verb.

3. Write a sentence in which the indefinite pronoun *nobody* or *anything* is the subject.

4. Write a sentence with the compound subjects *manager* and *employees*. Underline the subject of your sentence and circle the verb.

Reflective Activity

1. Look at the paragraph about the apartment that you revised above. Which rule involving subject-verb agreement gave you the most trouble? How did you figure out the correct answer?

2. Five situations involving subject-verb agreement have been discussed in this chapter. Explain which one is most likely to cause you problems.

■ **Review Test 1**

Complete each of the following sentences, using *is, are, was, were, have,* or *has.* Underline the subject of each of these verbs. In some cases you will need to provide that subject.

Example   The <u>hot dogs</u> in that luncheonette *are hazardous to your health.* _____

1. In my glove compartment _____

2. The cat and her three kittens _____

3. I frequently see people who _____

4. Neither of the wrestlers _____

5. Scattered across the parking lot _____

6. The dust balls under my bed _____

7. There are _____

8. My friend and his brother _____

9. The newspapers that accumulate in my garage _____

_____

10. It was one of those movies that _____

_____

■ **Review Test 2**

Draw one line under the subject. Then draw two lines under the correct verb in parentheses.

1. The plants in the window (grows, grow) quickly because they have plenty of sunlight.

2. Nobody (walks, walk) on the streets of this neighborhood at night.

3. Here (is, are) the keys you need to get into the apartment.

4. A dropped pass and two fumbles (was, were) the reasons the team lost the football game.

5. There (is, are) billboards all along the road warning drivers to stay sober.

6. A paper plate fitted over the dog's head (prevents, prevent) the animal from biting its stitches.

7. Since I gained weight, neither my old suits nor my new shirt (fits, fit) me.

8. What (does, do) my marital status have to do with my qualifications for the job?

9. Sitting silently off in the distance in the bright moonlight (was, were) the wolf and his mate.

10. Neither the security guard nor the police officer (was, were) able to figure out how the thief got into the building.

■ Review Test 3

There are ten mistakes in subject-verb agreement in the following passage. Cross out each incorrect verb and write the correct form above it. In addition, underline the subject of each of the verbs that must be changed.

After more than thirty years on television, there is few honors that *Sesame Street* has not won. The awards are deserved, for *Sesame Street* is a show that treat children with respect. Most children's programs consists of cheaply made cartoons that is based on the adventures of a superhero or a video-game character. Unfortunately, children's TV programs are generally so poor because quality kids' shows does not make the profits that the networks demand. Both the superhero story and the video-game story is easy to slap together. By contrast, the producers of *Sesame Street* spends enormous amounts of time and money researching how children learn. Another reason for the low profits are the nature of the audience. Because children have little money to spend on sponsors' products, each of the networks charge bottom rates for advertising during children's programs. *Sesame Street*, a nonprofit show, does not even accept ads. And income from the sale of *Sesame Street* products are used to do an even better job of producing the show.

11 Consistent Verb Tense

Introductory Activity

See if you can find and underline the two mistakes in verb tense in the following selection.

> When Computer Warehouse had a sale, Alex decided to buy a new personal computer. He planned to set up the machine himself and hoped to connect it to the Internet right away. When he arrived home, however, Alex discovers that hooking up the wires to the computer could be complicated and confusing. The directions sounded as if they had been written for electrical engineers. After two hours of frustration, Alex gave up and calls a technician for help.

Now try to complete the following statement:

Verb tenses should be consistent. In the selection above, two verbs have to be changed because they are mistakenly in the (*present, past*) _____ tense while all the other verbs in the selection are in the (*present, past*) _____ tense.

Answers are on page 685.

Keeping Tenses Consistent

18.5

Do not shift tenses unnecessarily. If you begin writing a paper in the present tense, don't shift suddenly to the past. If you begin in the past, don't shift without reason to the present. Notice the inconsistent verb tenses in the following example:

> Smoke spilled from the front of the overheated car. The driver opens up the hood, then jumped back as steam billows out.

The verbs must be consistently in the present tense:

> Smoke spills from the front of the overheated car. The driver opens up the hood, then jumps back as steam billows out.

Or the verbs must be consistently in the past tense:

> Smoke spilled from the front of the overheated car. The driver opened up the hood, then jumped back as steam billowed out.

Practice

In each item, one verb must be changed so that it agrees in tense with the other verbs. Cross out the incorrect verb and write the correct form in the space at the left.

looked   Example   I gave away my striped sweater after three people told me I ~~look~~ like a giant bee.

_____   1. The wet dog, delighted that its bath was over, raced madly around the living room and rolls all over the carpet.
Change _rolls_ to past tense to agree with the rest of the sentence.

_____   2. On vacation, I couldn't face another restaurant meal, so I purchase cheese and crackers and ate in my room.

_____   3. The excited crowd clapped and cheered when the performers step onto the stage.

_____   4. Before the rain stopped, mud slid down the hill and crashes into the houses in the valley.

_____   5. When my little brother found my new box of markers, he snatches one and made green circles all over our front steps.

_____   6. The old house looked as if it hadn't been cleaned in years. Dust cover everything, and the smell of mildew hung in the air.

_____   7. The outfielder tumbled, made a spectacular catch, and lifts the ball up for the umpire to witness.

_____   8. Annie talks aloud to her favorite soap opera character; she argued and fights with the woman over her decisions.

_____   9. At the pie-eating contest, Leo stuffed in the last piece of blueberry pie, swallows it all, and then flashed a purple grin for the photographer.

_____ 10. The supermarket seemed empty on Sunday morning; shopping carts stood in long lines, bakery shelves were bare, and the lights over the meat counter glow dimly.

■ Review Test 1

Change the verbs where needed in the following selection so that they are consistently in the past tense. Cross out each incorrect verb and write the correct form above it, as shown in the example. You will need to make nine corrections.

> ¹Years ago, I ~~live~~ lived in an old apartment house where I got little peace and quiet. ²For one thing, I often heard the constant fights that went on in the adjoining apartment. ³The husband yells about killing his wife, and she screamed right back about leaving him or having him arrested. ⁴In addition, the people in the apartment above me have four noisy kids. ⁵Sometimes it seem as if football games were going on upstairs. ⁶The noise reach a high point when I got home from work, which also happened to be the time the kids return from school. ⁷If the kids and neighbors were not disturbing me, I always had one other person to depend on—the superintendent, who visits my apartment whenever he felt like it. ⁸He always had an excuse, such as checking the water pipes or caulking the windows. ⁹But each time he came, I suspect he just wants to get away from his noisy family, which occupied the basement apartment. ¹⁰I move out of that apartment as soon as I was able to.

■ Review Test 2

Change verbs as necessary in the following selection so that they are consistently in the past tense. Cross out each incorrect verb and write the correct form above it. You will need to make ten corrections in all.

[1]As a kid, I never really enjoyed the public swimming pool. [2]First, there were all sorts of rules that prevent me from having much fun in the water. [3]One was that children under the age of fourteen had to be accompanied by an adult. [4]I didn't like having to beg a parent or a neighbor to take me swimming every time I want to go. [5]Another rule was that girls are not allowed in the water without bathing caps. [6]The required bathing cap was so tight that it cause a heavy pressure mark on my forehead. [7]Also, it often gives me a headache. [8]Second, I wasn't a very good swimmer then. [9]Most of the time I find myself hanging on to the side of the pool. [10]And whenever I attempted a graceful dive, I end up doing a belly flop. [11]Finally, many of the kids tease me. [12]Some of them liked splashing water into my face, which force me to swallow chlorine and a dead bug or two. [13]Even worse was the boy who sneaks up behind me all summer long to dump ice cubes down the back of my swimsuit.

12 Additional Information about Verbs

The purpose of this special chapter is to provide additional information about verbs. Some people will find the grammatical terms here a helpful reminder of earlier school learning about verbs. For them, these terms will increase their understanding of how verbs function in English. Other people may welcome more detailed information about terms used elsewhere in the text. In either case, remember that the most common mistakes people make when writing verbs have been treated in earlier sections of the book.

Verb Tense

18.2

Verbs tell us the time of an action. The time that a verb shows is usually called *tense.* The most common tenses are the simple present, past, and future. In addition, there are nine other tenses that enable us to express more specific ideas about time than we could with the simple tenses alone. Following are the twelve verb tenses, with examples. Read them to increase your sense of the many different ways of expressing time in English.

Tenses	Examples
Present	I *work.*
	Jill *works.*
Past	Howard *worked* on the lawn.
Future	You *will work* overtime this week.
Present perfect	Gail *has worked* hard on the puzzle.
	They *have worked* well together.
Past perfect	They *had worked* eight hours before their shift ended.
Future perfect	The volunteers *will have worked* many unpaid hours.
Present progressive	I *am* not *working* today.
	You *are working* the second shift.
	The clothes dryer *is* not *working* properly.
Past progressive	She *was working* outside.
	The plumbers *were working* here this morning.
Future progressive	The sound system *will be working* by tonight.
Present perfect progressive	Married life *has* not *been working* out for that couple.
Past perfect progressive	I *had been working* overtime until recently.
Future perfect progressive	My sister *will have been working* at that store for eleven straight months by the time she takes a vacation next week.

The perfect tenses are formed by adding *have, has,* or *had* to the past participle (the form of the verb that ends, usually, in *-ed*). The progressive tenses are formed by adding *am, is, are, was,* or *were* to the present participle (the form of the verb that ends in *-ing*). The perfect progressive tenses are formed by adding *have been, has been,* or *had been* to the present participle.

Certain tenses are explained in more detail on the following pages.

Present Perfect
(*have* or *has* + past participle)

The present perfect tense expresses an action that began in the past and has recently been completed or is continuing in the present.

The city *has* just *agreed* on a contract with the sanitation workers.

Tony's parents *have lived* in that house for twenty years.

Lola *has enjoyed* mystery novels since she was a little girl.

Past Perfect
(*had* + past participle)

The past perfect tense expresses a past action that was completed before another past action.

Lola *had learned* to dance by the time she was five.

The class *had* just *started* when the fire bell rang.

Bad weather *had* never *been* a problem on our vacations until last year.

Present Progressive
(*am, is,* or *are* + the *-ing* form)

The present progressive tense expresses an action still in progress.

I *am taking* an early train into the city every day this week.

Karl *is playing* softball over at the field.

The vegetables *are growing* rapidly.

Past Progressive
(*was* or *were* + the *-ing* form)

The past progressive expresses an action that was in progress in the past.

I *was spending* twenty dollars a week on cigarettes before I quit.

Last week, the store *was selling* many items at half price.

My friends *were driving* over to pick me up when the accident occurred.

Practice

For the sentences that follow, fill in the present or past perfect or the present or past progressive of the verb shown. Use the tense that seems to express the meaning of each sentence best.

Example park This summer, Mickey _is parking_ cars at a French restaurant.

dry
1. The afternoon sun was so hot it _____ our jeans in less than an hour.

plan
2. My parents _____ a trip to the seashore until they heard about the sharks.

grow
3. This year, Aunt Anita _____ tomatoes; she must have two hundred already.

throw
4. The pitcher _____ the ball to second; unfortunately, the runner was on third.

carve
5. Everyone at the dinner table continued to complain about the way Henry _____ the Thanksgiving turkey.

open
6. The excited child _____ all her birthday presents before her father could load his camera.

care
7. Erica answered an ad for a baby-sitter and now _____ for three children, two dogs, and twenty houseplants.

watch
8. Helen is a television athlete; she _____ almost every football and baseball game televised this year.

walk
9. The hiker _____ for over twenty miles before she stopped for a short rest.

try
10. Last winter my brothers _____ to get a job bagging groceries at the supermarket.

Verbals

18.4

Verbals are words formed from verbs. Verbals, like verbs, often express action. They can add variety to your sentences and vigor to your writing style. The three kinds of verbals are *infinitives, participles,* and *gerunds.*

Infinitive

An infinitive is *to* plus the base form of the verb.

> I started *to practice.*
> Don't try *to lift* that table.
> I asked Russ *to drive* me home.

Participle

A participle is a verb form used as an adjective (a descriptive word). The present participle ends in *-ing.* The past participle ends in *-ed* or has an irregular ending.

> *Favoring* his *cramped* leg, the *screaming* boy waded out of the pool.
> The *laughing* child held up her *locked* piggy bank.
> *Using* a shovel and a bucket, I scooped water out of the *flooded* basement.

Gerund

A gerund is the *-ing* form of a verb used as a noun.

> *Studying* wears me out.
> *Playing* basketball is my main pleasure during the week.
> Through *jogging,* you can get yourself in shape.

Practice

In the space beside each sentence, identify the italicized word as a participle (*P*), an infinitive (*I*), or a gerund (*G*).

_____ 1. Carmine preferred the *reclining* chair for his bad back.
    Reclining is used as a descriptive word.

_____ 2. Doctors believe that *walking* is one of the most beneficial forms of exercise.

_____ 3. Once the pan was hot enough, Granddad was ready *to cook* his famous blueberry pancakes.

_____ 4. It isn't *flying* that makes Elsa anxious but the airline food.

_____ 5. *Scratching* its back against a tree, the bear looked deceptively harmless.

———————   6. *To make* the room more cheerful, Alice painted the dark cabinets yellow.

———————   7. *Observing* gorillas' mating behavior is part of that zookeeper's job.

———————   8. During the entire movie, the couple continued *to talk* loudly.

———————   9. My brother's *receding* hairline makes him look older than he really is.

———————   10. At the front door of the hospital, workers found a blanket *containing* a healthy newborn baby.

Active and Passive Verbs

ALLWRITE!
18.7

When the subject of a sentence performs the action of a verb, the verb is in the *active voice*. When the subject of a sentence receives the action of a verb, the verb is in the *passive voice*.

The passive form of a verb consists of a form of the verb *be* plus the past participle of the main verb. Look at the active and passive forms of the verbs below.

Active	*Passive*
Lola *ate* the vanilla pudding. (The subject, *Lola,* is the doer of the action.)	The vanilla pudding *was eaten* by Lola. (The subject, *pudding,* does not act. Instead, something happens to it.)
The plumber *replaced* the hot water heater. (The subject, *plumber,* is the doer of the action.)	The hot water heater *was replaced* by the plumber. (The subject, *heater,* does not act. Instead, something happens to it.)

In general, active verbs are more effective than passive verbs. Active verbs give your writing a simpler and more vigorous style. The passive form of verbs is appropriate, however, when the performer of an action is unknown or is less important than the receiver of the action. For example:

My house was vandalized last night.

(The performer of the action is unknown.)

Mark was seriously injured as a result of your negligence.

(The receiver of the action, *Mark,* is being emphasized.)

Practice

Change the following sentences from passive voice to active voice. Note that in some cases you may have to add a subject.

Examples   The motorcycle was ridden by Tony.
Tony rode the motorcycle.

The basketball team was given a standing ovation.
The crowd gave the basketball team a standing ovation.

(Here a subject had to be added.)

1. The bus was boarded by a man with a live parrot on his shoulder.
   Who boarded the bus? Make him the subject.

   _____

   _____

2. The stained-glass window was broken by a large falling branch.

   _____

   _____

3. Baseballs for hospitalized children were autographed by the entire team.

   _____

   _____

4. The hotel was destroyed by a fire that started with a cigarette.

   _____

   _____

5. The pressures of dealing with life and death must be faced by doctors.

   _____

   _____

6. The missile was directed to its target by a sophisticated laser system.

   _____

   _____

7. The kitchen shelves were covered by a thick layer of yellowish grease.

   _____

   _____

8. Trash in the neighborhood park was removed by a group of volunteers.

_____

_____

9. Most of the escaped convicts were captured within a mile of the jail by the state police.

_____

_____

10. Prizes were awarded by the judges for hog-calling and stone-skipping.

_____

_____

■ Review Test

On separate paper, write three sentences for each of the following forms:

1. Present perfect tense
2. Past perfect tense
3. Present progressive tense
4. Past progressive tense
5. Infinitive
6. Participle
7. Gerund
8. Passive voice (when the performer of the action is unknown or is less important than the receiver of an action—see page 192)

Personal → I, you, He

Relative — Who that which

Demonstrative— This that
                    these Those

Reflexive myself himself
                themselves

Indefinite— Anyone some one
                 some body

13 Pronoun Reference, Agreement, and Point of View

Introductory Activity

Read each pair of sentences below, noting the underlined pronouns. Then see if you can circle the correct letter in each of the statements that follow.

1. a. None of the nominees for "best actress" showed their anxiety as the names were being read.
   b. None of the nominees for "best actress" showed her anxiety as the names were being read.

2. a. At the mall, they are already putting up Christmas decorations.
   b. At the mall, shop owners are already putting up Christmas decorations.

3. a. I go to the steak house often because you can get inexpensive meals there.
   b. I go to the steak house often because I can get inexpensive meals there.

In the first pair, (a, b) uses the underlined pronoun correctly because the pronoun refers to *None,* which is a singular word.

In the second pair, (a, b) is correct because otherwise the pronoun reference would be unclear.

In the third pair, (a, b) is correct because the pronoun point of view should not be shifted unnecessarily.

Answers are on page 685.

195

Pronouns are words that take the place of nouns (persons, places, or things). In fact, the word *pronoun* means *for a noun*. Pronouns are shortcuts that keep you from unnecessarily repeating words in writing. Here are some examples of pronouns:

> Martha shampooed *her* dog. (*Her* is a pronoun that takes the place of *Martha*.)
>
> As the door swung open, *it* creaked. (*It* replaces *door*.)
>
> When the motorcyclists arrived at McDonald's, *they* removed *their* helmets. (*They* and *their* replace *motorcyclists*.)

This section presents rules that will help you avoid three common mistakes people make with pronouns. The rules are as follows:

1 A pronoun must refer clearly to the word it replaces.

2 A pronoun must agree in number with the word or words it replaces.

3 Pronouns should not shift unnecessarily in point of view.

Pronoun Reference

19.5

A sentence may be confusing and unclear if a pronoun appears to refer to more than one word, as in this sentence:

> I locked my suitcase in my car, and then it was stolen.

What was stolen? It is unclear whether the suitcase or the car was stolen.

> I locked my suitcase in my car, and then my car was stolen.

A sentence may also be confusing if the pronoun does not refer to any specific word. Look at this sentence:

> We never buy fresh vegetables at that store because they charge too much.

Who charges too much? There is no specific word that *they* refers to. Be clear.

> We never buy fresh vegetables at that store because the owners charge too much.

Here are additional sentences with unclear pronoun reference. Read the explanations of why they are unclear and look carefully at the ways they are corrected.

handwritten: 11/08/06

Unclear

Lola told Gina that she had gained weight.

(*Who* had gained weight: Lola or Gina? Be clear.)

handwritten: Noun its referring to

My older brother is an electrician, but I'm not interested in it.

(There is no specific word that *it* refers to. It would not make sense to say, "I'm not interested in electrician.")

handwritten: personal pronoun

Our instructor did not explain the assignment, which made me angry.

(Does *which* mean that the instructor's failure to explain the assignment made you angry, or that the assignment itself made you angry? Be clear.)

Clear

Lola told Gina, "You've gained weight."

(Quotation marks, which can sometimes be used to correct an unclear reference, are explained in Chapter 25.)

My older brother is an electrician, but I'm not interested in becoming one.

I was angry that our instructor did not explain the assignment.

Practice

Rewrite each of the following sentences to make clear the vague pronoun reference. Add, change, or omit words as necessary.

Example   Lana thanked Amy for the gift, which was very thoughtful of her.

handwritten: Lana thanked Amy for the thoughtful gift.

1. Fran removed the blanket from the sofa bed and folded it up.
   What does *it* stand for?   *handwritten: the blanket up*

   _____

   _____

2. The defendant told the judge he was mentally ill.
   handwritten: The defendant told the judge I am men

   _____

3. Before the demonstration, they passed out signs for us to carry.

   _____

   _____

handwritten left margin: Answers 6 85

4. Cindy complained to Rachel that her boyfriend was being dishonest.

_____

_____

5. Because I didn't rinse last night's dishes, it smells like a garbage can.

_____

_____

6. The students watched a film on endangered species, which really depressed them.

_____

_____

7. The veterinarian said that if I find a tick on my dog, I should get rid of it immediately.

_____

_____

8. My sister removed the curtains from the windows so that she could wash them.

_____

_____

9. Richard said his acupuncture therapist could help my sprained shoulder, but I don't believe in it.

_____

_____

10. I discovered when I went to sell my old textbooks that they've put out new editions, and nobody wants to buy them.

_____

_____

Pronoun Agreement

ALLWRITE!
17.8

A pronoun must agree in number with the word or words it replaces. If the word a pronoun refers to is singular, the pronoun must be singular; if the word is plural, the pronoun must be plural. (Note that the word a pronoun refers to is known as the *antecedent.*)

Lola agreed to lend me her Jewel albums.

The gravediggers sipped coffee during their break.

In the first example, the pronoun *her* refers to the singular word *Lola;* in the second example, the pronoun *their* refers to the plural word *gravediggers.*

Practice

Write the appropriate pronoun (*they, their, them, it*) in the blank space in each of the following sentences.

Example   My credit cards got me into debt, so I burned ___them___.

1. The two girls in identical dresses were surprised when __they__ saw each other at the prom.
    Which word best takes the place of *the two girls?*

2. Flies often lay __their__ eggs on the bodies of dead animals.

3. I put my family pictures in a photo album, but then I lost __it__.

4. I used to collect baseball cards and comic books, but then I gave __them__ to my little brother.

5. When the children are watching television, it's impossible to get __their__ attention.

Indefinite Pronouns

17.5

The following words, known as *indefinite pronouns,* are always singular.

Indefinite Pronouns		
(*-one* words)	(*-body* words)	
one	nobody	each
anyone	anybody	either
everyone	everybody	neither
someone	somebody	

(handwritten: Antecedent — Noun — the one that describes it)

Either of the apartments has *its* drawbacks.

One of the girls lost *her* skateboard.

Everyone in the class must hand in *his* paper tomorrow.

In each example, the pronoun is singular because it refers to one of the indefinite pronouns. There are two important points to remember about indefinite pronouns.

Point 1   The last example above suggests that everyone in the class is male. If the students were all female, the pronoun would be *her*. If the students were a mixed group of males and females, the pronoun form would be *his or her.*

Everyone in the class must hand in *his or her* paper tomorrow.

Some writers still follow the traditional practice of using *his* to refer to both men and women. Many now use *his or her* to avoid an implied sexual bias. Perhaps the best practice, though, is to avoid using either *his* or the somewhat awkward *his or her.* This can often be done by rewriting a sentence in the plural:

All students in the class must hand in *their* papers tomorrow.

Here are some examples of sentences that can be rewritten in the plural.

A young child is seldom willing to share her toys with others.
Young children are seldom willing to share their toys with others.

Anyone who does not wear his seat belt will be fined.
People who do not wear their seat belts will be fined.

A newly elected politician should not forget his or her campaign promises.
Newly elected politicians should not forget their campaign promises.

Point 2   In informal spoken English, *plural* pronouns are often used with indefinite pronouns. Instead of saying

Everybody has *his or her* own idea of an ideal vacation.

(handwritten left margin: 1st) Identify pronoun   2) Identify the antecedent)

we are likely to say   11–08/06

> Everybody has *their* own idea of an ideal vacation.

Here are other examples:

> Everyone in the class must pass in *their* papers.
>
> Everybody in our club has *their* own idea about how to raise money.
>
> No one in our family skips *their* chores.

In such cases, the indefinite pronouns are clearly plural in meaning. Also, the use of such plurals helps people avoid the awkward *his or her.* In time, the plural pronoun may be accepted in formal speech or writing. Until that happens, however, you should use the grammatically correct singular form in your writing.

Practice

Underline the correct pronoun.

Example   Neither of those houses has (<u>its</u>, their) own garage.

1. Neither of the men was aware that (<u>his</u>, their) voice was being taped.
   Neither requires a singular pronoun.
2. One of the waiters was fired for failing to report all (<u>his</u>, their) tips.
3. We have three dogs, and each of them has (<u>its</u>, their) own bowl.
4. During the intermission, everyone had to wait a while for (<u>her</u>, their) turn to get into the ladies' room.
5. All of the presents on the table had tiny gold bows on (it, <u>them</u>).   *indefinite pronoun*
6. Mr. Alvarez refuses to let anyone ride in his car without using (<u>his or her</u>, their) seat belt.
7. It seems that neither of the mothers is comfortable answering (<u>her</u>, their) teenager's questions about sex.
8. If anybody in the men's club objects to the new rules, (<u>he</u>, they) should speak up now.
9. Nobody on the women's basketball team had enough nerve to voice (<u>her</u>, their) complaints to the coach.
10. Before being allowed to go on the class trip, each student had to have (<u>his or her</u>, their) parents sign a permission form.   *sub of the clause*

11-08-06

Pronoun Point of View

Pronouns should not shift their point of view unnecessarily. When writing a paper, be consistent in your use of first-, second-, or third-person pronouns.

Type of Pronoun	Singular	Plural
First-person pronouns	I (my, mine, me)	we (our, us)
Second-person pronouns	you (your)	you (your)
Third-person pronouns	he (his, him)	they (their, them)
	she (her)	
	it (its)	

Note   Any person, place, or thing, as well as any indefinite pronoun like *one, anyone, someone,* and so on (see page 199), is a third-person word.

For instance, if you start writing in the first-person *I,* don't jump suddenly to the second-person *you.* Or if you are writing in the third-person *they,* don't shift unexpectedly to *you.* Look at the examples.

Inconsistent	Consistent
One reason that *I* like living in the city is that *you* always have a wide choice of sports events to attend.	One reason that *I* like living in the city is that *I* always have a wide choice of sports events to attend.
(The most common mistake people make is to let a *you* slip into their writing after they start with another pronoun.)	
Someone who is dieting should have the help of friends; *you* should also have plenty of willpower.	*Someone* who is dieting should have the help of friends; *he* or *she* should also have plenty of willpower.
Students who work while *they* are going to school face special problems. For one thing, *you* seldom have enough study time.	Students who work while *they* are going to school face special problems. For one thing, *they* seldom have enough study time.

12-08-06

Pronoun goes after noun

Number

person

& Gender

Practice

Cross out inconsistent pronouns in the following sentences and write the correction above the error.

Example   I work much better when the boss doesn't hover over ~~you~~ *me* with instructions on what to do.

1. A good horror movie makes my bones feel like ice and gets ~~your~~ *my* blood running cold.
   Since this sentence begins in first person, change *your* to a first-person pronoun.

2. People buy groceries from that supermarket because ~~you~~ *they* know it has the best prices in the area.

3. One experience that almost everyone fears is when ~~you have~~ *he/or she has* to speak in front of a crowd of people.

4. If students attend class regularly and study hard, ~~you~~ *they* should receive a good grade.

5. I drive on back roads instead of major highways because ~~you~~ *I* can avoid traffic.

6. The spread of many illnesses, such as the flu and common cold, could be reduced if people just washed ~~your~~ *their* hands.

7. Andy enjoys watching soap operas because then ~~you~~ *he* can worry about someone else's problems instead of ~~your~~ *his* own.

8. Our street was so slippery after the ice storm that ~~you~~ *we* could barely take a step without falling down.

9. Mrs. Almac enjoys working the three-to-eleven shift because that way ~~you~~ *she* can still have a large part of ~~your~~ *her* day free.

10. All of us at work voted to join the union because we felt it would protect ~~your~~ *our* rights.

■ Review Test 1

Underline the correct word in the parentheses.

1. Devan slammed the phone down on the table so hard that (it, the phone) broke.

2. During the boring movie, people started to squirm in (his or her, their) seats.

3. I love living alone because (you, I) never have to answer to anyone else.

4. Almost all the magazines I subscribe to arrive with (its, their) covers torn.

5. My father disagrees with my husband about almost everything because (he, my father) is so stubborn.

6. I like driving on that turnpike because (they, state officials) don't allow bill-boards there.

7. Neither one of the umpires wanted to admit that (he, they) had made a mistake.

8. When Ed went to the bank for a home improvement loan, (they, the loan officers) asked him for three credit references.

9. Even if you graduate from that business school, (they, the placement officers) don't guarantee they will find you a job.

10. Not one of the women in the audience was willing to raise (her, their) hand when the magician asked for a female volunteer.

■ Review Test 2

Cross out the pronoun error in each sentence and write the correction in the space provided. Then circle the letter that correctly describes the type of error that was made.

Examples ~~Anyone~~ turning in their papers late will be penalized.

      __Students__

Mistake in: a. pronoun reference   (b.) pronoun agreement

When Clyde takes his son Paul to the park, ~~he~~ enjoys himself.

      __Paul__

Mistake in: (a.) pronoun reference   b. pronoun point of view

From where we stood, ~~you~~ could see three states.

      __we__

Mistake in: a. pronoun agreement   (b.) pronoun point of view

1. A good salesperson knows that ~~you~~ should be courteous to customers.

      _____

Mistake in: a. pronoun agreement   (b.) pronoun point of view

2. Neither of the girls who flunked bothered to bring ~~their~~ report card home.

      _____

Mistake in: a. pronoun reference   (b.) pronoun agreement

Hotel employees

3. When the shabbily dressed woman walked into the fancy hotel, they weren't very polite to her.

   _____

   Mistake in: a. pronoun agreement   b. pronoun reference   *specify who*

4. Nobody seems to add or subtract without their pocket calculator anymore.

   _____

   Mistake in: a. pronoun agreement   b. pronoun point of view

5. Denise went everywhere with Nita until she moved to Texas last year.   *Nita*

   _____

   Mistake in: a. pronoun agreement   b. pronoun reference

6. Everyone on my street believes they saw a strange glow in the sky last night.   *he/she*

   _____

   Mistake in: a. pronoun agreement   b. pronoun point of view   *Don't agree*

7. In baking desserts, people should follow the directions carefully or you are likely to end up with something unexpected.   *Plural*   *they*

   _____

   Mistake in: a. pronoun reference   b. pronoun point of view

8. When Jerry added another card to the delicate structure, it fell down.   *the structure*

   _____

   Mistake in: a. pronoun reference   b. pronoun point of view

9. Anyone who wants to join the car pool should leave their name with me.   *Sing*   *his/her*

   _____

   Mistake in: a. pronoun agreement   b. pronoun reference

10. Any working mother knows that you need at least a twenty-five hour day.   *she*

   _____

   Mistake in: a. pronoun agreement   b. pronoun point of view

Hint   In item 10, you will also need to correct a verb form.

Shift from one person

14 Pronoun Types

Introductory Activity

In each pair, write a check beside the sentence that you think uses pronouns correctly.

Andy and *I* enrolled in a computer course. _____

Andy and *me* enrolled in a computer course. _____

The police officer pointed to my sister and *me*. _____

The police officer pointed to my sister and *I*. _____

Lola prefers men *whom* take pride in their bodies. _____

Lola prefers men *who* take pride in their bodies. _____

The players are confident that the league championship is *theirs'*.

_____

The players are confident that the league championship is *theirs*.

_____

Them concert tickets are too expensive. _____

Those concert tickets are too expensive. _____

Our parents should spend some money on *themself* for a change.

_____

Our parents should spend some money on *themselves* for a change.

_____

Answers are on page 686.

This chapter describes some common types of pronouns: subject and object pronouns, relative pronouns, possessive pronouns, demonstrative pronouns, and reflexive pronouns.

Subject and Object Pronouns

Pronouns change their form depending on the place they occupy in a sentence. Here is a list of subject and object pronouns:

Subject Pronouns	Object Pronouns
I	me
you	you (no change)
he	him
she	her
it	it (no change)
we	us
they	them

Subject Pronouns

19.2a

Subject pronouns are subjects of verbs.

They are getting tired. (*They* is the subject of the verb *are getting.*)
She will decide tomorrow. (*She* is the subject of the verb *will decide.*)
We women organized the game. (*We* is the subject of the verb *organized.*)

Several rules for using subject pronouns, and mistakes people sometimes make, are explained starting below.

Rule 1   Use a subject pronoun in a sentence with a compound (more than one) subject.

Incorrect	*Correct*
Nate and *me* went shopping yesterday.	Nate and *I* went shopping yesterday.
Him and *me* spent lots of money.	*He* and *I* spent lots of money.

If you are not sure which pronoun to use, try each pronoun by itself in the sentence. The correct pronoun will be the one that sounds right. For example, "*Me* went shopping yesterday" does not sound right; "*I* went shopping yesterday" does.

Rule 2   Use a subject pronoun after forms of the verb *be*. Forms of *be* include *am, are, is, was, were, has been, have been,* and others.

> It was *I* who telephoned.
>
> It may be *they* at the door.
>
> It is *she*.

The sentences above may sound strange and stilted to you, since this rule is seldom actually followed in conversation. When we speak with one another, forms such as "It was me," "It may be them," and "It is her" are widely accepted. In formal writing, however, the grammatically correct forms are still preferred. You can avoid having to use a subject pronoun after *be* simply by rewording a sentence. Here is how the preceding examples could be reworded:

> *I* was the one who telephoned.
>
> *They* may be at the door.
>
> *She* is here.

Rule 3   Use subject pronouns after *than* or *as* when a verb is understood after the pronoun.

> You read faster than I (read). (The verb *read* is understood after *I*.)
>
> Tom is as stubborn as I (am). (The verb *am* is understood after *I*.)
>
> We don't go out as much as they (do). (The verb *do* is understood after *they*.)

Notes

a Avoid mistakes by mentally adding the "missing" verb at the end of the sentence.

b Use object pronouns after *as* or *than* when a verb is not understood after the pronoun.

> The law applies to you as well as me.
>
> Our boss paid Monica more than me.

Object Pronouns

ALLWRITE!
19.2b

Object pronouns (*me, him, her, us, them*) are objects of verbs or prepositions. (Prepositions are connecting words like *for, at, about, to, before, by, with,* and *of.* See also page 91.)

> Raisa chose *me*. (*Me* is the object of the verb *chose*.)
>
> We met *them* at the ballpark. (*Them* is the object of the verb *met*.)
>
> Don't mention UFOs to *us*. (*Us* is the object of the preposition *to*.)
>
> I live near *her*. (*Her* is the object of the preposition *near*.)

People are sometimes uncertain about what pronoun to use when two objects follow the verb.

Incorrect	*Correct*
I spoke to George and *he*.	I spoke to George and *him*.
She pointed at Linda and *I*.	She pointed at Linda and *me*.

Hint   If you are not sure which pronoun to use, try each pronoun by itself in the sentence. The correct pronoun will be the one that sounds right. For example, "I spoke to he" doesn't sound right; "I spoke to him" does.

Practice 1

Underline the correct subject or object pronoun in each of the following sentences. Then show whether your answer is a subject or an object pronoun by circling the *S* or *O* in the margin.

S   O   1. I left the decision to (her, she).
             The correct pronoun is the object of the preposition *to*.

S   O   2. (She, Her) and Louise look enough alike to be sisters.

S   O   3. Just between you and (I, me), these rolls taste like sawdust.

S   O   4. The certified letter was addressed to both (she, her) and (I, me).

S   O   5. If (he, him) and Vic are serious about school, why are they absent so much?

S   O   6. Practically everyone is better at crossword puzzles than (I, me).

S   O   7. It was (they, them) who left the patio furniture outside during the rainstorm.

S   O   8. The creature that climbed out of the coffin scared Boris and (I, me) half to death.

S   O   9. (We, Us) tenants are organizing a protest against the dishonest landlord.

S   O   10. When we were little, my sister and (I, me) invented a secret language.

Practice 2

For each sentence, in the space provided, write an appropriate subject or object pronoun. Try to use as many different pronouns as possible.

1. Gerald and _____ forgot to lock the door the night our restaurant was robbed.

    Along with *Gerald,* this pronoun is part of the sentence's subject.

2. The referee disqualified Tyray and _____ for fighting.

3. I have seldom met two people as boring as _____.

4. If you and _____ don't lose patience, we'll finish sanding this floor by tonight.

5. Our professor told _____ students that our final exam would be a take-home test.

6. Ernie and _____ drove on the interstate highway for ten hours with only one stop.

7. I don't follow sports as much as _____.

8. You know better than _____ how to remove lipstick stains.

9. Maggie and _____ spent several hours yesterday looking for the lost puppy.

10. The store manager praised _____ for being the best cashiers in the department.

Relative Pronouns

Relative pronouns do two things at once. First, they refer to someone or something already mentioned in the sentence. Second, they start a short word group which gives additional information about this someone or something. Here is a list of relative pronouns:

<table>
<tr><td colspan="2">*Relative Pronouns*</td></tr>
<tr><td>who</td><td>which</td></tr>
<tr><td>whose</td><td>that</td></tr>
<tr><td>whom</td><td></td></tr>
</table>

Here are some sample sentences:

The only friend *who* really understands me is moving away.
The child *whom* Ben and Arlene adopted is from Korea.
Chocolate, *which* is my favorite food, upsets my stomach.
I guessed at half the questions *that* were on the test.

In the example sentences, *who* refers to *friend, whom* refers to *child, which* refers to *chocolate,* and *that* refers to *questions.* In addition, each of the relative pronouns begins a group of words that describes the person or thing being referred to. For example, the words *whom Ben and Arlene adopted* tell which child the sentence is about, and the words *which is my favorite food* give added information about chocolate.

Points to Remember about Relative Pronouns

Point 1   *Whose* means *belonging to whom.* Be careful not to confuse *whose* with *who's,* which means *who is.*

Point 2   *Who, whose,* and *whom* all refer to people. *Which* refers to things. *That* can refer to either people or things.

I don't know *whose* book this is.
Don't sit on the chair *which* is broken.
Let's elect a captain *that* cares about winning.

Point 3   *Who, whose, whom,* and *which* can also be used to ask questions. When they are used in this way, they are called *interrogative* pronouns:

Who murdered the secret agent?
Whose fingerprints were on the bloodstained knife?
To *whom* have the detectives been talking?
Which suspect is going to confess?

Note   In informal usage, *who* is generally used instead of *whom* as an interrogative pronoun. Informally, we can say or write, "*Who* are you rooting for in the game?" or "*Who* did the instructor fail?" More formal usage would call for *whom:* "*Whom* are you rooting for in the game?" "*Whom* did the instructor fail?"

Point 4   *Who* and *whom* are used differently. *Who* is a subject pronoun. Use *who* as the subject of a verb:

Let's see *who* will be teaching the course.

Whom is an object pronoun. Use *whom* as the object of a verb or a preposition:

Dr. Kelsey is the instructor *whom* I like best.
I haven't decided for *whom* I will vote.

You may want to review the material on subject and object pronouns on pages 208–210.

Here is an easy way to decide whether to use *who* or *whom*. Find the first verb after the place where the *who* or *whom* will go. See if it already has a subject. If it does have a subject, use the object pronoun *whom*. If there is no subject, give it one by using the subject pronoun *who*. Notice how *who* and *whom* are used in the sentences that follow:

I don't know *who* sideswiped my car.
The suspect *whom* the police arrested finally confessed.

In the first sentence, *who* is used to give the verb *sideswiped* a subject. In the second sentence, the verb *arrested* already has a subject, *police*. Therefore, *whom* is the correct pronoun.

Practice 1

Underline the correct pronoun in each of the following sentences.

1. One activity (that, who) my father and I both enjoy is cooking.
   *Who refers only to people; it cannot refer to *activity.*
2. On a bright, sunny day, some office buildings (who, that) have glass walls look like giant icicles.
3. My sister, (who, whom) loves ballet, walks around the house on her toes.
4. The new highway, (who, which) was supposed to lessen traffic jams, only made them worse.
5. The supervisor (who, whom) everybody dislikes was just given thirty days' notice.

Practice 2

On separate paper, write five sentences using *who, whose, whom, which,* and *that.*

Possessive Pronouns

Possessive pronouns show ownership or possession.

> Clyde shut off the engine of *his* motorcycle.
> The keys are *mine*.

Here is a list of possessive pronouns:

Possessive Pronouns	
my, mine	our, ours
your, yours	your, yours
his	their, theirs
her, hers	
its	

Points to Remember about Possessive Pronouns

Point 1   A possessive pronoun *never* uses an apostrophe. (See also page 299.)

Incorrect	*Correct*
That coat is *hers'*.	That coat is *hers*.
The card table is *theirs'*.	The card table is *theirs*.

Practice

Cross out the incorrect pronoun form in each of the sentences that follow. Write the correct form in the space at the left.

___My___   Example   ~~Me~~ car has broken down again.

_____   1. Is this pen yours' or mine?
                      The possessive pronoun *yours* never uses an apostrophe.

_____   2. Only relatives of him are allowed to visit while he is in the hospital.

_____   3. My sisters think that every new dress I buy is theirs' too.

_____   4. Are you going to eat all of you hamburger, or can I have half?

_____   5. The thermos that is mines is held together with duct tape.

Demonstrative Pronouns

Demonstrative pronouns point to or single out a person or thing. There are four demonstrative pronouns:

> ### Demonstrative Pronouns
>
> | | |
> |---|---|
> | this | these |
> | that | those |

Generally speaking, *this* and *these* refer to things close at hand; *that* and *those* refer to things farther away.

> Is anyone using *this* spoon?
>
> I am going to throw away *these* magazines.
>
> I just bought *that* old white pickup at the curb.
>
> Pick up *those* toys in the corner.

Note   Do not use *them, this here, that there, these here,* or *those there* to point out. Use only *this, that, these,* or *those.*

Incorrect	*Correct*
Them tires are badly worn.	*Those* tires are badly worn.
This here book looks hard to read.	*This* book looks hard to read.
That there candy is delicious.	*That* candy is delicious.
Those there squirrels are pests.	*Those* squirrels are pests.

Practice 1

Cross out the incorrect form of the demonstrative pronoun and write the correct form in the space provided.

Those   Example   ~~Them~~ clothes need washing.

_____   1. This here town isn't big enough for both of us, Tex.
                This here is not standard.

_____   2. Let's hurry and get them seats before someone else does.

_____   3. That there dress looked better on the hanger than it does on you.

_____   4. Let me try one of those there candies before they're all gone.

_____   5. Watch out for them potholes the next time you drive my car.

Practice 2

Write four sentences using *this, that, these,* and *those.*

_____

_____

_____

_____

Reflexive Pronouns

Reflexive pronouns are pronouns that refer to the subject of a sentence. Here is a list of reflexive pronouns:

Reflexive Pronouns	
myself	ourselves
yourself	yourselves
himself	themselves
herself	
itself	

Sometimes a reflexive pronoun is used for emphasis:

You will have to wash the dishes *yourself*.

We *ourselves* are willing to forget the matter.

The manager *himself* stole merchandise from the store.

Points to Remember about Reflexive Pronouns

Point 1   In the plural *-self* becomes *-selves*.

Lola covered *herself* with insect repellent.

They treated *themselves* to a Bermuda vacation.

Point 2   Be careful that you do not use any of the following incorrect forms as reflexive pronouns.

Incorrect	*Correct*
He believes in *hisself*.	He believes in *himself*.
We drove the children *ourself*.	We drove the children *ourselves*.
They saw *themself* in the fun house mirror.	They saw *themselves* in the fun house mirror.
I'll do it *meself*.	I'll do it *myself*.

Practice

Cross out the incorrect form of the reflexive pronoun and write the correct form in the space at the left.

<u>themselves</u>   Example   She believes that God helps those who help ~~themself~~.

_____   1. Shoppers stop and stare when they see themself on the closed-circuit TV overhead.
Themself is not standard.

_____   2. The restaurant owner herselve came out to apologize to us.

_____   3. When my baby brother tries to dress hisself, the results are often funny.

_____   4. The waiter was busy, so we poured ourself coffee from a nearby pot.

_____   5. These housepainters seem to be making more work for theirselves than is necessary.

Review Test 1

Underline the correct word in the parentheses.

1. The waitress finally brought Dolores and (I, me) our order.
2. I hope my son behaves (hisself, himself) at preschool.
3. Hand me (that, that there) fiddle and I'll play you a tune.
4. If it were up to (she, her), men wouldn't have the right to vote.
5. Roger, (who, whom) has worked here for almost thirty years, is ready to retire.
6. Vera dressed much more casually than (I, me) for the party.
7. You won't get very far on the bike unless you add more air to (its, it's) tires.
8. We'll be reading (this, this here) stack of books during the semester.
9. The apartment of (his, him) is next to a chemical processing plant.
10. The ducks circled the lake until they were sure that no one was around but (theirselves, themselves).

Review Test 2

Cross out the pronoun error in each sentence and write the correct form in the space at the left.

_____I_____ Example   Terry and ~~me~~ have already seen the movie.

_____ 1. The chili that Manny prepared was too spicy for we to eat.

_____ 2. I checked them wires, but I couldn't find any faulty connections.

_____ 3. The old Chevy, who has 110,000 miles on it, is still running well.

_____ 4. When him and his partner asked me to step out of my car, I knew I was in trouble.

_____ 5. Omar realized that he would have to change the tire hisself.

_____ 6. My husband is much more sentimental than me.

_____ 7. I hope you'll come visit us in July while the garden is looking its' best.

_____ 8. The CDs are mines, but you can listen to them whenever you wish.

_____ 9. This here dog is friendly as long as you move slowly.

_____ 10. Vicky and me are going to the concert at the fairgrounds.

■ Review Test 3

On separate paper, write sentences that use each of the following words.

Example   Peter and him *The coach suspended Peter and him.* _____

1. yourselves
2. Jasmine and me
3. these
4. the neighbors and us
5. Victor and he
6. slower than I
7. its
8. which
9. you and I
10. Maria and them

15 Adjectives and Adverbs

Introductory Activity

Write in an appropriate word or words to complete each of the sentences below.

1. The teenage years were a _____ time for me.
2. The mechanic listened _____ while I described my car problem.
3. Basketball is a _____ game than football.
4. My brother is the _____ person in our family.

Now see if you can complete the following sentences.

The word inserted in the first sentence is an (adjective, adverb); it describes the word *time.*

The word inserted in the second sentence is an (adjective, adverb);

it probably ends in the two letters _____ and describes the word *listened.*

The word inserted in the third sentence is a comparative adjective;

it may be preceded by *more* or end in the two letters _____.

The word inserted in the fourth sentence is a superlative adjective;

it may be preceded by *most* or end in the three letters _____.

Answers are on page 687.

221

Adjectives and adverbs are descriptive words. Their purpose is to make the meaning of the words they describe more specific.

Adjectives

What Are Adjectives?

Adjectives describe nouns (names of persons, places, or things) or pronouns.

> Charlotte is a *kind* woman. (The adjective *kind* describes the noun *woman*.)
> He is *tired*. (The adjective *tired* describes the pronoun *he*.)

An adjective usually comes before the word it describes (as in *kind woman*). But it can also come after forms of the verb *be* (*is, are, was, were,* and so on). Less often, an adjective follows verbs such as *feel, look, smell, sound, taste, appear, become,* and *seem.*

> The bureau is *heavy*. (The adjective *heavy* describes the bureau.)
> These pants are *itchy*. (The adjective *itchy* describes the pants.)
> The children seem *restless*. (The adjective *restless* describes the children.)

Using Adjectives to Compare

For most short adjectives, add *-er* when comparing two things and *-est* when comparing three or more things.

> I am *taller* than my brother, but my father is the *tallest* person in the house.
> The farm market sells *fresher* vegetables than the corner store, but the *freshest* vegetables are the ones grown in my own garden.

For most *longer* adjectives (two or more syllables), add *more* when comparing two things and *most* when comparing three or more things.

> Backgammon is *more enjoyable* to me than checkers, but chess is the *most enjoyable* game of all.
> My mother is *more talkative* than my father, but my grandfather is the *most talkative* person in the house.

Points to Remember about Adjectives

Point 1 Be careful not to use both an *-er* ending and *more,* or both an *-est* ending and *most.*

Incorrect	*Correct*
Football is a *more livelier* game than baseball.	Football is a *livelier* game than baseball.
Tod Traynor was voted the *most likeliest* to succeed in our high school class.	Tod Traynor was voted the *most likely* to succeed in our high school class.

Point 2 Pay special attention to the following words, each of which has irregular forms.

	Comparative (Two)	*Superlative (Three or More)*
bad	worse	worst
good, well	better	best
little	less	least
much, many	more	most

Practice 1

Fill in the comparative or superlative forms for the following adjectives. Two are done for you as examples.

	Comparative (Two)	*Superlative (Three or More)*
firm	firmer	firmest
organized	more organized	most organized
tough		
practical		
quiet		
aggressive		
clear		

Practice 2

Add to each sentence the correct form of the adjective in the margin.

Example *bad* The _____*worst*_____ day of my life was the one when my house
caught fire.

good   1. I hope the _____ days of my life are still to come.
               What is the superlative from of good?

dirty   2. The water in Mudville is _____ than the name of the town.

considerate 3. If Tyrone were _____, he would have more friends.

bad   4. The announcement of a surprise quiz gave me a _____ headache
               than this morning's traffic did.

scary   5. The _____ scene in the horror movie was when dead people began
               crawling out of their graves.

little   6. As hard as it is to believe, he is an even _____ dependable worker
               than his brother.

stylish   7. In an effort to look _____, Bob replaced his big glasses with small
               lightweight ones.

silly   8. June is even _____ than her sister; she once burst out laughing at
               a wedding and had to run out of the church.

slow   9. The computers in the library must be the _____ machines on Earth.

fattening   10. Estella ordered a tossed salad as her main course, so she could have the

               _____ dessert on the menu.

Adverbs

What Are Adverbs?

20.6

Adverbs describe verbs, adjectives, or other adverbs. An adverb usually ends in *-ly*.

Charlotte spoke *kindly* to the confused man. (The adverb *kindly* describes the
verb *spoke*.)

The man said he was *completely* alone in the world. (The adverb *completely*
describes the adjective *alone*.)

Charlotte listened *very* sympathetically to his story. (The adverb *very*
describes the adverb *sympathetically*.)

A Common Mistake with Adjectives and Adverbs

Perhaps the most common mistake that people make with adjectives and adverbs is to use an adjective instead of an adverb after a verb.

Incorrect	*Correct*
Tony breathed *heavy.*	Tony breathed *heavily.*
I rest *comfortable* in that chair.	I rest *comfortably* in that chair.
She learned *quick.*	She learned *quickly.*

Practice

Underline the adjective or adverb needed.

1. I need a vacation (bad, badly).
   An adverb is required to describe the verb *need.*
2. The police reacted (harsh, harshly) to the noisy demonstrators.
3. The truck groaned as it crept up the (steep, steeply) grade.
4. My boss tells me (frequent, frequently) that I do a good job.
5. Did you answer every question in the interview (truthful, truthfully)?
6. If you think your decision was right, you'll sleep (peaceful, peacefully).
7. Walter the werewolf smiled at the (bright, brightly) moonlight shining through his bedroom window.
8. Nate was playing the stereo so (loud, loudly) that both the dog and the cat were cowering in the basement.
9. The surgeon stitched the wound very (careful, carefully), so that the scar would not be noticeable.
10. Eli dressed (nice, nicely) for his first meeting with his girlfriend's parents.

Well and *Good*

Two words often confused are *well* and *good. Good* is an adjective; it describes nouns. *Well* is usually an adverb; it describes verbs. *Well* (rather than *good*) is also used when referring to a person's health.

Here are some examples:

I became a *good* swimmer. (*Good* is an adjective describing the noun *swimmer.*)

For a change, two-year-old Rodney was *good* during the church service. (*Good* is an adjective describing Rodney and comes after *was,* a form of the verb *be.*)

Maryann did *well* on that exam. (*Well* is an adverb describing the verb *did.*)

I explained that I wasn't feeling *well.* (*Well* is used in reference to health.)

Practice

Write *well* or *good* in the sentences that follow.

1. Fortunately, the new stepbrothers and stepsisters get along _____.
   An adverb is needed to describe the verb *get along.*

2. The dog did a _____ job of chewing our sofa.

3. Crystal did so _____ on her placement exam that she was put into an advanced math course.

4. My idea of a _____ date is to talk over dinner.

5. Although I didn't feel _____ , I tried to keep doing my work.

■ Review Test 1

Underline the correct word in the parentheses.

1. When I found out that the landlord intended to increase my rent, I moved back in with my parents (immediate, immediately).

2. During the massage, the therapist pressed (deep, deeply) into the muscles of my neck and shoulders.

3. For as long as I can remember, my teachers have tried to get me to write more (neat, neatly).

4. Judy's parents were deeply disturbed that her grades were (worse, more worse) than ever.

5. My grandfather says that teenagers acted just as (unpredictable, unpredictably) when he was a boy as they do today.

6. The plane taxied (rapid, rapidly) down the runway but then came to a complete stop.

7. The crowd booed (loud, loudly) when the referee ejected the player from the game.

8. Although Al thought his accounting test was the (difficultest, most difficult) test he had ever taken, he got an A on it.

9. Holding the purple felt-tipped pen (loose, loosely), Gina drew graceful spirals in her notebook.

10. Phil played so (good, well) in the soccer game that the coach asked him to join the team.

■ **Review Test 2**

Write a sentence that uses each of the following adjectives and adverbs correctly.

1. confident _____

_____

2. nervously _____

_____

3. well _____

_____

4. more impulsive _____

_____

5. better _____

_____

6. cleverly _____

_____

7. worst _____

_____

8. rough _____

_____

9. most annoying _____

_____

10. sweeter _____

_____

16 Misplaced Modifiers

Introductory Activity

Because of misplaced words, each of the sentences below has more than one possible meaning. In each case, see if you can explain both the intended meaning and the unintended meaning.

1. The farmers sprayed the apple trees wearing masks.

   Intended meaning: _____

   Unintended meaning: _____

2. The woman reached out for the faith healer who had a terminal disease.

   Intended meaning: _____

   Unintended meaning: _____

Answers are on page 687.

What Misplaced Modifiers Are and How to Correct Them

ALLWRITE!

16.2

Misplaced modifiers are words that, because of awkward placement, do not describe the words the writer intended them to describe. Misplaced modifiers often confuse the meaning of a sentence. To avoid them, place words as close as possible to what they describe.

Misplaced Words	Correctly Placed Words
They could see the Goodyear blimp *sitting on the front lawn.*	Sitting on the front lawn, they could see the Goodyear blimp.
(The *Goodyear blimp* was sitting on the front lawn?)	(The intended meaning—that the Goodyear blimp was visible from the front lawn—is now clear.)
We had a hamburger after the movie, *which was too greasy for my taste.*	After the movie, we had a hamburger, which was too greasy for my taste.
(The *movie* was too greasy for your taste?)	(The intended meaning—that the hamburger was greasy—is now clear.)
Our phone *almost rang* fifteen times last night.	Our phone rang almost fifteen times last night.
(The phone *almost rang* fifteen times, but in fact did not ring at all?)	(The intended meaning—that the phone rang a little under fifteen times—is now clear.)

Other single-word modifiers to watch out for include *only, even, hardly, nearly,* and *often.* Such words should be placed immediately before the word they modify.

Practice 1

Underline the misplaced word or words in each sentence. Then rewrite the sentence, placing related words together to make the meaning clear.

Example   Anita returned the hamburger to the supermarket that <u>was spoiled</u>.

Anita returned the hamburger that was spoiled to the supermarket.

1. The tiger growled at a passerby at the back of his cage.
   Who is *at the back of the cage?*

   _____

   _____

2. Lee hung colorful scarves over her windows made of green and blue silk.

   _____

   _____

3. We watched the fireworks standing on our front porch.

   _____

   _____

4. Jason almost has two hundred baseball cards.

   _____

   _____

5. The salesclerk exchanged the blue sweater for a yellow one with a smile.

   _____

   _____

6. We all stared at the man in the front row of the theater with curly purple hair.

   _____

   _____

7. I love the cookies from the bakery with the chocolate frosting.

   _____

   _____

8. The faculty decided to strike during their last meeting.

   _____

   _____

9. Larry looked on as his car burned with disbelief.

   _____

   _____

10. My cousin sent me instructions on how to get to her house in a letter.

    _____

    _____

Practice 2

Rewrite each sentence, adding the *italicized* words. Make sure that the intended meaning is clear and that two different interpretations are not possible.

Example   I borrowed a pen for the essay test. (Insert *that ran out of ink.*)
For the essay test, I borrowed a pen that ran out of ink.

1. My mother sat lazily in the hot sun watching her grandchildren play. (Insert *with a glass of lemonade.*)
   Who has the *glass of lemonade?*

   _____

   _____

2. My father agreed to pay for the car repairs. (Insert *over the phone.*)

   _____

   _____

3. I found a note on the kitchen bulletin board. (Insert *from Jeff.*)

   _____

   _____

4. The fires destroyed the entire forest. (Insert *almost.*)

   _____

   _____

5. Jon read about how the American Revolution began. (Insert *during class.*)

   _____

   _____

■ Review Test 1

Write *M* for *misplaced* or *C* for *correct* in front of each sentence.

_____   1. I keep a ten-dollar bill under the car seat for emergencies.

_____   2. I keep a ten-dollar bill for emergencies under the car seat.

_____   3. This morning, I planned my day in the shower.

_____   4. In the shower this morning, I planned my day.

_____   5. While skating, Bert ran over a dog's tail.

_____   6. Bert ran over a dog's tail skating.

_____   7. I could hear my neighbors screaming at each other through the apartment wall.

_____   8. Through the apartment wall, I could hear my neighbors screaming at each other.

_____   9. For the family reunion, we cooked hamburgers and hot dogs on an outdoor grill.

_____   10. For the family reunion on an outdoor grill we cooked hamburgers and hot dogs.

_____   11. Virgil visited the old house, still weak with the flu.

_____   12. Virgil, still weak with the flu, visited the old house.

_____   13. While still weak with the flu, Virgil visited the old house.

_____   14. My teenage son nearly grew three inches last year.

_____   15. My teenage son grew nearly three inches last year.

_____   16. The instructor explained how to study for the final exam at the end of her lecture.

_____   17. The instructor explained how to study at the end of her lecture for the final exam.

_____   18. At the end of her lecture, the instructor explained how to study for the final exam.

_____   19. In the library, I read that a deadly virus was spread through an air-conditioning system.

_____   20. I read that a deadly virus was spread through an air-conditioning system in the library.

■ Review Test 2

Underline the five misplaced modifiers in the passage below. Then, in the spaces that follow, show how you would correct them.

> [1]The young teenagers who almost hang out in our town library every night are becoming a major nuisance. [2]They show up every weeknight and infuriate the otherwise mild librarians throwing spitballs and paper airplanes. [3]Some of the kids hide out behind stacks of bookcases; others indulge in continual adolescent flirting games. [4]The noise many of these teenagers make is especially offensive to some of the older library patrons, who often give looks to the clusters of young people that are disapproving. [5]One time there was so much noise that a librarian lost her temper and yelled at some boys to be quiet or leave the library at the top of her lungs. [6]The worst recent offense took place when a soaking-wet dog was led into the middle of the library by a junior high school boy with a stubby tail and the meanest-looking face one could ever imagine.

Sentence number: _____

Correction:

_____

Sentence number: _____

Correction:

_____

Sentence number: _____

Correction:

_____

Sentence number: _____

Correction:

_____

Sentence number: _____

Correction:

_____

17 Dangling Modifiers

Introductory Activity

Because of dangling words, each of the sentences below has more than one possible meaning. In each case, see if you can explain both the intended meaning and the unintended meaning.

1. Munching leaves from a tall tree, the children were fascinated by the eighteen-foot-tall giraffe.

   Intended meaning: _____

   _____

   Unintended meaning: _____

   _____

2. Arriving home after ten months in the army, Michael's neighbors threw a block party for him.

   Intended meaning: _____

   _____

   Unintended meaning: _____

   _____

Answers are on page 688.

What Dangling Modifiers Are and How to Correct Them

16.4

A modifier that opens a sentence must be followed immediately by the word it is meant to describe. Otherwise, the modifier is said to be *dangling,* and the sentence takes on an unintended meaning. For example, look at this sentence:

> While sleeping in his backyard, a Frisbee hit Bill on the head.

The unintended meaning is that the *Frisbee* was sleeping in his backyard. What the writer meant, of course, was that *Bill* was sleeping in his backyard. The writer should have placed *Bill* right after the modifier, revising the rest of the sentence as necessary:

> While sleeping in his backyard, *Bill* was hit on the head by a Frisbee.

The sentence could also be corrected by adding the missing subject and verb to the opening word group:

> While *Bill* was sleeping in his backyard, a Frisbee hit him on the head.

Other sentences with dangling modifiers follow. Read the explanations of why they are dangling and look carefully at how they are corrected.

Dangling	*Correct*
Having almost no money, my survival depended on my parents.	Having almost no money, *I* depended on my parents for survival.
(*Who* has almost no money? The answer is not *survival* but *I*. The subject *I* must be added.)	*Or:* Since *I* had almost no money, I depended on my parents for survival.
Riding his bike, a German shepherd bit Tony on the ankle.	Riding his bike, *Tony* was bitten on the ankle by a German shepherd.
(*Who* is riding the bike? The answer is not *German shepherd,* as it unintentionally seems to be, but *Tony.* The subject *Tony* must be added.)	*Or:* While *Tony* was riding his bike, a German shepherd bit him on the ankle.

When trying to lose weight,
all snacks are best avoided.

When trying to lose weight,
you should avoid all snacks.

(*Who* is trying to lose weight?
The answer is not *snacks* but *you*.
The subject *you* must be added.)

Or: When *you* are trying to
lose weight, avoid all snacks.

These examples make clear two ways of correcting a dangling modifier. Decide on a logical subject and do one of the following:

1 Place the subject *within* the opening word group:

Since *I* had almost no money, I depended on my parents for survival.

Note   In some cases an appropriate subordinating word such as *since* must be added, and the verb may have to be changed slightly as well.

2 Place the subject right *after* the opening word group:

Having almost no money, *I* depended on my parents for survival.

Sometimes even more rewriting is necessary to correct a dangling modifier. What is important to remember is that a modifier must be placed as close as possible to the word that it modifies.

Practice 1

Rewrite each sentence to correct the dangling modifier. Mark the one sentence that is correct with a *C.*

1. Hanging safely on a wall, a security guard pointed to the priceless painting.
   What is hanging safely on a wall?

   _____

   _____

2. At the age of five, my mother bought me a chemistry set.

   _____

   _____

3. While it was raining, shoppers ran into the stores.

   _____

   _____

4. Having turned sour, I would not drink the milk.

_____

_____

5. Talking on the phone, my hot tea turned cold.

_____

_____

6. Piled high with dirty dishes, Pete hated to look at the kitchen sink.

_____

_____

7. Having locked my keys in the car, the police had to open it for me.

_____

_____

8. Drooping and looking all dried out, the children watered the plants.

_____

_____

9. After sitting through a long lecture, my foot was asleep.

_____

_____

10. Being late, stopping for coffee was out of the question.

_____

_____

Practice 2

Complete the following sentences. In each case, a logical subject should follow the opening words.

Example　Checking the oil stick, _I saw that my car was a quart low._____

1. While taking a bath, _____

2. Before starting the car, _____

3. Frightened by the noise in the basement, _____

4. Realizing it was late, _____

5. Though very expensive, _____

■ Review Test 1

Write *D* for *dangling* or *C* for *correct* in front of each sentence. Remember that the opening words are a dangling modifier if they are not followed immediately by a logical subject.

_____ 1. Burning quickly, the firefighters turned several hoses on the house.

_____ 2. Because it was burning quickly, the firefighters turned several hoses on the house.

_____ 3. While focusing the camera, several people wandered out of view.

_____ 4. While I focused the camera, several people wandered out of view.

_____ 5. When I peered down from the thirtieth floor, the cars looked like toys.

_____ 6. Peering down from the thirtieth floor, the cars looked like toys.

_____ 7. The cars looked like toys peering down from the thirtieth floor.

_____ 8. Riding in the rear of the bus, the sudden starts and stops were sickening.

_____ 9. For passengers riding in the rear of the bus, the sudden starts and stops were sickening.

_____ 10. Speaking excitedly, the phone seemed glued to Sara's ear.

_____ 11. The phone seemed glued to Sara's ear as she spoke excitedly.

_____ 12. In a sentimental frame of mind, the music brought tears to Beth's eyes.

_____ 13. As Beth was in a sentimental frame of mind, the music brought tears to her eyes.

_____ 14. When Helen suddenly became sick, I drove her to the doctor's office.

_____ 15. Suddenly sick, I drove Helen to the doctor's office.

_____ 16. The pancake was browned on one side, so Mark flipped it over.

_____ 17. Browned on one side, Mark flipped the pancake over.

_____ 18. Hanging by her teeth, the acrobat's body swung back and forth.

_____ 19. Hanging by her teeth, the acrobat swung back and forth.

_____ 20. While hanging by her teeth, the acrobat's body swung back and forth.

■ Review Test 2

Underline the five dangling modifiers in this passage. Then correct them in the spaces provided.

[1]Have you ever thought about what life was like for the first generation of your family to come to America? [2]Or have you wondered what your grandparents did for fun when they were your age? [3]Family stories tend to

be told for two or three generations and then disappear because no one ever records them. 4Using a tape recorder, these stories can be saved for the future. 5Here are some hints for conducting interviews with older members of your family. 6Thinking hard about what you really want to know, good questions can be prepared in advance. 7Try to put the people you interview at ease by reassuring them that you value what they have to say. 8Nervous about the tape recorder, stories might not come so easily to them otherwise. 9Remember that most people have never been interviewed before. 10Listening carefully to everything the person says, your interview will be more successful. 11By respecting their feelings, your older relatives will be delighted to share their stories. 12The tapes you make will be valued by your family for many years to come.

Sentence number: _____
Correction:

_____

_____

Sentence number: _____
Correction:

_____

_____

Sentence number: _____
Correction:

_____

_____

Sentence number: _____
Correction:

_____

_____

Sentence number: _____
Correction:

_____

_____

18 Faulty Parallelism

Introductory Activity

Read aloud each pair of sentences below. Write a check mark beside the sentence that reads more smoothly and clearly and sounds more natural.

Pair 1

_____ I use my TV remote control to change channels, to adjust the volume, and for turning the set on and off.

_____ I use my TV remote control to change channels, to adjust the volume, and to turn the set on and off.

Pair 2

_____ One option the employees had was to take a cut in pay; the other was longer hours of work.

_____ One option the employees had was to take a cut in pay; the other was to work longer hours.

Pair 3

_____ The refrigerator has a cracked vegetable drawer, one of the shelves is missing, and a strange freezer smell.

_____ The refrigerator has a cracked vegetable drawer, a missing shelf, and a strange freezer smell.

Answers are on page 688.

241

Parallelism Explained

16.5

Words in a pair or a series should have parallel structure. By balancing the items in a pair or a series so that they have the same kind of structure, you will make the sentence clearer and easier to read. Notice how the parallel sentences that follow read more smoothly than the nonparallel ones.

Nonparallel (Not Balanced)	*Parallel (Balanced)*
Fran spends her free time reading, listening to music, and she works in the garden.	Fran spends her free time reading, listening to music, and working in the garden. (A balanced series of *-ing* words: *reading, listening, working.*)
After the camping trip I was exhausted, irritable, and wanted to eat.	After the camping trip I was exhausted, irritable, and hungry. (A balanced series of descriptive words: *exhausted, irritable, hungry.*)
My hope for retirement is to be healthy, to live in a comfortable house, and having plenty of money.	My hope for retirement is to be healthy, to live in a comfortable house, and to have plenty of money. (A balanced series of *to* verbs: *to be, to live, to have.*)
Nightly, Fred puts out the trash, checks the locks on the doors, and the burglar alarm is turned on.	Nightly, Fred puts out the trash, checks the locks on the doors, and turns on the burglar alarm. (Balanced verbs and word order: *puts out the trash, checks the locks, turns on the burglar alarm.*)

Balanced sentences are not a skill you need to worry about when you are writing first drafts. But when you rewrite, you should try to put matching words and ideas into matching structures. Such parallelism will improve your writing style.

Practice 1

The one item in each list that is not parallel in form to the other items is crossed out. In the space provided, rewrite that item in parallel form. The first one has been done for you as an example.

1. fresh food
   attractive setting
   ~~service that is fast~~
   fast service _____

2. screaming children
   dogs that howl
   blaring music

   _____

3. slow
   speaks rudely
   careless

   _____

4. to hike
   swimming
   boating

   _____

5. noisy neighbors
   high rent
   security that is poor

   _____

6. cleaning of the apartment
   paid the bills
   did the laundry

   _____

7. looking good
   to have fun
   feeling fine

   _____

8. healthy soups
   tasty sandwiches
   desserts that are inexpensive

   _____

9. under the desk drawers
   the floor of the closet
   behind the bedroom curtains

   _____

10. works at the supermarket
    member of the church choir
    coaches the Little League team

    _____

Practice 2

The unbalanced part of each sentence is *italicized.* Rewrite this part so that it matches the rest of the sentence.

Example   In the afternoon, I changed two diapers, ironed several shirts, and *was watching* soap operas. _watched_ _____

1. Annie dropped a coin into the slot machine, pulled the lever, and *was waiting* to strike it rich.
   To be parallel, all three verbs should end in *-ed.*

   _____

2. Studying a little each day is more effective than *to cram.*

   _____

3. Many old people fear loneliness, *becoming ill,* and poverty.

   _____

4. My pet peeves are screeching chalk, *buses that are late,* and dripping sinks.

   _____

5. The magazine cover promised stories on losing weight quickly, *how to attract* a rich spouse, and finding the perfect haircut.

   _____

6. As smoke billowed around her, Paula knew her only choices were to jump or *suffocation.*

   _____

7. The principal often pestered students, yelled at teachers, and *was interrupting* classes.

   _____

8. People immigrate to America with hopes of finding freedom, happiness, and *in order to become financially secure.*

   _____

9. Once inside the zoo gates, Julio could hear lions roaring, *the chirping of birds,* and elephants trumpeting.

   _____

10. As a child I had nightmares about a huge monster that came out of a cave, *was breathing fire,* and wanted to barbecue me.

    _____

Practice 3

Complete the following statements. The first two parts of each statement are parallel in form; the part that you add should be parallel in form as well.

Example   Three things I like about myself are my sense of humor, my thought-
fulness, and *my self-discipline.*

1. I always celebrate my birthday by sleeping late, eating a good dinner, and
   To be parallel, all three verbs should end in *-ing.*

   _____

2. When Anita gets home from work, she likes to kick off her shoes, turn on
   some soft music, and _____

   _____

3. Despite the salesman's pitch, I could see that his "wonderful" used car had worn tires, rusting fenders, and _____

_____

4. Trying to realize that it was only a machine, Tina sat down in front of the computer, took a deep breath, and _____

_____

5. Three qualities I look for in a friend are loyalty, a sense of humor, and

_____

Collaborative Activity

Part A: Editing and Rewriting

Working with a partner, read carefully the short paragraph below and cross out the five instances of faulty parallelism. Then use the space provided to correct the instances of faulty parallelism. Feel free to discuss the rewrite quietly with your partner and refer back to the chapter when necessary.

[1]Running is an exercise that can be good for you mentally, physically, and also be helpful for your emotions. [2]A beginning runner should keep three things in mind: the warm-up session, the actual time that you are running, and the cool-down period. [3]Never start a run without first having warmed up through stretching exercises. [4]Stretching reduces muscle stiffness, decreases the possibility of injury, and it's a good method to gradually increase the heart rate. [5]During the run itself, move at a comfortable pace. [6]Your breathing should be steady and with depth. [7]Finally, remember to cool down after a run. [8]An adequate cool-down period allows time for the body to relax and the normalizing of the heart rate.

_____

_____

_____

_____

Continued

_____

_____

_____

_____

_____

Part B: Creating Sentences

Working with a partner, make up your own short test on faulty parallelism, as directed.

1. Write a sentence that includes three things you want to do tomorrow. One of those things should not be in parallel form. Then correct the faulty parallelism.

   Nonparallel _____

   _____

   Parallel _____

   _____

2. Write a sentence that names three positive qualities of a person you like or three negative qualities that you don't like.

   Nonparallel _____

   _____

   Parallel _____

   _____

3. Write a sentence that includes three everyday things that annoy you.

   Nonparallel _____

   _____

   Parallel _____

   _____

Reflective Activity

1. Look at the paragraph that you revised above. How does parallel form improve the paragraph?
2. How would you evaluate your own use of parallel form? When you write, do you use it almost never, at times, or often? How would you benefit from using it more?

■ Review Test 1

Cross out the unbalanced part of each sentence. Then rewrite the unbalanced part so that it matches the other item or items in the sentence.

Example   I enjoy watering the grass and ~~to work~~ in the garden.
           working

1. When someone gives you advice, do you listen, laugh, or are you just ignoring it?

   _____

2. After finding an apartment, we signed a lease, made a deposit, and preparing to move in.

   _____

3. The little girl came home from school with a tear-streaked face, a black eye, and her shirt was torn.

   _____

4. Ruby watched television, was talking on the phone, and studied all at the same time.

   _____

5. My Halloween shopping list included one bottle of blue nail polish, fake blood, and a wig that was colored purple.

   _____

6. Carmen went to class prepared to take notes, to volunteer answers, and with questions to ask.

   _____

7. The severe thunderstorm brought winds that were strong, dangerous lightning, and heavy rain to the entire county.

_____

8. When I got back from vacation, my refrigerator contained rotting vegetables, milk that was soured, and moldy cheese.

_____

9. The guide demonstrated how colonial Americans made iron tools, crushed grain for flour, and were making their own cloth.

_____

10. When my roommate blasts her stereo, I shut her door, put cotton in my ears, and am running the vacuum cleaner.

_____

■ Review Test 2

Each group of sentences contains two errors in parallelism. Underline these errors. Then, on the lines below, rewrite each item that doesn't match to make it parallel with the other item or items in the sentence.

1. When Phil left for work, he felt bright and cheerful. But by midafternoon he was coughing, wheezing, and shivers ran throughout his body. He left work, drove home, and was crawling into bed, where he stayed for the next four days.

   a. _____

   b. _____

2. I never spend money on fancy wrapping paper. When people get a present, they generally want to rip off the paper and be looking at what's inside. So I wrap my gifts in either plain brown grocery bags or Sunday comics that are colorful.

   a. _____

   b. _____

3. Failing students can be kinder than to pass them. There is little benefit to passing a student to a level of work he or she can't do. In addition, it is cruel to graduate a student from high school who has neither the communication skills nor the skills at math needed to get along in the world.

   a. _____

   b. _____

4. The little boy drew back from his new baby-sitter. Her long red nails, black eye makeup, and jewelry that jangled all frightened him. He was sure she was either a bad witch or a queen that was evil.

   a. _____

   b. _____

5. An actress stopped in the middle of a Broadway show and scolded flash photographers in the audience. She said they can either have a photo session or they can be enjoying the show, but they can't do both. The photographers sank down in their seats, their cameras were put away, and quietly watched the show.

   a. _____

   b. _____

■ Review Test 3

Cross out the five nonparallel parts in the following passage. Correct them in the spaces between the lines.

[1]When a few people in one community decided to form a homeowners' association, many of their neighbors were skeptical. [2]Some objected to stirring things up, and others were feeling the dues were too high. [3]But many neighbors joined, and their first big success was a garage sale. [4]They scheduled a day for everybody in the neighborhood to bring unwanted items to a community center. [5]Big appliances and other items that are heavy were picked up by volunteers with trucks. [6]The association promoted the sale by placing ads in newspapers and with the distribution of fliers at local shopping centers. [7]Dozens of families took part. [8]After that, the association helped plant trees, start a Crime Watch Program, and in repairing cracked sidewalks. [9]Members now receive discounts from local merchants and theater owners. [10]This association's success has inspired many more neighbors to join and people in other neighborhoods, who are starting their own organizations.

19 Sentence Variety II

Like Chapter 7, this chapter will show you a variety of ways to write effective and varied sentences. You will increase your sense of the many ways available to you for expressing your ideas. The practices here will also reinforce much of what you have learned in this section about modifiers and the use of parallelism.

-ing Word Groups

Use an *-ing* word group at some point in a sentence. Here are examples:

> The doctor, *hoping* for the best, examined the x-rays.
>
> *Jogging* every day, I soon raised my energy level.

More information about *-ing* words, also known as *present participles,* appears on page 191.

Practice 1

Combine each pair of sentences below into one sentence by using an *-ing* word and omitting repeated words. Use a comma or commas to set off the *-ing* word group from the rest of the sentence.

Example   • The diesel truck chugged up the hill.
            • It spewed out smoke.

                Spewing out smoke, the diesel truck chugged up the hill.

     or   *The diesel truck, spewing out smoke, chugged up the hill.*

1. • The tourists began to leave the bus.
   • They picked up their cameras.

   _____

   _____

2. • I was almost hit by a car.
   • I was jogging on the street.

   _____

   _____

3. • Barbara untangled her snarled hair from the brush.
   • She winced with pain.

   _____

   _____

4. • The singer ran to the front of the stage.
   • She waved her arms at the excited crowd.

   _____

   _____

5. • The team braced itself for a last-ditch effort.
   • It was losing by one point with thirty seconds left to play.

   _____

   _____

Practice 2

On separate paper, write five sentences of your own that contain *-ing* word groups.

-ed Word Groups

Use an *-ed* word group at some point in a sentence. Here are examples:

Tired of studying, I took a short break.

Mary, *amused* by the joke, told it to a friend.

I opened my eyes wide, *shocked* by the red "F" on my paper.

More information about *-ed* words, also known as *past participles,* appears on page 191.

Practice 1

Combine each of the following pairs of sentences into one sentence by using an *-ed* word and omitting repeated words. Use a comma or commas to set off the *-ed* word group from the rest of the sentence.

Example • Tim woke up with a start.
    • He was troubled by a dream.
      <u>Troubled by a dream, Tim woke up with a start.</u>

   or <u>Tim, troubled by a dream, woke up with a start.</u>

1. • Mary sat up suddenly in bed.
   • She was startled by a thunderclap.

   _____

   _____

2. • My parents decided to have a second wedding.
   • They have been married for fifty years.

   _____

   _____

3. • Erica wouldn't leave her car.
   • She was frightened by the large dog near the curb.

   _____

   _____

4. • The old orange felt like a marshmallow.
   • It was dotted with mold.

   _____

   _____

5. • Ernie made a huge sandwich and popped popcorn.
   • He was determined to have plenty to eat during the movie.

   _____

   _____

Practice 2

On separate paper, write five sentences of your own that contain *-ed* word groups.

-*ly* Openers

Use an -*ly* word to open a sentence. Here are examples:

Gently, he mixed the chemicals together.

Anxiously, the contestant looked at the game clock.

Skillfully, the quarterback rifled a pass to his receiver.

More information about -*ly* words, which are also known as *adverbs,* appears on page 224.

Practice 1

Combine each of the following pairs of sentences into one sentence by starting with an -*ly* word and omitting repeated words. Place a comma after the opening -*ly* word.

Example   • I gave several yanks to the starting cord of the lawn mower.

         • I was angry.

         Angrily, I gave several yanks to the starting cord of the lawn

         mower.

1. • We ate raw carrots and celery sticks.

   • We were noisy.
   Begin your revised sentence with *noisily.*

                    _____

                    _____

2. • Cliff spoke to his sobbing little brother.

   • He was gentle.

                    _____

                    _____

3. • The father picked up his baby daughter.

   • He was tender.

                    _____

                    _____

4. • I paced up and down the hospital corridor.
   • I was anxious.

   _____

   _____

5. • Anita repeatedly dived into the pool to find her engagement ring.
   • She was frantic.

   _____

   _____

Practice 2

On separate paper, write five sentences of your own that begin with *-ly* words.

To Openers

Use a *to* word group to open a sentence. Here are examples:

To succeed in that course, you must attend every class.
To help me sleep better, I learned to quiet my mind through meditation.
To get good seats, we went to the game early.

The combination of *to* and a verb, also known as an *infinitive,* is explained on page 191.

Practice 1

Combine each of the following pairs of sentences into one sentence by starting with a *to* word group and omitting repeated words. Use a comma after the opening *to* word group.

Example • I fertilize the grass every spring.
         • I want to make it greener.
           To make the grass greener, I fertilize it every spring.

1. • Sally put a thick towel on the bottom of the tub.
   • She did this to make the tub less slippery.
   Your combined sentence should omit these words: *she did this.*

   _____

   _____

2. • We now keep our garbage in the garage.
   • We do this to keep raccoons away.

   _____

   _____

3. • Bill pressed two fingers against the large vein in his neck.
   • He did this to count his pulse.

   _____

   _____

4. • My aunt opens her dishwasher when it begins drying.
   • She does this to steam her face.

   _____

   _____

5. • We looked through our closets for unused clothing.
   • We did this to help out the homeless.

   _____

   _____

Practice 2

On separate paper, write five sentences of your own that begin with *to* word groups.

Prepositional Phrase Openers

Use prepositional phrase openers. Here are examples:

From the beginning, I disliked my boss.
In spite of her work, she failed the course.
After the game, we went to a movie.

Prepositional phrases include words like *in, from, of, at, by,* and *with.* A list of common prepositions appears on page 91.

Practice 1

Combine each of the following groups of sentences into one sentence by omitting repeated words. Start each sentence with a suitable prepositional phrase and put the other prepositional phrases in places that sound right. Generally, you should use a comma after the opening prepositional phrase.

Example   • A fire started.

• It did this at 5 A.M.

• It did this inside the garage.
    At 5 A.M., a fire started inside the garage.

1. • We have dinner with my parents.

   • We do this about once a week.

   • We do this at a restaurant.
   Begin with *About once a week.*

   _____

   _____

2. • I put the dirty cups away.

   • I did this before company came.

   • I put them in the cupboard.

   _____

   _____

3. • My eyes roamed.

   • They did this during my English exam.

   • They did this around the room.

   • They did this until they met the instructor's eye.

   _____

   _____

4. • The little boy drew intently.

   • He did this in a comic book.

   • He did this for twenty minutes.

   • He did this without stopping once.

   _____

   _____

5. • A playful young orangutan wriggled.
   • He did this at the zoo.
   • He did this in a corner.
   • He did this under a paper sack.

_____

_____

Practice 2

On separate paper, write five sentences of your own, each beginning with a prepositional phrase and containing at least one other prepositional phrase.

Series of Items

Use a series of items. Following are two of the many items that can be used in a series: adjectives and verbs.

Adjectives in Series

Adjectives are descriptive words. Here are examples:

The *husky young* man sanded the *chipped, weather-worn* paint off the fence.

Husky and *young* are adjectives that describe *man; chipped* and *weather-worn* are adjectives that describe *paint.* More information about adjectives appears on page 222.

Practice 1

Combine each of the following groups of sentences into one sentence by using adjectives in a series and omitting repeated words. Use a comma between adjectives only when *and* inserted between them sounds natural.

Example • I sewed a set of buttons onto my coat.

- The buttons were shiny.
- The buttons were black.
- The coat was old.
- The coat was green.

I sewed a set of shiny black buttons onto my old green coat.

1. • The shingles blew off the roof during the storm.
   - The shingles were old.
   - The shingles were peeling.
   - The storm was blustery.

   Begin with *The old, peeling shingles.*

   _____

   _____

2. • The dancer whirled across the stage with his partner.
   - The dancer was lean.
   - The dancer was powerful.
   - The partner was graceful.
   - The partner was elegant.

   _____

   _____

3. • A rat scurried into the kitchen of the restaurant.
   - The rat was large.
   - The rat was furry.
   - The kitchen was crowded.

   _____

   _____

4. • The moon lit up the sky like a street lamp.
   - The moon was full.
   - The moon was golden.
   - The sky was cloudy.
   - The street lamp was huge.
   - The street lamp was floating.

   _____

   _____

5. • The doorbell of the house played a tune.
   • The doorbell was oval.
   • The doorbell was plastic.
   • The house was large.
   • The house was ornate.
   • The tune was loud.
   • The tune was rock.

_____

_____

Practice 2

On separate paper, write five sentences of your own that contain a series of adjectives.

Verbs in Series

Verbs are words that express action. Here are examples:

In my job as a cook's helper, I *prepared* salads, *sliced* meat and cheese, and *made* all kinds of sandwiches.

Basic information about verbs appears on pages 88–89.

Practice 1

Combine each group of sentences below into one sentence by using verbs in a series and omitting repeated words. Use a comma between verbs in a series.

Examples • In the dingy bar Sam shelled peanuts.
   • He sipped a beer.
   • He talked up a storm with friends.

In the dingy bar Sam shelled peanuts, sipped a beer, and talked up a storm with friends.

1. • The flea-ridden dog rubbed itself against the fence.
   • It bit its tail.
   • It scratched its neck with its hind leg.
   What three things did the dog do?

   _____

   _____

2. • I put my homework on the table.
   • I made a cup of coffee.
   • I turned the radio up full blast.

   _____

   _____

3. • The driver stopped the school bus.
   • He walked to the back.
   • He separated two children.

   _____

   _____

4. • I rolled up my sleeve.
   • I glanced at the nurse nervously.
   • I shut my eyes.
   • I waited for the worst to be over.

   _____

   _____

5. • The parents applauded politely at the program's end.
   • They looked at their watches.
   • They exchanged looks of relief.
   • They reached for their coats.

   _____

   _____

   _____

Practice 2

On separate paper, write five sentences of your own that use verbs in a series.

Note   The chapter on parallelism (pages 241–249) gives you practice in some of the other kinds of items that can be used in a series.

■ Review Test 1

Combine each group of short sentences into one sentence. Various combinations are possible. Choose the combination that reads most smoothly and clearly and that sounds most appropriate in the context of surrounding sentences.

Note   In combining short sentences into one sentence, omit repeated words where necessary. Use separate paper. The story continues in the next review test.

Dracula's Revenge

- Mickey Raines had a dislike.
- The dislike was of horror movies.
- His friends were different.
- They loved to see such movies.

- They would always invite Mickey to go with them.
- He would always refuse.

- He thought horror films were stupid.
- The actors were covered with fake blood.
- They were pretending to writhe in agony.

- Mickey thought their behavior was disgusting.
- He did not think their behavior was frightening.

- Once his friends persuaded him to come with them.
- They went to see a movie.
- The movie was called *Halloween 14— The Horror Continues.*

- Mickey found it ridiculous.
- He laughed aloud through parts of the movie.
- They were the scariest parts.

- His friends were embarrassed.
- They were so embarrassed they moved.
- They moved away from him.
- They moved to another part of the theater.

- Then one night Mickey was alone.
- He was alone in his house.
- His mother was out for the evening.
- He turned on the television.

- A movie was playing.
- It was called *Nosferatu.*

- It was the original film version of the Dracula story.
- The film version was silent.
- It was made in Germany.
- It was made in 1922.

■ Review Test 2

Combine each group of short sentences into one sentence. Various combinations are possible. Choose the combination that reads most smoothly and clearly and that sounds most appropriate in the context of surrounding sentences.

Note   In combining short sentences into one sentence, omit repeated words where necessary. Use separate paper. The story continues from the previous review test.

- The movie was not gory at all.
- There were no teenage girls in it getting chased.
- There were no teenage girls in it getting murdered.

- The villain was a vampire.
- He was hideous.
- He was shriveled.
- He was terrifying.

- His victims did not die.
- His victims grew weaker.
- They grew weaker after every attack.

- The vampire reminded Mickey of a parasite.
- The parasite was terrible.
- It was a dead thing.
- It was feeding off the living.

- Mickey trembled.
- He was trembling at the thought of such a creature.
- It could be lurking just out of sight.
- It could be lurking in the darkness.

- Then he heard a scraping noise.
- The noise was at the front door.
- He almost cried out in terror.

- The door opened quickly.
- Cold air rushed in.
- His mother appeared.
- She was back from her date.

- His mother smiled at him.
- She called out "Hello."
- She paused in the foyer to take off her coat.

- Mickey was relieved to see her.
- His relief was enormous.
- He rushed up to greet her.

- The spell of the movie was broken.
- Mickey locked the door on the night.

20 Paper Format

Introductory Activity

Check the paper opening below that seems clearer and easier to read.

___ A

	Dangers of Prescription Drugs
	Careless consumers can harm themselves with
	prescription drugs. To begin with, consumers should always
	be aware of the possible side effects of a prescription drug.

___ B

	"dangers of prescription drugs"
	Careless consumers can harm themselves with prescription drugs.
	To begin with, consumers should always be aware of the possib-
	le side effects of a prescription drug. They should take the time

What are four reasons for your choice?

_____

_____

_____

_____

Answers are on page 690.

Guidelines for Preparing a Paper

Here are guidelines to follow in preparing a paper for an instructor.

1 Use full-sized theme or typewriter paper, 8½ by 11 inches.

2 Leave wide margins (1 to 1½ inches) all around the paper. In particular, do not crowd the right-hand or bottom margin. This white space makes your paper more readable; also, the instructor has room for comments.

3 If you write by hand:

- Use a pen with blue or black ink (*not* a pencil).
- Be careful not to overlap letters and not to make decorative loops on letters.
- On narrow-ruled paper, write on every other line.
- Make all your letters distinct. Pay special attention to *a, e, i, o*, and *u*—five letters that people sometimes write illegibly.

4 Center the title of your paper on the first line of the first page. Do not put quotation marks around the title. Do not underline the title. Capitalize all the major words in a title, including the first word. Short connecting words within a title, such as *of, for, the, in*, and *to,* are not capitalized.

5 Skip a line between the title and the first line of your text. Indent the first line of each paragraph about five spaces (half an inch) from the left-hand margin.

6 Make commas, periods, and other punctuation marks firm and clear. Leave a slight space after each period. When you type, leave a double space after a period.

7 If you break a word at the end of a line, break only between syllables (see page 341). Do not break words of one syllable.

8 Put your name, date, and course number where your instructor asks for them.

Remember these points about the title and the first sentence of your paper.

9 The title should be several words that tell what the paper is about. It should usually *not* be a complete sentence. For example, if you are writing a paper about your jealous sister, the title could simply be "My Jealous Sister."

10 Do not rely on the title to help explain the first sentence of your paper. The first sentence must be independent of the title. For instance, if the title of your paper is "My Jealous Sister," the first sentence should *not* be, "She has been this way as long as I can remember." Rather, the first sentence might be, "My sister has always been a jealous person."

Practice 1

Identify the mistakes in format in the following lines from a student composition. Explain the mistakes in the spaces provided. One mistake is described for you as an example.

	"Being a younger sister"
	When I was young, I would gladly have donated my older si-
	ster to another family. First of all, most of my clothes were
	hand-me-downs. I rarely got to buy anything new to wear. My
	sister took very good care of her clothes, which only made the
	problem worse. Also, she was always very critical of everything.

1. *Break words at correct syllable divisions (sis-ter).*

2. _____

3. _____

4. _____

5. _____

6. _____

Practice 2

As already stated, a title should tell in several words what a paper is about. Often a title can be based on the sentence that expresses the main idea of a paper.

Following are five main-idea sentences from student papers. Write a suitable specific title for each paper, basing the title on the main idea.

Example   Title: *Aging Americans as Outcasts* _____
Our society treats aging Americans as outcasts in many ways.

1. Title: _____
   What is a three-word subject for this paper?
   Pets offer a number of benefits to their owners.

2. Title: _____
   Since I have learned to budget carefully, I no longer run out of money at the end of the week.

3. Title: _____

   Studying regularly with a study group has helped me raise my grades.

4. Title: _____

   Grandparents have a special relationship with their grandchildren.

5. Title: _____

   My decision to eliminate junk food from my diet has been good for my health and my budget.

Practice 3

In four of the five following sentences, the writer has mistakenly used the title to help explain the first sentence. But as has been noted, you must *not* rely on the title to explain your first sentence. Rewrite the sentences so that they are independent of the title. Write *Correct* under the one sentence that is independent.

Example   Title: Flunking an Exam

First sentence: I managed to do this because of several bad habits.

Rewritten: _I managed to flunk an exam because of several bad_

habits.

1. Title: The Best Children's Television Shows

   First sentence: They educate while they entertain, and they are not violent. Indicate the words that *they* stands for.

   Rewritten: _____

   _____

2. Title: Women in the Workplace

   First sentence: They have made many gains there in the last decade.

   Rewritten: _____

   _____

3. Title: The Generation Gap

   First sentence: It results from differing experiences of various age groups.

   Rewritten: _____

   _____

4. Title: My Ideal Job

First sentence: My ideal job would be to manage a pop singer and make a lot of money.

Rewritten: _____

_____

5. Title: Important Accomplishments

First sentence: One of them was to finish high school despite my parents' divorce.

Rewritten: _____

_____

■ Review Test

Use the space provided below to rewrite the following sentences from a student paper, correcting the mistakes in format.

	"my nursing-home friends"
	I now count some of them among my good friends. I first went there just to keep a relative of mine company.
	That is when I learned some of them rarely got any visitors.
	Many were starved for conversation and friendship.
	At the time, I did not want to get involved. But what I

21 Capital Letters

Introductory Activity

You probably know a good deal about the uses of capital letters. Answering the questions below will help you check your knowledge.

1. Write the full name of a person you know: _____

2. In what city and state were you born? _____

3. What is your present street address? _____

4. Name a country where you would like to travel: _____

5. Name a school that you attended: _____

6. Give the name of a store where you buy food: _____

7. Name a company where you or anyone you
   know works: _____

8. Which day of the week gives you the best chance to relax? _____

9. What holiday is your favorite? _____

10. Which brand of toothpaste do you use? _____

11. Give the brand name of a candy or chewing gum you like: _____

12. Name a song or a television show you enjoy: _____

13. Write the title of a magazine or newspaper
    you read: _____

Items 14–16   Three capital letters are needed in the example below. Underline the words you think should be capitalized. Then write them, capitalized, in the spaces provided.

on Super Bowl Sunday, my roommate said, "let's buy some
snacks and invite a few friends over to watch the game." i knew
my plans to write a term paper would have to be changed.

14. _____   15. _____   16. _____

Answers are on page 690.

Main Uses of Capital Letters

25.1

Capital letters are used with:

1   First word in a sentence or direct quotation
2   Names of persons and the word *I*
3   Names of particular places
4   Names of days of the week, months, and holidays
5   Names of commercial products
6   Titles of books, magazines, articles, films, television shows, songs, poems, stories, papers that you write, and the like
7   Names of companies, associations, unions, clubs, religious and political groups, and other organizations

Each use is illustrated on the pages that follow.

First Word in a Sentence or Direct Quotation

> Our company has begun laying people off.
> The doctor said, "This may hurt a bit."
> "My husband," said Martha, "is a light eater. When it's light, he starts to eat."

Note   In the third example above, *My* and *When* are capitalized because they start new sentences. But *is* is not capitalized, because it is part of the first sentence.

Names of Persons and the Word *I*

> At the picnic, I met Tony Curry and Lola Morrison.

Names of Particular Places

> After graduating from Gibbs High School in Houston, I worked for a summer at a nearby Holiday Inn on Clairmont Boulevard.

But   Use small letters if the specific name of a place is not given.

> After graduating from high school in my hometown, I worked for a summer at a nearby hotel on one of the main shopping streets.

Names of Days of the Week, Months, and Holidays

This year, Memorial Day falls on the last Thursday in May.

But   Use small letters for the seasons—summer, fall, winter, spring.

In the early summer and fall, my hay fever bothers me.

Names of Commercial Products

The consumer magazine gave high ratings to Cheerios breakfast cereal, Breyer's ice cream, and Progresso chicken noodle soup.

But   Use small letters for the *type* of product (breakfast cereal, ice cream, chicken noodle soup, and the like).

Titles of Books, Magazines, Articles, Films, Television Shows, Songs, Poems, Stories, Papers That You Write, and the Like

My oral report was on *The Diary of a Young Girl,* by Anne Frank.

While watching *The Young and the Restless* on television, I thumbed through *Cosmopolitan* magazine and the *New York Times.*

Names of Companies, Associations, Unions, Clubs, Religious and Political Groups, and Other Organizations

A new bill before Congress is opposed by the National Rifle Association.

My wife is Jewish; I am Roman Catholic. We are both members of the Democratic Party.

My parents have life insurance with Prudential, auto insurance with Allstate, and medical insurance with Blue Cross and Blue Shield.

Practice

In the sentences that follow, cross out the words that need capitals. Then write the capitalized forms of the words in the space provided. The number of spaces tells you how many corrections to make in each case.

Example   Rhoda said, "~~why~~ should I bother to *eat* this ~~hershey~~ bar? I should just apply it directly to my hips."   _____Why_____   _____Hershey_____

1. Sometimes i still regret not joining the boy scouts when I was in grade school.
   The word *I* and names of organizations are capitalized.

   _____   _____   _____

2. On the friday after thanksgiving, Carole went to target to buy gifts for her family.

   _____   _____   _____

3. In the box office of the regal cinema is a sign saying, "if you plan to see an R-rated movie, be ready to show your ID."

   _____   _____   _____

4. In many new england towns, republicans outnumber democrats five to one.

   _____   _____   _____   _____

5. Nelson was surprised to learn that both state farm and nationwide have insurance offices in the prudential building.

   _____   _____   _____   _____   _____

6. Magazines such as *time* and *newsweek* featured articles about the fires that devastated part of southern california.

   _____   _____   _____

7. The rose grower whom Manny works for said that the biggest rose-selling holidays are valentine's day and mother's day.

   _____   _____   _____   _____

8. With some pepsis and fritos nearby, the kids settled down to play a game on the macintosh computer.

   _____   _____   _____

9. Bob's ford taurus was badly damaged when he struck a deer last saturday.

   _____   _____   _____

10. Though Julie Andrews excelled in the broadway version of *my fair lady,* Audrey Hepburn was cast as the female lead in the movie version.

    _____   _____   _____   _____

Other Uses of Capital Letters

Capital letters are also used with:

1   Names that show family relationships
2   Titles of persons when used with their names
3   Specific school courses
4   Languages
5   Geographic locations
6   Historic periods and events
7   Races, nations, and nationalities
8   Opening and closing of a letter

Each use is illustrated on the pages that follow.

Names That Show Family Relationships

Aunt Fern and Uncle Jack are selling their house.

I asked Grandfather to start the fire.

Is Mother feeling better?

But   Do not capitalize words like *mother, father, grandmother, grandfather, uncle, aunt,* and so on when they are preceded by *my* or another possessive word.

My aunt and uncle are selling their house.

I asked my grandfather to start the fire.

Is my mother feeling better?

Titles of Persons When Used with Their Names

I wrote an angry letter to Senator Blutt.

Can you drive to Dr. Stein's office?

We asked Professor Bushkin about his attendance policy.

But   Use small letters when titles appear by themselves, without specific names.

I wrote an angry letter to my senator.

Can you drive to the doctor's office?

We asked our professor about his attendance policy.

Specific School Courses

My courses this semester include Accounting I, Introduction to Data Processing, Business Law, General Psychology, and Basic Math.

But   Use small letters for general subject areas.

This semester I'm taking mostly business courses, but I have a psychology course and a math course as well.

Languages

Lydia speaks English and Spanish equally well.

Geographic Locations

I lived in the South for many years and then moved to the West Coast.

But   Use small letters in giving directions.

Go south for about five miles and then bear west.

Historic Periods and Events

One essay question dealt with the Battle of the Bulge in World War II.

Races, Nations, and Nationalities

The census form asked whether I was African American, Native American, Hispanic, or Asian.

Last summer I hitchhiked through Italy, France, and Germany.

The city is a melting pot for Koreans, Vietnamese, and Mexican Americans.

But   Use small letters when referring to *whites* or *blacks*.

Both whites and blacks supported our mayor in the election.

Opening and Closing of a Letter

Dear Sir: Sincerely yours,

Dear Madam: Truly yours,

Note   Capitalize only the first word in a closing.

Practice

Cross out the words that need capitals in the following sentences. Then write the capitalized forms of the words in the spaces provided. The number of spaces tells you how many corrections to make in each case.

1. The nervous game show contestant couldn't remember how long the hundred years' war lasted.
   Capitalize the name of the historic event.

   _____   _____   _____

2. My sister and I always plead with aunt sophie to sing polish songs whenever she visits us.

   _____   _____   _____

3. While in Philadelphia, we visited independence hall and saw the liberty bell.

   _____   _____   _____   _____

4. The readings for the first semester of world history end with the middle ages.

   _____   _____   _____   _____

5. The Miami area has many fine cuban restaurants, several spanish-language newspapers, and annual hispanic cultural festivals.

   _____   _____   _____

Unnecessary Use of Capitals

Practice

Many errors in capitalization are caused by adding capitals where they are not needed. Cross out the incorrectly capitalized letters in the following sentences and write the correct forms in the spaces provided. The number of spaces tells you how many corrections to make in each sentence.

1. Antonio's Grandmother makes the best Spaghetti with Meatballs I've ever tasted.
   No words need capitals.

   _____   _____   _____

2. In our High School, the American history teacher was also the Basketball Coach.

   _____   _____   _____   _____

3. A Shop at Westville Mall sells copies of all the trendy clothes shown in various Fashion Magazines.

   _____   _____   _____

4. Several Parents' Groups protested the Ads for the new horror movie, which showed Santa Claus as a Maniac with a knife.

   _____   _____   _____   _____

5. When I complained to the Manager of the Restaurant about the poor service, she gave me a free Dessert.

   _____   _____   _____

Collaborative Activity

Part A: Editing and Rewriting

Working with a partner, read the short paragraph below and mark off the fifteen spots where capital letters are missing. Then use the space provided to rewrite the passage, adding capital letters where needed. Feel free to discuss the passage quietly with your partner and refer back to the chapter when necessary.

[1]The morning that I visited the lincoln memorial, it was raining. [2]It was a quiet thursday in late october, and the air was cold. [3]I was with my uncle walt, and we had spent the morning visiting the smithsonian institution together. [4]After lunch, my uncle said to me, "now we're going to go someplace that you'll never forget." [5]When we arrived, I was overwhelmed by lincoln's massive statue, which dwarfed everything around it—just as the man had done in life. [6]To my left I was aware of the silently flowing potomac river. [7]Engraved on one of the marble walls was the gettysburg address. [8]I read those familiar words and remained there for a time in

Continued

silence, touched by the simple eloquence of that speech. [9]I then snapped just one picture with my kodak camera and walked down the stone steps quietly. [10]The photograph still sits on my desk today as a reminder of that special visit.

_____

_____

_____

_____

_____

_____

_____

_____

_____

_____

Part B: Creating Sentences

Working with a partner, write a sentence (or two) as directed. Pay special attention to capital letters.

1. Write about a place you like (or want) to visit. Be sure to give the name of the place, including the city, state, or country where it is located.

2. Write a sentence (or two) in which you state the name of your elementary school, your favorite teacher or subject, and your least favorite teacher or subject.

3. Write a sentence (or two) that includes the names of three brand-name products that you often use. You may begin the sentence with the words, "Three brand-name products I use every day are . . ."

4. Think of the name of your favorite musical artist or performer. Then write a sentence in which you include the musician's name and the title of one of his or her songs.

5. Write a sentence in which you describe something you plan to do two days from now. Be sure to include the date and day of the week.

Reflective Activity

1. What would writing be like without capital letters? Use an example or two to help show how capital letters are important to writing.
2. What three uses of capital letters are most difficult for you to remember? Explain, giving examples.

■ Review Test 1

Cross out the words that need capitals in the following sentences. Then write the capitalized forms of the words in the spaces provided. The number of spaces tells you how many corrections to make in each sentence.

Example   During halftime of the ~~saturday~~ afternoon football game, my sister said, "~~let's~~ get some hamburgers from ~~wendy's~~ or put a pizza in the oven."

_____Saturday_____   _____Let's_____   _____Wendy's_____

1. When he saw the exercise commercial that said "just do it," Lance put on his nike running shoes and went to the store to get some ice cream.

_____   _____

2. Millions of years ago, america's midwest was covered by a great inland sea.

_____   _____

3. One of our thanksgiving traditions is sending a check to an organization such as greenpeace, which helps protect the environment.

_____   _____

4. If you drive onto route 10 in tallahassee, florida, and stay on that road, you'll eventually end up in california.

_____   _____   _____   _____

5. Just before english class this morning, Arlene titled her final paper "my argument for an A."

_____   _____   _____

6. I read in the book *royal lives* that when an ancient egyptian king died, his servants were often killed and buried with him.

_____   _____   _____

7. dear mr. Bradford:

This is the third and final time I will write to complain about the leak in my bathroom.

sincerely,

Anne Morrison

_____   _____   _____

8. "After age eighty," grandma ida would say, "time passes very quickly. it seems as though it's time for breakfast every fifteen minutes."

_____   _____   _____

9. Dr. Green, who teaches a course called cultural anthropology, spent last summer on an archaeological dig in israel.

_____   _____   _____

10. During the singing of "the star-spangled banner," many fans at yankee stadium drank sodas, read their programs, or chatted with each other.

_____   _____   _____

_____   _____   _____

■ Review Test 2

On separate paper, write:

- Seven sentences demonstrating the seven main uses of capital letters.
- Eight sentences demonstrating the eight other uses of capital letters.

22 Numbers and Abbreviations

Introductory Activity

Write a check mark beside the item in each pair that you think uses numbers correctly.

I finished the exam by 8:55, but my grade was only 65 percent. _____

I finished the exam by eight-fifty-five, but my grade was only sixty-five percent. _____

9 people are in my biology lab, but there are 45 in my lecture group. _____

Nine people are in my biology lab, but there are forty-five in my lecture group. _____

Write a check mark beside the item in each pair that you think uses abbreviations correctly.

Both of my bros. were treated by Dr. Lewis after the mt. climbing accident. _____
Both of my brothers were treated by Dr. Lewis after the mountain climbing accident. _____

I spent two hrs. finishing my Eng. paper and handed it to my teacher, Ms. Peters, right at the deadline. _____
I spent two hours finishing my English paper and handed it to my teacher, Ms. Peters, right at the deadline. _____

Answers are on page 690.

Numbers

25.2

Rule 1 Spell out numbers that take no more than two words. Otherwise, use numerals—the numbers themselves.

> Last year Tina bought nine new records.
>
> Ray struck out fifteen batters in Sunday's softball game.
>
> *But*
>
> Tina now has 114 records in her collection.
>
> Already this season Ray has recorded 168 strikeouts.

You should also spell out a number that begins a sentence.

> One hundred fifty first-graders throughout the city showed flu symptoms today.

Rule 2 Be consistent when you use a series of numbers. If some numbers in a sentence or paragraph require more than two words, then use numbers themselves throughout the selection.

> That executive who tried to cut 250 employees' salaries owns 8 cars, 4 homes, 3 boats, and 1 jet.

Rule 3 Use numbers to show dates, times, addresses, percentages, exact sums of money, and parts of a book.

> John F. Kennedy was killed on November 22, 1963.
>
> My job interview was set for 10:15. (*But:* Spell out numbers before *o'clock.* For example: The time was then changed to eleven o'clock.)
>
> Janet's new address is 118 North 35 Street.
>
> Almost 40 percent of my meals are eaten at fast-food restaurants.
>
> The cashier rang up a total of $18.35. (*But:* Round amounts may be expressed as words. For example: The movie has an eight-dollar admission charge.)
>
> Read Chapter 6 in your math textbook and answer questions 1 to 5 on page 250.

Practice

Use the three rules to make the corrections needed in these sentences.

1. Almost every morning I get up at exactly six-fifteen.
   Use numerals to show time.

2. But on Sunday mornings, I sleep until 9 o'clock.

3. Sue and George got married on July twenty-eighth, 2004.

4. Joanne got really nervous when she saw there were only 6 other people in her English class.

5. Please send your complaints to sixteen hundred Pennsylvania Avenue.

6. 43 stores in the New England area were closed by a retail workers' strike.

7. Martin's computer system, including a printer, cost nine hundred thirty dollars and twenty cents.

8. Pages sixty through sixty-four of my biology book are stuck together.

9. Hollywood starlet Fifi LaFlamme's closet stores twenty-seven evening gowns, fifty-two designer suits, and 132 pairs of shoes.

10. Since over fifty percent of the class failed the midterm exam, the instructor decided not to count the grades.

Abbreviations

While abbreviations are a helpful time-saver in note-taking, you should avoid most abbreviations in formal writing. Listed below are some of the few abbreviations that are acceptable in compositions. Note that a period is used after most abbreviations.

1 Mr., Mrs., Ms., Jr., Sr., Dr., when used with proper names:

Mr. Rollin   Ms. Peters   Dr. Coleman

2 Time references:

A.M. or a.m.   P.M. or p.m.   B.C. or A.D.

3 First or middle initial in a name:

T. Alan Parker   Linda M. Evans

4 Organizations, technical words, and trade names known primarily by initials:

ABC   CIA   UNESCO   GM   AIDS   DNA

Practice

Cross out the words that should not be abbreviated and correct them in the spaces provided.

1. After I placed the "bike for sale" ad in the newsp., the tele. rang nonstop for a week.
   No words should be abbreviated.

   _____   _____

2. Sharon bought two bush. of ripe tomatoes at the farm mkt. on Rt. 73.

   _____   _____   _____

3. On Mon., NASA will announce its plans for a Sept. flight to Mars.

   _____   _____

4. The psych. class was taught by Dr. Aronson, a noted psychiatrist from Eng.

   _____   _____

5. The best things on the menu are the chick. pot pie and the mac. and cheese.

   _____   _____

6. Several baby opossums (each of which weighs less than an oz.) can fit into a tbsp.

   _____   _____

7. I didn't have time to study for my chem. test on Sun., but I studied for four hrs. yesterday.

   _____   _____   _____

8. Every Jan., our co. gives awards for the best employee suggestions of the previous yr.

   _____   _____   _____

9. Lawrence T. Johnson lost his lic. to practice medicine when the state board discovered he never went to med. school.

   _____   _____

10. Mick, a vet. who served in Iraq, started his own photography bus. after graduating from a community coll.

    _____   _____   _____

■ Review Test

Cross out the mistake or mistakes in numbers and abbreviations and correct them in the spaces provided.

1. Sears' 4-day sale starts this coming Thurs.

   _____   _____

2. One suspect had blue eyes and brn. hair and was over 6 ft. tall.

   _____   _____   _____

3. Answers to the chpt. questions start on p. two hundred and ninety-three.

   _____   _____   _____

4. With Dec. twenty-fifth only hrs. away, little Rhonda couldn't eat or sleep.

   _____   _____   _____

5. Over 200 children helped in the collection of seven hundred and thirty-two dollars for UNICEF.

   _____   _____

6. My growing 15-year-old son wears sz. 11 shoes that look like boats.

   _____   _____

7. My 3 years of Spanish in h.s. helped me to get a job in the city health clinic.

   _____   _____   _____

8. The robber was sentenced to 10 yrs. in prison for holding up a bank on Pacific Blvd.

   _____   _____   _____

9. I canceled my appt. when I got an emerg. call that my mother had been taken to the hosp.

   _____   _____   _____

10. When city employees staged a strike on Mon., more than 70 pct. of them didn't show up for work.

    _____   _____

23 End Marks

Introductory Activity

Add the end mark needed in each of the following sentences.

1. All week I have been feeling depressed
2. What is the deadline for handing in the paper
3. The man at the door wants to know whose car is double-parked
4. That truck ahead of us is out of control

Answers are on page 691.

A sentence always begins with a capital letter. It always ends with a period, a question mark, or an exclamation point.

Period (.)

23.1a

Use a period after a sentence that makes a statement.

More single parents are adopting children.
It has rained for most of the week.

Use a period after most abbreviations.

Mr. Brady	B.A.	Dr. Ballard
Ms. Peters	A.M.	Tom Ricci, Jr.

Question Mark (?)

23.1b

Use a question mark after a *direct* question.

When is your paper due?
How is your cold?
Tom asked, "When are you leaving?"
"Why can't we all stop arguing?" Rosa asked.

Do *not* use a question mark after an *indirect* question (a question not in the speaker's exact words).

She asked when the paper was due.
He asked how my cold was.
Tom asked when I was leaving.
Rosa asked why we couldn't all stop arguing.

Exclamation Point (!)

ALLWRITE!
23.1d

Use an exclamation point after a word or sentence that expresses strong feeling.

Come here!

Ouch! This pizza is hot!

That truck just missed us!

Note   Be careful not to overuse exclamation points.

Practice

Add a period, question mark, or exclamation point as needed to each of the following sentences.

1. Is it possible for a fish to drown
   This item is a *direct* question.
2. Thomas Jefferson was a redhead
3. I asked Jill for the time of day, but she wouldn't give it to me
4. When Eva learned she had won the lottery, she jumped up and down, yelling, "I don't believe it "
5. Because Americans watch so much television, one writer has called us a nation of "vidiots "
6. I questioned whether the police officer's report was accurate
7. If you had one year left to live, what would you do with the rest of your life
8. The last thing I heard before waking up in the hospital was someone screaming, "Look out for that truck "
9. On the plane from New York to Chicago, Dominic said, "Must I turn my watch back one hour—or forward "
10. Carlos asked himself on the way to his wedding whether he was sure he wanted to get married

■ **Review Test**

Add a period, question mark, or exclamation point as needed to each of the following sentences.

1. My birthday present was wrapped in old newspapers and yellowed Scotch tape

2. Did you know that washing in very hot water can dry out your skin

3. The bride stunned everyone when she appeared in a purple lace gown

4. Don't eat that poisonous mushroom

5. How did you get a wad of gum in your hair

6. That boy is waving a loaded gun

7. All through the interview, my stomach grumbled and my hands shook

8. If you won the lottery, what would you do with the prize money

9. I wonder if we should have a New Year's Eve party this year

10. Look out for that swerving car

24 Apostrophe

Introductory Activity

Look carefully at the three items below. Then see if you can answer the questions that follow each item.

1. the desk of the manager   = the manager's desk
   the car of Hakim   = Hakim's car
   the teeth of my dog   = my dog's teeth
   the smile of the woman   = the woman's smile
   the briefcase of my mother = my mother's briefcase

   What is the purpose of the apostrophe in the examples above?

   _____

2. He is my best friend.   = He's my best friend.
   I am afraid of spiders.   = I'm afraid of spiders.
   Do not watch too much TV. = Don't watch too much TV.
   They are an odd couple.   = They're an odd couple.
   It is a wonderful movie.   = It's a wonderful movie.

   What is the purpose of the apostrophe in the examples above?

   _____

3. Several buildings were damaged by the severe storm. One building's roof was blown off and dropped in a nearby field.

   Why does the apostrophe belong in the second sentence but not the first?

   _____

   _____

Answers are on page 691.

24.6

The two main uses of the apostrophe are:

1 To show the omission of one or more letters in a contraction

2 To show ownership or possession

Each use is explained on the pages that follow.

Apostrophe in Contractions

A contraction is formed when two words are combined to make one word. An apostrophe is used to show where letters are omitted in forming the contraction. Here are two contractions:

> have + not = haven't (the *o* in *not* has been omitted)
>
> I   + will = I'll (the *wi* in *will* has been omitted)

The following are some other common contractions:

I	+ am	= I'm	it	+ is	= it's
I	+ have	= I've	it	+ has	= it's
I	+ had	= I'd	is	+ not	= isn't
who	+ is	= who's	could	+ not	= couldn't
do	+ not	= don't	I	+ would	= I'd
did	+ not	= didn't	they	+ are	= they're
let	+ us	= let's	there	+ is	= there's

Note   The combination *will* + *not* has an unusual contraction: *won't*.

Practice 1

Combine the following words into contractions. One is done for you.

she	+ is	= _she's_	you	+ will	= _____
you	+ have	= _____	we	+ would	= _____
have	+ not	= _____	could	+ not	= _____
he	+ has	= _____	they	+ will	= _____
we	+ are	= _____	does	+ not	= _____

Practice 2

Write the contraction for the words in parentheses.

Example   He (could not) _couldn't_ come.

1. I (did not) _____ like the movie, but the popcorn (was not) _____
    bad.
    An apostrophe replaces the letter *o* in both answers.

2. Tara (does not) _____ hide her feelings well, so if (she is) _____
    angry you will know it.

3. (You are) _____ taking the wrong approach with Len, as he (cannot)
    _____ stand being lectured.

4. This (is not) _____ the first time (you have) _____ embarrassed me
    in public.

5. (We would) _____ love to have you stay for dinner if you (do not)
    _____ mind eating leftovers.

Note   Even though contractions are common in everyday speech and in written dialogue, usually it is best to avoid them in formal writing.

Practice 3

Write five sentences using the apostrophe in different contractions.

1. _____
2. _____
3. _____
4. _____
5. _____

Four Contractions to Note Carefully

Four contractions that deserve special attention are *they're, it's, you're,* and *who's.* Sometimes these contractions are confused with the possessive words *their, its, your,* and *whose.* The following list shows the difference in meaning between the contractions and the possessive words.

Contractions	*Possessive Words*
they're (means *they are*)	their (means *belonging to them*)
it's (means *it is* or *it has*)	its (means *belonging to it*)
you're (means *you are*)	your (means *belonging to you*)
who's (means *who is*)	whose (means *belonging to whom*)

Note   Possessive words are explained further on page 299.

Practice

Underline the correct form (the contraction or the possessive word) in each of the following sentences. Use the contraction whenever the two words of the contraction (*they are, it is, you are, who is*) would also fit.

1. (It's, Its) wonderful that (you're, your) grandmother is still so strong and active at eighty.

    The sentence contains one contraction and one possessive word.

2. I don't know (who's, whose) fault it is that the car battery is dead, but I know (who's, whose) the primary suspect.

3. (You're, Your) feeling nauseated because you did not open any windows while staining (you're, your) living-room floor.

4. (They're, There) are some people who insist on acting gloomy no matter how well (they're, their) lives are going.

5. (It's, Its) hard to be pleasant to neighbors who always keep (they're, their) stereo on too loud.

Apostrophe to Show Ownership or Possession

To show ownership or possession, we can use such words as *belongs to, owned by,* or (most commonly) *of.*

the knapsack *that belongs to* Lola

the grades *possessed by* Travis

the house *owned by* my mother

the sore arm *of* the pitcher

But the apostrophe plus *s* (if the word does not end in *-s*) is often the quickest and easiest way to show possession. Thus we can say:

Lola's knapsack

Travis's grades

my mother's house

the pitcher's sore arm

Points to Remember

1 The *'s* goes with the owner or possessor (in the examples given, *Lola, Travis, mother,* and *pitcher*). What follows is the person or thing possessed (in the examples given, *knapsack, grades, house,* and *sore arm*). An easy way to determine the owner or possessor is to ask the question "Who owns it?" In the first example, the answer to the question "Who owns the knapsack?" is *Lola.* Therefore, the *'s* goes with *Lola.*

2 In handwriting, there should always be a break between the word and the *'s.*

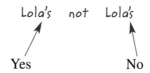

3 A singular word ending in *-s* (such as *Travis* in the earlier example) also shows possession by adding an apostrophe plus *s* (Travis's).

Practice 1

Rewrite the italicized part of each sentence below, using *'s* to show possession. Remember that the *'s* goes with the owner or possessor.

Examples   *The motorcycle owned by Clyde* is a frightening machine.
Clyde's motorcycle

The roommate of my brother is a sweet and friendly person.
My brother's roommate

1. The *voice of the singer* had a relaxing effect on the crowd.
   Who owns the *voice?*

2. *The garage of Dawn* has so much furniture stored in it that there's no room for her car.

3. *The law of Murphy* states, "Anything that can go wrong will go wrong."

_____

4. All the financial-planning information has been stored in the *memory of the computer.*

_____

5. Because *the mother of my wife* is in jail for forgery, I call her my mother-outlaw.

_____

6. Where is the rest of *the meat loaf of yesterday,* which I was planning to eat for lunch?

_____

7. *The promotion of my sister* to vice president of the company was well earned.

_____

8. *The bratty little brother of Alexis* has grown up to become a charming young man.

_____

9. The judges reversed *the call of the referee* after they viewed the videotaped replay.

_____

10. Thousands of gallons of crude oil spilled into the ocean when *the hull of the tanker* ruptured in the storm.

_____

Practice 2

Underline the word in each sentence that needs *'s*. Then write the word correctly in the space at the left.

_____   1. The trainer removed a nail from the horse hoof.
                    The hoof belongs to the horse.

_____   2. My brother appetite is like a bottomless pit.

_____   3. Arnie pulled his young son hand away from the kerosene heater.

_____   4. The comedian trademarks were long cigars and red socks.

_____   5. No matter when you dial the landlord number, nobody answers the phone.

_____   6. The assistant manager always takes credit for Ted ideas.

_____ 7. We all froze when the bank teller wig fell off.

_____ 8. Some people never feel other people problems are their concern.

_____ 9. Nita hires an accountant to prepare her dance studio tax returns each year.

_____ 10. The screen door slammed on the little girl fingers.

Practice 3

Add *'s* to each of the following words to make it the possessor or owner of something. Then write sentences using the words. Your sentences can be serious or playful. One is done for you as an example.

1. Cary _____ Cary's _____

   Cary's hair is bright red. _____

2. teacher _____

   _____

3. insect _____

   _____

4. husband _____

   _____

5. salesperson _____

   _____

Apostrophe versus Possessive Pronouns

Do not use an apostrophe with possessive pronouns. They already show ownership. Possessive pronouns include *his, hers, its, yours, ours,* and *theirs.*

Incorrect	Correct
The bookstore lost its' lease.	The bookstore lost its lease.
The racing bikes were theirs'.	The racing bikes were theirs.
The change is yours'.	The change is yours.
His' problems are ours', too.	His problems are ours, too.
Her' cold is worse than his'.	Her cold is worse than his.

Apostrophe versus Simple Plurals

When you want to make a word plural, just add *s* at the end of the word. Do *not* add an apostrophe. For example, the plural of the word *movie* is *movies,* not *movie's* or *movies'.*

Look at this sentence:

When Sally's cat began catching birds, the neighbors called the police.

The words *birds* and *neighbors* are simple plurals, meaning more than one bird, more than one neighbor. The plural is shown by adding *-s* only. (More information about plurals starts on page 352.) On the other hand, the *'s* after *Sally* shows possession—that Sally owns the cat.

Practice

In the spaces provided under each sentence, add the one apostrophe needed and explain why the other words ending in *s* are simple plurals.

Example   Originally, the cuffs of mens pants were meant for cigar ashes.

cuffs: *simple plural meaning more than one cuff*

mens: *men's, meaning "belonging to men"*

ashes: *simple plural meaning more than one ash*

1. The pizza parlors aromas seeped through the vents to our second-floor apartment.
   What possesses the *aromas?*

   parlors: _____

   aromas: _____

   vents: _____

2. A police cars siren echoed through the streets and buildings of the city.

   cars: _____

   streets: _____

   buildings: _____

3. Karens tomato plants are taller than the six-foot stakes she used to support them.

   Karens: _____

   plants: _____

   stakes: _____

4. Because of the lakes high bacteria level, officials prohibited boating, swimming, and fishing there.

lakes: _____

officials: _____

5. I have considered applying for many positions, but an exterminators job is not one of them.

positions: _____

exterminators: _____

6. The candlelights glow fell gently on the pale white plates and ruby-red goblets.

candlelights: _____

plates: _____

goblets: _____

7. Crackers layered with cheese and apple slices are my fathers favorite snack.

Crackers: _____

slices: _____

fathers: _____

8. Within a day that insects eggs will turn into glistening white worms.

insects: _____

eggs: _____

worms: _____

9. Seabirds skidding along the oceans edge at midnight looked like miniature moonlight surfers.

Seabirds: _____

oceans: _____

surfers: _____

10. My daughters prayers were answered when the heavy snow caused all the schools in the area to close for the rest of the week.

daughters: _____

prayers: _____

schools: _____

Apostrophe with Plural Words Ending in -s

Plurals that end in -s show possession simply by adding the apostrophe, rather than an apostrophe plus *s*.

Both of my *neighbors'* homes have been burglarized recently.

The many *workers'* complaints were ignored by the company.

All the *campers'* tents were damaged by the hailstorm.

Practice

Add an apostrophe where needed.

1. The nurses union protested my layoff.
   Whose *union* is it?
2. My two sisters feet are the same size, so they share their shoes.
3. The lions keeper has worked with those lions since birth.
4. The Tylers new television set was mistakenly delivered to our house.
5. The photo album that was lost contained my parents wedding pictures.

Collaborative Activity

Part A: Editing and Rewriting

Working with a partner, read the short paragraph below. Underline ten places where you could rewrite, using apostrophes to indicate contractions and possessives. Then rewrite those parts in the spaces that follow. Feel free to discuss the rewrite quietly with your partner and refer back to the chapter when necessary.

¹The dog of my neighbor is evil. ²For one thing, it barks constantly, even when there is nothing to bark at. ³Because of the constant barking of the dog, I can not sleep at night. ⁴The dog also growls menacingly whenever it sees me. ⁵One time, it tried to charge at me through the fence of my landlord. ⁶Luckily for me, the fence was strong enough to restrain the dog. ⁷I have tried to talk to my neighbor about the problem, but he refuses to listen. ⁸He thinks there is nothing wrong with the behavior of the dog. ⁹But that is because the dog does not show its fangs to him.

Continued

_____

_____

_____

_____

_____

Part B: Creating Sentences

Working with a partner, write sentences that use apostrophes as directed.

1. Write a sentence describing something a friend owns. For instance, you might mention a pet or a material possession.

   _____

2. Using an apostrophe to show a contraction, write a sentence about something at school or work that you feel is wrong and needs to be changed.

   _____

3. Write a sentence that correctly uses the word *teachers*. Then write a second sentence that correctly uses the word *teacher's*.

   _____

   _____

Reflective Activity

1. Look at the paragraph about the dog that you revised above. How has adding apostrophes affected the paragraph?
2. Explain what it is about apostrophes that you find most difficult to remember and apply. Use an example to make your point clear.

■ Review Test 1

In each sentence, cross out the two words that need apostrophes. Then write the words correctly in the spaces provided.

1. That authors latest horror novel isnt so horrifying.

    _____   _____

2. "I dont get it," I confessed after hearing Pams long, complicated joke.

    _____   _____

3. Luckily, the motorcycles gas tank hadnt been scratched in the collision.

    _____   _____

4. Whos been stealing the Sunday papers from my doorstep before Im awake?

    _____   _____

5. Nadias aunts never start the day without asking an astrologers advice.

    _____   _____

6. I too would like to take a shower, if theres any water left by the time youre finished.

    _____   _____

7. Olivia watched sadly as the highway departments bulldozer demolished the house shed grown up in.

    _____   _____

8. Sylvia wasnt on time for her first day of work because her mothers car broke down on the highway.

    _____   _____

9. The coach said theres no room on the team for players who dont want to win.

    _____   _____

10. The authorities guess is that a radical protest group put the toxic chemical in the towns water supply.

    _____   _____

■ Review Test 2

Rewrite the following sentences, changing the underlined words into either a contraction or a possessive.

1. Joe <u>was not</u> happy to hear the high-pitched sound of the <u>drill of the dentist</u>.

   _____

   _____

2. The weather <u>forecast of today</u> assured us that <u>it is</u> definitely going to be sunny, cloudy, or rainy.

   _____

   _____

3. The enthusiasm of my brother Manny for baseball is so great that <u>he will</u> even wear his glove and cap when he watches a game on TV.

   _____

   _____

4. Many parents think <u>the influence of television</u> is to blame for <u>the poor performance of their children</u> in school.

   _____

   _____

5. I was shocked by the <u>announcement of my friend</u> that he was going to marry a girl <u>he had</u> dated for only two months.

   _____

   _____

25 Quotation Marks

Introductory Activity

Read the following scene and underline all the words enclosed within quotation marks. Your instructor may also have you dramatize the scene with one person reading the narration and three persons acting the speaking parts—Clyde, Charlotte, and Sam. The two speakers should imagine the scene as part of a stage play and try to make their words seem as real and true-to-life as possible.

At a party that Clyde and his wife Charlotte recently hosted, Clyde got angry at a guy named Sam who kept bothering Charlotte. "Listen, man," Clyde said, "what's this thing you have for my wife? There are lots of other women at this party."

"Relax," Sam replied. "Charlotte is very attractive, and I enjoy talking with her."

"Listen, Sam," Charlotte said. "I've already told you three times that I don't want to talk to you anymore. Please leave me alone."

"Look, there's no law that says I can't talk to you if I want to," Sam challenged.

"Sam, I'm only going to say this once," Clyde warned. "Lay off my wife, or leave this party *now*."

Sam grinned at Clyde smugly. "You've got good liquor here. Why should I leave? Besides, I'm not done talking with Charlotte."

Clyde went to his basement and was back a minute later holding a two-by-four. "I'm giving you a choice," Clyde said. "Leave by the door or I'll slam you out the window."

Sam left by the door.

1. On the basis of the above selection, what is the purpose of quotation marks?

   _____

2. Do commas and periods that come after a quotation go inside or outside the quotation marks?

   _____

Answers are on page 692.

ALLWRITE!
24.3

The two main uses of quotation marks are as follows. Each use is explained here.

1 To set off the exact words of a speaker or writer

2 To set off the titles of short works

Quotation Marks to Set Off the Words of a Speaker or Writer

Use quotation marks when you want to show the exact words of a speaker or writer.

"Who left the cap off the toothpaste?" Lola demanded.
(Quotation marks set off the exact words that Lola spoke.)

Ben Franklin wrote, "Keep your eyes wide open before marriage, half shut afterward."
(Quotation marks set off the exact words that Ben Franklin wrote.)

"You're never too young," Aunt Fern told me, "to have a heart attack."
(Two pairs of quotation marks are used to enclose the aunt's exact words.)

Maria complained, "I look so old some days. Even makeup doesn't help. I feel as though I'm painting a corpse!"
(Note that the end quotes do not come until the end of Maria's speech. Place quotation marks before the first quoted word of a speech and after the last quoted word. As long as no interruption occurs in the speech, do not use quotation marks for each new sentence.)

Punctuation Hint   In the four examples above, notice that a comma sets off the quoted part from the rest of the sentence. Also observe that commas and periods at the end of a quotation always go *inside* quotation marks.

Complete the following statements, which explain how capital letters, commas, and periods are used in quotations. Refer to the four examples as guides.

• Every quotation begins with a _____ letter.

• When a quotation is split (as in the sentence about Aunt Fern), the second part does not begin with a capital letter unless it is a _____ sentence.

• _____ are typically used to separate the quoted part of a sentence from the rest of the sentence.

- Commas and periods that come at the end of a quotation go _____ quotation marks.

The answers are *capital, new, Commas,* and *inside.*

Practice 1

Insert quotation marks where needed in the sentences that follow.

1. The chilling bumper sticker read, You can't hug children with nuclear arms.
   Put quotes around the words on the sticker.

2. One day we'll look back on this argument, and it will seem funny, Bruce assured Rosa.

3. Hey, lady, this is an express line! shouted the cashier to the woman with a full basket.

4. My grandfather was fond of saying, Happiness is found along the way, not at the end of the road.

5. When will I be old enough to pay the adult fare? the child asked.

6. On his deathbed, Oscar Wilde is supposed to have said, Either this wallpaper goes or I do.

7. The sign on my neighbor's front door reads, Never mind the dog. Beware of owner.

8. I'm not afraid to die, said Woody Allen. I just don't want to be there when it happens.

9. My son once told me, Sometimes I wish I were little again. Then I wouldn't have to make so many decisions.

10. I don't feel like cooking tonight, Eve said to Adam. Let's just have fruit.

Practice 2

Rewrite the following sentences, adding quotation marks where needed. Use a capital letter to begin a quotation and use a comma to set off a quoted part from the rest of the sentence.

Example   I'm getting tired Sally said.
          "I'm getting tired," Sally said.

1. Simon said take three giant steps forward.
   Add a comma and put quotes around Simon's words.

   _____

   _____

2. Please don't hang up before leaving a message stated the telephone recording.

_____

_____

3. Clark Kent asked a man on the street where is the nearest phone booth?

_____

_____

4. You dirtied every pan in the kitchen just to scramble some eggs Rico said in disgust.

_____

_____

5. Nothing can be done for your broken little toe, the doctor said. You have to wait for it to heal.

_____

_____

Practice 3

1. Write three quotations that appear in the first part of a sentence.

    Example   *"Let's go shopping," I suggested.*

    a. _____

    b. _____

    c. _____

2. Write three quotations that appear at the end of a sentence.

    Example   *Bob asked, "Have you had lunch yet?"*

    a. _____

    b. _____

    c. _____

3. Write three quotations that appear at the beginning and end of a sentence.

    Example   *"If the bus doesn't come soon," Mary said, "we'll freeze."*

    a. _____

    b. _____

    c. _____

Indirect Quotations

An indirect quotation is a rewording of someone else's comments rather than a word-for-word direct quotation. The word *that* often signals an indirect quotation.

Direct Quotation	*Indirect Quotation*
George said, "My son is a daredevil." (George's exact spoken words are given, so quotation marks are used.)	George said that his son is a daredevil. (We learn George's words indirectly, so no quotation marks are used.)
Carol's note to Arnie read, "I'm at the neighbors'. Give me a call." (The exact words that Carol wrote in the note are given, so quotation marks are used.)	Carol left a note for Arnie saying that she would be at the neighbors' and he should give her a call. (We learn Carol's words indirectly, so no quotation marks are used.)

Practice 1

Rewrite the following sentences, changing words as necessary to convert the sentences into direct quotations. The first one is done for you as an example.

1. Agnes told me as we left work that Herb got a raise.
   Agnes said to me as we left work, "Herb got a raise."

2. I said that it was hard to believe, since Herb is a do-nothing.

   _____

   _____

3. Agnes replied that even so, he's gone up in the world.

   _____

   _____

4. I told her that she must be kidding.

   _____

   _____

5. Agnes laughed and said that Herb was moved from the first to the fourth floor today.

   _____

   _____

Practice 2

Rewrite the following sentences, converting each direct quotation into an indirect statement. In each case you will have to add the word *that* or *if* and change other words as well.

Example   The barber asked Fred, "Have you noticed how your hair is thinning?"
The barber asked Fred if he had noticed how his hair was thinning.

_____

1. My doctor said, "You need to lose weight."
   Begin the sentence with *My doctor said that.*

   _____

   _____

2. Lola asked Tony, "Don't you ever wash your car?"

   _____

   _____

3. The police officer asked me, "Do you know how fast you were going?"

   _____

   _____

4. Jane whispered, "Harold's so boring he lights up a room when he leaves it."

   _____

   _____

5. The instructor said, "Movies are actually a series of still pictures."

   _____

   _____

Quotation Marks to Set Off the Titles of Short Works

24.3c

Titles of short works are usually set off by quotation marks, while titles of long works are underlined. Use quotation marks to set off the titles of short works such as articles in books, newspapers, or magazines; chapters in a book; and short stories, poems, and songs. On the other hand, you should underline the titles of books, newspapers, magazines, plays, movies, music albums, and television shows. See the following examples.

Quotation Marks	*Underlines*
the article "The Toxic Tragedy"	in the book <u>Who's Poisoning America</u>
the article "New Cures for Headaches"	in the newspaper the <u>New York Times</u>
the article "When the Patient Plays Doctor"	in the magazine <u>Family Health</u>
the chapter "Connecting with Kids"	in the book <u>Straight Talk</u>
the story "The Dead"	in the book <u>Dubliners</u>
the poem "Birches"	in the book <u>The Complete Poems of Robert Frost</u>
the song "Some Enchanted Evening"	in the album <u>South Pacific</u>
	the television show <u>Friends</u>
	the movie <u>Rear Window</u>

Note In printed form, the titles of long works are set off by italics—slanted type that looks *like this.*

Practice

Use quotation marks or underlines as needed.

1. My sister programmed her VCR so she won't have to miss any more episodes of General Hospital.
   Underline the name of the TV show.

2. Rita grabbed the National Enquirer and eagerly began to read the article I Had a Space Alien's Baby.

3. Our exam will cover two chapters, The Study of Heredity and The Origin of Diversity, in our biology textbook, Life.

4. The last song on the bluegrass program was called I Ain't Broke but I'm Badly Bent.

5. The classic 1980s movie Stand By Me was actually based on The Body, a short story written by Stephen King.

6. At last night's performance of Annie Get Your Gun, the audience joined the cast in singing There's No Business Like Show Business.

7. A typical article in Cosmopolitan will have a title like How to Hook a Man without Letting Him Know You're Fishing.

8. One way Joanne deals with depression is to get out her Man of La Mancha album and play the song The Impossible Dream.

9. I read the article How Good Is Your Breakfast? in Consumer Reports while munching a doughnut this morning.

10. According to a Psychology Today article titled Home on the Street, there are 36,000 people living on New York City's sidewalks.

Other Uses of Quotation Marks

Here are two more uses of quotation marks.

1 To set off special words or phrases from the rest of a sentence (when italic is not used for this purpose):

Many people spell the words "all right" as one word, "alright," instead of correctly spelling them as two words.

I have trouble telling the difference between "principal" and "principle."

2 To mark off a quotation within a quotation. For this purpose, single quotation marks (' ') are used:

Ben Franklin said, "The noblest question in the world is, 'What good may I do in it?'"

"If you want to have a scary experience," Nick told Fran, "read Stephen King's story 'The Mangler' in his book *Night Shift.*"

Collaborative Activity

Part A: Editing and Rewriting

Working with a partner, read the short paragraph below and circle the places where quotation marks are needed. Then use the space provided to rewrite the paragraph, adding quotation marks where needed. Feel free to discuss the rewrite quietly with your partner and refer back to the chapter when necessary.

Continued

[1]Harry and his friend Susan got stuck in an elevator. [2]Another man was stuck with them. [3]Harry turned to Susan and asked, Has this ever happened to you before?

[4]Once, she said. [5]About ten years ago in a department store. [6]We weren't stuck long.

[7]Harry took a deep breath. [8]We're lucky only three of us are here. [9]I don't like being closed up in small places, especially crowded ones.

[10]Then the other man asked, Is there a phone or something here so we can talk to somebody?

[11]Susan looked around and noticed a small panel in the corner of the elevator. [12]A sign just over the panel read Open in Case of Emergency.

[13]I think it might be in there, she said, pointing to the sign.

[14]The man opened the panel, found a telephone, and dialed the security number written nearby. [15]Can anyone hear me? he asked.

[16]A voice on the phone said, Yes, and we know you're stuck. [17]Just wait a few minutes.

[18]When Harry heard that people knew about their problem, he let out a sigh. [19]I sure hope they can fix this quickly, he said softly, wringing his hands.

[20]Susan put her arm around him and smiled. [21]Don't worry. [22]We'll be out of here in no time.

_____

_____

_____

_____

_____

_____

_____

_____

_____

_____

Continued

Part B: Creating Sentences

Working with a partner, write sentences that use quotation marks as directed.

1. Write a sentence in which you quote a favorite expression of someone you know. Identify the person's relationship to you.

   Example   My brother Sam often says after a meal, "That wasn't bad at all."

   _____

   _____

2. Write a quotation that contains the words *Tony asked Lola*. Write a second quotation that includes the words *Lola replied*.

   _____

   _____

3. Write a sentence that interests or amuses you from a book, magazine, or newspaper. Identify the title and author of the book, magazine article, or newspaper article.

   Example   In her book <u>At Wit's End</u>, Erma Bombeck advises, "Never go to a doctor whose office plants have died."

   _____

   _____

Reflective Activity

1. Look at the paragraph about the elevator that you revised above. Explain how adding quotation marks has affected the paragraph.

2. What would writing be like without quotation marks? Explain, using an example, how quotation marks are important to understanding writing.

3. Explain what it is about quotation marks that is most difficult for you to remember and apply. Use an example to make your point clear. Feel free to refer back to anything in this chapter.

■ Review Test 1

Place quotation marks around the exact words of a speaker or writer in the sentences that follow.

1. Give me a break! Charlie shouted to no one in particular.
2. My mother always says, Some are wise, and some are otherwise.
3. Why do men continue to wear ties when they serve no purpose? asked Paul.
4. Take all you want, but eat all you take, read the sign in the cafeteria.
5. One of Mark Twain's famous lines is, Man is the only animal that blushes— or needs to.
6. My friend the radio announcer loses his voice every time we drive under a bridge, said the comedian.
7. The first time my daughter had a headache, she told me, Mommy, I have a pain in my brain.
8. If your parachute doesn't open, the skydiving instructor joked, bring it back, and we'll give you a new one.
9. The novelist ended a letter to his brother by saying, I'm sorry for writing such a long letter. I didn't have time for a shorter one.
10. Work fascinates me, said the comedian. I could sit and watch it for hours.

■ Review Test 2

Place quotation marks around the exact words of a speaker in the sentences that follow. Three of the sentences contain indirect quotations and do not require quotation marks.

Example   Soon after moving into their new house, Mike said to Marian, "Why don't we have a party? It'd be a good way to meet all our neighbors."

1. Nice idea, said Marian, but way too much work.
2. It won't be that bad. We'll grill hamburgers and ask everybody to bring a side dish, Mike answered.
3. Marian said that she would agree to the idea if Mike called all the guests.
4. Hi, this is Mike Josephs, your new neighbor in 44B, Mike said each time he called someone.
5. Afterward he told Marian that everything was under control.
6. I told them we'd provide burgers and plenty of drinks, Mike explained, and they'll bring everything else.

7. When the party started, the first guests arrived saying, We brought potato salad—we hope that's all right!

8. Then guests number two, three, and four arrived, also announcing that they had brought potato salad.

9. As the sixth bowl of potato salad arrived, Mike mumbled to Marian, Maybe I should have made some more suggestions about what people should bring.

10. Oh, well, I really love potato salad, Marian said.

■ Review Test 3

Go through the comics section of a newspaper to find a comic strip that amuses you. Be sure to choose a strip where two or more characters are speaking to each other. Write a full description that will enable people who have not read the comic strip to visualize it clearly and appreciate its humor. Describe the setting and action in each panel and enclose the words of the speakers in quotation marks.

26 Comma

Introductory Activity

Commas often (though not always) signal a minor break or pause in a sentence. Each of the six pairs of sentences below illustrates one of six main uses of the comma. Read each pair of sentences aloud and place a comma wherever you feel a slight pause occurs. Then choose the rule that applies from the box at the bottom of the page, and write its letter on the line provided.

___ 1. You can use a credit card write out a check or provide cash.

The old house was infested with red ants roaches and mice.

___ 2. To start the car depress the accelerator and turn the ignition key.

Before you go hiking buy a comfortable pair of shoes.

___ 3. Leeches creatures that suck human blood are valuable to medical science.

George Derek who was just arrested was a classmate of mine.

___ 4. Our professor said the exam would be easy but I thought it was difficult.

Wind howled through the trees and rain pounded against the window.

___ 5. Emily asked "Why is it so hard to remember your dreams the next day?"

"I am so tired after work" Lily said "that I fall asleep right away."

___ 6. Bert has driven 1500000 accident-free miles in his job as a trucker.

The Gates Trucking Company of Newark New Jersey gave Bert an award on August 26 2004 for his superior safety record.

---

a.	separate items in a list
b.	separate introductory material from the sentence
c.	separate words that interrupt the sentence
d.	separate complete thoughts in a sentence
e.	separate direct quotations from the rest of the sentence
f.	separate numbers, addresses, and dates in everyday writing

Answers are on page 693.

Six Main Uses of the Comma

23.2

Commas are used mainly as follows:

1 To separate items in a series

2 To set off introductory material

3 On both sides of words that interrupt the flow of thought in a sentence

4 Between two complete thoughts connected by *and, but, for, or, nor, so, yet*

5 To set off a direct quotation from the rest of a sentence

6 For certain everyday material

You may find it helpful to remember that the comma often marks a slight pause, or break, in a sentence. These pauses or breaks occur at the points where the six main comma rules apply. Sentence examples for each of the comma rules are given on the following pages; read these sentences aloud and listen for the minor pauses or breaks that are signaled by commas.

However, you should keep in mind that commas are far more often overused than underused. As a general rule, you should *not* use a comma unless a given comma rule applies or unless a comma is otherwise needed to help a sentence read clearly. A good rule of thumb is that "when in doubt" about whether to use a comma, it is often best to "leave it out."

After reviewing each of the comma rules that follow, you will practice adding commas that are needed and omitting commas that are not needed.

1 Comma between Items in a Series

Use a comma to separate items in a series.

Magazines, paperback novels, and textbooks crowded the shelves.

Hard-luck Sam needs a loan, a good-paying job, and a close friend.

Pat sat in the doctor's office, checked her watch, and flipped nervously through a magazine.

Lola bit into the ripe, juicy apple.

More and more people entered the crowded, noisy stadium.

Note   A comma is used between two descriptive words in a series only if *and* inserted between the words sounds natural. You could say:

Lola bit into the ripe *and* juicy apple.

More and more people entered the crowded *and* noisy stadium.

But notice in the following sentences that the descriptive words do not sound natural when *and* is inserted between them. In such cases, no comma is used.

The model wore a classy black dress. ("A classy *and* black dress" doesn't sound right, so no comma is used.)

Dr. Van Helsing noticed two tiny puncture marks on the patient's neck. ("Two *and* tiny puncture marks" doesn't sound right, so no comma is used.)

Practice 1

Place commas between items in a series.

1. Many of the refugees wandered around without work food or a place to live.
2. Ice cream crushed candy Pepsi and popcorn formed a glue-like compound on the movie theater's floor.
3. We finally drove across the Arizona–New Mexico border after eight hours four hundred miles and three rest stops.

Practice 2

For each item, cross out the one comma that is not needed. Add the one comma that is needed between items in a series.

1. I discovered gum wrappers, pennies and a sock hidden, under the seats when I vacuumed my car.
2. Squirrels Canadian geese, two white swans, and clouds of mosquitoes, populate Farwell Park.
3. Lewis dribbled twice, spun to his left and lofted his patented hook shot over the outstretched arms, of the Panthers' center.

2 Comma after Introductory Material

Use a comma to set off introductory material.

Fearlessly, Lola picked up the slimy slug.

Just to annoy Tony, she let it crawl along her arm.

Although I have a black belt in karate, I decided to go easy on the demented bully who had kicked sand in my face.

Mumbling under her breath, the woman picked over the tomatoes.

Note   If the introductory material is brief, the comma is sometimes omitted. In the activities here, you should include the comma.

Practice 1

Place commas after introductory material.

1. When all is said and done a lot more is said than done.
   The last introductory word is *done.*
2. If you mark your suitcase with colored tape it will be easier to find at the baggage counter.
3. Feeling brave and silly at the same time Anita volunteered to go onstage and help the magician.

Practice 2

For each item, cross out the one comma that is not needed. Add the one comma that is needed after introductory material.

1. Using metallic cords from her Christmas presents young Ali made several bracelets for herself. After that, she took a long ribbon, and tied a bow around her dog's head.
   Add a comma to the first sentence and omit the comma in the second.
2. As the bride smiled and strolled past me down the aisle I saw a bead of sweat roll, from her forehead down her cheek. Remembering my own wedding, I knew she wasn't sweating from the heat.
3. When my children were young, I wrote interesting anecdotes about them in a notebook. For example I wrote a note to remind me, that my son once wanted to be a yo-yo maker.

3 Comma around Words
Interrupting the Flow of Thought

Use a comma before and after words that interrupt the flow of thought in a sentence.

The car, cleaned and repaired, is ready to be sold.

Martha, our new neighbor, used to work as a bouncer at Rexy's Tavern.

Taking long walks, especially after dark, helps me sort out my thoughts.

Usually you can "hear" words that interrupt the flow of thought in a sentence. However, when you are not sure if certain words are interrupters, remove them from the sentence. If it still makes sense without the words, you know that the words are interrupters and that the information they give is nonessential. Such nonessential information is set off with commas. In the following sentence,

Susie Hall, who is my best friend, won a new car in the *Reader's Digest* sweepstakes.

the words *who is my best friend* are extra information, not needed to identify the subject of the sentence, *Susie Hall.* Put commas around such nonessential information. On the other hand, in the sentence

The woman who is my best friend won a new car in the *Reader's Digest* sweepstakes.

The words *who is my best friend* supply essential information that we need to identify the woman. If the words were removed from the sentence, we would no longer know which woman won the sweepstakes. Commas are not used around such essential information.

Here is another example:

The Shining, a novel by Stephen King, is the scariest book I've ever read.

Here the words *a novel by Stephen King* are extra information, not needed to identify the subject of the sentence, *The Shining.* Commas go around such nonessential information. On the other hand, in the sentence

Stephen King's novel *The Shining* is the scariest book I've ever read.

the words *The Shining* are needed to identify the novel. Commas are not used around such essential information.

Most of the time you will be able to "hear" words that interrupt the flow of thought in a sentence and will not have to think about whether the words are essential or nonessential.*

Practice 1

Add commas to set off interrupting words.

1. The dancer aided by members of the chorus hobbled across the stage toward the wings.
   The interrupting words are *aided by members of the chorus.*

2. Mr. and Mrs. Anderson who were married on the Fourth of July named their first child "Freedom."

3. The repairman unaware of the grease on his shoes left a black trail from our front door to the washing machine.

*Some instructors refer to nonessential or extra information that is set off by commas as a *nonrestrictive clause.* Essential information that interrupts the flow of thought is called a *restrictive clause.* No commas are used to set off a restrictive clause.

Practice 2

For each item, cross out the one comma that is not needed. Add the comma that is needed to complete the setting off of interrupting words.

1. All trees, even the most gigantic are only 1 percent living tissue; the rest, is deadwood.

   The interrupting words are *even the most gigantic.*

2. The city council in a rare fit, of wisdom, established a series of bicycle paths around town.

3. John Adams and Thomas Jefferson, the second and third presidents, of the United States died on the same day in 1826.

4. My aunt, a talkative, woman married a patient man who is a wonderful listener.

4 Comma between Complete Thoughts Connected by a Joining Word

Use a comma between two complete thoughts connected by *and, but, for, or, nor, so, yet.*

My parents threatened to throw me out of the house, so I had to stop playing the drums.

The polyester bedsheets had a gorgeous design, but they didn't feel as comfortable as plain cotton sheets.

The teenage girls walked along the hot summer streets, and the teenage boys drove by in their shined-up cars.

Notes

a The comma is optional when the complete thoughts are short:

Hal relaxed but Bob kept working.

The soda was flat so I poured it away.

We left school early for the furnace had broken down.

b Be careful not to use a comma in sentences having *one* subject and a *double* verb. The comma is used only in sentences made up of two complete thoughts (two subjects and two verbs). In the sentence

Mary lay awake that stormy night and listened to the thunder crashing.

there is only one subject (*Mary*) and a double verb (*lay* and *listened*). No comma is needed. Likewise, the sentence

The quarterback kept the ball and plunged across the goal line for a touch-down.

has only one subject (*quarterback*) and a double verb (*kept* and *plunged*); therefore, no comma is needed.

Practice

Place a comma before a joining word that connects two complete thoughts (two subjects and two verbs). Remember, do *not* place a comma within sentences that have only one subject and a double verb. Mark sentences that are correct with a *C*.

1. The apartment Kate looked at was clean and spacious but the rent was too expensive for her budget.
   But connects two complete thoughts.
2. Our power went out during the thunderstorm so we decided to eat dinner by candlelight.
3. Eddie is building a kayak in his garage and plans to take it down the Columbia River next year.
4. I desperately need more storage space for I can't seem to throw anything away.
5. The helicopter hovered overhead and lowered a rescue line to the downed pilot.
6. Travis was going to quit his job at the supermarket but he changed his mind after getting a raise.
7. One of the men got ready to leave work at four but put his coat away upon seeing his boss.
8. The family expected Valerie to go to college but she went to work after eloping with her boyfriend.
9. Bobby pleaded with his parents to buy him a personal computer for his schoolwork but he spends most of his time playing games on it.
10. The doctor examined me for less than ten minutes and then presented me with a bill for ninety dollars.

5 Comma with Direct Quotations

Use a comma to set off a direct quotation from the rest of a sentence.

"Please take a number," said the deli clerk.

Fred told Martha, "I've just signed up for a course on web-page design."

"Those who sling mud," a famous politician once said, "usually lose ground."

"Reading this book," complained Stan, "is about as interesting as watching paint dry."

Note   Commas and periods at the end of a quotation go inside quotation marks. See also page 308.

Practice 1

In each sentence, add the one or more commas needed to set off the quoted material.

1. The five-year-old boy said "Mommy, I have a bad headache in my tummy."
   Add a comma before the quoted material.
2. "The best way to get rid of a temptation" Oscar Wilde advised "is to yield to it."
3. "The movie will scare the whole family" wrote the reviewer.

Practice 2

In each item, cross out the one comma that is not needed to set off a quotation. Add the comma that is needed to set off a quotation from the rest of the sentence.

1. "If you're looking for a career change," read the poster, in the subway station "consider the US Armed Forces."
   Add a comma before the quoted material.
2. "Your arms look fine" said the swimming instructor, "but you keep forgetting, to kick."
3. "Did you really think" the judge asked, the defendant, "you could kill both your parents and then ask for mercy because you're an orphan?"

6 Comma with Everyday Material

Use a comma with certain everyday material, as shown in the following sections.

Persons Spoken To

I think, Sally, that you should go to bed.

Please turn down the stereo, Mark.

Please, sir, can you spare a dollar?

Dates

Our house was burglarized on June 28, 2004, and two weeks later on July 11, 2004.

Addresses

Lola's sister lives at 342 Red Oak Drive, Los Angeles, California 90057.
She is moving to Manchester, Vermont, after her divorce.

Note   No comma is used before a zip code.

Openings and Closings of Letters

Dear Marilyn,	Sincerely,
Dear John,	Truly yours,

Note   In formal letters, a colon is used after the opening:

Dear Sir:
Dear Madam:

Numbers

Government officials estimate that Americans spend about 785,000,000
hours a year filling out federal forms.

Practice

Place commas where needed.

1. Excuse me madam but your scarf is in my soup.
   Two commas are needed.
2. Before age eighteen the average child spends 6000 hours in school and 15000
   hours watching television.
3. The famous ocean liner *Titanic* sank in the Atlantic Ocean on April 15 1912.
4. Dear Teresa

   What do you think of this psychology lecture? Will you meet me for lunch
   after class? I'll treat. Pass me your answer right away.

                                                            Love
                                                            Jeff
5. The zoo in Washington D.C. purchases 50000 pounds of meat; 6500 loaves
   of bread; 114,000 live crickets; and other foods for its animals each year.

Unnecessary Use of Commas

Remember that if no clear rule applies for using a comma, it is usually better not to use a comma. As stated earlier, "When in doubt, leave it out." Following are some typical examples of unnecessary commas.

Incorrect

Sharon told me, that my socks were different colors.

(A comma is not used before *that* unless the flow of thought is interrupted.)

The union negotiations, dragged on for three days.

(Do not use a comma between a simple subject and verb.)

I waxed all the furniture, and cleaned the windows.

(Use a comma before *and* only with more than two items in a series or when *and* joins two complete thoughts.)

Sharon carried, the baby into the house.

(Do not use a comma between a verb and its object.)

I had a clear view, of the entire robbery.

(Do not use a comma before a prepositional phrase.)

Practice

Cross out commas that do not belong. Some commas are correct. Do not add any commas.

1. We grew a pumpkin last year, that weighed over one hundred pounds.
   The comma is not needed.
2. Anyone with a failing grade, must report to the principal.
3. Last weekend a grizzly bear attacked a hiker, who got too close to its cubs.
4. After watching my form, on the high diving board, Mr. Riley, my instructor, asked me if I had insurance.
5. Rosa flew first to Los Angeles, and then she went to visit her parents, in Mexico City.
6. The tall muscular man wearing the dark sunglasses, is a professional wrestler.
7. Onions, radishes, and potatoes, seem to grow better in cooler climates.
8. Whenever Vincent is in Las Vegas, you can find him at the blackjack table, or the roulette wheel.

9. While I watched in disbelief, my car rolled down the hill, and through the front window of a Chinese restaurant.

10. The question, sir, is not, whether you committed the crime, but, when you committed the crime.

Collaborative Activity

Part A: Editing and Rewriting

Working with a partner, read carefully the short paragraph below and cross out the five misplaced commas. Then insert the ten additional commas needed. Feel free to discuss the rewrite quietly with your partner and refer back to the chapter when necessary.

Dear Teresa,

On Tuesday, May 4 2004 my husband, and I were unable to sleep because of the loud music coming from your apartment. When I first heard the music I didn't say anything to you because it was still early. But the music, along with loud, laughter and talking, continued until around four o'clock in the morning. At midnight, my husband went into the hallway to see what was happening and he ran into one of your guests. The man who seemed very drunk stared at him, and said "Go back to bed, old man." The next morning, we found beer cans pizza boxes, and cigarette butts, piled outside our door. This is unacceptable. We have written this letter to you as a warning. The next time something like this happens we will call the police, and the building manager. We don't want to cause trouble with you but we will not tolerate another incident like what happened that night.

Sincerely,

Rose Connelly

Continued

Part B: Creating Sentences

Working with a partner, write sentences that use commas as directed.

1. Write a sentence mentioning three items you want to get the next time you go to the store.

   _____

   _____

2. Write two sentences describing how you relax after getting home from school or work. Start the first sentence with *After* or *When*. Start the second sentence with *Next*.

   _____

   _____

3. Write a sentence that tells something about your favorite movie, book, television show, or song. Use the words *which is my favorite movie* (or *book, television show,* or *song*) after the name of the movie, book, television show, or song.

   _____

   _____

4. Write two complete thoughts about a person you know. The first thought should mention something that you like about the person. The second thought should mention something you don't like. Join the two thoughts with *but*.

   _____

   _____

5. Invent a line that Lola might say to Tony. Use the words *Lola said* in the sentence. Then include Tony's reply, using the words *Tony responded*.

   _____

   _____

6. Write a sentence about an important event in your life. Include the day, month, and year of the event.

   _____

   _____

Reflective Activity

1. Look at the letter that you revised above. Explain how adding commas has affected the paragraph.
2. What would writing be like without the comma? How do commas help writing?
3. What is the most difficult comma rule for you to remember and apply? Explain, giving an example.

■ **Review Test 1**

Insert commas where needed. In the space provided under each sentence, summarize briefly the rule that explains the use of the comma or commas.

1. As the usher turned his head two youngsters darted into the movie theater.

   _____

2. My boss it is rumored is about to be fired.

   _____

3. I found my father's dusty water-stained yearbook behind some pipes in the basement.

   _____

4. "Be careful what you wish for" an old saying goes "or you may get it."

   _____

5. My final mortgage payment on December 3 2011 seems light-years away.

   _____

6. We sat together on the riverbank watched the sun disappear and made plans for our divorce.

   _____

7. I panicked when I saw the flashing red lights behind me but the policeman just wanted to pass.

   _____

8. The burly umpire his shoes and trousers now covered with dirt pulled off his mask and angrily ejected the St. Louis manager from the game.

   _____

9. "Knock off the noise" Sam yelled to the children. "I'm talking long distance to your grandmother."

_____

10. Rubbing her eyes and clearing her throat Stella tried to sound human as she answered the early-morning call.

_____

■ Review Test 2

Insert commas where needed. One sentence does not need commas.

1. Some people believe that television can be addictive but I think they're wrong.
2. While there are people who turn on their sets upon waking up in the morning I don't do that.
3. I turn on my set only upon sitting down for breakfast and then I watch the _Today_ show with Katie Couric and Matt Lauer.
4. I don't need to watch game shows soap operas and situation comedies to get through the day.
5. Instead I watch all these programs simply because I enjoy them.
6. I also keep the television turned on all evening because thanks to cable there is always something decent to watch.
7. If I did not have good viewing choices I would flick the set off without hesitation.
8. Lots of people switch channels rapidly to preview what is on.
9. I on the other hand turn immediately to the channel I know I want.
10. In other words I am not addicted; I am a selective viewer who just happens to select a lot of shows.

■ Review Test 3

On separate paper, write six sentences, with each sentence demonstrating one of the six main comma rules.

27 Other Punctuation Marks

Introductory Activity

Each sentence below needs one of the following punctuation marks.

; — - ( ) :

See if you can insert the correct mark in each case.

1. The following items were on my mother's grocery list eggs, tomatoes, milk, and cereal.
2. A life size statue of her cat adorns the living room of Diana's penthouse.
3. Sigmund Freud, the pioneer of psychoanalysis 1856–1939, was a habitual cocaine user.
4. As children, we would put pennies on the railroad track we wanted to see what they would look like after being run over by a train.
5. The stuntwoman was battered, broken, barely breathing but alive.

Answers are on page 694.

Colon (:)

ALLWRITE!

24.2

The colon is a mark of introduction. Use the colon at the end of a complete statement to do the following:

1 Introduce a list.

My little brother has three hobbies: playing video games, racing his Hot Wheels cars all over the floor, and driving me crazy.

2 Introduce a long quotation.

Janet's paper was based on a passage from George Eliot's novel *Middlemarch:* "If we had a keen vision and feeling of all ordinary human life, it would be like hearing the grass grow and the squirrel's heart beat, and we should die of that roar which lies on the other side of silence. As it is, the quickest of us walk about well wadded with stupidity."

3 Introduce an explanation.

There are two ways to do this job: the easy way and the right way.

Two minor uses of the colon are after the opening in a formal letter (*Dear Sir or Madam:*) and between the hour and the minute in writing the time (*The bus will leave for the game at 11:45*).

Practice

Place colons where needed.

1. Roger is on a "see-food" diet if he sees food, he eats it.
   Add a colon before the explanation.

2. Brenda had some terrible problems last summer her mother suffered a heart attack, her husband lost his job, and one of her children was arrested for shoplifting.

3. Andy Rooney wrote in one of his columns "Doctors should never talk to ordinary people about anything but medicine. When doctors talk politics, economics, or sports, they reveal themselves to be ordinary mortals, idiots just like the rest of us. That isn't what any of us wants our doctors to be."

Semicolon (;)

24.1

The semicolon signals more of a pause than the comma alone but not quite the full pause of a period. Use a semicolon to do the following:

1 Join two complete thoughts that are not already connected by a joining word such as *and, but, for,* or *so.*

> The chemistry lab blew up; Professor Thomas was fired.
>
> I once stabbed myself with a pencil; a black mark has been under my skin ever since.

2 Join two complete thoughts that include a transitional word such as *however, otherwise, moreover, furthermore, therefore,* or *consequently.*

> I changed and made the bed; moreover, I cleaned the entire bedroom.
>
> Sally finished typing the paper; however, she forgot to bring it to class.

> Note   The first two uses of the semicolon are treated in more detail on pages 124–127.

3 Separate items in a series when the items themselves contain commas.

> This fall I won't have to work on Labor Day, September 7; Veterans Day, November 11; or Thanksgiving Day, November 26.
>
> At the final Weight Watchers' meeting, prizes were awarded to Sally Johnson, for losing 20 pounds; Irving Ross, for losing 26 pounds; and Betty Mills, the champion loser, who lost 102 pounds.

Practice

Place semicolons where needed.

1. Manny worked four extra hours at his job last night consequently, he has been like a zombie in class today.
   Add a semicolon before the transitional word.

2. We could tell it was still raining all the puddles looked as if they were being shot at.

3. My grocery shopping has to take into account my daughter, who's a vegetarian my mother, who is diabetic and my husband, who wants meat at every meal.

Dash (—)

ALLWRITE!
24.4

A dash signals a degree of pause longer than a comma but not as complete as a period. Use the dash to set off words for dramatic effect.

I suggest—no, I insist—that you stay for dinner.

The prisoner walked toward the electric chair—grinning.

A meaningful job, a loving wife, and a car that wouldn't break down all the time—these are the things he wanted in life.

Practice

Place dashes where needed.

1. The members of the Polar Bear Club marched into the icy sea shivering.
   One dash is needed.
2. The actress's wedding her third in three years included a dozen bridesmaids and a flock of white doves.
3. My sociology class meets at the worst possible time eight o'clock on Monday morning.

Hyphen (-)

Use a hyphen in the following ways:

1 With two or more words that act as a single unit describing a noun.

The society ladies nibbled at the deep-fried grasshoppers.
A white-gloved waiter then put some snails on their table.

Your dictionary will often help when you are unsure about whether to use a hyphen between words.

2 To divide a word at the end of a line of writing or typing.

Although it had begun to drizzle, the teams decided to play the championship game that day.

Notes

a Divide a word only between syllables. Use your dictionary (see page 339) to be sure of correct syllable divisions.

b Do not divide words of one syllable.

c Do not divide a word if you can avoid dividing it.

Practice

Place hyphens where needed.

1. Why do I always find myself behind a slow moving car when I'm in a no passing zone?
   Two hyphens are needed.

2. To convince herself that she was still on a diet, Paula ordered a sugar free cola with her double cheese pizza.

3. Twirling his mustache, the hard hearted villain chuckled as he tied the teary eyed heroine to the railroad tracks.

Parentheses ( )

24.5

Use parentheses to do the following:

1 Set off extra or incidental information from the rest of a sentence.

The chapter on drugs in our textbook (pages 234–271) contains some frightening statistics.

The normal body temperature of a cat (101° to 102°) is 3° higher than the temperature of its owner.

2 Enclose letters or numbers that signal items in a series.

Three steps to follow in previewing a textbook are to (1) study the title, (2) read the first and last paragraphs, and (3) study the headings and subheadings.

Note   Do not use parentheses too often in your writing.

Practice

Add parentheses where needed.

1. According to the 2000 Census, a majority of Americans 80 percent had earned a high school diploma.
   Put the extra information in parentheses.

2. That instructor's office hours 3 to 4 P.M. are impossible for any student with an afternoon job.

3. Since I am forgetful, I often 1 make a list and then 2 check off items I have done. Now where did I put my list?

■ Review Test 1

At the appropriate spot or spots, insert the punctuation mark shown in the margin.

Example   ;   The singles dance was a success; I met several people I wanted to see again.

:   1. That catalog lists some unusual items a sausage stuffer, an electric foot warmer, and a remote-control car starter.

—   2. My brother's jokes none of which I can repeat are unfunny and tasteless.

-     3. These days, many two career couples have decided not to have children.

( )   4. The section on space travel in my daughter's science book Chapters 10–11 is sadly out of date.

:   5. Anne Frank wrote in her diary "It's a wonder I haven't abandoned all my ideals; they seem so absurd and impractical. Yet I cling to them because I still believe, in spite of everything, that people are truly good at heart."

;   6. The frightened hamster darted from room to room finally, it crawled under a dresser.

—   7. Credit card bills, the mortgage payment, and car repairs no wonder my paycheck doesn't last till the end of the month.

-     8. Someone once defined a self confident person as one who does crossword puzzles in pen instead of pencil.

( )   9. Three ways to save money on home repairs are 1 get several estimates, 2 avoid costly designer products, and 3 do it yourself.

;   10. I ordered several items from Sears: two suitcases, one maroon and one blue an extra-large, machine-washable sweater and a canvas gym bag.

■ Review Test 2

On separate paper, write two sentences using each of the following punctuation marks: colon, semicolon, dash, hyphen, parentheses.

28 Dictionary Use

Introductory Activity

The dictionary is an indispensable tool, as will be apparent if you try to answer the following questions *without* using the dictionary.

1. Which one of the following words is spelled incorrectly?

   fortutious   macrobiotics   stratagem

2. If you wanted to hyphenate the following word correctly, at which points would you place the syllable divisions?

   h i e r o g l y p h i c s

3. What common word has the sound of the first *e* in the word *chameleon?* _____

4. Where is the primary accent in the following word?

   o c t o g e n a r i a n

5. What are the two separate meanings of the word *earmark?*

   _____

   _____

Your dictionary is a quick and sure authority on all these matters: spelling, syllabication, pronunciation, and word meanings. And as this chapter will show, it is also a source for many other kinds of information.

Answers are on page 694.

The dictionary is a valuable tool. To take advantage of it, you need to understand the main kinds of information that a dictionary gives about a word. Look at the information provided for the word *dictate* in the following entry from the *American Heritage Dictionary,* fourth paperback edition.*

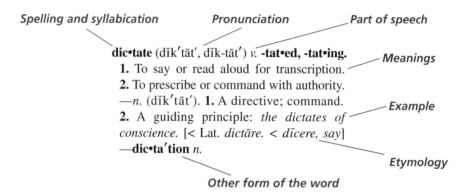

Spelling and syllabication   Pronunciation   Part of speech

dic•tate (dĭk′tāt′, dĭk-tāt′) *v.* **-tat•ed, -tat•ing.** — Meanings
1. To say or read aloud for transcription.
2. To prescribe or command with authority.
—*n.* (dĭk′tāt′). **1.** A directive; command. — Example
2. A guiding principle: *the dictates of*
conscience. [< Lat. *dictāre.* < *dīcere, say*]
—**dic•ta′tion** *n.* — Etymology

Other form of the word

Spelling

The first bit of information, in the **boldface** (heavy type) entry itself, is the spelling of *dictate*. You probably already know the spelling of *dictate,* but if you didn't, you could find it by pronouncing the syllables in the word carefully and then looking it up in the dictionary.

Use your dictionary to correct the spelling of the following words:

wellcome _____   persistant _____

quiting _____   proformance _____

consentration _____   oppurtinity _____

perfessional _____   desision _____

recieving _____   roomate _____

aranged _____   envolvment _____

extremly _____   diferance _____

nesasary _____   catagory _____

exciteing _____   priveledge _____

---

*©2001 Houghton Mifflin Company. Reprinted by permission from *American Heritage Dictionary of the English Language,* Fourth Paperback Edition.

Syllabication

The second bit of information that the dictionary gives, also within the boldface entry, is the syllabication of *dic•tate*. Note that a dot separates each syllable (or part) of the word. Use your dictionary to mark the syllable divisions in the following words. Also indicate how many syllables are in each word.

v e n t u r e   (_____ syllables)

o b s e s s i o n   (_____ syllables)

e n e r g e t i c   (_____ syllables)

i n s p i r a t i o n a l   (_____ syllables)

Noting syllable divisions will enable you to *hyphenate* a word: divide it at the end of one line of writing and complete it at the beginning of the next line. You can correctly hyphenate a word only at a syllable division, and you may have to check your dictionary to make sure of the syllable divisions for a particular word.

Pronunciation

The third bit of information in the dictionary entry is the pronunciation of *dictate: (dik'tat')* or *(dik-tat')*. You already know how to pronounce *dictate,* but if you did not, the information within the parentheses would serve as your guide.

Vowel Sounds

You will probably use the pronunciation key in your dictionary mainly as a guide to pronouncing different vowel sounds (*vowels* are the letters *a, e, i, o,* and *u*). Here is the pronunciation key that appears on every other page of the paperback *American Heritage Dictionary:*

ă pat ā pay â care ä father ĕ pet ē be ĭ pit ī tie î pier ŏ pot ō toe ô paw, for oi noise o͝o took o͞o boot ou out th thin *th* this ŭ cut û urge yo͞o abuse zh vision ə about, item, edible, gallop, circus

This key tells you, for example, that the short *a* is pronounced like the *a* in *pat,* the long *a* is like the *a* in *pay,* and the short *i* is like the *i* in *pit.*

Now look at the pronunciation key in your own dictionary. The key is probably located in the front of the dictionary or at the bottom of every page. What common word in the key tells you how to pronounce each of the following sounds?

ĕ _____   ō _____

ī _____   ŭ _____

ŏ _____   o͞o _____

(Note that a long vowel always has the sound of its own name.)

The Schwa (ə)

The symbol ə looks like an upside-down *e*. It is called a *schwa,* and it stands for the unaccented sound in such words as *about, item, edible, gallop,* and *circus.* More approximately, it stands for the sound *uh*—like the *uh* that speakers some-times make when they hesitate. Perhaps it would help to remember that *uh,* as well as ə, could be used to represent the schwa sound.

Here are three of the many words in which the schwa sound appears: *socialize* (sō'shə līz or sō'shuh līz); *legitimate* (lə jĭt'ə mĭt or luh jĭt'uh mĭt); *oblivious* (ə blĭv'ē əs or uh blĭv'ē uhs). Open your dictionary to any page, and you will almost surely be able to find three words that make use of the schwa in the pro-nunciation in parentheses after the main entry. Write three such words and their pronunciations in the following spaces:

1. _____

2. _____

3. _____

Accent Marks

Some words contain both a primary accent, shown by a heavy stroke ('), and a secondary accent, shown by a lighter stroke ('). For example, in the word *vicis-situde* (vĭ sĭs'ĭ to͞od'), the stress, or accent, goes chiefly on the second syllable (sĭs'), and, to a lesser extent, on the last syllable (to͞od').

Use your dictionary to add stress marks to the following words:

notorious (nō tôr ē əs)   enterprise (ĕn tər prīz)

instigate (ĭn stĭ gāt)   irresistible (ĭr ĭ zĭs tə bəl)

equivocate (ĭ kwĭv ə kāt)   probability (prŏb ə bĭl ĭ tē)

millennium (mə lĕn ē əm)   representative (rĕp rĭ zen tə tĭv)

Full Pronunciation

Use your dictionary to write out the full pronunciation (the information given in parentheses) for each of the following words:

1. magnate _____

2. semblance _____

3. satiate _____

4. bastion _____

5. celestial _____

6. extraneous _____

7. edifice _____

8. incipient _____

9. fallacious _____

10. ostracize _____

11. phlegmatic _____

12. proximity _____

13. anachronism _____

14. felicitous _____

15. extemporaneous

_____

Now practice pronouncing each word. Use the pronunciation key in your dictionary as an aid to sounding out each syllable. Do *not* try to pronounce a word all at once; instead, work on mastering *one syllable at a time.* When you can pronounce each of the syllables in a word successfully, then say them in sequence, add the accent, and pronounce the entire word.

Other Information about Words

Parts of Speech

The dictionary entry for *dictate* includes the abbreviation *v.* This indicates that the meanings of *dictate* as a verb will follow. The abbreviation *n.* is then followed by the meanings of *dictate* as a noun.

At the front of your dictionary, you will probably find a key that will explain the meanings of abbreviations used in the dictionary. Use the key to fill in the meanings of the following abbreviations:

pl.   = _____

sing. = _____

adj. = _____

adv. = _____

Principal Parts of Irregular Verbs

Dictate is a regular verb and forms its principal parts by adding *-d, -d,* and *-ing* to the stem of the verb. When a verb is irregular, the dictionary lists its principal parts. For example, with *begin* the present tense comes first (the entry itself, *begin*). Next comes the past tense (*began*), and then the past participle (*begun*)— the form of the verb used with such helping words as *have, had,* and *was.* Then comes the present participle (*beginning*)—the *-ing* form of the word.

Look up the principal parts of the following irregular verbs and write them in the spaces provided. The first one has been done for you.

Present	*Past*	*Past Participle*	*Present Participle*
see	*saw*	*seen*	*seeing*
choose			
know			
speak			

Plural Forms of Irregular Nouns

The dictionary supplies the plural forms of all irregular nouns. (Regular nouns form the plural by adding *-s* or *-es.*) Write the plurals of the following nouns:

thief   _____

cavity   _____

hero   _____

thesis   _____

Note   See page 352–353 for more information about plurals.

Meanings

When a word has more than one meaning, its meanings are numbered in the dictionary, as with the verb *dictate.* In many dictionaries, the most common meanings are presented first. The introductory pages of your dictionary will explain the order in which meanings are presented.

Use the sentence context to try to explain the meaning of the underlined word in each of the following sentences. Write your definition in the space provided. Then look up and record the dictionary meaning of the word. Be sure to select the meaning that fits the word as it is used in the sentence.

1. Honesty is a cardinal rule in my family.

   Your definition: _____

   _____

   Dictionary definition: _____

   _____

2. The union strike put management in a ticklish situation.

   Your definition: _____

   _____

   Dictionary definition: _____

   _____

3. Ben lacks confidence, probably because his parents constantly railed at him.

   Your definition: _____

   _____

   Dictionary definition: _____

   _____

Etymology

Etymology refers to the history of a word. Many words have origins in foreign languages, such as Greek (abbreviated Gk in the dictionary) or Latin (L). Such information is usually enclosed in brackets and is more likely to be present in a hardbound desk dictionary than in a paperback one. A good desk dictionary will tell you, for example, that the word *cannibal* derives from the name of the man-eating tribe, the Caribs, that Christopher Columbus discovered on Cuba and Haiti.

The following are good desk dictionaries:

The American Heritage Dictionary
Random House College Dictionary
Webster's New Collegiate Dictionary
Webster's New World Dictionary

See if your dictionary says anything about the origins of the following words.

magazine _____

anatomy _____

frankfurter _____

Usage Labels

As a general rule, use only standard English words in your writing. If a word is not standard English, your dictionary will probably give it a usage label such as *informal, nonstandard, slang, vulgar, obsolete, archaic,* or *rare.*

Look up the following words and record how your dictionary labels them. Remember that a recent hardbound desk dictionary will always be the best source of information about usage.

sharp (meaning *attractive*)

_____

hard-nosed

_____

sass (meaning *to talk impudently*)

_____

ain't

_____

put-down

_____

Synonyms

A *synonym* is a word that is close in meaning to another word. Using synonyms helps you avoid unnecessary repetition of the same word in a paper. A paperback dictionary is not likely to give you synonyms for words, but a good desk dictionary will. (You might also want to own a *thesaurus,* a book that lists synonyms and antonyms. An *antonym* is a word approximately opposite in meaning to another word.)

Consult a desk dictionary that gives synonyms for the following words, and write some of the synonyms in the spaces provided.

desire _____

ask _____

cry _____

■ Review Test

Items 1–5   Use your dictionary to answer the following questions.

1. How many syllables are in the word *neurosurgery?* _____

2. Where is the primary accent in the word *elevation?* _____

3. In the word *evasion,* the *a* is pronounced like

    a.   short *o*

    b.   short *a*

    c.   schwa

    d.   long *a*

4. In the word *nobility,* the *y* is pronounced like

    a.   schwa

    b.   short *a*

    c.   long *e*

    d.   short *e*

5. In the word *data,* the second *a* is pronounced like

    a.   short *a*

    b.   schwa

    c.   short *i*

    d.   long *e*

Items 6–10   There are five misspelled words in the following sentence. Cross out each misspelled word and write the correct spelling in the spaces provided.

Some freinds and I are planning to go to the libary on Wensday to do some research for an importent paper for our litrature class.

6. _____

7. _____

8. _____

9. _____

10. _____

29 Spelling Improvement

Introductory Activity

See if you can circle the word that is misspelled in each of the following pairs:

akward	*or*	awkward
exercise	*or*	exercize
business	*or*	buisness
worried	*or*	worryed
shamful	*or*	shameful
begining	*or*	beginning
partys	*or*	parties
sandwichs	*or*	sandwiches
heroes	*or*	heros

Answers are on page 694.

Poor spelling often results from bad habits developed in the early school years. With work, such habits can be corrected. If you can write your name without misspelling it, there is no reason why you can't do the same with almost any word in the English language. Following are seven steps you can take to improve your spelling.

Step 1: Using the Dictionary

Get into the habit of using the dictionary. When you write a paper, allow yourself time to look up the spelling of all the words you are unsure about. Do not underestimate the value of this step just because it is such a simple one. By using the dictionary, you can probably make yourself a 95 percent better speller.

Step 2: Keeping a Personal Spelling List

Keep a list of words you misspell, and study those words regularly. Use the chart on the inside front cover of this book as a starter. When you accumulate additional words, you may want to use a back page of your English notebook.

Hint   When you have trouble spelling long words, try to break each word into syllables and see whether you can spell the syllables. For example, *misdemeanor* can be spelled easily if you can hear and spell in turn its four syllables: *mis-de-mean-or.* The word *formidable* can be spelled easily if you hear and spell in turn its four syllables: *for-mi-da-ble.* Remember, then: try to see, hear, and spell long words in terms of their syllables.

Step 3: Mastering Commonly Confused Words

Master the meanings and spellings of the commonly confused words on pages 365–383. Your instructor may assign twenty words for you to study at a time and give you a series of quizzes until you have mastered all the words.

Step 4: Using Electronic Aids

There are two electronic aids that may help your spelling.
    First, a *computer with a spell-checker* will identify incorrect words and suggest correct spellings. If you know how to write on a computer, you will have no trouble learning how to use the spell-check feature.

Second, *electronic spell-checkers* are pocket-size devices that look much like the pocket calculator you may carry to your math class. They are the latest example of how technology can help the learning process. Electronic spellers can be found in the computer section of any discount store, at prices in the $100 range. The checker has a tiny keyboard. You type out the word the way you think it is spelled, and the checker quickly provides you with the correct spelling of related words. Some of these checkers even *pronounce* the word aloud for you.

Step 5: Understanding Basic Spelling Rules

Explained briefly here are three rules that may improve your spelling. While exceptions sometimes occur, these rules hold true most of the time.

1 *Change y to i.* When a word ends in a consonant plus *y*, change *y* to *i* when you add an ending.

try   + ed = tried   marry + es   = marries
worry + es = worries   lazy   + ness = laziness
lucky + ly = luckily   silly   + est = silliest

2 *Final silent e.* Drop a final *e* before an ending that starts with a vowel (the vowels are *a, e, i, o,* and *u*).

hope + ing = hoping   sense + ible = sensible
fine + est = finest   hide + ing = hiding

Keep the final *e* before an ending that starts with a consonant.

use + ful = useful   care + less   = careless
life + like = lifelike   settle + ment = settlement

3 *Doubling a final consonant.* Double the final consonant of a word when all the following are true:

a The word is one syllable or is accented on the last syllable.
b The word ends in a single consonant preceded by a single vowel.
c The ending you are adding starts with a vowel.

sob   + ing = sobbing   big   + est = biggest
drop + ed = dropped   omit + ed = omitted
admit + ing = admitting   begin + ing = beginning

Practice

Combine the following words and endings by applying the three rules above.

1. hurry   + ed = _____   6. commit + ed = _____
     Change y to i.

2. admire + ing = _____   7. dive   + ing = _____

3. deny   + es = _____   8. hasty   + ly = _____

4. jab   + ing = _____   9. propel + ing = _____

5. magnify + ed = _____   10. nudge + es = _____

Step 6: Understanding Plurals

Most words form their plurals by adding *-s* to the singular.

Singular	*Plural*
blanket	blankets
pencil	pencils
street	streets

Some words, however, form their plurals in special ways, as shown in the rules that follow.

1 Words ending in *-s, -ss, -z, -x, -sh,* or *-ch* usually form the plural by adding *-es.*

kiss	kisses	inch	inches
box	boxes	dish	dishes

2 Words ending in a consonant plus *y* form the plural by changing *y* to *i* and adding *-es.*

party	parties	county	counties
baby	babies	city	cities

3 Some words ending in *f* change the *f* to *v* and add *-es* in the plural.

leaf	leaves	life	lives
wife	wives	yourself	yourselves

4 Some words ending in *o* form their plurals by adding *-es.*

| potato | potatoes | mosquito | mosquitoes |
| hero | heroes | tomato | tomatoes |

5 Some words of foreign origin have irregular plurals. When in doubt, check your dictionary.

| antenna | antennae | crisis | crises |
| criterion | criteria | medium | media |

6 Some words form their plurals by changing letters within the word.

| man | men | foot | feet |
| tooth | teeth | goose | geese |

7 Combined words (words made up of two or more words) form their plurals by adding *-s* to the main word.

| brother-in-law | brothers-in-law |
| passerby | passersby |

Practice

Complete these sentences by filling in the plural of the word at the left.

bus
1. No _____ are permitted on the Channel Bridge.
   A word ending in *s* forms the plural by adding *-es.*

grocery
2. Many of the _____ spilled out of the bags in my trunk when I braked suddenly.

potato
3. Baked _____ complement almost any main dish.

taxi
4. Just after I decided to take the crowded bus, four _____ passed us on Market Street.

themself
5. The owners of the failed curried-pizza restaurant have no one but _____ to blame.

theory
6. The essay question asked us to describe two _____ of evolution.

passerby
7. When I had a flat tire after work, several _____ stopped to ask if they could help.

alumnus   8. More presidents of the United States were _____ of Harvard than of any other university.

sandwich   9. The best short-order cook I ever met could make thirty bacon, lettuce, and tomato _____ in ten minutes.

mouse   10. During the sanitation workers' strike, _____ scurried along the street between bags of uncollected trash.

Step 7: Mastering a Basic Word List

Make sure you can spell all the words in the following list. They are some of the words used most often in English. Again, your instructor may assign twenty words for you to study at a time and give you a series of quizzes until you have mastered the words.

ability	apply	business
absent	approve	careful
accident	argue	careless
across	around	cereal
address	attempt	certain
advertise	attention	change
advice	awful	cheap
after	awkward	chief
again	balance	children
against	bargain	church
all right	beautiful	cigarette
almost	because	clothing
a lot	become	collect
although	before	color
always	begin	comfortable
among	being	company
angry	believe	condition
animal	between	conversation **60**
another	bottom **40**	daily
answer **20**	breathe	danger
anxious	building	daughter

death	holiday	mountain
decide	house **100**	much
deposit	however	needle
describe	hundred	neglect
different	hungry	newspaper
direction	important	noise
distance	instead	none **140**
doubt	intelligence	nothing
dozen	interest	number
during	interfere	ocean
each	kitchen	offer
early	knowledge	often
earth	labor	omit
education	language	only
either	laugh	operate
English	leave	opportunity
enough **80**	length	original
entrance	lesson	ought
everything	letter	pain
examine	listen	paper
exercise	loneliness	pencil
expect	making **120**	people
family	marry	perfect
flower	match	period
foreign	matter	personal
friend	measure	picture
garden	medicine	place **160**
general	middle	pocket
grocery	might	possible
guess	million	potato
happy	minute	president
heard	mistake	pretty
heavy	money	problem
height	month	promise
himself	morning	property

psychology	smoke	tongue
public	something	tonight
question	soul	touch
quick	started	travel **220**
raise	state	truly
ready	straight	understand
really	street	unity
reason	strong **200**	until
receive	student	upon
recognize	studying	usual
remember	success	value
repeat **180**	suffer	vegetable
restaurant	surprise	view
ridiculous	teach	visitor
said	telephone	voice
same	theory	warning
sandwich	thought	watch
send	thousand	welcome
sentence	through	window
several	ticket	would
shoes	tired	writing
should	today	written
since	together	year
sleep	tomorrow	yesterday **240**

■ Review Test

Items 1–10   Use the three spelling rules to spell the following words.

1. admire   + able   =   _____

2. drop   + ing   =   _____

3. big   + est   =   _____

4. gamble   + ing   =   _____

5. luxury   + es   =   _____

6. immediate   + ly   =   _____

7. imply   + es   = _____

8. plan   + ed   = _____

9. involve   + ment   = _____

10. refer   + ed   = _____

Items 11–14 Circle the correctly spelled plural in each pair.

11. daisies   daisys
12. bookshelfs   bookshelves
13. mosquitos   mosquitoes
14. crisis   crises

Items 15–20 Circle the correctly spelled word (from the basic word list) in each pair.

15. tommorrow   tomorrow
16. height   hieght
17. needel   needle
18. visiter   visitor
19. hungry   hungery
20. writting   writing

30 Omitted Words and Letters

Introductory Activity

Some people drop small connecting words such as *of, and,* or *in* when they write. They may also drop the *-s* endings of plural nouns. See if you can find the six places in the passage below where letters or words have been dropped. Supply whatever is missing.

Two glass bottle of apple juice lie broken the supermarket aisle. Suddenly, a toddler who has gotten away from his parents appears at the head of the aisle. He spots the broken bottles and begins to run toward them. His chubby body lurches along like wind-up toy, and his arm move excitedly up and down. Luckily, alert shopper quickly reacts to the impending disaster and blocks the toddler's path. Then the shopper waits with crying, frustrated little boy until his parents show up.

Answers are on page 695.

Be careful not to leave out words or letters when you write. The omission of words like *a, an, of, to,* or *the* or the *-s* ending needed on nouns or verbs may confuse and irritate your readers. They may not want to read what they regard as careless work.

Finding Omitted Words and Letters

Finding omitted words and letters, like finding many other sentence-skills mistakes, is a matter of careful proofreading. You must develop your ability to look carefully at a page to find places where mistakes may exist.

The exercises here will give you practice in finding omitted words and omitted *-s* endings on nouns. Another section of this book (pages 153–154) gives you practice in finding omitted *-s* endings on verbs.

Omitted Words

Practice

Add the missing word (*a, an, the, of,* or *to*) as needed.

Example   Some people regard television as *a* tranquilizer that provides temporary relief from *the* pain and anxiety *of* modern life.

1. I grabbed metal bar on roof of subway car as the train lurched into station.
   Four changes are needed.

2. For most our country's history, gold was basis the monetary system.

3. Maggie made about a quart French-toast batter—enough soak few dozen slices.

4. Several pairs sneakers tumbled around in dryer and banged against glass door.

5. To err is human and to forgive is divine, but never make a mistake in the first place takes lot of luck.

6. Raccoons like wash their food in stream with their nimble, glove-like hands before eating.

7. When I got the grocery store, I realized I had left my shopping list in glove compartment my car.

8. Game shows are inexpensive way for networks make high profit.

9. Soap operas, on other hand, are very expensive to produce because the high salaries of many cast members.

10. One memorable Friday the thirteenth, a friend mine bought black cat, broke mirror, and walked under ladder. He had a wonderful day!

Omitted -s Ending

The plural form of regular nouns usually ends in -s. One common mistake that some people make with plurals is to omit this -s ending. People who drop the ending from plurals when speaking also tend to do it when writing. This tendency is especially noticeable when the meaning of the sentence shows that a word is plural.

> Ed and Mary pay two hundred dollar a month for an apartment that has only two room.

The -s ending has been omitted from *dollars* and *rooms*.

The activities that follow will help you correct the habit of omitting the -s endings from plurals.

Practice 1

Add -s endings where needed.

Example   Bill beat me at several game of darts.

1. Many sightseer flocked around the disaster area like ghoul.
   Two -s endings are needed.

2. Martha has two set of twins, and all of their name rhyme.

3. Dozen of beetle are eating away at the rosebush in our yard.

4. Since a convention of dentist was in town, all the restaurant had waiting line.

5. Until the first of the year, worker in all department will not be permitted any overtime.

6. Blinking light, such as those on video game or police car, can trigger seizures in person with epilepsy.

7. Ray and his friends invented several game using an old rubber radiator hose and two plastic ball.

8. My thirteen-year-old has grown so much lately that she doesn't fit into the shoe and jean I bought for her a couple of month ago.

9. While cleaning out her desk drawers, Ann found a page of postage stamp stuck together and a couple of dried-up pen.

10. Worker fed large log and chunk of wood into the huge machine, which spit out chip and sawdust from its other end.

Practice 2

Write sentences that use plural forms of the following pairs of words.

Example   girl, bike *The little girls raced their bikes down the street.*

1. college, student

   _____

   _____

2. shopper, bargain

   _____

   _____

3. car, driver

   _____

   _____

4. instructor, grade

   _____

   _____

5. vampire, victim

   _____

   _____

Note   People who drop the *-s* ending on nouns also tend to omit endings on verbs. Pages 153–155 will help you correct the habit of dropping endings on verbs.

■ Review Test 1

Insert the two small connecting words needed in each sentence.

1. When I opened freezer door, box of ice cream fell out.

2. Hiking along trail next to the lake, we came to very muddy stretch.

3. The newlyweds rented apartment with two rooms and bath.

4. I had walk all the way up to our fifth-floor office because elevator was broken.

5. Unfortunately, the road leading wealth is a lot longer than one leading to poverty.

■ Review Test 2

Insert the two *-s* endings needed in each sentence.

1. The tallest building in the city has 67 floor and 75,010 doorknob.

2. Student who receive the highest grades are usually the one who study the most.

3. The trash cans by the picnic benches attracted dozen of bee.

4. Tiny crack were visible in all the wall of the building after the earthquake.

5. The fruit basket we received included instruction for ripening fresh fruit and a booklet of recipe.

31 Commonly Confused Words

Introductory Activity

Circle the five words that are misspelled in the following passage. Then write their correct spellings in the spaces provided.

If your a resident of a temperate climate, you may suffer from feelings of depression in the winter and early spring. Scientists are now studying people who's moods seem to worsen in winter, and there findings show that the amount of daylight a person receives is an important factor in "seasonal depression." When a person gets to little sunlight, his or her mood darkens. Its fairly easy to treat severe cases of seasonal depression; the cure involves spending a few hours a day in front of full-spectrum fluorescent lights that contain all the components of natural light.

1. _____
2. _____
3. _____
4. _____
5. _____

Answers are on page 695.

Homonyms

The commonly confused words shown below are known as *homonyms;* they have the same sounds but different meanings and spellings. Complete the activities for each set of words, and check off and study the words that give you trouble.

Common Homonyms

all ready	pair	threw
already	pear	through
brake	passed	to
break	past	too
coarse	peace	two
course	piece	wear
hear	plain	where
here	plane	weather
hole	principal	whether
whole	principle	whose
its	right	who's
it's	write	your
knew	than	you're
new	then	
know	their	
no	there	
	they're	

---

all ready   completely prepared
already   previously, before

We were *all ready* to go, for we had eaten and packed *already* that morning.

Fill in the blanks: Phil was _____ for his driver's test, since he had _____ memorized the questions and regulations.

Write sentences using *all ready* and *already.*

_____

_____

brake   stop
break   come apart

Dot slams the *brake* pedal so hard that I'm afraid I'll *break* my neck in her car.

Fill in the blanks: While attempting to _____ a speed record, the racecar driver had to _____ for a spectator who had wandered onto the track.

Write sentences using *brake* and *break.*

_____

_____

coarse   rough
course   part of a meal; a school subject; direction; certainly (with *of*)

During the *course* of my career as a waitress, I've dealt with some very *coarse* customers.

Fill in the blanks: The instructor in my electronics _____ is known to use _____ language.

Write sentences using *coarse* and *course.*

_____

_____

hear   perceive with the ear
here   in this place

If I *hear* another insulting ethnic joke *here,* I'll leave.

Fill in the blanks: Unless you sit right _____ in one of the front rows, you won't be able to _____ a single thing the soft-spoken lecturer says.

Write sentences using *hear* and *here.*

_____

_____

hole   empty spot
whole   entire

If there is a *hole* in the tailpipe, I'm afraid we will have to replace the *whole* exhaust assembly.

Fill in the blanks: If you eat the _____ portion of chili, it will probably burn a _____ in your stomach.

Write sentences using *hole* and *whole.*

_____

_____

its   belonging to it
it's   contraction of *it is* or *it has*

The kitchen floor has lost *its* shine because *it's* been used as a roller skating rink by the children.

Fill in the blanks: Our living-room carpet has lost _____ vivid color since _____ been exposed to so much sunlight.

Write sentences using *its* and *it's.*

_____

_____

knew   past tense of *know*
new   not old

We *knew* that the *new* television comedy would be canceled quickly.

Fill in the blanks: As soon as we brought our _____ microwave home, we _____ it wouldn't fit where we planned to put it.

Write sentences using *knew* and *new.*

_____

_____

know   to understand
no   a negative

I never *know* who might drop in even though *no* one is expected.

Fill in the blanks: I _____ there are _____ openings in your company at present, but please keep my résumé in case anything turns up.

Write sentences using *know* and *no.*

_____

_____

pair   set of two
pear   fruit

The dessert consisted of a *pair* of thin biscuits topped with vanilla ice cream and poached *pear* halves.

Fill in the blanks: We spotted a _____ of bluejays on our dwarf _____ tree.

Write sentences using *pair* and *pear.*

_____

_____

passed   went by; succeeded in; handed to
past   time before the present; by, as in "I drove past the house."

After Edna *passed* the driver's test, she drove *past* all her friends' houses and honked the horn.

Fill in the blanks: Norman couldn't understand why he'd been _____ over for the promotion, because his _____ work had been very good.

Write sentences using *passed* and *past.*

_____

_____

peace   calm
piece   part

The *peace* of the little town was shattered when a *piece* of a human body was found in the town dump.

Fill in the blanks: We ate in _____ until my two brothers started fighting over who would get the last _____ of blueberry pie.

Write sentences using *peace* and *piece*.

_____

_____

plain   simple
plane   aircraft

The *plain* box contained a very expensive model *plane* kit.

Fill in the blanks: The _____ truth is that unless you can land this _____ within the next twenty minutes, it will run out of fuel and crash.

Write sentences using *plain* and *plane*.

_____

_____

principal   main; a person in charge of a school; amount of money borrowed
principle   law or standard

My *principal* goal in child rearing is to give my daughter strong *principles* to live by.

Fill in the blanks: My _____ reason for turning down the part-time job is that it's against my _____s to work on weekends.

Write sentences using *principal* and *principle*.

_____

_____

Note   It might help to remember that the *e* in *principle* is also in *rule*—the meaning of *principle*.

right   correct; opposite of *left;* something to which one is entitled
write   to put words on paper

It is my *right* to refuse to *write* my name on your petition.

Fill in the blanks: The instructor said if the students' outlines were not
_____, they would have to _____ them again.

Write sentences using *right* and *write.*

_____

_____

than   used in comparisons
then   at that time

I glared angrily at my boss, and *then* I told him our problems were more
serious *than* he suspected.

Fill in the blanks: Felix hiked seven miles and _____ chopped firewood;
he was soon more tired _____ he'd been in years.

Write sentences using *than* and *then.*

_____

_____

Note   It might help to remember that *then* (the word spelled with an *e*) is a time
signal (*time* also has an *e*).

their   belonging to them
there   at that place; a neutral word used with verbs like *is, are, was, were,*
           have, and *had*
they're   contraction of *they are*

The tenants *there* are complaining because *they're* being cheated by *their*
landlords.

Fill in the blanks: The music next door is so loud that I'm going over _____
to tell my neighbors to turn _____ stereo down before _____
arrested for disturbing the peace.

Write sentences using *their, there,* and *they're.*

_____

_____

threw   past tense of *throw*
through   from one side to the other; finished

    When a character in a movie *threw* a cat *through* the window, I had to close my eyes.

Fill in the blanks: When Lee was finally _____ studying for her psychology final, she _____ her textbook and notes into her closet.

Write sentences using *threw* and *through.*

_____

_____

to   verb part, as in *to smile;* toward, as in "I'm going to school."
too   overly, as in "The pizza was too hot"; also, as in "The coffee was hot, too."
two   the number 2

    Lola drove *to* the store *to* get some ginger ale. (The first *to* means *toward;* the second *to* is a verb part that goes with *get.*)
    The jacket is *too* tight; the pants are tight, *too.* (The first *too* means *overly;* the second *too* means *also.*)
    The *two* basketball players leaped for the jump ball. (2)

Fill in the blanks: My _____ daughters are _____ young _____ wear much makeup.

Write sentences using *to, too,* and *two.*

_____

_____

wear   to have on
where   in what place

    I work at a nuclear reactor, *where* one must *wear* a radiation-detection badge at all times.

Fill in the blanks: At the college _____ Ann goes, almost all the students _____ very casual clothes to class.

Write sentences using *wear* and *where.*

_____

_____

weather   atmospheric conditions
whether   if it happens that; in case; if

Because of the threatening *weather,* it's not certain *whether* the game will be played.

Fill in the blanks: After I hear the _____ report, I'll decide _____ I'll drive or take a train to my sister's house.

Write sentences using *weather* and *whether.*

_____

_____

whose   belonging to whom
who's   contraction of *who is* and *who has*

The man *who's* the author of the latest diet book is a man *whose* ability to cash in on the latest craze is well known.

Fill in the blanks: The cousin _____ visiting us is the one _____ car was just demolished by a tractor trailer.

Write sentences using *whose* and *who's.*

_____

_____

your   belonging to you
you're contraction of *you are*

Since *your* family has a history of heart disease, *you're* the kind of person who should take extra health precautions.

Fill in the blanks: If _____ not going to eat any more, could I have what's left on _____ plate?

Write sentences using *your* and *you're.*

_____

_____

Other Words Frequently Confused

Following is a list of other words that people frequently confuse. Complete the activities for each set of words, and check off and study the ones that give you trouble.

Commonly Confused Words

a	among	desert	learn
an	between	dessert	teach
accept	beside	does	loose
except	besides	dose	lose
advice	can	fewer	quiet
advise	may	less	quite
affect	clothes	former	though
effect	cloths	latter	thought

a   Both *a* and *an* are used before other words to mean, approximately, *one.*
an

Generally you should use *an* before words starting with a vowel (*a, e, i, o, u*):

an absence   an exhibit   an idol   an offer   an upgrade

Generally you should use *a* before words starting with a consonant (all other letters):

a pen   a ride   a digital clock   a movie   a neighbor

Fill in the blanks: When it comes to eating, I am lucky; I can eat like _____ elephant and stay as thin as _____ snake.

Write sentences using *a* and *an.*

_____

_____

accept   receive; agree to
except   exclude; but

    If I *accept* your advice, I'll lose all my friends *except* you.

Fill in the blanks: Everyone _____ my parents was delighted when I decided to _____ the out-of-town job offer.

Write sentences using *accept* and *except.*

_____

_____

advice   noun meaning *an opinion*
advise   verb meaning *to counsel, to give advice*

    Jake never listened to his parents' *advice,* and he ended up listening to a cop *advise* him of his rights.

Fill in the blanks: My father once gave me some good _____: never _____ people on anything unless they ask you to.

Write sentences using *advice* and *advise.*

_____

_____

affect   verb meaning *to influence*
effect   verb meaning *to bring about something;* noun meaning *result*

    My sister Sally cries for *effect,* but her act no longer *affects* my parents.

Fill in the blanks: Some school officials think suspension will _____ students positively, but many students think its main _____ is time off from school.

Write sentences using *affect* and *effect.*

_____

_____

| among | implies three or more |
| between | implies only two |

    We selfishly divided the box of candy *between* the two of us rather than *among* all the members of the family.

Fill in the blanks: _____ my souvenirs from high school is a scrapbook with a large pink rose pressed _____ two of its pages.

Write sentences using *among* and *between.*

_____

_____

| beside | along the side of |
| besides | in addition to |

    Fred sat *beside* Martha. *Besides* them, there were ten other people at the Tupperware party.

Fill in the blanks: Elena refused to sit _____ Carlos in class because he always fidgeted, and, _____, he couldn't keep his mouth shut.

Write sentences using *beside* and *besides.*

_____

_____

| can | refers to the ability to do something |
| may | refers to permission or possibility |

    If you *can* work overtime on Saturday, you *may* take Monday off.

Fill in the blanks: Joanne certainly _____ handle the project, but she _____ not have time to complete it by the deadline.

Write sentences using *can* and *may.*

_____

_____

clothes   articles of dress
cloths   pieces of fabric

    I tore up some old *clothes* to use as polishing *cloths.*

Fill in the blanks: I keep a bag of dust _____ in the corner of my _____ closet.

Write sentences using *clothes* and *cloths.*

_____

_____

desert   a stretch of dry land; to abandon one's post or duty
dessert   last part of a meal

    Don't *desert* us now; order a sinful *dessert* along with us.

Fill in the blanks: I know my willpower will _____ me whenever there are brownies for _____.

Write sentences using *desert* and *dessert.*

_____

_____

does   form of the verb *do*
dose   amount of medicine

    Martha *does* not realize that a *dose* of brandy is not the best medicine for the flu.

Fill in the blanks: A _____ of aspirin _____ wonders for Sally's arthritis.

Write sentences using *does* and *dose.*

_____

_____

fewer   used with things that can be counted
less   refers to amount, value, or degree

I missed *fewer* writing classes than Rafael, but I wrote *less* effectively than he did.

Fill in the blanks: Florence is taking _____ courses this semester because she has _____ free time than she did last year.

Write sentences using *fewer* and *less.*

_____

_____

former   refers to the first of two items named
latter   refers to the second of two items named

I turned down both the job in the service station and the job as a shipping clerk; the *former* involved irregular hours and the *latter* offered very low pay.

Fill in the blanks: My mother does both calisthenics and yoga; the _____ keeps her weight down while the _____ helps her relax.

Write sentences using *former* and *latter.*

_____

_____

Note   Be sure to distinguish *latter* from *later* (meaning *after some time*).

learn   to gain knowledge
teach   to give knowledge

After Roz *learns* the new dance, she is going to *teach* it to me.

Fill in the blanks: My dog is very smart; she can _____ any new trick I _____ her in just minutes.

Write sentences using *learn* and *teach.*

_____

_____

loose   not fastened; not tight-fitting
lose   misplace; fail to win

   I am afraid I'll *lose* my ring; it's too *loose* on my finger.

Fill in the blanks: Those slippers are so _____ that every time I take a step, I _____ one.

Write sentences using *loose* and *lose.*

_____

_____

quiet   peaceful
quite   entirely; really; rather

   After a busy day, the children were not *quiet,* and their parents were *quite* tired.

Fill in the blanks: After moving furniture all day, Vince was _____ exhausted, so he found a _____ place and lay down for a nap.

Write sentences using *quiet* and *quite.*

_____

_____

though   despite the fact that
thought   past tense of *think*

   Though I enjoyed the dance, I *thought* the cover charge of ten dollars was too high.

Fill in the blanks: Even _____ my paper was two weeks late, I _____ the instructor would accept it.

Write sentences using *though* and *thought.*

_____

_____

Incorrect Word Forms

Following is a list of incorrect word forms that people sometimes use in their writing. Complete the activities for each word, and check off and study the words that give you trouble.

Incorrect Word Forms

being that	could of	should of
can't hardly	irregardless	would of
couldn't hardly	must of	

---

being that   Incorrect! Use *because* or *since*.

                              because
    I'm going to bed now ~~being that~~ I must get up early tomorrow.

Correct the following sentences.

1. Being that our stove doesn't work, we'll have tuna salad for dinner.

2. I never invite both of my aunts over together, being that they don't speak to each other.

3. I'm taking a day off tomorrow, being that it's my birthday.

can't hardly   Incorrect! Use *can hardly* or *could hardly.*
couldn't hardly

                         can
    Small store owners ~~can't~~ hardly afford to offer large discounts.

Correct the following sentences.

1. I can't hardly concentrate when the teacher looks over my shoulder.

2. James couldn't hardly believe the bill for fixing his car's brakes.

3. You couldn't hardly hear the music because the audience was so loud.

could of   Incorrect! Use *could have.*

       have
I could ~~of~~ done better in that test.

Correct the following sentences.

1. The sidewalk was so hot you could of toasted bread on it.

2. The moon was so bright you could of read by it.

3. The peach pie was so good that I could of eaten it all.

irregardless   Incorrect! Use *regardless.*

   Regardless
~~Irregardless~~ of what anyone says, he will not change his mind.

Correct the following sentences.

1. Irregardless of your feelings about customers, you must treat them with courtesy.

2. Jay jogs every day irregardless of the weather.

3. Anyone can learn to read irregardless of age.

must of   Incorrect! Use *must have, should have, would have.*
should of
would of

       have
I should ~~of~~ applied for a loan when my credit was good.

Correct the following sentences.

1. I must of dozed off during the movie.

2. If Marty hadn't missed class yesterday, he would of known about today's test.

3. You should of told me to stop at the supermarket.

■ **Review Test 1**

These sentences check your understanding of *its, it's; there, their, they're; to, too, two;* and *your, you're.* Underline the correct word in the parentheses. Rather than guess, look back at the explanations of the words when necessary.

1. It seems whenever (your, you're) at the doctor's office, (your, you're) symptoms disappear.

2. The boss asked his assistant (to, too, two) rearrange the insurance files, placing each in (its, it's) proper sequence.

3. You'll get (your, you're) share of the pizza when (its, it's) cool enough (to, too, two) eat.

4. (Its, It's) a terrible feeling when (your, you're) (to, too, two) late (to, too, two) help someone.

5. (To, Too, Two) eat insects, most spiders use their (to, too, two) fangs to inject a special poison that turns (there, their, they're) victim's flesh into a soupy liquid they can drink.

6. (Its, It's) a fact that (there, their, they're) are (to, too, two) many violent shows on TV.

7. (There, Their, They're) is no valid reason for the (to, too, two) of you (to, too, two) have forgotten about turning in (your, you're) assignments.

8. If you (to, too, two) continue (to, too, two) drive so fast, (its, it's) likely you'll get ticketed by the police.

9. "My philosophy on guys is that (there, their, they're) just like buses," said Lola. "If you miss one, (there, their, they're) is always another one coming by in a little while."

10. "(Its, It's) about time you (to, too, two) showed up," the manager huffed. "(There, Their, They're) is already a line of customers waiting outside."

■ **Review Test 2**

The sentences that follow check your understanding of a variety of commonly confused words. Underline the correct word in the parentheses. Rather than guess, look back at the explanations of the words when necessary.

1. When (your, you're) (plain, plane) arrives, call us (weather, whether) (its, it's) late or not.

2. You (should have, should of) first found out (whose, who's) really (to, too, two) blame before coming in (hear, here) and making false accusations.

3. When Jack drove (threw, through) his old neighborhood, he (could hardly, couldn't hardly) recognize some of the places he (knew, new) as a child.

4. The (affect, effect) of having drunk (to, too, two) much alcohol last night was something like having (a, an) jackhammer drilling (among, between) my ears.

5. I was (quiet, quite) surprised to learn that in the (passed, past), (our, are) town was the site of (a, an) Revolutionary War battle.

6. Of (coarse, course) (its, it's) important to get good grades while (your, you're) in school, but it (does, dose) not hurt to (know, now, no) the (right, write) people when (your, you're) looking for a job.

7. If (your, you're) interested in listening to a great album, take my (advice, advise) and pick up a copy of *Sgt. Pepper's Lonely Hearts Club Band;* (its, it's) been voted the most popular rock album in history.

8. (Being that, Since) Barry has failed all five quizzes and one major exam and didn't hand in the midterm paper, he (though, thought) it would be a good idea (to, too, two) drop the (coarse, course).

9. (Their, There, They're) is (know, no) greater feeling (than, then) that of walking (threw, through) a forest in the spring.

10. I spent the (hole, whole) day looking (threw, through) my history notes, but when it came time to take the exam, I still (could hardly, couldn't hardly) understand the similarities (among, between) the Korean War, World War I, and World War II.

■ Review Test 3

On separate paper, write short sentences using the ten words shown below.

their	effect
your	passed
it's	here
then	brake
too (meaning *also*)	whose

32 Effective Word Choice

Introductory Activity

Put a check beside the sentence in each pair that makes more effective and appropriate use of words.

1. After a bummer of a movie, we pigged out on a pizza. _____

   After a disappointing movie, we devoured a pizza. _____

2. Feeling blue about the death of his best friend, Tennyson wrote the tearjerker "In Memoriam." _____

   Mourning the death of his best friend, Tennyson wrote the moving poem "In Memoriam." _____

3. The personality adjustment inventories will be administered on Wednesday in the Student Center. _____

   Psychological tests will be given on Wednesday in the Student Center. _____

4. The referee in the game, in my personal opinion, made the right decision in the situation. _____

   I think the referee made the right decision. _____

Now see if you can circle the correct number in each case:

Pair (1, 2, 3, 4) contains a sentence with slang; pair (1, 2, 3, 4) contains a sentence with a cliché; pair (1, 2, 3, 4) contains a sentence with pretentious words; and pair (1, 2, 3, 4) contains a wordy sentence.

Answers are on page 696.

Choose your words carefully when you write. Always take the time to think about your word choices, rather than simply using the first word that comes to mind. You want to develop the habit of selecting words that are appropriate and exact for your purposes. One way you can show sensitivity to language is by avoiding slang, clichés, pretentious words, and wordiness.

Slang

21.3a

We often use slang expressions when we talk because they are so vivid and colorful. However, slang is usually out of place in formal writing. Here are some examples of slang expressions:

Last night's party was a *real train wreck.*

I don't want to *lay a guilt trip* on you.

My boss *dissed* me last night when he said I was a bad employee.

Dad *flipped out* when he learned that Jan had *totaled* the car.

Someone *ripped off* Ken's new Adidas running shoes from his locker.

After the game, we *stuffed our faces* at the diner.

I finally told my parents to *get off my case.*

The movie really *grossed me out.*

Slang expressions have a number of drawbacks. They go out of date quickly, they become tiresome if used excessively in writing, and they may communicate clearly to some readers but not to others. Also, the use of slang can be an evasion of the specific details that are often needed to make one's meaning clear in writing. For example, in "The party was a real horror show," the writer has not provided the specific details about the party necessary for us to understand the statement clearly. Was it the setting, the food and drink (or lack of them), the guests, the music, or the hosts that made the party such a dreadful experience? In general, then, you should avoid slang in your writing. If you are in doubt about whether an expression is slang, it may help to check a recently published hardbound dictionary.

Practice

Rewrite the following sentences, replacing the italicized slang words with more formal ones.

Example   I was *so beat* Friday night that I decided *to ditch* the birthday party.

I was so exhausted Friday night that I decided not to go to the

birthday party.

1. If you keep *putting it away,* you're going to be *a blimp.*
   What does "putting it away" mean; what does "blimp" mean?

   _____

   _____

2. My parents always *shoot me down* when I ask them for some *bucks* to buy new CDs.

   _____

3. The entire city was *psyched up* when the basketball team *creamed* its opponent in the playoffs.

   _____

4. If Ellen would *lighten up* and stop talking about her troubles, a date with her wouldn't be such a *downer.*

   _____

   _____

5. I'm going to have to *sweat it out* for the next couple of days, hoping the boss doesn't discover the *goof* I made.

   _____

   _____

Clichés

Clichés are expressions that have been worn out through constant use. Some typical clichés are listed below.

Common Clichés

all work and no play	sad but true
at a loss for words	saw the light
better late than never	short and sweet
drop in the bucket	sigh of relief
easier said than done	singing the blues
had a hard time of it	taking a big chance
in the nick of time	time and time again
in this day and age	too close for comfort
it dawned on me	too little, too late
it goes without saying	took a turn for the worse
last but not least	under the weather
make ends meet	where he (*or* she) is coming from
needless to say	word to the wise
on top of the world	work like a dog

Clichés are common in speech but make your writing seem tired and stale. Also, they are often an evasion of the specific details that you must work to provide in your writing. You should, then, avoid clichés and try to express your meaning in fresh, original ways.

Practice 1

Underline the cliché in each of the following sentences. Then substitute specific, fresh words for the trite expression.

Example   My parents supported me through some <u>trying times</u>.
              rough years

1. To make a long story short, my sister decided to file for divorce.
   To make a long story short is a cliché.

   _____

2. As quick as a wink, the baby tipped over the open box of oatmeal.

   _____

3. Any advice my friends give me goes in one ear and out the other.

   _____

4. I felt like a million dollars when I got my first A on a college test.

   _____

5. These days, well-paying jobs for high school graduates are few and far between.

   _____

Practice 2

Write a short paragraph describing the kind of day you had yesterday. Try to put as many clichés as possible into your writing. For example, "I had a long hard day. I had a lot to get done, and I kept my nose to the grindstone." By making yourself aware of clichés in this way, you should lessen the chance that they will appear in your writing.

Pretentious Words

Some people feel that they can improve their writing by using fancy, elevated words rather than simpler, more natural words. They use artificial and stilted language that more often obscures their meaning than communicates it clearly.

Here are some unnatural-sounding sentences:

The football combatants left the gridiron.

His instructional technique is a very positive one.

At the counter, we inquired about the arrival time of the aircraft.

I observed the perpetrator of the robbery depart from the retail establishment.

The same thoughts can be expressed more clearly and effectively by using plain, natural language, as below:

The football players left the field.

He is a good teacher.

At the counter, we asked when the plane would arrive.

I saw the robber leave the store.

Following is a list of some other inflated words and the simple words that could replace them.

Inflated Words	Simpler Words
component	part
delineate	describe
facilitate	help
finalize	finish
initiate	begin
manifested	shown
subsequent to	after
to endeavor	to try
transmit	send

Practice

Cross out the two pretentious words in each sentence. Then substitute clear, simple language for the pretentious words.

Example   Sally was ~~terminated~~ from her ~~employment~~.
Sally was fired from her job.

1. Please query one of our sales associates.
   Replace *query* and *associates* with simpler words.

   _____

   _____

2. The meteorological conditions are terrible today.

   _____

   _____

3. My parents desire me to obtain a college degree.

   _____

   _____

4. Do not protrude your arm out of the car, or an accident might ensue.

   _____

   _____

5. Many conflagrations are caused by the careless utilization of portable heaters.

_____

_____

Wordiness

22

Wordiness—using more words than necessary to express a meaning—is often a sign of lazy or careless writing. Your readers may resent the extra time and energy they must spend when you have not done the work needed to make your writing direct and concise.

Here is a list of some wordy expressions that could be reduced to single words.

Wordy Form	Short Form
a large number of	many
a period of a week	a week
arrive at an agreement	agree
at an earlier point in time	before
at the present time	now
big in size	big
due to the fact that	because
during the time that	while
five in number	five
for the reason that	because
good benefit	benefit
in every instance	always
in my opinion	I think
in the event that	if
in the near future	soon
in this day and age	today
is able to	can
large in size	large
plan ahead for the future	plan
postponed until later	postponed
red in color	red
return back	return

Here are examples of wordy sentences:

At this point in time in our country, the amount of violence seems to be increasing every day.

I called to the children repeatedly to get their attention, but my shouts did not get any response from them.

Omitting needless words improves these sentences:

Violence is increasing in our country.

I called to the children repeatedly, but they didn't respond.

Practice

Rewrite the following sentences, omitting unnecessary words.

Example   Starting as of the month of June, I will be working at the store on a full-time basis.

As of June, I will be working at the store full time.
_____

1. It is a well-known and proven fact that there is no cure as of yet for the common cold.
    The first part of the sentence and *as of yet* are wordy.

    _____

2. The main point that I will try to make in this paper is that our state should legalize and permit gambling.

    _____

3. Due to the fact that Chen's car refused to start up, he had to take public transportation by bus to his place of work.

    _____

4. When I was just a little boy, I already knew in my mind that my goal was to be a stockbroker in the future of my life.

    _____

5. The exercises that Susan does every day of the week give her more energy with which to deal with the happenings of everyday life.

    _____

■ Review Test 1

Certain words are italicized in the following sentences. In the space provided, identify whether the words are slang (*S*), clichés (*C*), or pretentious words (*PW*). Then replace them with more effective words.

_____   1. Donna *came out of her shell* after she joined a singing group at school.

_____

_____   2. I *totally lost it* when my little brother *got busted* for underage drinking.

_____

_____   3. I'm *suffering from a temporary depletion of all cash reserves.*

_____

_____   4. Our manager *flipped out* when a cashier gave the wrong change to a customer.

_____

_____   5. I got angry at the park visitors who did not put their *waste materials* in the *trash receptacle.*

_____

_____   6. Hearing I had passed the accounting final really *took a load off my mind.*

_____

_____   7. We all thought it was *too good to be true* when the instructor said that most of us would get A's in the course.

_____

_____   8. Fred *asserted to* the collection agency that he had sent the *remuneration.*

_____

_____   9. My old Toyota just *bit the dust,* so I'm *checking out* new cars.

_____

_____   10. This book was written by a millionaire who *didn't have a dime to his name* as a boy.

_____

■ **Review Test 2**

Rewrite the following sentences, omitting unnecessary words.

1. At 6 A.M. early this morning, I suddenly heard a loud and noisy banging by someone at the front door of my apartment.

   _____

   _____

2. The fact of the matter is that I did not remember until, of course, just now that I had an appointment to meet you.

   _____

   _____

3. We are very pleased to have the opportunity to inform you that your line of credit on your credit card with us has just been increased.

   _____

   _____

4. At this point in time, the company has no plan of adding to anyone's salary by giving a raise in pay in the near or distant future.

   _____

   _____

5. If you are out on the job market seeking a job, you just might benefit from professional help to assist you in your search for employment.

   _____

   _____

Part Three

Reinforcement of the Skills

Introduction

To reinforce the sentence skills presented in Part Two, this part of the book—Part Three—provides mastery tests, combined mastery tests, proofreading tests, and editing tests. There are four *mastery tests* for each of the skills where errors occur most frequently and two *mastery tests* for each of the remaining skills. A series of *combined mastery tests* will reassure your understanding of important related skills. *Editing and proofreading tests* offer practice in finding and correcting one kind of error in a brief passage. *Combined editing tests* then offer similar practice—except that each of these passages contains a variety of mistakes. Both the editing and the proofreading tests will help you become a skilled editor and proofreader. All too often, students can correct mistakes in practice sentences but are unable to do so in their own writing. You must learn to look carefully for sentence-skills errors and to make close checking a habit.

Appendix F at the end of the book provides progress charts that will help you keep track of your performance on these tests.

Mastery Tests

Subjects and Verbs

■ **Mastery Test 1**

Draw one line under subjects and two lines under verbs. Cross out prepositional phrases as necessary to help find subjects. (Be sure to underline all the parts of a verb. Also, remember that you may find more than one subject and one verb in a sentence.)

1. The sailboat drifted for hours on the calm sea.
2. Career Day at my high school was a big success.
3. Tall pine trees hid the farmhouse from view.
4. Sandy's revealing swimsuit attracted stares from everyone at the swimming pool.
5. Televisions, radios, and microwave ovens are on sale at greatly reduced prices.
6. All the fish in that lake have become contaminated.
7. Several garbage cans lined the weathered fence behind the old hotel.
8. Gloria often buys secondhand clothes and brightens them up by dyeing or embroidering them.
9. Weapons from police raids are kept under lock and key.
10. The old lady got back on her feet and surprised her attacker with a karate chop.

Score Number correct _____ × 10 = _____ %

9-25-06

Subjects and Verbs

■ Mastery Test 2

Draw one line under subjects and two lines under verbs. Cross out prepositional phrases as necessary to help find subjects. (Be sure to underline all the parts of a verb. Also, remember that you may find more than one subject and one verb in a sentence.)

1. Sharks swim continuously in their search for food.
2. The spider floated down from the ceiling and landed on my arm.
3. Most of the applicants for the office job arrived early for the interview.
4. The elderly man sat on the park bench and carefully opened his newspaper.
5. The shrubs are growing too close to the side of the house.
6. Andrew wants to learn to repair watches but does not have enough time on his hands.
7. All my friends, except my boyfriend, like my new hairstyle.
8. Carl washed his sports car every weekend and polished it once a month to protect the finish.
9. With only a day till the wedding, the bride and groom were having second thoughts.
10. Astrologers and astronomers agree on the importance of the stars but disagree on almost everything else.

(of) Set off a subject

Score Number correct _____ × 10 = _____ %

Subjects and Verbs

■ Mastery Test 3

Draw one line under subjects and two lines under verbs. Cross out prepositional phrases as necessary to help find subjects. (Be sure to underline all the parts of a verb. Also, remember that you may find more than one subject and one verb in a sentence.)

1. Blue wildflowers fill the empty lot.
2. No quarrel between good friends lasts for very long.
3. We borrowed my uncle's truck to move the refrigerator.
4. A young boy paid for the lollipop with a fistful of pennies.
5. Fewer people have been attending the school games this year.
6. Toward evening, my appetite seems to increase by the minute.
7. The woman in front of me was wearing a straw hat with a large daisy.
8. After a long search, I found my sweater in my sister's closet.
9. Giant lions and camels once roamed the American West.
10. An ancient footbridge formerly spanned the narrow stream but now lies under water.

Score   Number correct _____ × 10 = _____ %

9-25-06

Subjects and Verbs

■ Mastery Test 4

Draw one line under subjects and two lines under verbs. Cross out prepositional phrases as necessary to help find subjects. (Be sure to underline all the parts of a verb. Also, remember that you may find more than one subject and one verb in a sentence.)

1. The sharp edge of a book page slit my finger.
2. Floyd should have waxed his car in the shade.
3. A maze of gopher tunnels winds under our lawn.
4. I am planning to protest the school's suspension policy.
5. The thick coating on the fried chicken slipped off like a jacket.
6. My sister and I have agreed to share only our everyday clothes.
7. An angry player yelled at the umpire during the game and was ejected from the ballpark.
8. Canned salmon and tuna contain significant amounts of calcium.
9. A small dog followed me home and waited on my doorstep.
10. Dexter and Gale are taking their vacations at the same time and will visit Disney World for three days.

action word subject connect

passive voice

When the action is commenced upon subject

future tense

Score   Number correct _____ × 10 = _____ %

Fragments

■ Mastery Test 1

Each word group in the student paragraph below is numbered. In the space provided, write *C* if a word group is a complete sentence; write *frag* if it is a fragment. You will find ten fragments in the paragraph.

1. _____

2. _____

3. _____

4. _____

5. _____

6. _____

7. _____

8. _____

9. _____

10. _____

11. _____

12. _____

13. _____

14. _____

15. _____

16. _____

17. _____

18. _____

19. _____

20. _____

¹If an advertisement captures your interest. ²It may be because some proven psychological methods of gaining attention are being used. ³Such as change. ⁴A flashing light, for example, is more noticeable than a continuously lit one. ⁵Which is why many signs flash on and off. ⁶And change colors and shapes. ⁷Another advertising device is repetition. ⁸We remember many advertising slogans and jingles because we have heard them so often. ⁹In a thirty-second commercial, for instance, a message to use a certain toothpaste might be repeated five or six times. ¹⁰In addition, frequent appearances of such ads. ¹¹Contrast, too, gains people's interest. ¹²An advertiser may make a bright gold bracelet more appealing by placing it on a black velvet background. ¹³Creating a dramatic visual effect. ¹⁴Finally, to grab our attention. ¹⁵Advertisers also use novelty. ¹⁶Since people are drawn to the new and different, companies often change their products slightly. ¹⁷Or make new products that are just variations of the old ones. ¹⁸Then they emphasize the newness in their ads with various slogans. ¹⁹Including "new and improved" and "different from anything you've ever tried before." ²⁰Even if the products are not very new and different.

Score Number correct _____ × 5 = _____ %

Fragments

■ Mastery Test 2

Underline the fragment in each item. Then make whatever changes are needed to turn the fragment into a sentence.

Example   In grade school, I didn't want to wear glasses_x <u>And avoided having to</u>

<u>get them by memorizing the Snellen eye chart.</u>

 1. Lee went to the beauty parlor. To have her nails done for the vampire party.

 2. When the Millers moved away last winter. The entire town was mystified. They had left all their furniture behind.

 3. Nobody knew when the next train would arrive. Impatient commuters waited in line. And checked their watches every few minutes.

 4. Richard brought a stepladder to the parade. Planning to sell seats on the top rungs. Several police officers vetoed that idea.

 5. I don't like to go to the bank. Except on Friday. That's when I deposit money.

 6. Dawn is almost always early for work. But was late this morning. The boss told her not to worry.

 7. Sitting on the boat dock. Jesse was lost in thought. The rising sun climbed slowly in the sky.

 8. Nan felt around for the scissors at the back of the crowded drawer. She realized she had found them. When they stabbed her.

 9. The battery in Frank's Chevy is five years old. And barely able to start the engine on a cold morning. He is waiting to buy a new battery on sale.

10. We had to wait at the airport for quite a while. All departing flights were delayed. Because a small private plane had to make an emergency landing.

Score   Number correct _____ × 10 = _____ %

Fragments

■ Mastery Test 3

Underline the fragment in each item. Then make whatever changes are needed to turn the fragment into a sentence.

1. The police recruits lined up on the practice range. And loaded their pistols with bullets. Then they began firing at the targets in the distance.

2. Having gone on an all-day hike. We walked into the restaurant with dusty clothes and dirty faces. The hostess led us to a table in back by the kitchen.

3. The sanitation workers made quite a racket this morning. Also bent my new metal trash can. If they continue to be so rough, the can will soon be trash.

4. Sometimes my boss disappoints me. He can be very rude. For example, interrupting me while I'm making excuses.

5. My son wants to buy all the toys advertised on TV. Even if we had the money for them all. We wouldn't have the space.

6. I put off studying for the test until the last minute. As a result, being up all night. During the test the next morning, I was too tired to think clearly.

7. Nancy likes to be a know-it-all. She pretends to identify the stars on camping trips. But consults her map when no one is looking.

8. George and Charlotte got up at four this morning. To stand in line at the box office. They wanted front-row seats for the rock concert.

9. The boss gave all the secretaries bonuses at Christmas. Even Ms. Foster, who just joined the company in November. Many people felt he was too generous.

10. The newest ride at the amusement park is the "Elevator." You are hauled to the top of a tall shaft. And then dropped four stories to the ground. Fortunately, the brakes prevent your death.

Score   Number correct _____ × 10 = _____ %

Fragments

■ Mastery Test 4

Underline and then correct the ten fragments in the following passage.

My cousin Darryl is the worst driver I know. When he picks me up for school in the morning, he screeches to a halt outside my door. And peels away again in a cloud of blue exhaust fumes. Before hitting the highway, we speed through several narrow streets. Doing forty-five in twenty-miles-an-hour zones. On the four-lane road, Darryl weaves from lane to lane, tailgating cars six inches from their rear bumpers. Then passes them with a burst of stomach-flattening acceleration. To pass a car that's moving somewhat slowly in the passing lane. Darryl will get behind it, beep his horn, and even flash his high beams. Nothing infuriates him more than the "idiots," as he calls them. Who ignore these hints to move over. As we approach the jug-handle turn leading to school, Darryl speeds up. He is determined to make the light allowing cars to cross the highway into campus. If the light turns red and a car has already stopped. Darryl tromps on the brake pedal at the last possible second before impact and curses various things. Such as the red light and the car that stopped for it. Once in the parking lot, he finishes with a flourish. Pulling into a parking space at thirty-five miles an hour. As I reach out a limp hand to open the car door. I usually vow that I soon will buy my own car. Or find another ride to school.

Score Number correct _____ × 10 = _____ %

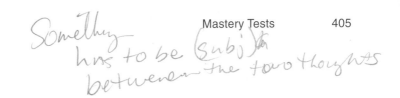

Something has to be (subj) ʃʃ between the two thoughts

Run-Ons

■ **Mastery Test 1**

In the space provided, write *R-O* beside run-on sentences. Write *C* beside the one sentence that is punctuated correctly. Some of the run-ons have no punctuation between the two complete thoughts; others have only a comma.

   Correct each run-on by using (1) a period and a capital letter, (2) a comma and a joining word, or (3) a semicolon. Do not use the same method of correction for every sentence.

Examples

___R-O___ I applied for the job, *but* I never got called in for an interview.

___R-O___ Carla's toothache is getting worse *. S* she should go to a dentist soon.

___R-O___ 1. He enjoys watching a talk show, she prefers watching a late movie.

___R-O___ 2. Elena tried an herbal shampoo, her hair smelled like a meadow.

___R-O___ 3. My last vacation trip was very broadening *but* I gained five pounds.

___R-O___ 4. Some people prefer very loud music, their bodies vibrate with the sound.

___C___ 5. Lorenzo is determined to find a new job, for his old one has given him an ulcer. *makes it complete*

___R-O___ 6. The rain fell softly outside, it was a relaxing day to stay indoors.

___R-O___ 7. A little girl toddled down the street she was attached to her mother by a chest harness and leash.

___R-O___ 8. The school bus stopped at the corner children scattered like leaves in the wind.

___R-O___ 9. The restaurant was closing *so* waiters were already stacking chairs on the tables for the night.

___R-O___ 10. His nose had become very cold, he pressed the warm underside of his forearm against it.

Score Number correct _____ × 10 = _____ %

Run-Ons

■ Mastery Test 2

In the space provided, write *R-O* beside run-on sentences. Write *C* beside the one sentence that is punctuated correctly. Some of the run-ons have no punctuation between the two complete thoughts; others have only a comma.

Correct each run-on by using (1) a period and capital letter, (2) a comma and a joining word, or (3) a semicolon. Do not use the same method of correction for every sentence.

_____   1. This semester our instructor gained a lot of weight he opened his belt another notch every two weeks.

_____   2. First Darlene washes her hair, then she goes to the hairdresser.

_____   3. The blue whale is an endangered animal, its population has been reduced to near extinction by whaling.

_____   4. Barbara saw a funeral on television she thought of her brother's recent death.

_____   5. I began to get sleepy during the long ride, so I opened all the windows and pinched myself.

_____   6. A flock of crows settled on a dimly lit tree their silhouettes stood out against the moon.

_____   7. The average American teenager spends thirty-eight hours a week on schoolwork the average Japanese teenager spends about sixty.

_____   8. Many people complained that the proposed apartment building would obstruct the scenery the water tower was bad enough.

_____   9. I spoke to the growling dog in a friendly tone. I hoped his owner would show up soon.

_____   10. At the crack of dawn, our neighbor started his lawnmower our "Saturday morning symphony" had begun.

> **Score**   Number correct _____ × 10 = _____ %

Run-Ons

■ Mastery Test 3

In the space provided, write *R-O* beside run-on sentences. Write *C* beside the two sentences that are punctuated correctly. Some of the run-ons have no punctuation between the two complete thoughts; others have only a comma.

    Correct each run-on by using (1) a period and capital letter, (2) a comma and a joining word, or (3) a semicolon. Do not use the same method of correction for every sentence.

_____   1. The early bird catches the worm, the early worm is not so lucky.

_____   2. A mountain of garbage bags stood on the curb I wondered about the fate of all that plastic.

_____   3. Some cities sponsor odd food festivals one celebrates spring with a dandelion-eating spree.

_____   4. Confinement in bed was the worst part of my illness, for I had to use a bedpan.

_____   5. At first, Regina forgot to serve the dinner rolls the smoke from the oven reminded her.

_____   6. The roadside trees were infested webbed caterpillar nests filled the tree branches.

_____   7. Al slammed the New York City phone book down with disgust it was impossible to find the right John Smith in it.

_____   8. Few trout live in the stream its once-clear waters are cloudy with the runoff from the new subdivision.

_____   9. The dashboard lights flickered on and off there was a short in the electrical system.

_____   10. The children enjoyed seeing the animals at the zoo, but the high points of their visit were the cotton candy and popcorn.

Score   Number correct _____ × 10 = _____ %

Run-Ons

■ Mastery Test 4

In the space provided, write *R-O* beside run-on sentences. Write *C* beside the one sentence that is punctuated correctly. Some of the run-ons have no punctuation between the two complete thoughts; others have only a comma.

Correct each run-on by using (1) a period and capital letter, (2) a comma and a joining word, or (3) a semicolon. Do not use the same method of correction for every sentence.

_____ 1. The sky in the country seems to have more stars, no city pollution blocks the view.

_____ 2. An old engraving of New York City shows a startling fact pigs once ran loose on Broadway.

_____ 3. Sandy sat quietly in the empty church it was better than any tranquilizer.

_____ 4. On the way home, Linda wanted to get her gas tank filled the stations she passed were all closed.

_____ 5. Numerous shrubs lined the driveway they were a pruner's nightmare.

_____ 6. Victor turned to look at the unexpected face in the window it was his own reflection.

_____ 7. An elephant's thin ears cool the animal in two ways they fan the body and cool blood on its way to the heart.

_____ 8. A vigorous wind lashed through the forest trees nodded and bowed toward each other like old men in conversation.

_____ 9. Theo chose a bad time to teach his tardy wife a lesson, for he showed up four hours late for dinner on the night of his surprise birthday party.

_____ 10. Soldiers in the Revolutionary Army had to be at least sixteen they also had to have good teeth in order to tear the paper cartridges filled with gunpowder.

Score   Number correct _____ × 10 = _____ %

Sentence Variety I

■ Mastery Test 1

Combine each group of short sentences into one sentence. Various combinations are possible. Choose the combination that reads most smoothly and clearly and that sounds most appropriate in the context of surrounding sentences.

Note   In combining short sentences into one sentence, omit repeated words where necessary. Use separate paper. The story about the mother's advice continues in the next mastery test.

Helpful Advice

- People repeat common sayings.
- People do this often.
- People do this without thinking about them.

- These sayings are old proverbs.
- They are based on a lot of experience.
- They can be good advice.

- My mother told me a proverb.
- My mother told it to me many years ago.
- My mother lived by this proverb.

- This old saying still rings in my ears.
- The ringing is often.
- The saying is "Don't sweat the small stuff."

- My mother realized she worried about problems.
- My mother realized she worried for too long.
- The problems were trivial.
- The problems were soon forgotten.

Score Number correct _____ × 20 = _____ %

Sentence Variety I

■ Mastery Test 2

Combine each group of short sentences into one sentence. Various combinations are possible. Choose the combination that reads most smoothly and clearly and that sounds most appropriate in the context of surrounding sentences.

Note   In combining short sentences into one sentence, omit repeated words where necessary. Use separate paper. The story about the mother's advice continues from the previous mastery test.

- She kept this saying in mind.
- The saying reminded her not to fret about little things.
- The fretting was needless.

- I lie in bed sleepless.
- I do this sometimes.
- I worry about the dent in my car.
- I worry about the way my clothes fit.
- I worry about a remark someone made.

- I do something then.
- I put things in perspective.
- I do this by remembering my mother's words.
- I decide not to "sweat the small stuff."

- My mother's advice is like a pill.
- The pill is for sleeping.
- The pill allows me to rest.

- I am able to save my worrying.
- My worrying will be for important matters.
- My worrying will not be for the small stuff.

Score   Number correct _____ × 20 = _____ %

Standard English Verbs

■ Mastery Test 1

Underline the correct words in the parentheses.

1. Bert's car (have, has) a horn that (play, plays) six different tunes.
2. When the pile of rags (start, started) to catch on fire, Dave (reach, reached) for the hose.
3. I (don't, doesn't) think my mother (has, have) gone out to a movie in years.
4. When she (is, be) upset, Mimi (tell, tells) her troubles to her houseplants.
5. The play (was, were) ruined when the quarterback (fumble, fumbled) the handoff.
6. My husband (think, thinks) more clearly in the morning than he (do, does) at night.
7. I (want, wanted) to take off my rings, but they (was, were) stuck on my swollen fingers.
8. Dolores (has, have) only three more courses before she (earn, earns) her degree.
9. Sometimes I (think, thinks) the happiest people (be, are) those with the lowest expectations of life.
10. The street musician (count, counted) the coins in his donations basket and (pack, packed) his trumpet in its case.

Score Number correct _____ × 10 = _____ %

Standard English Verbs

■ Mastery Test 2

Cross out the nonstandard verb form and write the correct form in the space provided.

seems   Example   The job offer ~~seem~~ too good to be true.

_____   1. Billy always clown around in the back of the class.

_____   2. When the last guests left our party, we was exhausted but happy.

_____   3. The computer in the library keep saying, "System error."

_____   4. Today my counselor advise me to drop one of my courses.

_____   5. My sister Louise walk a mile to the bus stop every day.

_____   6. I don't think that Juan have thought enough about his future.

_____   7. The fans all stood up and cheer when the home team made a goal-line stand.

_____   8. Dora's husband don't like to talk about his experiences in Vietnam.

_____   9. After fumbling with his papers, the nervous announcer pronounce the president's name wrong.

_____   10. Some students heads for the parking lot between classes to sit in their cars and blast their radios.

Score   Number correct _____ × 10 = _____ %

Standard English Verbs

■ Mastery Test 3

Part 1   Fill in each blank with the appropriate standard verb form of *be, have,* or *do* in the present or past tense.

I _____ this problem called a little brother. Though I _____ always
     1   2

nice to him, he enjoys embarrassing me. The other night, for example, I _____ my
                                                            3

boyfriend over to the house. The lights were turned down low, and my boyfriend and

I _____ alone on the living-room couch. At least I thought so. The nosy spy who
      4

_____ my brother crawled into the living room with a video camera. My
     5

boyfriend and I _____ not notice him because we _____ started kissing.
                 6   7

It _____ the next night when I discovered what that little brat _____ been
       8   9

up to. In front of my parents, he showed them what he filmed. His plan _____ a
                                                                10

big success because I felt embarrassed to death.

Part 2   Fill in the correct form of the regular verb in parentheses.

Shopping at a convenience store isn't always so convenient. The other night I (stop)

_____ off at the local Seven-Eleven to pick up a two-liter bottle of diet soda and a
     1

package of chips. After I had (park) _____ my car and gone inside, I was (greet)
                                          2

_____ by the sight of a long line of customers, which was (back) _____
     3   4

up down one aisle. Since Seven-Eleven was the only place still open at that time of

night, I (decide) _____ to stay. I (pick) _____ up my soda and potato chips
                     5   6

and (walk) _____ to the end of the line. I saw that the delay was (cause)
               7

_____ by a woman who had (place) _____ a large order for lunch meat.
     8   9

And the teenage boy waiting on her (move) _____ like someone in a slow-motion
                                                10

film.

Score	Number correct _____ × 5 = _____ %

Standard English Verbs

■ **Mastery Test 4**

Part 1   Fill in each blank with the appropriate standard verb form of *be, have,* or *do* in the present or past tense.

There _____ one thing my mother does better than anybody else in the
                    1
world—make requests. It seems she _____ to start right in as soon as I wake up.
                                              2
"_____ you make your bed, Arnold?" she always asks me. "_____ you
        3   4
going to wear that nice sport shirt I pressed for you last night? _____ not forget to
                                                                              5
put out the trash before you leave for school, dear. _____ you still going to paint
                                                                  6
the basement this weekend? _____ you remember to stop by the grocery on your
                                        7
way home from school?" She _____ an endless supply of such appeals. I think I
                                        8
_____ to get out of here. Maybe it _____ time to get married, which
          9   10
happens to be another thing she wants me to do.

Part 2   Fill in each blank with the appropriate form of the regular verb shown in parentheses. Use present or past tense as needed.

Driving on trips with my three-year-old son has its drawbacks. For one thing he (find)
_____ it difficult to sit still for long. Besides that, when he (eat) _____ in
          1   2
the car, which is frequently, he (scatter) _____ crumbs all over the backseat and
                                                      3
floor. And after each time he (snack) _____ on something, he (insist)
                                                  4
_____ on touching everything in sight with his dirty hands. My mother (believe)
          5
_____ he actually (enjoy) _____ smudging the windows with grease. Last
          6   7
week, driving (affect) _____ his stomach, which (require) _____ an
                                8   9
unpleasant stop at the side of the road. The only good thing about traveling with my son is
that he still (take) _____ naps a couple of times a day.
                              10

Score   Number correct _____ × 5 = _____ %

Irregular Verbs

■ Mastery Test 1

Underline the correct word in the parentheses.

1. (Lying, Laying) in the hot sun is bad for the skin.
2. Last night I (saw, seen) a dead collie on the road.
3. My girlfriend (teached, taught) me how to make curtains for my van.
4. The judge reminded Daniel that he had (sworn, swore) to tell the truth.
5. My boss has (chosen, chose) to treat me the way a baby treats a diaper.
6. Whenever I had an important date, my brother (lended, lent) me his good jacket.
7. Molly has finally (took, taken) aspirin for the headache she's had all day.
8. Five different people had (bringed, brought) huge bowls of potato salad to the barbecue.
9. I scratched the spot where the hornet (stinged, stung) me till I bled.
10. The picture I (drawed, drew) in art class ended up looking like a plate of spaghetti.
11. Taking care of two of the neighbor's children this week has (worn, wore) me out.
12. I left the wine in the freezer to cool, and it (froze, freezed) into wine slush.
13. The thief (hid, hided) in the shadows until the guard left the area.
14. Stan's truck (rises, raises) a cloud of dust when it comes down the dirt road.
15. My research paper is due in two weeks, and I haven't even (begun, began) to work on it.
16. Having (slept, sleeped) all day, Dracula looked forward to a bite to eat.
17. I accidentally (throwed, threw) away the parking ticket when I cleaned out my glove compartment.
18. After playing touch football all afternoon, Jake (drunk, drank) a quart of Gatorade.
19. Since Carol left a third of the answer spaces blank, she (knew, knowed) she had failed the psychology exam.
20. After you have (broke, broken) up with a boyfriend or girlfriend, every day feels like a cloudy, cold Monday morning.

Score Number correct _____ × 5 = _____ %

Irregular Verbs

■ Mastery Test 2

Cross out the incorrect verb form in each sentence. Write the correct form in the space provided.

_____   1. The phone rung once and then stopped.

_____   2. Rosie spended an entire week's salary on a new pair of boots.

_____   3. No one had broke the news to Rich that he had not made the team.

_____   4. The hurricane winds blowed several beach houses off their foundations.

_____   5. I've swam in this lake for years, and I've never seen it so shallow.

_____   6. That trucker has drove over a million accident-free miles.

_____   7. How did the police know where the kidnappers had hid their victim?

_____   8. My cotton sweater shranked so much in the wash that I gave it to my daughter.

_____   9. If I had took more notes in that class, I would have done better on the exam.

_____   10. The receiver escaped the defender, catched the football, and dashed into the end zone for a touchdown.

Score   Number correct _____ × 10 = _____ %

Irregular Verbs

■ Mastery Test 3

Write in the space provided the correct form of the verb shown at the left.

grow

1. My nephew must have _____ six inches since last summer.

drive

2. We _____ almost seven hundred miles before pulling over for a break.

fall

3. Frowning, the building inspector stood where the store's sign had _____.

fight

4. My parents _____ with the IRS for a year before finally paying the additional tax.

break

5. During last night's storm, lightning _____ the clock over the town hall.

write

6. The police found the hit-and-run driver because Aunt Edith had _____ the license number down.

eat

7. Hank's dog climbed onto the kitchen table at night and _____ most of the chocolate chip cookies.

tear

8. After he _____ the cartilage in his knee for the third time, Bubba decided to retire from football.

take

9. The orchestra arrived two hours late for the New Year's Eve party because the bus driver had _____ a wrong turn.

go

10. When his boss caught him sleeping at his desk, Norman wished he had _____ to bed earlier the night before.

Score Number correct _____ × 10 = _____ %

Irregular Verbs

■ Mastery Test 4

Write in the space provided the correct form of the verb shown at the left.

see
1. My roommate and I _____ that new horror film last night.

bring
2. I should have _____ a gift to the office Christmas party.

speak
3. Has the supervisor _____ to Marcia yet about being late for work?

come
4. Just as we were talking about Rob's new pickup truck, Rob _____ up the driveway.

throw
5. Huey _____ out his back trying to put a new air conditioner in his bedroom window.

sing
6. I could have _____ professionally, but I lacked the determination to pursue a career.

sit
7. When I have company for dinner, I _____ in the middle of the table rather than at one end.

speak
8. Our guest is a former police detective who has _____ all over the country on the subject of teenage drug abuse.

choose
9. I know I should have _____ a different major, but I don't want to start from the beginning now.

give
10. The state trooper _____ Harley a warning for riding his motor-cycle on the interstate without a safety helmet.

Score Number correct _____ × 10 = _____ %

Subject-Verb Agreement

■ **Mastery Test 1**

Underline the correct verb in the parentheses. Note that you will first have to determine the subject in each sentence. To help find subjects in certain sentences, you may find it helpful to cross out prepositional phrases.

1. Many stories in the *National Enquirer* (seems, seem) hard to believe.
2. Where (has, have) all the pens gone in this house?
3. One of my sweaters (has, have) moth holes in the sleeves.
4. There (is, are) plenty of reasons for not going to the party tonight.
5. Each of the marathon runners (receives, receive) a special T-shirt.
6. The movies in my DVD collection (is, are) arranged alphabetically.
7. Football players who (scores, score) touchdowns get most of the glory.
8. The major story on all the news programs (concerns, concern) the president's operation.
9. Both of the drive-in windows at the bank (closes, close) at three o'clock.
10. Here (is, are) my address and phone number, so you can get in touch.
11. On the front page of the newspaper (was, were) a story about my accident.
12. Someone (keeps, keep) calling me and hanging up when I answer.
13. How (does, do) the weather forecasters determine if it's partly sunny or partly cloudy?
14. Growing in the middle of our flower bed (was, were) a single stalk of wild asparagus.
15. Every one of the boxers (seems, seem) to follow a different training regimen.
16. Each of my little boys (needs, need) a warmer jacket for the winter.
17. The level of water in local reservoirs (has, have) dropped dramatically recently.
18. The figure that intrigues Wayne most in his geometry class (belongs, belong) to the girl sitting next to him.
19. Why (does, do) many appliances stop working as soon as their warranties expire?
20. Orange slices and ginger ale still (needs, need) to be added to the punch.

Score   Number correct _____ × 5 = _____ %

Subject-Verb Agreement

■ Mastery Test 2

In the space provided, write the correct form of the verb shown in the margin.

cares, care   1. Gina seems like the kind of person who _____ more about style than about substance.

was, were   2. There _____ five people absent from last night's class.

runs, run   3. The portable television and the radio _____ on batteries or house current.

snarls, snarl   4. Either construction work or accidents _____ expressway traffic every morning.

has, have   5. Along with the two graduate assistants, the professor _____ conducted the experiment hundreds of times.

is, are   6. At least a few of the gray hairs on your poor father's head _____ due to you and that no-good brother of yours.

finds, find   7. Each runner, summoning all the courage and adrenaline he has left, _____ that the ultimate challenger is himself.

is, are   8. Lined up outside the movie theater _____ dozens of impatient children and their angry parents.

seems, seem   9. Politicians, I have noticed, often _____ to choose words very carefully, as if selecting stones to step on while crossing a stream.

was, were   10. I found it almost impossible to believe that this seventy-year-old man, with his rumpled clothes, _____ a mass murderer.

Score   Number correct _____ × 10 = _____ %

Subject-Verb Agreement

■ **Mastery Test 3**

Cross out the incorrect form of the verb. In addition, underline the subject that goes with the verb. Then write the correct form of the verb in the space provided. Mark the one sentence that is correct with a *C*.

_____ 1. Each of the secretaries work from nine to five.

_____ 2. The price of the theater tickets seem much too high.

_____ 3. A salad, beverage, and dessert accompanies the meal.

_____ 4. There was only three pieces of wood left in the pile.

_____ 5. The new tenant and her little boy makes a lot of noise.

_____ 6. Corn on the cob, iced tea, and watermelon is symbolic of summer.

_____ 7. One of the most regal-looking animals in the zoo are the big-horned sheep.

_____ 8. The picture on the cover of that paperback gives the wrong idea of the book's story.

_____ 9. Neither Brenda nor her sisters has enough money to go to the movies tonight.

_____ 10. The roots of the tree on the beach was exposed by erosion from the surf.

Score Number correct _____ × 10 = _____ %

Subject-Verb Agreement

■ Mastery Test 4

Cross out the incorrect form of the verb. In addition, underline the subject that goes with the verb. Then write the correct form of the verb in the space provided. Mark the one sentence that is correct with a *C*.

_____	1. When is Kay and her parents going on vacation?
_____	2. One of the patients wander aimlessly down the halls.
_____	3. My sister and her husband takes my father bowling every Thursday night.
_____	4. Each of the fast-food restaurants now have a breakfast special.
_____	5. Next to the newborn chicks were one of the barn rats.
_____	6. Whenever the coach gets angry, both sides of his mouth curls up in a sneer.
_____	7. The clouds part, and the warming rays of the sun shine through, bringing instant heat with them.
_____	8. Anyone who comes in late to Mr. Barker's class have to have a good excuse.
_____	9. Snuggling under the covers feel wonderful on Saturday mornings.
_____	10. A box of shredded wheat last about a year in our house, since the kids call it "shredded steel wool."

Score Number correct _____ × 10 = _____ %

Consistent Verb Tense

■ Mastery Test 1

In each item, one verb must be changed so that it agrees in tense with the other verb or verbs. Cross out the inconsistent verb and write the correct form in the space provided.

_____   1. Sofia asked the grouchy cashier for change, and he counts out twenty-five pennies.

_____   2. After dinner, my parents watched the news while the children clear the table and washed the dishes.

_____   3. I walked through town yesterday, and a friend from grade school calls to me.

_____   4. Rose tried to avoid breathing the fumes as she sprays her houseplants with pesticide.

_____   5. When we arrived at the theater, I suddenly remember that I had left the oven turned on at home.

_____   6. Annie sighed as her little boy repeatedly guides the spoonful of mashed carrots to his ear.

_____   7. I drank the ice water too quickly; sharp pains rush to my temple and forced me to stop walking for a minute.

_____   8. Upon finding a seat on the bus, Victor unfolded his newspaper, turns to the sports section, and began to read.

_____   9. Polar bear cubs stay with their mothers for two years; then they leave home and faced the Arctic winter alone.

_____   10. Our family car was in sad shape; the tires were worn, the chrome is pitted, and the paint came off if you rubbed it too hard.

Score Number correct _____ × 10 = _____ %

Consistent Verb Tense

■ Mastery Test 2

In each item, one verb must be changed so that it agrees in tense with the other verb or verbs. Cross out the inconsistent verb and write the correct form in the space provided.

_____ 1. Hana eats a nutritious breakfast, skipped lunch, and then enjoys a big dinner.

_____ 2. The circus performer balanced on one foot, juggles knives, and joked with the crowd.

_____ 3. Tears streamed down little Heather's face as her father combs her tangled hair.

_____ 4. The restaurant near the wharf opened in May, stays busy all summer, and then closes for the winter.

_____ 5. At the game, Danny hums along with the national anthem when he forgot some of the words.

_____ 6. Terri buys and reads several romance novels every month, for she wanted to escape from her dull daily routine.

_____ 7. When he prepared the omelet, the chef grated fresh cheese, chopped an onion, and slices a crisp green pepper.

_____ 8. To make the dress fit, Inez shortened the shoulder straps, moved a button, and tightens the waist.

_____ 9. Stu got his driver's license after he had an eye exam, took a written quiz, and passes a driving-skills test.

_____ 10. Before she decided to buy the wall calendar, Magda turns its pages and looked at all the pictures.

Score   Number correct _____ × 10 = _____ %

11-13-06

Pronoun Reference, Agreement, and Point of View

■ **Mastery Test 1**

Underline the correct word in the parentheses.

who became upset

1. As Jill argued with her mother, (she, Jill) became more and more upset.

2. One of the female astronauts will take (her, their) first space walk during the flight.

3. If you stay up too late watching television, (one, you) may walk around like a zombie the next day.

4. At the library, (they, the librarian) showed me how to use the microfilm machines.

5. Everyone who works in this company must have (his or her, their) chest x-rayed every two years.

6. The nurse finally penetrated my vein with a large needle, although (it, the vein) had been hard to find.

7. I like living in a large apartment house because (I, you) have more chances to meet people.

8. Jesse's brother called to say that (he, Jesse) had gotten bad news from the doctor.

9. Although I was an announcer on my college radio station, I wouldn't want to make a career of (announcing, it).

10. Anybody who lives to (their, his or her) ninetieth year is eligible to receive a birthday card from the president.

Score   Number correct _____ × 10 = _____ %

Pronoun Reference, Agreement, and Point of View

14-13-06 (handwritten)

■ **Mastery Test 2**

In the space provided, write *PE* beside sentences that contain pronoun errors. Write *C* beside the two sentences that use pronouns correctly. Then cross out each pronoun error and write the correction above it.

_____PE_____   Example   Each of the boys explained ~~their~~ *his* project.

_____Pe_____   1. Vincent doesn't like visiting his in-laws because ~~you~~ *Vincent* never feel like part of the family.

_____Pe_____   2. Nadine told her niece that ~~she~~ *her niece* would be famous someday.

_____Pe_____   3. I ordered three novels from the company's website, but ~~they~~ *the company* never sent them.

_____PE_____   4. We are treated horribly at work; ~~they~~ *supervisor* must think we're slaves.

_____C_____   5. Someone on the team shared his complaints with a reporter.

_____Pe_____   6. Ernie placed the ladder against the wall of the garage and then leaned against ~~it~~ *the wall* for a moment.

_____C_____   7. Each of these jobs has its advantages: one has good pay, and the other has short hours.

_____Pe_____   8. I like to watch TV quiz shows because ~~you~~ *I* can learn a lot from their questions.

_____Pe_____   9. The college instructors made sure the students understood that ~~they~~ *college inst.* were bright and capable.

_____Pe_____   10. Any salesperson in our office will win a free trip to Hawaii if ~~they~~ *he/she* can sell one house in the next twenty-four hours.

Score Number correct _____ × 10 = _____ %

Pronoun Reference, Agreement, and Point of View

11-13-06

■ Mastery Test 3

In the spaces provided, write *PE* beside sentences that contain pronoun errors. Write *C* beside the two sentences that use pronouns correctly. Then cross out each pronoun error and write the correction above it.

Pe   1. When the car banged into the wall, ~~it~~ *the car* was damaged.

Pe   2. One of my friends entered ~~their~~ *his/her* dog in a Frisbee tournament.

Pe   3. One of the floorboards is warped, and I keep tripping on ~~them~~ *she*.

Pe   4. As I slowed down at the scene of the accident, ~~you~~ *I* could see long black skid marks on the highway.

C   5. As we looked out the plane window, we could see roads and buildings get smaller and smaller.

C   6. All visitors should stay in their cars while driving through the wild animal park.

Pe   7. Tisha avoids office parties because ~~one~~ *She* always has to watch out for the office Romeos.

Pe   8. I always shopped at that market because ~~they~~ *the market or (It)* had such a large selection.

Pe   9. A person who likes to criticize others often objects when someone teases ~~them~~ *his/her*.

Pe   10. If anyone works with an irresponsible lab partner, ~~you~~ *he/she* will find it difficult to complete experiments successfully.

Score Number correct _____ × 10 = _____ %

Pronoun Reference, Agreement, and Point of View

■ **Mastery Test 4**

In the spaces provided, write *PE* beside sentences that contain pronoun errors. Write *C* beside the two sentences that use pronouns correctly. Then cross out each pronoun error and write the correction above it. One item needs to be rewritten altogether. Identify it and rewrite it in the space at the bottom.

_____   1. Bill spent a half hour complaining to Gary about his girlfriend.

_____   2. As I watched the pro wrestling match, you could tell the violence was faked.

_____   3. Each gymnast has to develop his or her own floor routine.

_____   4. I arrived late for the final exam in English, which is why I failed it.

_____   5. Anybody willing to volunteer their time to work at the shelter for the homeless should sign up here.

_____   6. My sister and I fought a lot as children, but you learned to get along better as grown-ups.

_____   7. Sally received an ad in the mail that said she could make one thousand dollars a month addressing envelopes.

_____   8. One of the players on the women's basketball team scored their thousandth point yesterday.

_____   9. Mr. Penge invited his students to his home to meet a famous scientist, which made them feel special.

_____   10. During my first year in college, I stayed in a dorm where they chose a roommate for me.

Rewritten Version of Item :_____

_____

_____

Score   Number correct _____ × 10 = _____ %

Pronoun Types

■ Mastery Test 1

Underline the correct word in parentheses.

1. Paul is a much faster typist than (I, me).
2. (That, That there) tree will probably fall over with the next strong wind.
3. Since I'm about to get sick, that last drink is (yours, yours') if you want it.
4. My neighbor asked Eric and (I, me) to help him unload his new living-room furniture.
5. The students raised the money for the class trip (theirselves, themselves).
6. Our neighbors take (they, their) dog with them whenever they go for a ride.
7. My sister and (I, me) have gotten part-time jobs at the same store.
8. I feel certain that Steven will speak for (hisself, himself) at the meeting tonight.
9. Before I dated Don, I dated a number of friends of (his, his').
10. It was up to Kelly and (I, me) to fix the loose handrail on the back porch.
11. (Them, Those) strawberries we picked should taste delicious on our home-made ice cream.
12. After the riot, the band members (theirselves, themselves) decided to go on with the concert.
13. My father always said to remember to give each man the respect due to (he, him).
14. Julie is the one student (who, whom) is doing well in that class.
15. The audience laughed when Mario and (he, him) walked onstage in the carrot costumes.
16. Terry left some old books of (her's, hers) when she moved out of the apartment.
17. Telemarketers insist on calling my wife and (I, me) during dinner.
18. If any of you want tickets to the play-offs, you will have to pick them up (yourselfs, yourselves).
19. I couldn't decide to (who, whom) I should tell the secret.
20. If we don't get overtime pay for working on the holiday, (we, us) employees are going to file a complaint.

Score Number correct _____ × 5 = _____ %

Pronoun Types

■ **Mastery Test 2**

Cross out the incorrect pronoun in each sentence and write the correct form in the space provided at the left.

_____ 1. That there house across the street has been vacant for two years now.

_____ 2. The wallet that was stolen from the health club is hers'.

_____ 3. Give Chet and I a few hours, and we'll have that washing machine running again.

_____ 4. Rodney convinced hisself he would win the bowling match, and he did.

_____ 5. If I have to be marooned on a desert island with someone, I hope it is him.

_____ 6. Carla has put everything of yours' in the hall closet.

_____ 7. Just between you and I, the mayor is a horrible womanizer.

_____ 8. The coaches themself took full blame for the loss of the football game.

_____ 9. You two have a better attitude about school than them.

_____ 10. Please clear your books off the table, so I can set these here dishes down.

_____ 11. At the meeting, the store buyers told we salespeople about the new fall line.

_____ 12. The tornado destroyed everything in its' path.

_____ 13. If you were as nervous as him, your forehead would be sweating too.

_____ 14. When our whispering started to annoy her, the librarian asked Paula and I to leave.

_____ 15. You can tell them plants haven't been watered in ages because their leaves are turning brown.

_____ 16. After the police released us from the station, my stepfather lectured my brother and I for two hours.

_____ 17. Margo did not recognize the man whom stood at her apartment door.

_____ 18. Our students seem to have less school spirit than theirs'.

_____ 19. We asked ourself why such a young girl would try to take her own life.

_____ 20. Although we got a late start, Herbie and me collected enough aluminum cans along the highway to fill three plastic trash bags.

Score Number correct _____ × 5 = _____ %

Adjectives and Adverbs

■ Mastery Test 1

Part 1 Cross out the incorrect adjectival and adverbial form in each sentence. Then write the correct form in the space provided.

1. I did my work silent, but I was seething inside.

   _____

2. The children's smiles were so sweetly that I knew they were up to something.

   _____

3. Sarita was proud that she had stuck to her diet faithful for two weeks.

   _____

4. The students gazed longing at the clock as the instructor's voice droned on.

   _____

5. Signs warn motorists to drive slow near the school.

   _____

Part 2 Cross out the error in comparison in each sentence. Then write the correct form in the space provided.

6. Roy can't pitch, but he catches good.

   _____

7. You gave me a more smaller slice of pizza than you gave Bud.

   _____

8. A king-size bed is much comfortabler than a single bed.

   _____

9. Mrs. Patridge owns several banks, but she's the most stingiest person I know.

   _____

10. My coach said I had the most good chance of any person on the team of becoming a professional ballplayer.

    _____

Score Number correct _____ × 10 = _____ %

Adjectives and Adverbs

■ Mastery Test 2

Part 1   Cross out the incorrect adjectival and adverbial form in each sentence. Then write the correct form in the space provided.

1. Too many children complain that their parents don't take them serious.

   _____

2. The president's spouse greeted all the guests at the reception warm.

   _____

3. He is the most fiendishly culprit the police have ever encountered.

   _____

4. Fran polished the dull chrome tabletop until she could see her face clear in it.

   _____

5. The doctor said I wasn't good enough to travel, but I stubbornly refused to listen to him.

   _____

Part 2   Add to each sentence the correct form of the word at the left.

good   6. Of the two hundred applicants, Olivia was easily the _____.

few   7. _____ people live in Los Angeles than in New York.

boring   8. Of all the new television shows I have watched this year, that comedy is the

          _____.

high   9. Because his house was so drafty, Pat had to turn the thermostat even

          _____ to keep warm.

scary   10. *The Night of the Living Dead* is the _____ movie I have ever
          seen.

> *Score*   Number correct _____ × 10 = _____ %

Misplaced Modifiers

■ Mastery Test 1

Underline the misplaced word or words in each sentence. Then rewrite the sentence, placing related words together and making the meaning clear.

1. Barry decided to quit smoking while jogging.

   _____

   _____

2. The suburbs nearly had five inches of rain.

   _____

   _____

3. I decided to send fewer Christmas cards out this year in October.

   _____

   _____

4. My mother talked about her plans to start a garden while preparing dinner.

   _____

   _____

5. The car was parked along the side of the road with a flat tire.

   _____

   _____

6. Olivia stretched out on the lounge chair wearing her bathing suit.

   _____

   _____

7. Caryl read an article about starting your own business in the dentist's office.

   _____

   _____

8. A cake baked by my brother covered with coconut and candies was the prizewinner.

   _____

   _____

> **Score**   Number correct _____ × 12.5 = _____ %

Misplaced Modifiers

■ **Mastery Test 2**

Underline the misplaced word or words in each sentence. Then rewrite the sentence, placing related words together and making the meaning clear.

1. I replaced the shingle on the roof that was loose.

   _____

   _____

2. The instructor explained why cheating was wrong on Friday.

   _____

   _____

3. Jamal ordered a large pizza for his family topped with extra cheese.

   _____

   _____

4. The helicopter filmed the migrating antelope hovering overhead.

   _____

   _____

5. I bought a jacket at our neighborhood sporting goods store that is water resistant.

   _____

   _____

6. The magician almost held his breath for five minutes while escaping from the submerged trunk.

   _____

   _____

7. Neighborhood children watched the new family move in from the street corner.

   _____

   _____

8. Newspapers ran the story of the congressman's lies in every part of the country.

   _____

   _____

Score Number correct _____ × 12.5 = _____ %

Dangling Modifiers

■ Mastery Test 1

Underline the dangling modifier in each sentence. Then rewrite the sentence, correcting the dangling modifier.

1. Being on a diet, my pie had no whipped cream.

   _____

   _____

2. Walking through the woods, the trees shaded George from the sun.

   _____

   _____

3. After a nap in my room, my mother always gave me a snack.

   _____

   _____

4. Running to catch the ball at full speed, my cap went flying into the wind.

   _____

   _____

5. While looking for bargains at Sears, an exercise bike caught my eye.

   _____

   _____

6. Filled with sand, Debbie took off her shoes before going into the house.

   _____

   _____

7. Pedaling as fast as possible, Todd's bike pulled away from the snapping dog.

   _____

   _____

8. Punctured by a pin, Dexter mended his water bed with a plastic bandage.

   _____

   _____

Score Number correct _____ × 12.5 = _____ %

Dangling Modifiers

■ **Mastery Test 2**

Underline the dangling modifier in each sentence. Then rewrite the sentence, correcting the dangling modifier.

1. Being hungry as a bear, my dinner was enormous.

   _____

   _____

2. Feet spread, the police frisked the suspects for weapons.

   _____

   _____

3. Blown over in the hurricane, Roberto had to build a new garage.

   _____

   _____

4. Stolen from the mall parking lot, my girlfriend spotted my sports car the next day.

   _____

   _____

5. Even before being housebroken, I thought the beagle was lovable.

   _____

   _____

6. Walking down the weedy path, the old, weathered house loomed larger than I had remembered.

   _____

   _____

7. While dreaming about the beach, the alarm suddenly woke Lynn up.

   _____

   _____

8. After spending most of the night outdoors in a tent, the sun rose, and we went into the house.

   _____

   _____

Score   Number correct _____ × 12.5 = _____ %

Faulty Parallelism

■ Mastery Test 1

The unbalanced part of each sentence is italicized. Rewrite this part so that it matches the rest of the sentence.

1. The theater popcorn was greasy, stale, and *had too much salt.*

   _____

2. I would rather have you call me on the phone than *sending me a letter.*

   _____

3. The orchestra leader had slick black hair, a long thin nose, and *eyes that were dark blue.*

   _____

4. Whenever I get home, my dog barks, *is running to get his ball,* and drops it at my feet.

   _____

5. The job applicant—well dressed, well spoken, and *with a good education*—impressed the interviewer.

   _____

6. I stood for two hours in the hot sun in my heavy wool dress, long-sleeved jacket, and *shoes that were tight.*

   _____

7. After his family's weekend visit ended, Enrique was exhausted and relieved but *was feeling lonely.*

   _____

8. Before assembling the casserole, Marty had to sauté the onions and *stirring them into the ground meat.*

   _____

9. As they neared the ocean, they could hear the waves, smell the salt water, and *the dampness was felt by them.*

   _____

10. For fifty years, Jessie spent each spring plowing his fields, planting his seeds, and *watered* his crops.

   _____

Score   Number correct _____ × 10 = _____ %

Faulty Parallelism

■ Mastery Test 2

Draw a line under the unbalanced part of each sentence. Then rewrite the unbalanced part so that it matches the other items in the sentence.

1. The movie contains adult language, nudity, and it is violent.

   _____

2. My doctor told me to stop smoking and that I should lose weight.

   _____

3. Holly was frightened, upset, and a nervous wreck; she had three exams in the next two days.

   _____

4. We had a choice of chocolate-flavored coffee or coffee flavored with cinnamon.

   _____

5. After moving the furniture, spreading a drop cloth, and the wall edges were taped, we were ready to paint.

   _____

6. Toshio promised his girlfriend he would be more reliable, less moody, and jealous less often.

   _____

7. I've tried several cures for my headaches, including medication, exercise, meditation, and massaging my head.

   _____

8. The astronauts' concerns were landing on the satellite, to take off again, and reentering the earth's atmosphere.

   _____

9. I'm attending college to gain knowledge, to meet people, and preparation for a good job.

   _____

10. For his date with Gina, Troy cooked a homemade meal, playing some music that was soft, and read a romantic poem.

   _____

Score   Number correct _____ × 10 = _____ %

Sentence Variety II

■ Mastery Test 1

Combine each group of short sentences into one sentence. Various combinations are possible. Choose the combination that reads most smoothly and clearly and that sounds most appropriate in the context of surrounding sentences.

Note   In combining short sentences into one sentence, omit repeated words where necessary. Use separate paper. The story about the snake continues in the next mastery test.

The Snake and the Frog

- An unusual thing happened.
- It happened in my backyard.
- It happened while I was mowing the grass.

- There is an old wall in the yard.
- It is a stone wall.
- It is bordered by high weeds.

- I approached the wall with the mower.
- I saw a snake.
- The snake was yellow and black.
- I saw it in the weeds.

- I thought the snake had been crushed.
- I thought this at first.
- The snake's "neck" was widened and bulging.

- I grabbed my metal hoe.
- I slid it under the snake.
- I began to lift the snake.
- I did this carefully.

Score   Number correct _____ × 20 = _____ %

Sentence Variety II

■ Mastery Test 2

Combine each group of short sentences into one sentence. Various combinations are possible. Choose the combination that reads most smoothly and clearly and that sounds most appropriate in the context of surrounding sentences.

Note   In combining short sentences into one sentence, omit repeated words where necessary. Use separate paper. The story about the snake continues from the previous mastery test.

- The snake shuddered.
- The snake opened its mouth wide.
- The snake began to regurgitate something.

- I watched in horror.
- The snake coughed up a frog.
- The frog was large.
- The frog was green.

- I had interrupted the snake.
- He had been digesting a fresh meal.
- I did this unknowingly.

- The snake crawled away.
- The snake was suddenly slim.
- The snake slithered into a cranny in the stone wall.

- I was amazed.
- I was shocked.
- I stood staring at the frog.
- The frog was dead.

Score   Number correct _____ × 20 = _____ %

Capital Letters

■ Mastery Test 1

Cross out the two capitalization errors in each of the following sentences. Then write the corrections in the spaces provided.

_____
_____   1. One of our thanksgiving traditions is sending a check to an organization dedicated to relieving World hunger.

_____
_____   2. Josh couldn't understand why the U.S. Naval academy would want to have a goat for a Mascot.

_____
_____   3. Until he actually walked on the boardwalk in Atlantic City, my Brother thought it was just a blue strip on the monopoly game board.

_____
_____   4. I spent my vacation visiting grandmom and grandpop in New York City.

_____
_____   5. To get to the Lake, go West for five miles until you see a Honda billboard.

_____
_____   6. There are only a few people in Louisiana who still speak cajun, a language similar to french.

_____
_____   7. In uncle Charlie's last letter, he wrote that he was thinking of retiring and moving to the south.

_____
_____   8. Vern's old chevy finally broke down outside a wendy's a few blocks from his home.

_____
_____   9. Count dracula asked doctor Frankenstein to make a donation to the annual blood drive.

_____
_____   10. When the red cross arrived, many of the flood victims were wandering the muddy streets in a daze.

Score Number correct _____ × 10 = _____ %

Capital Letters

■ Mastery Test 2

Cross out the two capitalization errors in each of the following sentences. Then write the corrections in the spaces provided.

_____
_____

1. A sign on a closed office door at the Kennedy Space center read, "out to launch."

_____
_____

2. While I was driving my toyota to canada, the state police stopped me for speeding.

_____
_____

3. Dr. quinn told me that if I didn't lose twenty pounds, I'd be risking a Heart attack.

_____
_____

4. Laura was happy that Mr. Armstrong would be teaching technical writing II this semester.

_____
_____

5. It was mr. Spock in the original TV series *Star Trek* who said, "live long and prosper."

_____
_____

6. Lena and I wrote to the National Park service for information on camping sites out west.

_____
_____

7. My brother james benefits from my poor spelling whenever we play scrabble.

_____
_____

8. Carlos, an exchange student from latin America, spent last Summer living with our family.

_____
_____

9. Each Christmas, big motion picture studios such as MGM and paramount release new films aimed at attracting huge Holiday audiences.

_____
_____

10. The makers of Cigarettes such as eve and Virginia Slims try to lure women consumers by using pastel colors and slender shapes.

Score   Number correct _____ × 10 = _____ %

Capital Letters

■ Mastery Test 3

Cross out the two capitalization errors in each of the following sentences. Then write the corrections in the spaces provided.

_____   1. Is it possible to order a Steak sandwich at a chinese restaurant?
_____

_____   2. Many romances that blossom in Spring wilt by september.
_____

_____   3. Doctor jekyll seemed to do better with the women when he turned into
_____   mr. Hyde.

_____   4. Nicole feels sentimental every time the beatles' song "yesterday" is played
_____   on the radio.

_____   5. At Sears there is a Sale on Levi's jeans until tuesday.
_____

_____   6. My Brother's idea of a balanced meal is pizza followed by a snickers bar.
_____

_____   7. I've been thinking of converting to Hinduism, because hindus believe in
_____   Reincarnation.

_____   8. My father died for his country, so we regularly visit washington, D.C., to see
_____   his name carved on the vietnam memorial.

_____   9. The instructor explained, "by the end of the course, you should be very
_____   comfortable writing on a Computer."

_____   10. i never could understand how every time Clark Kent decides to become
_____   superman, he can find an empty phone booth.

Score Number correct _____ × 10 = _____ %

Capital Letters

■ Mastery Test 4

Cross out the two capitalization errors in each of the following sentences. Then write the corrections in the spaces provided.

_____   1. Do you think february is too early to start planning a Summer vacation?
_____

_____   2. Because of the severe storm, i missed my flight and had to sleep at the
_____   philadelphia International Airport.

_____   3. Before she could stop Herself, Clarice had bought three boxes of girl Scout
_____   cookies.

_____   4. Since I did so well in introduction to Sociology, my adviser suggested I take
_____   an Advanced course.

_____   5. "I can never win at scrabble," Nellie complained, "Because I'm always at a
_____   loss for words."

_____   6. It seems the minute I turn on the television to watch the News, my Telephone
_____   rings.

_____   7. Many Walt Disney Films, such as *cinderella,* are timeless.
_____

_____   8. The Video store on Baltimore avenue will let us rent as many as four movies
_____   at a time.

_____   9. The Knights of Columbus convention was the reason all the motels along the
_____   beach in ocean city, Maryland, were so crowded last weekend.

_____   10. My little brother's favorite Bible story is the one about Adam and eve; He
_____   loves hearing about other people who get into trouble.

Score   Number correct _____ × 10 = _____ %

Numbers and Abbreviations

■ Mastery Test 1

Cross out the mistake in numbers or abbreviations in each sentence and correct it in the space provided.

_____ 1. Robert was arrested for doing 80 miles an hour on Skyline Drive.

_____ 2. Our tel. bill listed three long-distance calls to someone in Australia.

_____ 3. When I retire, I want to sleep until ten-thirty every morning.

_____ 4. Convicted speeders will lose their driver's lic. in this state.

_____ 5. The corn crop was cut in half this year owing to 2 months of hot, dry weather.

_____ 6. Three different classmates called Francisco and urged him to attend the ten-year reunion of his h.s. class.

_____ 7. I never seem to be able to find a gas sta. open before six o'clock in the morning.

_____ 8. Billy has about 250 baseball cards and almost one thousand clippings from *Sports Illustrated.*

_____ 9. Dr. Goldsmith's secretary called to confirm my Wed. dental appointment.

_____ 10. I won twenty-five dollars and fifty cents in the lottery after spending at least five times that much to buy tickets.

Score Number correct _____ × 10 = _____ %

Numbers and Abbreviations

■ Mastery Test 2

Cross out the mistake in numbers or abbreviations in each sentence and correct it in the space provided. Mark the one sentence that is correct with a *C*.

_____   1. My dr. told me the best way to lose weight is little by little.

_____   2. The third baseman struck out ten of his last eleven times at bat.

_____   3. My aunt has a patriotic address: seventeen seventy six North Street.

_____   4. My car performs very well if I don't go over thirty miles an hr.

_____   5. I enjoy watching shows on the 3 major networks, but I prefer the shows on PBS.

_____   6. Grandma Belle jokingly gives her birth date as nineteen hundred and one B.C.

_____   7. I started working as a part-time salesperson at Sears in nineteen ninety-six.

_____   8. At about 1:30 last night I woke up and made myself a ham sand. on rye.

_____   9. The instructor said our class is bankrupt when it comes to Chapter Eleven in our economics text.

_____   10. My little bro. wants to join the FBI so he can snoop into other people's business.

Score   Number correct _____ × 10 = _____ %

End Marks

■ Mastery Test 1

Add a period, question mark, or exclamation point, as needed, to each of the following sentences.

Note   End marks always go *inside* the quotation marks that appear in some sentences.

1. Sometimes I wonder why I always seem to learn lessons the hard way
2. Look out or you'll smash the car
3. When you finish with the dishes, please put them neatly in the cupboards
4. Do you always find time to read the Sunday newspaper
5. I asked Heather where her club's party is being held
6. Claudio had to cut one of his sneakers to make room for his swollen toe
7. All the game show contestant could do was yell, "I won, I won"
8. People often buy through a mixture of rational and irrational motives
9. Jerry looked up from the stack of bills and asked, "Whose idea was it to have teenagers"
10. Staci shouted, "If that's the way you feel, you can take back your ring"
11. There's a woman at the door asking if we want to save our souls
12. Will you still need me, and will you still feed me, when I'm sixty-four
13. If it's noon here, what time is it in Tokyo
14. The patriot Tom Paine wrote: "These are the times that try men's souls"
15. Barbara always gets terrific bargains the day after Christmas
16. The larger pieces of farm equipment stood next to the empty barn, waiting for the auction to begin
17. "But Mr. Wilson," Ling said to the bank manager, "how can I be overdrawn when I still have four checks left"
18. Research has shown that most poverty comes about because of a life change such as divorce, sudden unemployment, or even the birth of a child
19. For the convenience of our customers, employees will no longer park in the spaces near the front entrance of the store
20. As the members of the cast took their bows, a woman called from the back of the audience, "That's my Bernie up there"

Score   Number correct _____ × 5 = _____ %

End Marks

■ Mastery Test 2

Add a period, question mark, or exclamation point, as needed, to each of the following sentences.

Note   End marks always go *inside* the quotation marks that appear in some sentences.

1. The dog's bite is worse than its bark
2. Please run down to the store and buy a loaf of rye bread
3. Hurry, Alan, the movie will be starting any minute
4. I wonder what Beethoven would think of the Beatles
5. What do you think about before you fall asleep
6. The young apprentice was inspired by the skill of the master carpenter
7. Judging by all the television ads, Americans are in great need of pain relief
8. Which is better, one long vacation a year or several shorter ones
9. Erica cried out in her sleep, "Please—somebody help me"
10. Len keeps a mug full of pencils on his desk, but every one of them has a broken point
11. Why do I always pick the slowest checkout line in the supermarket
12. If I catch you kids in my yard again, I'm calling the police
13. Because of a printing error, each month in the calendar had thirty-five days
14. The sign in front of Buckingham Palace seemed to scream, "Don't even think of parking here"
15. "Dear Abby," wrote Lana, "do you think you can love someone too much"
16. The first time I saw your car, I thought you must have strayed into the wrong neighborhood
17. Taylor sat for over an hour watching a pair of robins building a nest in the tree outside his bedroom window
18. The player won the championship game with a half-court basket, and the sportscaster shouted, "What a shot"
19. Because of the increase in sexually transmitted diseases, monogamous relationships are becoming more popular
20. Dried grapes are raisins, and dried plums are prunes, but dried apricots are always called "dried apricots"

Score   Number correct _____ × 5 = _____ %

Apostrophe

■ Mastery Test 1

In each sentence, cross out the word that needs an apostrophe. Then write the word correctly in the space provided.

_____ 1. That department stores prices are too high.

_____ 2. Christines aunt has a very deep voice for such a small woman.

_____ 3. The black rhino will eventually become extinct, because it wont breed in captivity.

_____ 4. As the snow fell harder, the children began to plan for tomorrows holiday from school.

_____ 5. When lost on the road, Carl will never ask questions or admit that he doesnt know the way.

_____ 6. The TV program dealt with a mothers concern about drugs and alcohol.

_____ 7. Matt stood silently in the darkened hallway and tried to remember why hed come there.

_____ 8. "If you pull that cats tail one more time," Rhona told her little daughter, "you will be very sorry."

_____ 9. Spectators were thrilled by the stunt pilots ability to put the biplane through breathtaking loops and rolls.

_____ 10. The elderly mans wallet was returned with all its contents intact.

Score   Number correct _____ × 10 = _____ %

Apostrophe

■ Mastery Test 2

In the spaces provided under each sentence, add the one apostrophe needed and explain why the other word ending in *s* is a simple plural.

1. Sallys grades in math began to improve after a session or two with a tutor.

   Sallys: _____

   grades: _____

2. Before the boys were halfway across the lake, their grandfathers old canoe sprang a leak.

   boys: _____

   grandfathers: _____

3. Oscars mother woke him and his sisters in the middle of the night to watch the meteor shower.

   Oscars: _____

   sisters: _____

4. The squeaking of the elevators outside Williams hotel room kept the poor man awake half the night.

   elevators: _____

   Williams: _____

5. Maria and her sister often watch music videos at Terrys house, since they aren't allowed to see them at home.

   videos: _____

   Terrys: _____

Score   Number correct _____ × 20 = _____ %

Apostrophe

■ Mastery Test 3

In each sentence two apostrophes are missing or are used incorrectly. Cross out the two errors and write the corrections in the spaces provided.

_____   1. The invitation's to the wedding arent being mailed until the bride and groom
_____   start speaking to each other again.

_____   2. On Wednesday morning, youre supposed to report to the boys gym for your
_____   physical.

_____   3. Tobys parents gave him a new leather briefcase on the morning he started his'
_____   new job at the insurance agency.

_____   4. Looking through the classified ads only reminded Roger of the many thing's
_____   he didnt know how to do.

_____   5. My cousins, Sharon and Ben, work for Meals on Wheels, a volunteer
_____   organization that provide's hot food to many of the towns senior citizens.

_____   6. The sight of Lolas tanned body in a black bikini was enough to make young
_____   mens heads spin around as if they were on ball bearings.

_____   7. With each new scandal in the athletic department, the universitys reputation
_____   for integrity slips' another notch.

_____   8. Grandmothers eye's were misty as she remembered the nights Grandfather
_____   called for her in a Model T Ford.

_____   9. A blue whales tongue weighs' as much as forty men.
_____

_____   10. Ricks decision to begin attending classes so close to the semesters end is like
_____   turning off the faucets on the sinking *Titanic*.

Score   Number correct _____ × 10 = _____ %

Apostrophe

■ Mastery Test 4

In each sentence two apostrophes are missing or are used incorrectly. Cross out the two errors and write the corrections in the spaces provided.

_____ 1. Whats mine is your's, darling, including the bills.

_____

_____ 2. "Stay away from my brothers stuff if you dont want your face removed," said Gladys.

_____

_____ 3. Slivers from the glass Id broken glistened like diamond's on the kitchen tile.

_____

_____ 4. The young mans hands were shaking as he dialed Colleens number on the phone.

_____

_____ 5. Craigs medical exam revealed that he has high blood pressure and that hes twenty pounds overweight.

_____

_____ 6. The pitcher whod given up the home run tipped his cap to the jeering spectator's as he exited.

_____

_____ 7. In considering new admissions, most colleges look at each applicants grades, extracurricular activities, test score's, and personal recommendations.

_____

_____ 8. If this weekends forecast for heavy rain and flash floods comes true, many peoples houses are in danger.

_____

_____ 9. Nick and Ellen havent seen their friends much since having the baby; they say shes more work than a full-time job.

_____

_____ 10. We wouldve won the sardine race after stuffing fifteen people into Annemaries Volkswagen, but she couldn't budge the gearshift to drive the car.

_____

_____
| |
| *Score*   Number correct _____ × 10 = _____ % |
|_____|

Quotation Marks

■ **Mastery Test 1**

Place quotation marks or underlines where needed.

1. A sign in a cluttered hardware store read, We've got it if we can find it.
2. Go ahead, make my day! snarled Dirty Harry.
3. I can't do the dishes, Tyrone said, because the cat is sitting on my lap.
4. This machine will do half your work for you, the salesclerk promised.
5. That's terrific, I replied. I'll take two of them.
6. Robert Frost's poem The Road Not Taken influenced Gordon's decision to be an architect.
7. When someone asked Willie Sutton why he kept robbing banks, he replied, Because that's where the money is.
8. I'd never date him, Celia said. He switches girlfriends at the blink of an eyelid.
9. One of Murphy's laws states: An optimist believes we live in the best of all possible worlds; a pessimist fears this is true.
10. The bittersweet song At the Ballet is one of several showstoppers in A Chorus Line, one of the longest-running musicals in Broadway history.

Score Number correct _____ × 10 = _____ %	

Quotation Marks

■ Mastery Test 2

Place quotation marks or underlines where needed.

1. Get back behind the railing! the zookeeper yelled to the little boy.

2. A New York subway sign showing little confidence in the public reads, No spitting.

3. The job is yours, Ms. Washburn said, as long as you're willing to work a fifty-hour week.

4. Mae West once said, It's better to be looked over than overlooked.

5. The only part of the income-tax form I like to read is the one called How to Claim Your Refund.

6. Why don't you watch where you're going? the drunk mumbled to the lamppost.

7. In a special section of Harper's magazine called Tools for Living, I saw an ad for a gadget that triples the life of a lightbulb.

8. Turning to his father during the ball game, Joey mimicked the nearby vendor and said, Hot dogs! Hot dogs! Get your son a hot dog right here.

9. One letter to Abigail Van Buren from a man named Henry read, Dear Abby: Between you and me, the people who write to you are either morons or just plain stupid.

10. Abby's response was, Dear Henry: Which are you?

Score   Number correct _____ × 10 = _____ %

Quotation Marks

■ Mastery Test 3

Place quotation marks or underlines where needed.

1. If life's a bowl of cherries, sighed Reggie, mine are canned.

2. My friends are mistaken when they say I'm afraid of flying, said my aunt.

3. Then she added, It's crashing I'm afraid of.

4. Stephen King's short story The Body was the basis for the successful movie Stand by Me.

5. The comedian said, I took a cab to the drive-in; the movie cost me ninety-five dollars.

6. If a tree falls in the forest and nobody is there to hear it, asked the philosophy instructor, is there a noise?

7. The late Spencer Tracy's advice on acting was, Remember your lines and don't bump into the furniture.

8. Here's some sound financial advice, Mr. Green said to his son, who was dressing for a date. Take her to a place that has a cook, not a chef.

9. Many music critics consider Nirvana's song Smells Like Teen Spirit to be one of the best rock songs of the last 25 years.

10. The difference between that weatherman and us, my father said as he watched the news, is that when it comes to telling the weather he has to stick his neck out, but we only have to stick our heads out.

Score   Number correct _____ × 10 = _____ %

Quotation Marks

■ Mastery Test 4

Place quotation marks or underlines where needed.

1. On our way to the doctor's office, Dad said, Dr. Cobb has been practicing medicine for forty years.
2. Hasn't he learned how to do it yet? my little brother asked.
3. No onions on that sandwich, please, Sharon told the deli clerk. I'm on my way to an interview.
4. Ever since my sixth-grade teacher made me memorize Carl Sandburg's poem The Grass, I've hated it.
5. A judge asked Oscar Wilde during Wilde's trial, Are you trying to show contempt for this court?
6. On the contrary—I'm trying to conceal it, Wilde replied.
7. Either that painting is crooked or our house is leaning, Teresa said to her husband. Please fix one of them.
8. The lion may be king of the beasts, but the majestic elegance of the giraffe certainly makes it part of the royal court, asserted the zoo tour guide.
9. Of course, I saw the play under unfortunate conditions, wrote the drama critic in the morning paper. The curtain was up.
10. I'm determined to grow roses this summer, my Aunt Freda said. So I bought a copy of McCall's Garden Book and began reading the first chapter, How to Cultivate Your Green Thumb.

Score   Number correct _____ × 10 = _____ %

Comma

■ Mastery Test 1

Add commas where needed. Then refer to the box below and write, in the space provided, the letter of the comma rule that applies in each sentence.

a. Between items in a series	d. Between complete thoughts
b. After introductory material	e. With direct quotations
c. Around interrupters	

_____ 1. The witness swore to tell the truth the whole truth and nothing but the truth.

_____ 2. When Mona loses her temper she speaks in a very subdued voice.

_____ 3. The coach told me it was his way or the highway so I hit the road.

_____ 4. The undertaker's sign stated "We're the last ones in the world to let you down."

_____ 5. Three sets of twins a hospital record were born on the same day.

_____ 6. "Park your car over there" the attendant said "and leave the keys in the ignition."

_____ 7. Entering the crystal blue ocean like a pin the cliff diver caused barely a ripple on the surface.

_____ 8. Helen's new food processor slices dices chops and makes mounds of julienne fries.

_____ 9. The next time you dare use language like that in my presence young man will be your last day in this school.

_____ 10. Rob is forty-one years old and runs his own business but his mother still wants to know when he's going to settle down.

Score Number correct _____ × 10 = _____ %

Comma

■ **Mastery Test 2**

Add commas where needed. Then refer to the box below to write, in the space provided, the letter of the one comma rule that applies in each sentence.

---

a.	Between items in a series	d.	Between complete thoughts
b.	After introductory material	e.	With direct quotations
c.	Around interrupters		

_____   1. As I opened the car door a wave of hot air spilled out of the baking interior.

_____   2. Cindy bought two lamps a beach chair and plastic salt and pepper shakers at a yard sale.

_____   3. Hal's instructions to the prospective models were "Don't just do something, stand there."

_____   4. Ved realized checkmate was inevitable so he conveniently knocked over the four pawns closest to him.

_____   5. Cary Grant a symbol of sophisticated charm for many moviegoers never won an Oscar the film industry's highest honor.

_____   6. After the wild dog had devoured my pet rabbits it disappeared into the woods behind our house.

_____   7. "This is the worst coffee I've ever had" protested Rochelle.

_____   8. The wrestler's face fleshy and pockmarked and dominated by big green eyes seemed too small for such a colossal body.

_____   9. Mrs. Evans scooped Tommy up as he headed for the mouthwash display but her unattended shopping cart smashed into a mountain of cereal boxes.

_____   10. The lifeguard had white-blond hair piercing blue eyes a deep bronze tan and a scraggly beard that the teenage girl mistook for a sign of maturity.

Score   Number correct _____ × 10 = _____ %

Comma

■ Mastery Test 3

Add commas where needed. Then refer to the box below to write, in the space provided, the letter of the one comma rule that applies in each sentence.

a.	Between items in a series	d.	Between complete thoughts
b.	After introductory material	e.	With direct quotations
c.	Around interrupters		

_____ 1. The dean of the law school I am told was arrested for fraud and embezzlement.

_____ 2. The accident outside the mall destroyed both cars but no one was killed.

_____ 3. After I flunked out of school I realized that studying might have been a good idea.

_____ 4. The thirsty sore and exhausted marathon runner collapsed as she staggered across the finish line.

_____ 5. The professor's stare so unexpectedly direct that it caused me to blush made me forget my question.

_____ 6. Mother tried to probe my eyes for the truth but I avoided her penetrating gaze.

_____ 7. "He's greyhound lean and wolf-pack mean" the sportscaster said in describing the middleweight boxing contender.

_____ 8. Ted Kelly one of my high school friends was nicknamed "Gingersnap" for the large freckles on his face.

_____ 9. Because the convict showed no remorse for his brutal crime the judge imposed the maximum sentence allowed under law.

_____ 10. The construction workers had already torn down the fence uprooted the trees and dug a trench across the front yard before they realized they were at the wrong address.

Score   Number correct _____ × 10 = _____ %

Comma

■ Mastery Test 4

Add commas where needed. Then refer to the box below to write, in the space provided, the letter of the one comma rule that applies in each sentence.

a. Between items in a series	d. Between complete thoughts
b. After introductory material	e. With direct quotations
c. Around interrupters	

_____ 1. I sat there open-mouthed and embarrassed listening to the class laugh at my answer.

_____ 2. Calvin couldn't sleep because the baby upstairs was crying a neighborhood dog was barking and someone nearby kept racing a car engine.

_____ 3. Franco has taken trumpet lessons for five years but most people agree they have been in vain.

_____ 4. The defendant had to be extremely careful of his testimony for the prosecutor was clever and determined.

_____ 5. "Stay tuned" said the announcer "for an important message for everyone who would like to become a millionaire."

_____ 6. My father shut his eyes put his hands on his lap and said a quiet prayer as he waited for the news from the doctor.

_____ 7. With the utmost care little Jenny placed the kitten in her coat pocket and headed for the school playground.

_____ 8. Tom Zydakis became tired of spelling his name over the telephone so he now orders all his pizzas for "Smith."

_____ 9. Irving Berlin composed "White Christmas" one of the most popular Christmas songs of all time while sitting by his swimming pool.

_____ 10. Realizing that every one of the six lottery numbers matched her ticket Roxanne could feel a surge of blood rush to her temples.

Score   Number correct _____ × 10 = _____ %

Other Punctuation Marks

■ Mastery Test 1

At the appropriate spot (or spots), place the punctuation mark shown in the margin.

—
1. He's so rich he doesn't count his money he weighs it.

;
2. Ruby's savings have dwindled to nothing she's been borrowing from me to pay her rent.

-
3. The quick witted little boy called the rescue squad for help.

:
4. Martha likes only two kinds of books cookbooks and bankbooks.

( )
5. The size of the lot two acres was just what Bob had been looking for.

-
6. The anti war activists staged a rally to protest the latest military actions of the government.

—
7. I think as a matter of fact, I'm positive I returned your power drill last week.

:
8. The novelist Jessamyn West once defined irony as follows "Irony is when you buy a suit with two pairs of pants and then burn a hole in the coat."

( )
9. If you're running out of storage space, there are only two solutions: 1 store your possessions more efficiently or 2 get rid of some of the junk you never use.

;
10. An old Chinese proverb says, "If you are planting for a year, sow rice if you are planting for a decade, plant trees and if you are planting for a lifetime, educate a person."

Score   Number correct _____ × 10 = _____ %

Other Punctuation Marks

■ **Mastery Test 2**

Each sentence below needs one of the following punctuation marks:

colon :	hyphen -	semicolon ;
dash —	parentheses ( )	

Insert the correct mark (or pair of marks) as needed.

1. Call the toll free number for quick service from our catalogue.

2. My sister is allergic to cats and dogs therefore, we never could have any pets when we were little.

3. The counseling center's hours 9:00 A.M. to 5:00 P.M. are inconvenient, since all my classes are at night.

4. My distinguished opponent is a highly qualified person if you ignore his long prison record.

5. There are two basic rules for travelers take half as many clothes and take twice as much money as you think you will need.

6. A sixty year old woman is entered in the marathon.

7. The crippled airliner landed safely the passengers and crew walked away unharmed.

8. Lola said, "My first boyfriend I'll never forget him proposed to me fifteen minutes after we met."

9. Before the party, Alicia had to stop at the cleaner's, where her dress was ready at the bakery, where she had ordered a decorated cake and at the convenience store, where she got ice.

10. In his book *On Writing Well,* William Zinsser wrote about wordiness "If you give me an article that runs to eight pages and I tell you to cut it to four, you'll howl and say it can't be done. Then you will go home and do it, and it will be infinitely better. After that comes the hard part: cutting it to three."

Score   Number correct _____ × 10 = _____ %

Dictionary Use

■ Mastery Test 1

Items 1–5   Use your dictionary to answer the following questions.

1. How many syllables are in the word *inconsequential?* _____

2. Where is the primary accent in the word *contemplation?* _____

3. In the word *frivolity,* the first *i* is pronounced like

    a.   long *e*

    b.   long *i*

    c.   schwa

    d.   short *i*

4. In the word *rudiment,* the *u* is pronounced like

    a.   short *u*

    b.   long *u*

    c.   short *a*

    d.   schwa

5. In the word *inhalation,* the first *a* is pronounced like

    a.   schwa

    b.   short *i*

    c.   short *a*

    d.   long *a*

Items 6–10   There are five misspelled words in the following sentence. Cross out each misspelled word and write in the correct spelling in the spaces provided.

I had a chance to work thirty hours a week at a restarant this semestir, but my parants told me that it was more importent to have sufficent time for studying.

6. _____   9. _____

7. _____   10. _____

8. _____

Score   Number correct _____ × 10 = _____ %

Dictionary Use

■ **Mastery Test 2**

Items 1–5   Use your dictionary to answer the following questions.

1. How many syllables are in the word *subsequently?* _____

2. Where is the primary accent in the word *fastidious?* _____

3. In the word *cantankerous,* the *e* is pronounced like
   a. short *i*
   b. short *e*
   c. long *e*
   d. schwa

4. In the word *demoniac,* the *o* is pronounced like
   a. short *a*
   b. short *i*
   c. short *o*
   d. long *o*

5. In the word *malleable,* the first *a* is pronounced like
   a. schwa
   b. short *a*
   c. long *a*
   d. short *e*

Items 6–10   There are five misspelled words in the following sentences. Cross out each misspelled word and write the correct spelling in the space provided.

My dauhter Judy wants to legaly change her name to "Violet" because she thinks "Judy" is too commen and "Violet" has a sence of mystery and glamer to it.

6. _____   9. _____

7. _____   10. _____

8. _____

Score   Number correct _____ × 10 = _____ %

Spelling Improvement

■ Mastery Test 1

Items 1–8   Use the three spelling rules to spell the following words.

1. inflate + able   =   _____   5. trim   + er   =   _____

2. ban   + ing   =   _____   6. plenty   + ful =   _____

3. thrifty + est   =   _____   7. concern + ed   =   _____

4. refer   + ed   =   _____   8. derive   + ing =   _____

Items 9–14   Circle the correctly spelled plural in each pair.

9. sheafs   sheaves   12. quarrys   quarries
10. pitches   pitchs   13. echos   echoes
11. pastries   pastrys   14. relays   relais

Items 15–20   Circle the correctly spelled word (from the basic word list) in each pair.

15. direction   direcion   18. awkwerd   awkward
16. wellcome   welcome   19. believe   beleive
17. generel   general   20. comfortible   comfortable

Score   Number correct _____ × 5 = _____ %

Spelling Improvement

■ Mastery Test 2

Items 1–8   Use the three spelling rules to spell the following words.

1. grip   + ed   =   _____   5. date   + ing   =   _____

2. fancy + ful   =   _____   6. employ + er   =   _____

3. imply + ed   =   _____   7. spine   + less =   _____

4. curve + ing =   _____   8. duty   + ful   =   _____

Items 9–14   Circle the correctly spelled plural in each pair.

9. embargoes   embargos   12. hobbys   hobbies

10. wolves   wolfs   13. guards   guardes

11. attorney-at-laws attorneys-at-law   14. reflexs   reflexes

Items 15–20   Circle the correctly spelled word (from the basic word list) in each pair.

15. atempt   attempt   18. several   severel

16. attenshun   attention   19. alot   a lot

17. personal   perssonal   20. diferent   different

| *Score*   Number correct _____ × 5 = _____ % |

Omitted Words and Letters

■ Mastery Test 1

Part 1   Write in the two short connecting words needed in each sentence. Use carets (∧) within the sentences to show where these words belong.

1. A carton milk leaked all over floor of my car.

2. I'd like introduce you to man I'm going to marry.

3. The supermarket was full shoppers who heard about big sale.

4. When spring is the air, most people seem feel especially happy.

5. After the torrents rain turned to ice, condition of the streets was treacherous.

Part 2   Add the two -s endings needed in each sentence. Use carets.

6. Between you and me, raisin make a better pie than apple do.

7. Darien spent forty-five minute balancing his checkbook and found four error.

8. The member of the sixth grade collected Christmas toy for needy children.

9. Together, my daughter and my husband have twenty-seven mateless sock.

10. There is little doubt remaining that many student cheated on several final examination.

Score   Number correct _____ × 10 = _____ %

Omitted Words and Letters

■ Mastery Test 2

Part 1   In the spaces provided, write in the two short connecting words needed in each sentence. Use carets (∧) within the sentences to show where these words belong.

1. I noticed number of anthills our backyard while I was mowing the lawn.

2. Please put timer on so you remember take the cookies out of the oven.

3. Without a doubt, Jenny's drawing was best all the students' art projects today.

4. My brother couldn't remember the name of book on which he had to write book report.

5. At first, the mountains looked like a foggy dream off the distance; then, as we approached, they seemed be almost too real.

Part 2   Add the two -*s* endings needed in each sentence. Use carets.

6. All the house in the neighborhood have decoration for the holiday.

7. In our basic math course, the final exam covers statistic and graph.

8. At the beginning of the football season, most of the defensive player got Mohawk haircut.

9. Your children left their coat on the sidewalk about two block away from here.

10. Too many cook may spoil the broth, but I still want as many helper in the kitchen as possible.

Score   Number correct _____ × 10 = _____ %

Commonly Confused Words

■ Mastery Test 1

Choose the correct words in each sentence and write them in the spaces provided.

_____ 1. If you want my (advice, advise), the (right, write) thing to do is apologize.
_____

_____ 2. (Being that, Because) Leon had (all ready, already) dropped off his last
_____   assignment, he prepared to leave campus for spring vacation.

_____ 3. I wish I (knew, new) (whose, who's) dog is responsible for the mess in my
_____   front yard.

_____ 4. You (to, too, two) troublemakers are (threw, through) with this team as of right
_____   this minute.

_____ 5. The reason I signed up for an accounting (coarse, course) is that I want to
_____   know the basic (principals, principles) of bookkeeping.

_____ 6. If you intend to continue living (hear, here), young man, (your, you're) going
_____   to have to follow my rules.

_____ 7. Ann and George's friendship developed into love as the years (passed, past),
_____   and now, in midlife, (their, there, they're) newlyweds.

_____ 8. (Beside, Besides) the fact that this car runs like a dream, (its, it's) trade-in
_____   value remains quite high.

_____ 9. Randy, you must have a (hole, whole) in your head if you really believe you
_____   can (right, write) a term paper in one night.

_____ 10. (Their, There, They're) was so much alcohol served with dinner that the noise
_____   at our table became (quite, quiet) loud.

Score Number correct _____ × 10 = _____ %

Commonly Confused Words

■ Mastery Test 2

Choose the correct words in each sentence and write them in the spaces provided.

_____   1. When my son's stereo broke, (their, there, they're) was finally some (peace,
_____   piece) around the house.

_____   2. By using pieces of her children's old (clothes, cloths), Lois gave her quilt a
_____   wonderfully colorful (affect, effect).

_____   3. The hosts of the New Year's Eve party (passed, past) glasses of champagne
_____   (among, between) the guests just after midnight.

_____   4. If you (knew, new) you weren't feeling well this morning, you (should have,
_____   should of) called in sick and stayed home.

_____   5. An easy way to eat (fewer, less) calories is to simply eliminate all (deserts,
_____   desserts) from your diet.

_____   6. Is it important (weather, whether) I use up all my vacation this year, or (can,
_____   may) I apply this year's leftover days to next year?

_____   7. I think I (would have, would of) collapsed any minute if the coach hadn't
_____   given us a (brake, break).

_____   8. I don't (know, no) a nicer couple than the Wenofs, who are just (plain, plane)
_____   folks despite their wealth.

_____   9. You (can't hardly, can hardly) blame people for avoiding you when you
_____   (loose, lose) your temper all the time.

_____   10. Our English professor is a tough grader, but students like her because she can
_____   (learn, teach) better (than, then) anyone else in the school.

Score   Number correct _____ × 10 = _____ %

Commonly Confused Words

■ **Mastery Test 3**

Cross out the two mistakes in usage in each sentence. Then write the correct words in the spaces provided.

_____   1. If you're family is starving, is it better to become a beggar then a thief?
_____

_____   2. If you ate less snacks between meals, you probably would loose some weight.
_____

_____   3. We're already for our vacation, accept for the usual last-minute packing.
_____

_____   4. Who's job was it to give the dog it's bath?
_____

_____   5. In the dessert, plant life has learned too survive with very little rainfall.
_____

_____   6. Write from the beginning, we could tell the knew professor was going to be a pushover.
_____

_____   7. The fog was so thick that Aaron couldn't hardly see the break lights of the car ahead of him.
_____

_____   8. Denzel would of learned his brother to play the drums, but their mother hid the drumsticks.
_____

_____   9. The acting principle of the new high school addressed the hole student body on the first day of school.
_____

_____ 10. As Wilma paddled along the quite stream, the only sounds she heard were the calls of a pear of doves.
_____

Score Number correct _____ × 10 = _____ %

Commonly Confused Words

■ Mastery Test 4

Cross out the two mistakes in usage in each sentence. Then write the correct words in the spaces provided.

_____   1. Charlotte has never learned to except an compliment without blushing.

_____

_____   2. I'd have less worries if I didn't let the opinions of others effect me so much.

_____

_____   3. Scott holds to the principal that true wisdom comes only threw experience.

_____

_____   4. I should of mowed the lawn as soon as I heard their was going to be a thunderstorm tonight.

_____   5. Chuck's car would of passed inspection accept for the hole in its muffler.

_____

_____   6. Being that the airport bus was late, we missed our flight and had to wait too hours for the next one.

_____   7. I new there was something questionable about the magazine when it arrived in a plane brown wrapper.

_____   8. Some guys think its a lot easier to break up with a girlfriend when they all ready have a replacement lined up.

_____   9. The friends must of past four theaters before they spotted a movie they all wanted to see.

_____   10. A California man once rode a skateboard down a mountainside coarse at speeds greater then seventy miles an hour.

_____

Score Number correct _____ × 10 = _____ %

Effective Word Choice

■ Mastery Test 1

Certain words are italicized in the following sentences. In the spaces at the left, identify whether those words are slang (*S*), clichés (*C*), or pretentious words (*PW*). Then replace the words with more effective diction.

_____ 1. I *get off* on horror *flicks*.

_____

_____ 2. You should file all office *memorandums* after *perusing* them.

_____

_____ 3. Building your own house is *easier said than done.*

_____

_____ 4. Because Ben realized he *had had one too many,* he decided to take a taxi home.

_____

_____ 5. My little brother's *demeanor* always *ameliorates* just before Christmas.

_____

_____ 6. Often when I am called on in school, *my brain is out to lunch.*

_____

_____ 7. When Flora tried to *bum* a *cancer stick* from me, I told her I quit smoking a week ago.

_____

_____ 8. The committee's *mission* is to *alleviate* scheduling problems.

_____

_____ 9. Because Marita kept forgetting to clean her room, our mother decided to *put her foot down.*

_____

_____ 10. The students *manifested* delight at the *communication* that classes would be canceled Tuesday morning.

_____

Score   Number correct _____ × 10 = _____ %

Effective Word Choice

■ Mastery Test 2

Certain words are italicized in the following sentences. In the spaces at the left, identify whether those words are slang (*S*), clichés (*C*), or pretentious words (*PW*). Then replace the words with more effective diction.

_____   1. Receiving an A on my final was *as sweet as pie.*

_____

_____   2. If you don't *get off my case,* I'll *punch your lights out.*

_____

_____   3. The school board's decision to drop football *had many parents up in arms.*

_____

_____   4. The interviewer *inquired as to the location of my permanent residence.*

_____

_____   5. Too many people *get hung up on* the way teenagers look, instead of trying to understand *where they're coming from.*

_____

_____   6. Our *refuse* cans were bent up by the *sanitation personnel.*

_____

_____   7. John, your mother and I *have had it up to here* with your careless attitude.

_____

_____   8. The instructor *chewed him out* for missing class, but Jed *kept his cool.*

_____

_____   9. *An excess of precipitation* has caused crop failure.

_____

_____   10. I *let out a sigh of relief* when I saw my grade for the paper.

_____

Score   Number correct _____ × 10 = _____ %

Effective Word Choice

■ **Mastery Test 3**

The following sentences include examples of wordiness. Rewrite the sentences in the spaces provided, omitting needless words.

1. A total of eight students in our class were given failing grades for the exam we took.

   _____

   _____

2. During the time that the Millers were off on vacation somewhere, their home was burglarized by unknown persons.

   _____

   _____

3. Holly took three hundred dollars from her bank account for the purpose of buying a television in the near future.

   _____

   _____

4. At this point in time, I have not as yet fully and completely made my decision concerning just what it is that I should do.

   _____

   _____

5. If you want to make sure that the answer you have come up with is correct, you should refer to the answer key that you will find by turning to the back of the book.

   _____

   _____

Score   Number correct _____ × 20 = _____ %

Effective Word Choice

■ Mastery Test 4

The following sentences include examples of wordiness. Rewrite the sentences in the spaces provided, omitting needless words.

1. Owing to the fact that I was half an hour late, I did not do very well on the test and failed it.

_____

_____

2. The actual true reason I don't watch much television is that there are too many television commercials to look at.

_____

_____

3. After a great deal of driving practice that she had with the family car, my sister said she felt she was finally ready to take and pass her driver's test.

_____

_____

4. In this day and age, the majority of people seem more than ever to want to get something of value in return for the money they pay out.

_____

_____

5. Because of the fact that the amount of my salary is less than the total sum of my expenses, it has been necessary for me to find a second job in addition to my present one.

_____

_____

Score   Number correct _____ × 20 = _____ %

Combined Mastery Tests

Fragments and Run-Ons

■ Combined Mastery Test 1

Each of the word groups below is numbered. In the space provided, write *C* if a word group is a complete sentence, write *F* if it is a fragment, and write *R-O* if it is a run-on.

1. _____
2. _____
3. _____
4. _____
5. _____
6. _____
7. _____
8. _____
9. _____
10. _____
11. _____
12. _____
13. _____
14. _____
15. _____
16. _____
17. _____
18. _____
19. _____
20. _____

[1]Richard was an angry young man a few years ago. [2]And still has some scars to prove it. [3]He once became so furious. [4]That he broke a window with his fist and cut his hand on the glass. [5]Another time, he threw a plate of spaghetti across a room through the years, his temper got him into many arguments. [6]And even fistfights. [7]Richard finally realized he had to bring his anger under control, or it would defeat him. [8]Making him the biggest victim of his own fury. [9]To get some perspective on the problem. [10]He asked his uncle Jay for help, Jay pointed out that Richard's explosions only made bad situations worse. [11]When a person has a lot of rage inside, Jay said. [12]His explosions often have little to do with the incidents that seem to cause the anger. [13]Jay suggested that Richard might get some insight into the problem. [14]By keeping a diary of his feelings and of his temper tantrums. [15]Jay also advised Richard to ask himself a question whenever he began to feel angry. [16]The question was, "Is it really important enough to get upset about?" [17]Richard took his uncle's advice, he began to seek new responses to situations that frustrated and angered him. [18]Although it hasn't been easy. [19]He has gradually learned how to control his temper even more important is that by examining his feelings, Richard has changed his outlook on life. [20]Which has resulted in less temper to control.

Score	Number correct _____ × 5 = _____ %	

Fragments and Run-Ons

■ Combined Mastery Test 2

In the space provided, indicate whether each item below contains a fragment (*F*) or a run-on (*R-O*). Then correct the error.

_____   1. A pungent odor filled the house cabbage was simmering on the stove. I suddenly felt hungry.

_____   2. Stella clips out many recipes. That she finds in the newspaper. However, she rarely tries them out.

_____   3. Hummingbirds eat half their weight every day. They are tiny, colorful creatures. Weighing no more than a dime.

_____   4. The impatient driver could hardly wait for the green light. He kept edging his car into the intersection, then he accelerated when the light turned green.

_____   5. Using Tupperware containers as molds. The children built an elaborate sand castle on the beach. A helpful wave filled in their moat.

_____   6. Pauline has taught in many elementary classes she finds first-graders the most rewarding to teach. Most of them still think school is fun.

_____   7. Some people feel we should bring our own bags to the supermarket. We could save millions of trees. Instead of throwing away usable paper.

_____   8. When I got home. I stuffed my wet shoes with newspaper. I didn't want the toes to curl up as they dried.

_____   9. On my way to class, I spied a dollar bill on the ground, of course, I stooped to pick it up. But as I bent over, I dropped and broke my twelve-dollar thermos.

_____   10. Andrea decorated her home with purchases from the novelty store where she worked. She put a red satin pillow shaped like a pair of lips on the couch. And a pink and green rug with a watermelon design on the floor.

> *Score*   Number correct _____ × 10 = _____ %

Verbs

■ Combined Mastery Test 1

Each sentence contains a mistake involving (1) standard English or irregular verb forms, (2) subject-verb agreement, or (3) consistent verb tense. Cross out the incorrect verb and write the correct form in the space provided.

_____ 1. Only two pieces of lemon meringue pie remains on the plate.

_____ 2. Every morning, he starts the car, tuned in the radio, and adjusts the heat.

_____ 3. The basketball team's center growed almost five inches between his freshman and sophomore seasons.

_____ 4. Uncle Edwin became frightened as we approached the airport, for he had never flew before.

_____ 5. Each of the cupcakes for Jenny's birthday were decorated with blue roses.

_____ 6. I came home, settled down for a short nap, and sleep for three hours.

_____ 7. On my way home, an oncoming car's headlights were so bright I have to slow down till it passed.

_____ 8. When the accident victim complained of dizziness, the paramedics told him to lay on the stretcher.

_____ 9. After I checked my bank balance, I realize I did not have enough money for a new stereo.

_____ 10. The full moon covered the beach with a cool blue light, and the water shimmers as a soft breeze blows off the lake.

Score Number correct _____ × 10 = _____ %

Verbs

■ Combined Mastery Test 2

Each sentence contains a mistake involving (1) standard English or irregular verb forms, (2) subject-verb agreement, or (3) consistent verb tense. Cross out the incorrect verb and write the correct form in the space provided.

_____   1. Travis chopped the wood from the dead maple tree and stack it against the shed.

_____   2. School closings because of bad weather is announced on the radio.

_____   3. By the time we reached our seats in the upper deck, the game had already began.

_____   4. Jasmine took down some books, thumbed through their indexes, and then returns them to the library shelf.

_____   5. Every morning, several people on the bus smokes cigarettes.

_____   6. He makes me so angry I can feel my blood pressure raise every time he's nearby.

_____   7. There is two fat pigeons strutting back and forth on my windowsill.

_____   8. An elderly, poorly dressed man came up to us on the sidewalk and asks if we had any spare change.

_____   9. Anne had not took the hamburger out of the freezer, so we had peanut butter sandwiches for dinner.

_____   10. Members of the rescue team climbed down the cliff, grabbed the frightened boy, and haul him to safety.

Score   Number correct _____ × 10 = _____ %

Pronouns

■ Combined Mastery Test 1

Choose the sentence in each pair that uses pronouns correctly. Then write the letter of that sentence in the space provided at the left.

_____ 1. a. The five students in our lab group developed a closeness that you could feel grow as the semester progressed.
  b. The five students in our lab group developed a closeness that we could feel grow as the semester progressed.

_____ 2. a. Carrie and he have a surprise for everyone at the dance tonight.
  b. Carrie and him have a surprise for everyone at the dance tonight.

_____ 3. a. This here fudge is the creamiest I've ever tasted.
  b. This fudge is the creamiest I've ever tasted.

_____ 4. a. Though we started our diets at the same time, Hal has lost twice as much weight as me.
  b. Though we started our diets at the same time, Hal has lost twice as much weight as I.

_____ 5. a. The teacher told the children that everyone could choose his or her partner for the class trip to the zoo.
  b. The teacher told the children that everyone could choose their partner for the class trip to the zoo.

Score Number correct _____ × 20 = _____ %

Pronouns

■ Combined Mastery Test 2

In the spaces provided, write *PE* for each of the nine sentences that contain pronoun errors. Write *C* for the sentence that uses pronouns correctly. Then cross out each pronoun error and write the correction in the space provided.

_____   1. Alma doesn't like them jelly-filled doughnuts.

_____   2. Neither of the candidates writes their own speeches.

_____   3. Mary asked her friend why she wasn't invited to the party.

_____   4. Most people who know my brother and me think I am more shy than him.

_____   5. What I don't like about eating a heavy lunch is that you always feel sleepy afterward.

_____   6. People who work with young children must have his or her share of patience.

_____   7. I want to get a part-time restaurant job, but they just won't give me a chance.

_____   8. Quincy decided to add a porch onto the house by hisself.

_____   9. Last Halloween, him and Anita went to the neighborhood center's party dressed as Mr. Ed, the talking horse.

_____   10. If you want to get along with others, you have to know how to be a good listener.

Score Number correct _____ × 10 = _____ %

Faulty Modifiers and Parallelism

■ Combined Mastery Test 1

In the spaces at the left, indicate whether each sentence contains a misplaced modifier (*MM*), a dangling modifier (*DM*), or faulty parallelism (*FP*). Then correct the error in the space under the sentence.

_____ 1. Being frightened, the skunk's odor filled the air.

_____

_____ 2. We watched the traffic pile up bumper to bumper from the window.

_____

_____ 3. A police officer needs an open mind, sharp eyes, and to be cool-headed.

_____

_____ 4. Wondering if my hair is naturally blond, I told Jim the truth.

_____

_____ 5. The biology students saw one-celled animals squirming through their microscopes.

_____

_____

_____ 6. Snuggling under the warm comforter, the cold room didn't bother me.

_____

_____ 7. After sitting through a long class, my foot was asleep.

_____

_____ 8. My lasagna recipe includes chopped spinach, grated cheese, and onions that have been sliced.

_____

_____ 9. While learning to shift gears, the Toyota crashed into the garage door.

_____

_____ 10. The new employee is not only intelligent but also friendly, dedicated, and can be relied on.

_____

_____

Score Number correct _____ × 10 = _____ %

Faulty Modifiers and Parallelism

■ Combined Mastery Test 2

In the spaces at the left, indicate whether each sentence contains a misplaced modifier (*MM*), a dangling modifier (*DM*), or faulty parallelism (*FP*). Then correct the error in the space under the sentence.

_____   1. The guests were hungry, noisy, and they messed up the room.

     _____

_____   2. The last of a set, I used the old cup as a pencil holder.

     _____

_____   3. Leroy and Ella watched the stars lying on their backs in the grass at dusk.

     _____

_____   4. Waiting in the icy rain for twenty minutes, the bus finally arrived.

     _____

_____   5. After bragging so much, Lester's friends became impatient with him.

     _____

_____   6. The receptionist opens the mail, sorts it, and it is piled neatly on her boss's desk.

     _____

_____   7. At the zoo, Hazel watched a hippopotamus that sat near a stone wall and ate a sandwich.

     _____

     _____

_____   8. Mrs. Sanchez has lived in the area for most of her life, and she almost knows everyone by name.

     _____

_____   9. Grateful for the relief from the heat, the air-conditioned library made it easier for Ruth to study.

     _____

     _____

_____   10. We couldn't decide whether taking a ride in the country, barbecuing in the backyard, or to go to the park was how we should spend the afternoon.

     _____

Score Number correct _____ × 10 = _____ %	

Capital Letters and Punctuation

■ Combined Mastery Test 1

Each of the following sentences contains an error in capitalization or punctuation. Refer to the box below and, in the space provided, write the letter identifying the error. Then correct the error.

a. missing capital	c. missing quotation marks
b. missing apostrophe	d. missing comma

_____ 1. The Texas flight attendant asked "Is everyone tied down to a seat?"

_____ 2. Todays paper had a story about a councilman who was arrested for drunk driving.

_____ 3. I had to write two papers during my first college english class.

_____ 4. "My cellar is so damp," the comedian said, that when I set a mousetrap there, I caught a herring."

_____ 5. You may not believe this, but I havent watched television in a week.

_____ 6. My little brothers worst trick was to hide a dead fish in my closet.

_____ 7. "One of the most important things a writer can do, the speaker told his audience, "is to satisfy the reader's curiosity."

_____ 8. Because of the noise of the dishwasher Emma didn't hear the doorbell ring.

_____ 9. Phan hates winter so much that he wishes he could go to sleep every november and not wake up until spring.

_____ 10. The little girl, her eyes filled with desperation believed the shadow on the wall of her bedroom was a monster.

Score Number correct _____ × 10 = _____ %

Capital Letters and Punctuation

■ Combined Mastery Test 2

Each of the following sentences contains an error in capitalization or punctuation. Refer to the box below and, in the space provided, write the letter identifying the error. Then correct the error.

<table>
<tr><td>a.</td><td>missing capital</td><td>c.</td><td>missing quotation marks</td></tr>
<tr><td>b.</td><td>missing apostrophe</td><td>d.</td><td>missing comma</td></tr>
</table>

_____   1. Its often not what you do but how you do it that counts.

_____   2. Kwan enjoys reading books of all kinds but she probably spends more time with nonfiction than with fiction.

_____   3. Photos taken on my new canon digital camera are not as sharp as those taken on an old 35-millimeter camera.

_____   4. "The trouble with this office, Darryl confided, "is that the only ones who are sharp are the pencils."

_____   5. Coffee tea, colas, and chocolate all contain caffeine.

_____   6. My father always told me, "when you drive, watch out for the other guy."

_____   7. In many rural areas of the west, mail deliveries are made at odd hours.

_____   8. My daughters purse is full of jelly beans and dandelions.

_____   9. Peter was amazed at his compact cars trunk space when he fit all the camping gear into it with room to spare.

_____   10. "It's not my fault that I'm having trouble with spelling, my little brother insisted. "The teacher keeps changing the words."

Score   Number correct _____ × 10 = _____ %

Word Use

■ Combined Mastery Test 1

Each of the following sentences contains a mistake identified in the left-hand margin. Underline the mistake and then correct it in the space provided.

Slang

1. Gene was all hyped up for the school marathon.

_____

Wordiness

2. At this point in time, I haven't decided which courses I'll take next semester.

_____

Cliché

3. I am so sick and tired of television commercials that I watch only cable shows.

_____

Pretentious language

4. After a year on the job, the foreman received an increase in remuneration.

_____

Adverb error

5. Balancing several plates on my arm careful, I turned and bumped into a customer.

_____

Error in comparison

6. That last game was the most bad one I ever bowled.

_____

Confusing word

7. For those who want help with the final exam, their will be a review on Thursday.

_____

Confusing word

8. We must have past ten service stations, but Lennie wouldn't stop until he found one that sold snacks.

_____

Confusing word

9. San Francisco's Golden Gate Bridge is constructed out of more then eighty thousand miles of wire.

_____

Confusing word

10. The mayor's remarks aggravated the all ready bad feelings that existed among the city's rival street gangs.

_____

Score   Number correct _____ × 10 = _____ %

Word Use

■ **Combined Mastery Test 2**

Each of the following sentences contains a mistake identified in the left-hand margin. Underline the mistake and then correct it in the space provided.

Slang

1. The boss has been on my case for leaving half an hour before quitting time.

_____

Wordiness

2. Violence seems to be increasing more and more every day in our cities.

_____

Cliché

3. The championship game slipped through our fingers when our best receiver dropped the ball in the end zone.

_____

Pretentious language

4. My husband and I have lost weight as a result of our reducing regimen.

_____

Adverb error

5. The water was coming out of the hose too slow, so I increased the pressure.

_____

Error in comparison

6. Accounting has been the usefulest course that I have ever taken.

_____

Confusing word

7. Irregardless of my beliefs, I am willing to listen to your views with an open mind.

_____

Confusing word

8. It's plane to see that nobody in this class studied for the exam.

_____

Confusing word

9. I asked my doctor what the side affects might be from the medicine he prescribed.

_____

Confusing word

10. In the passed few years, it seems that adults have become as interested in dressing up for Halloween as their children.

_____

Score Number correct _____ × 10 = _____ %

Editing and Proofreading Tests

The passages in this section can be used in either of two ways:

1 As Editing Tests   Each passage contains a number of mistakes involving a single sentence skill. For example, the first passage (on page 491) contains five sentence fragments. Your instructor may ask you to proofread the passage to locate the five fragments. Spaces are provided at the bottom of the page for you to indicate which word groups are fragments. Your instructor may also have you correct the errors, either in the text itself or on separate paper.

There are three passages for each skill area, and there are eleven skills covered in all. Here is a list of the skill areas:

2 As Guided Composition Activities   To give practice in proofreading as well, your instructor may ask you to do more than correct the skill mistakes in each passage. You may be asked to rewrite the passage, correcting it for skill mistakes *and also* copying the rest of the passage perfectly. Should you miss one skill mistake or make even one copying mistake (for example, omitting a word, dropping a verb ending, misspelling a word, or misplacing an apostrophe), you may be asked to rewrite a different passage that deals with the same skill.

Here is how you would proceed. You would start with sentence fragments, rewriting the first passage, proofreading your paper carefully, and then showing it to your instructor. He or she will check it quickly to see that all the fragments have been corrected and that no copying mistakes have been made. If the passage is error-free, the instructor will mark and initial the appropriate box in the progress chart on pages 701–702 and you can proceed to run-ons.

If even a single mistake is made, the instructor may question you briefly to see if you recognize and understand it. (Perhaps he or she will put a check beside the line in which the mistake appears, and then ask if you can correct it.) You may then be asked to write the second passage under a particular skill.

You will complete the program in guided composition when you successfully work through all eleven skills. Completing the eleven skills will strengthen your understanding of the skills, increase your ability to transfer the skills to actual writing situations, and markedly improve your proofreading.

In working on the passages, note the following points:

a   For each skill, you will be told how many mistakes appear in the passages. If you have trouble finding the mistakes, turn back and review the pages in this book that explain the skill in question.

b   Here is an effective way to go about correcting a passage. First, read it over quickly. Look for and mark off mistakes in the skill area involved. For example, in your first reading of a passage that has five fragments, you may locate and mark only three fragments. Next, reread the passage carefully so you can find the remaining errors in the skill in question. Finally, make notes in the margin about how to correct each mistake. Only at this point should you begin to rewrite the passage.

c   Be sure to proofread with care after you finish a passage. Go over your writing word for word, looking for careless errors. Remember that you may be asked to do another passage involving the same skill if you make even one mistake.

■ Test 1: Fragments

Mistakes in each passage: 5

Passage A

¹I can't remember a time when my sister didn't love to write. ²In school, when teachers assigned a composition or essay. ³Her classmates often groaned. ⁴She would join them in their protests. ⁵Because she didn't want to seem different. ⁶Secretly, though, her spirit would dance. ⁷Words were special to her. ⁸I remember an incident when she was in third grade. ⁹She wrote a funny story. ¹⁰About the time my dog made a mess out of our kitchen. ¹¹The teacher made my sister stand in front of the class and read it aloud. ¹²By the time she finished. ¹³The classroom was bedlam. ¹⁴Even the teacher wiped away tears of laughter. ¹⁵It was a magic moment. ¹⁶Which made my sister more in love with writing than ever.

Word groups that are fragments: _____ _____ _____ _____ _____

Passage B

      1Too little attention is paid to the common household problem of single socks. 2Although it seems missing socks must have fallen behind the washer or stuck to other clothing. 3Careful searches always end in failure. 4Some sock wearers react by buying only one type and color of socks. 5So that they can deny ever losing any. 6Accepting the inevitability of single socks is braver. 7Also, finding uses for them is a creative challenge. 8They are often transformed into containers for small items in drawers and suitcases. 9Or used to shine shoes. 10Many people even wear single socks that are only slightly mismatched. 11Deluding themselves into thinking the mismatch will go unnoticed. 12A better strategy is to be bold and wear pairs that do not match at all. 13Such as a bright red sock and a gray one. 14This establishes the wearer as a trendsetter and turns the appearance of a single sock into a welcome event.

Word groups that are fragments: _____ _____ _____ _____ _____

■ Test 2: Fragments

Mistakes in each passage: 5

Passage A

¹Your friend's new restaurant is a big success. ²Since it is attracting large numbers of customers. ³You know you should be thrilled for her. ⁴In secret, however, her achievement makes you feel slightly depressed. ⁵Maybe in the back of your mind you were secretly hoping that the restaurant would be a flop. ⁶If you occasionally have negative thoughts about people you like. ⁷You are not alone. ⁸Many people are secretly pleased. ⁹When their friends fail at something and are tortured with envy when they succeed. ¹⁰Psychologists believe that such feelings are the result of a poor self-image. ¹¹For example, people who have a poor opinion of themselves are likely to feel threatened. ¹²By their friends' success. ¹³Instead of feeling happy when a friend is successful. ¹⁴They feel unhappy with themselves—and their friend's achievement.

Word groups that are fragments: _____ _____ _____ _____ _____

Passage B

[1]Much has been written in newspapers and magazines about fear of heights. [2]As well as fear of open places and of closed spaces. [3]Another phobia, the fear of bridges, is less known but just as disabling. [4]People who have this phobia fear that they will get dizzy and faint. [5]When they drive on a bridge. [6]As a result, they drive very slowly. [7]Staying close to the protective railing. [8]Some people are also afraid they will be pulled through the railing. [9]Down into the water below. [10]One help for such drivers is provided by the police force. [11]On the Chesapeake Bay Bridge, our nation's longest-span bridge. [12]The police will drive motorists' cars for them. [13]The police perform this welcome service many times each day.

Word groups that are fragments: _____ _____ _____ _____ _____

■ Test 3: Run-Ons (Fused Sentences)

Mistakes in each passage: 5

Passage A

[1]A young girl looks at a fashion magazine she sees clothes modeled by women who weight 115 pounds although they are nearly six feet tall. [2]She receives a "teen doll" as a present and studies its proportions. [3]The doll has legs nearly two-thirds the length of its body it also has a tiny waist and nonexistent hips and thighs. [4]She goes to the movies the screen heroines resemble adolescent boys more than mature women. [5]Her favorite television shows are filled with commercials showing attractive men and women. [6]The commercials are for weight-loss programs these programs insist that a person must be slender to be desirable. [7]By the time the girl reaches her teens, she has been thoroughly brainwashed. [8]The media have given her the same messages over and over they all say that to be thin is the only acceptable option.

Word groups that are run-ons: ＿＿＿ ＿＿＿ ＿＿＿ ＿＿＿ ＿＿＿

Passage B

[1]Before there were Hindus, Christians, or Jews, there were Jains. [2]In all of its history, this religious group has avoided violence in fact, it has never fought a war. [3]Today ten million Jains live in India of these millions, not one has a criminal record. [4]Jains restrict themselves to occupations that do not destroy the environment or other living creatures they work as computer operators, teachers, and doctors. [5]In spite of these limitations, the Jains are India's most successful people. [6]They contribute more to charity than any other group they have built schools, hospitals, and shelters for the poor all over India. [7]Their kindness even extends to animals the Jains eat no meat and wear no skins or furs. [8]What is the secret of this remarkable people? [9]They not only teach nonviolence; they also live it.

Word groups that are run-ons: _____ _____ _____ _____ _____

■ Test 4: Run-Ons (Comma Splices)

Mistakes in each passage: 5

Passage A

[1]In any high school, three subcultures exist within the larger school environment. [2]The three groups are quite different, almost every student can be identified with one of them. [3]The first one is the delinquent subculture, this one is the least popular of the three groups. [4]Members of the delinquent group despise school, they hate the faculty, the staff, and any other symbols of authority. [5]The next step up the social ladder is the academic subculture, it is composed of hardworking students who value their education. [6]The third major student group is the fun subculture. [7]These students care most about looks, clothes, cars, and dates, for this group, social status is the most important thing in the world. [8]Needless to say, the fun subculture is the most popular of the three groups.

Word groups that are run-ons: _____ _____ _____ _____ _____

Passage B

[1]A trip to the supermarket can be quite frustrating, especially if you need only a few items. [2]When you arrive, you look for a parking space close to the store, you can't find one and have to walk half the distance of the parking lot. [3]Then you must find an empty cart, those which don't bounce or squeak are in short supply. [4]When you finally start shopping, you discover that the items you want are "out of stock until Tuesday" or that their prices have gone up since your last visit. [5]Eventually, you approach the so-called express lane. [6]You're supposed to have ten items or fewer for this lane, the person in front of you usually has many more. [7]It also seems that the store's slowest checkout person is assigned to that register. [8]But eventually it is your turn, and you pay for your order and leave. [9]Then, with a bag in each hand, you make the long walk back to your car, you are understandably frazzled at this point. [10]Struggling to unlock the car without dropping your bags, you decide to try the local mini-market next time, it's closer to home anyway.

Word groups that are run-ons: _____ _____ _____ _____ _____

■ Test 5: Standard English Verbs

Mistakes in each passage: 5

Passage A

¹Few issues generate more heated debate than gun control. ²Most of the controversy has center on the sale of handguns, which, because they can be concealed easily, are usually the weapons use in armed robberies and murders. ³For that reason, while it is often easy to buy a rifle, many localities ban private ownership of handguns or require owners to get licenses from the police. ⁴Advocates of gun control argue that these restrictions do not go far enough. ⁵They feel, for example, that selling handguns through the mail should be abolish. ⁶Their opponents maintain that further restrictions would prevent law-abiding citizens from buying guns for protection or recreation. ⁷Such debates have continue for years, with both sides frequently appealing to emotion rather than reason. ⁸Opponents of gun-control laws, for example, shout, "Guns don't kill people—people do," which is true enough but has little to do with the issue. ⁹And advocates of tougher laws accuse the other side of wanting guns in order to live out childish or macho fantasies. ¹⁰Because neither side attempt to understand the other, it has been difficult to reach a rational public consensus.

Sentences with nonstandard verbs (write down the number of a sentence twice if it has two nonstandard verbs): _____ _____ _____ _____ _____

Passage B

¹When I was a part-time library assistant at our public high school, I work the Friday afternoon shift. ²In the middle of an unusually hectic and complicated Friday morning of running errands, I realize that I would never make it to work by 12:30. ³I tried several times to telephone the high school but kept getting a busy signal. ⁴So I decided to just keep going and explain later, since I had never been late before. ⁵When I finally arrive at the library at 1:10, the librarian shot a glance at me and then look up at the wall clock. ⁶"I was in the neighborhood, so I thought I'd drop in," I quipped. ⁷We both laughed, and I went right to work. ⁸The librarian never ask me to explain, but I made a point of getting to work the following Monday forty minutes early.

Sentences with nonstandard verbs (write down the number of a sentence twice if it has two nonstandard verbs): _____ _____ _____ _____ _____

■ Test 6: Irregular Verbs

Mistakes in each passage: 10

Passage A

[1]Although Margo Carbone has hiked and skied in frigid weather, her greatest risk from cold was when her car breaked down in a rural area during a winter storm. [2]The temperature had fell below zero. [3]At first she stayed in her car and waited for help, but she was so cold she shaked. [4]She hoped that moving would warm her up, so she begun to walk briskly toward the nearest town. [5]Walking did warm her at first, but it also drained her energy reserves. [6]She knowed that her body was losing heat fast. [7]As she struggled against the wind, she started to feel disoriented. [8]She was afraid her low body temperature had begun to affect her brain. [9]If she did not get help soon, she could become too tired and confused to save herself. [10]Luckily, a car soon come plodding through the snow, and the driver insisted that Margo get in and then taked her to a nearby diner. [11]Once she drunk some hot tea, warmed up, and rested, she felt better. [12]However, she knew that she had been lucky. [13]She could have froze to death. [14]Her experience teached her a lesson. [15]Now she carries a blanket and candy bars in her car during the winter and always takes cold weather seriously.

Sentences with mistakes in irregular verbs (write down the number of a sentence twice if it contains two mistakes):

_____ _____ _____ _____ _____

_____ _____ _____ _____ _____

Passage B

[1]It was delightful to visit a day care center and watch children at play. [2]In the playground, some throwed colorful balls to one another while others swinged on the play equipment. [3]Inside, some of the children had took coloring books off a shelf. [4]They were laying on the floor and giving serious attention to their artwork. [5]Two others had began to build a castle with blocks, but it falled down when a little girl runned into it. [6]Then there was the little girl who played nurse to her doll. [7]She pretended that it had been bit by a dog and put a bandage on its finger. [8]I loved seeing all the children having such a good time while learning to play together. [9]After a while, the bell ringed, and all the children wented to take a nap.

Sentences with mistakes in irregular verbs (write down the number of a sentence twice or more if it contains two or more mistakes):

_____ _____ _____ _____ _____

_____ _____ _____ _____ _____

Test 7: Faulty Parallelism

Mistakes in each passage: 5

Passage A

[1]For many athletes, life after a sports career is a letdown. [2]While they are in the limelight, the athletes are praised for the records they break and winning games. [3]The public cheers them on and is seeking their autographs. [4]But what happens when a sports figure is no longer able to play? [5]Most athletes, because of the physical demands of the game or injuring themselves, are unable to play into their thirties. [6]While a few former athletes move on to success in other fields, most are not prepared for nonathletic careers and lives that are private. [7]Sadly, many former players are unable to find a second career. [8]Many suffer from depression, and with some there are suicide attempts. [9]Players' associations, having become aware of the problem, are investigating ways to prepare their members for life after athletics.

Sentences with faulty parallelism: _____ _____ _____ _____ _____

Passage B

[1]Humanity's longtime dream of flying remained just a dream until two brothers, Joseph and Etienne Montgolfier, built the first hot-air balloon. [2]Joseph had experimented with parachutes and mechanical devices. [3]Then Etienne decided to leave an architectural career and was working with his brother. [4]They came to believe that if one made a sufficiently light container and would fill it with a gas that was lighter than air, the container must rise. [5]Joseph proved this theory by building small paper balloons and filling them with air that was hot. [6]When these small balloons rose, the brothers made larger and larger paper balloons, and then the building of a paper balloon seven hundred cubic feet in size. [7]Eventually, they constructed a silk balloon, which they kept aloft for ten minutes. [8]It carried the first air passengers—a rooster, a duck, and a sheep. [9]The animals were placed in a basket that dangled below the balloon, arousing great interest, and it attracted crowds. [10]That balloon was launched September 19, 1783, and the rest, as they say, is history.

Sentences with faulty parallelism: _____ _____ _____ _____ _____

■ Test 8: Capital Letters

Mistakes in each passage: 10

Passage A

¹Orlando, an area in florida that used to be known primarily for citrus groves, has become one of the most popular vacation spots in the world. ²It all began with Disney World, a wildly successful theme park far bigger and more lavish than even disneyland in california. ³Disney World's success has drawn other tourist attractions to the orlando area. ⁴Sea World, featuring shamu, the killer whale, is the most successful of these, drawing over one million visitors a year. ⁵The Elvis Presley Museum, Flea World (a huge flea market), Reptile World, and the tupperware Museum, which exhibits food containers used through the ages, are other nearby attractions. ⁶But perhaps the most striking is Faith world, billed as "god's tourist attraction in central Florida." ⁷This church is in a huge red and white airline hangar that was formerly an air museum. ⁸In addition, hundreds of hotels, restaurants, and nightclubs have grown up in the area to accommodate an annual eight million visitors. ⁹Still, the center of attention remains Disney World itself, bringing millions to America's south to meet such international stars as Donald duck and Goofy.

Sentences with missing capitals (write the number of a sentence as many times as it contains capitalization mistakes):

_____ _____ _____ _____ _____

_____ _____ _____ _____ _____

Passage B

[1]Most immigrants who came to the United States by ship at the beginning of the century were thrilled at the sight of the statue of liberty. [2]But none were delighted with ellis island. [3]This drab little island off the southern tip of manhattan was the primary immigration center from january 1, 1902, until late in 1943. [4]The majority of immigrants came to this island from Europe. [5]On arrival, their first task was to prove they were physically and morally fit. [6]Herded into a big hall with all their possessions, these people were given medical and legal examinations. [7]Doctors had to certify that immigrants were not carrying or suffering from serious diseases; legal inspectors, asking questions in english, had to determine that the immigrants had a place to go, money, and potential employment. [8]Immigrants were asked questions such as "are you an anarchist?" and "do you have a criminal record?" [9]For most people, this investigation took three to five hours. [10]The immigrants were then free to join their waiting relatives and begin their new life in america.

Sentences with missing capitals (write the number of a sentence as many times as it contains capitalization mistakes):

_____ _____ _____ _____ _____

_____ _____ _____ _____ _____

■ Test 9: Apostrophes

Mistakes in each passage: 10

Passage A

[1]Sharon has worked at a convenience store long enough to spot three types of customers. [2]She recognizes customers of the first type by their haggard faces and bewildered expressions. [3]Such people may buy soft drinks or candy bars, but their main reason for coming in is to ask directions. [4]Unfortunately, they dont know north from south or any of the areas landmarks. [5]Although Sharons city has a population of forty thousand, they ask such questions as, "Do you know where Bill Hendersons house is?" [6]The second type buys more, but people in this category are never satisfied. [7]They complain that the dairy products arent fresh enough or act astonished that the store doesnt stock a product such as plum ketchup. [8]"Im an expert in these matters" seems to be this types attitude. [9]Luckily, Sharon sees many of her favorite customers, the friendly type, who often buy the same things each visit. [10]By the time one of her favorites, Mr. Clauser, reaches her counter each morning, she has gotten his coffee and roll and has begun to ring them up. [11]Mr. Clausers purchases are bagged so quickly that he has time to chat for a moment. [12]Without this type of customer, Sharon is sure she wouldve quit her job by now.

Sentences with missing apostrophes (write down the number of a sentence twice if it contains two missing apostrophes):

_____ _____ _____ _____ _____

_____ _____ _____ _____ _____

Passage B

[1]I love all kinds of food, but Ive a special fondness for fresh fruit. [2]There are many reasons for this. [3]An apples chewy skin covers a crispy treat. [4]An oranges rind is bitter, but the fruit beneath is sweet and juicy. [5]Peeling a bananas smooth skin reveals a mushy delight inside. [6]Other fruits offer more of a challenge and more of a reward. [7]It can be almost dangerous to remove a pineapples prickly exterior or a coconuts tough shell, but it is worth the effort to get to the delicious contents. [8]Another reason for eating fresh fruits is that theyre usually a good source of vitamins and fiber. [9]And theyre naturally sweet—an ideal substitute for foods with refined sugar. [10]Youll probably find that cake and candy are more popular, but you cant choose anything better for you than fresh fruit.

Sentences with missing apostrophes (write down the number of a sentence twice if it contains two missing apostrophes):

_____ _____ _____ _____ _____

_____ _____ _____ _____ _____

■ Test 10: Quotation Marks

Quotation marks needed in each passage: 10 pairs

Passage A

1 Tony and Lola were driving down the interstate highway at about sixty-five miles an hour. 2 You should slow down, Lola, Tony said. 3 We can't afford another ticket.

4 Oh, don't worry, Lola replied. 5 I haven't seen a police car all morning. 6 Besides, everyone else is driving just as fast.

7 Suddenly, a police car driving in the opposite direction made a quick U-turn, turned on its light and siren, and came up behind their car.

8 I knew it! Tony moaned. 9 Half a week's paycheck down the drain.

10 Now, this just isn't fair, Lola said to the officer as he walked toward the car. 11 It's not fair to stop us when everyone else is driving just as fast.

12 You may be right, the policeman answered, 13 but what's really unfair is that there's just one of me and so many speeders. 14 I can stop only one car at a time.

Sentences or sentence groups with missing quotation marks:

_____   _____   _____   _____   _____

_____   _____   _____   _____   _____

Passage B

1 The phone rang as the Parkers ate dinner. 2 I'll bet that's another nuisance call, said Mr. Parker, groaning as he got up to answer it.

3 Hello, my name is Marge. 4 May I speak to Mr. or Mrs. Parker?

5 This is Mr. Parker. 6 He rolled his eyes toward the ceiling.

7 Mr. Parker, you are probably aware of changes in the tax laws, inflated prices, and . . .

8 Yes, but I'm really not interested in buying anything, said Mr. Parker, trying to be patient.

9 Marge stumbled over a few words, cleared her throat, and said, I represent a service that will . . .

10 Perhaps you didn't understand me, said Mr. Parker, beginning to get angry. 11 I do not want to buy anything from you. 12 Now please hang up, because that's what I'm going to do.

13 But Mr. Parker . . .

14 The receiver slammed onto its base. 15 Mr. Parker returned to his dinner, sighed, and said, I hope I wasn't too rough on her. 16 I know she's just trying to earn a living, but I hate being interrupted at dinnertime.

Sentences or sentence groups with missing quotation marks:

_____ _____ _____ _____ _____

_____ _____ _____ _____ _____

■ Test 11: Commas

Mistakes in each passage: 10

Passage A

[1]How many homeless people live in the United States? [2]Estimates range as high as 3000000. [3]Today's homeless include not only single people but also families with small children. [4]Run-down boardinghouses and hotels the places where the poor once lived have been replaced by expensive houses and condominiums. [5]Although some of the homeless have jobs they do not make enough money to pay for food rent and other necessities. [6]Others are unable to find work. [7]Many of them have been released from mental hospitals but are still ill. [8]A few of the homeless refuse to live in shelters but most of them live on the street because they have nowhere else to go. [9]They are often seen sleeping in boxes or huddled in doorways. [10]To find enough food they search through garbage cans or accept handouts. [11]Life on the street is dangerous and short. [12]Our society is slow in realizing that these dirty poorly dressed people have not brought their problems on themselves. [13]They cannot solve their problems without help.

Sentences with missing commas (write down the number of a sentence as many times as it contains comma mistakes):

_____ _____ _____ _____ _____

_____ _____ _____ _____ _____

Passage B

[1]On one bitterly cold day a week ago I experienced one of the nicest features of rural life—old-fashioned neighborliness. [2]I had gotten a flat tire while driving to work on a back road so I walked to the nearest house and knocked at the door. [3]An elderly kind-eyed woman answered. [4]I quickly explained my problem and asked to use her telephone to call my boss and a gas station. [5]The woman graciously led me inside and then said her son might be willing to change the tire. [6]As I started to protest she left the room. [7]She soon returned to inform me that her son would change it. [8]Then she explained that she had to take her husband to a doctor. [9]She insisted however that I sit by the wood stove and have some coffee while I waited. [10]Too astonished and grateful to protest again I thanked her profusely as she left. [11]About twenty minutes later I saw from the window that her son was finishing with my tire. [12]I went out to my car. [13]"Thanks so much. [14]Please accept this for your kindness" I said as I offered him a bill from my wallet. [15]He waved it away. [16]"Hope your day gets better" he said as he headed back to his house.

Sentences with missing commas (write down the number of a sentence as many times as it contains comma mistakes):

_____ _____ _____ _____ _____

_____ _____ _____ _____ _____

■ Test 12: Commonly Confused Words

Mistakes in each passage: 10

Passage A

[1]How does a magician saw a woman in half? [2]Thought this illusion usually makes a strong impression on an audience, its an easy one for magicians, irregardless of experience. [3]In fact, it requires more skill on the part of a pear of female assistants than the magician. [4]The trick begins when a table holding the coffinlike box is rolled onstage. [5]One assistant is hiding inside that table. [6]When the magician displays the box to the audience, it is, of coarse, empty. [7]Than the magician asks an assistant on stage to climb into the box. [8]As she dose this, the hidden woman enters the box through a trapdoor in the table, sticks her feet out one end, and curls up with her head between her knees. [9]The other woman, drawing her knees up to her chin, puts her head out the other end. [10]Now the box appears to be holding one hole woman, and the magician can saw write through. [11]To complete the affect, the woman at the foot end slides back into the table as the magician reopens the box.

Sentences with commonly confused words (write the number of a sentence more than once if it contains more than one commonly confused word):

_____ _____ _____ _____ _____

_____ _____ _____ _____ _____

Passage B

1Increasing social pressure is encouraging many smokers to try to quit their habit. 2Many restaurants allow smoking only in special sections, and smoking has been banned in some other public places. 3When asked weather they would mind if a smoker lights up, people are more likely to object then they once were. 4At parties, smokers may be forced too sneak outside for a cigarette while their friends enjoy themselves inside. 5Less employers tolerate smoking, and family members also complain about smoke that reaches them threw the air. 6Its no wonder that many smokers are trying to quit. 7Succeeding is easy for a few people, but many find it almost impossible to brake the habit. 8Quitting is like ending a dozen habits, being that people smoke in so many different situations. 9They may light up when they wake up, when they have coffee or snacks, and when they drive there cars. 10In any such familiar situation, a person whose quit smoking is at risk of starting again. 11Luckily, the more times a person tries, the greater his or her chances are of quitting for good the next time.

Sentences with commonly confused words (write down the number of a sentence twice if it contains two commonly confused words):

_____ _____ _____ _____ _____

_____ _____ _____ _____ _____

Combined Editing Tests

Editing for Sentence-Skills Mistakes

The twenty editing tests in this section will give you practice in finding a variety of sentence-skills mistakes. People often find it hard to edit a paper carefully. They have put so much work, or so little work, into their writing, that it's almost painful for them to look at the paper one more time. You may simply have to *force* yourself to edit. Remember that eliminating sentence-skills mistakes will improve an average paper and help ensure a high grade on a good paper. Further, as you get into the habit of editing your papers, you will get into the habit of using the sentence skills consistently. They are a basic part of clear, effective writing.

In tests 3 through 10 and 16 through 20, the spots where errors occur have been underlined and/or numbered; your job is to identify each error. In tests 1 and 2 and 8 through 15, you must locate as well as identify the errors. Use the progress chart on page 703 to keep track of your performance on these tests.

515

■ Combined Editing Test 1

Identify the five mistakes in format in the student paper on the opposite page. From the box below, choose the letters that describe the five mistakes and write those letters in the spaces provided.

---

a. The title should not be underlined.

b. The title should not be set off in quotation marks.

c. There should not be a period at the end of a title.

d. All the major words in a title should be capitalized.

e. The title should be just several words, not a complete sentence.

f. The first line of a paper should stand independent of the title.

g. A line should be skipped between the title and the first line of the paper.

h. The first line of a paper should be indented.

i. The right-hand margin should not be crowded.

j. Hyphenation should occur only between syllables.

---

1. _____   2. _____   3. _____   4. _____   5. _____

"My worst job."

It was when I was working as a cashier last summer at Morgan's Department Store. Because I was the newest employee, I was given the hours no one else wanted. I usually had to work weekday evenings and weekend afternoons. I also got stuck working nearly every holiday. Further, Morgan's was very disorganized. Each Saturday, the store would run a large advertisement in our local newspaper offering fantastic sales on various products. However, there were usually only five or six of these items in stock. Once, there was a large advertisement offering barbecue grills for only $19.99. Unfortunately, we had sold the last grill within the first two hours of the day. For the rest of the afternoon, I had to deal with irate customers who complained that they had driven out of their way just for our sale. Between the long hours no one else wanted and the irate customers, I was happy when the summer came to a close and I could go back to being a full-time student.

■ Combined Editing Test 2

Identify the five mistakes in paper format in the student paper on the opposite page. From the box below, choose the letters that describe the five mistakes and write those letters in the spaces provided.

---

    a. The title should not be underlined.

    b. The title should not be set off in quotation marks.

    c. There should not be a period at the end of a title.

    d. All the major words in a title should be capitalized.

    e. The title should be just several words, not a complete sentence.

    f. The first line of a paper should stand independent of the title.

    g. A line should be skipped between the title and the first line of the paper.

    h. The first line of a paper should be indented.

    i. The right-hand margin should not be crowded.

    j. Hyphenation should occur only between syllables.

---

1. _____   2. _____   3. _____   4. _____   5. _____

Why Tabloids Are Popular

Tabloids have become famous for such headlines as "Aliens Steal Businessman on his Lunch Break" and "Woman Gives Birth to Fifty-Pound Baby." In fact, the weekly gossip sheets have become a multimillion-dollar business. Yet it is hard to believe that the people who buy these magazines actually believe the stories they read. Why, then, are these tabloids so popular? One reason for their popularity might be their entertainment value. The stories covered in such magazines as the National Enquirer are often so absurd that they are funny. To the weary shopper in a crowded checkout lane at a grocery store, these magazines may provide just the entertainment needed at the end of a long day. But, certainly, tabloids have not made their millions simply by being funny. In fact, their popularity may be a sad indicator of the state of many Americans' lives. The truth is that day-to-day life is often pathetically mundane. Thus, though the average tabloid reader may consciously know that the stories he or she reads are largely false, the articles may provide just the bit of imagination, the spark of controversy and extravagance, that the reader lacks in his or her everyday life.

■ Combined Editing Test 3

Identify the sentence-skills mistakes at the underlined spots in the selection that follows. From the box below, choose the letter that describes each mistake and write it in the space provided. (The same kind of mistake may appear more than once.) Then, in the space provided between the lines, correct each mistake.

a. fragment	d. missing capital letter
b. run-on	e. missing apostrophe
c. irregular verb mistake	

Did anyone ever <u>throwed</u> a surprise party for you? It's supposed to be fun, but I'm not
    ‾1‾
so sure about that anymore. I had one at the house of my girlfriend last week. When I

walked into <u>Ellens</u> living room, people hiding behind doors rushed out in a frenzy and
        ‾2‾
shouted, "<u>surprise!</u>" All that noise made me so nervous that I <u>felled</u> over a chair, <u>I couldn't</u>
        ‾3‾   ‾4‾
<u>believe this was happening to me.</u> <u>When everyone calmed down.</u> I noticed how dressed up
            ‾5‾   ‾6‾
they all were. My girlfriend had told me we were going to plant vegetables in her <u>mothers</u>
                                                                            ‾7‾
garden, <u>I was wearing old messy clothes.</u> Everyone <u>elses</u> clothes were at least clean and
        ‾8‾   ‾9‾
nice. I suppose it didn't really matter, but somehow I felt something was wrong. <u>About the

guest of honor being dressed like a slob.</u> On my next birthday, I want to go to a nice quiet
        ‾10‾
horror movie.

1. _____   2. _____   3. _____   4. _____   5. _____

6. _____   7. _____   8. _____   9. _____   10. _____

■ Combined Editing Test 4

Identify the sentence-skills mistakes at the underlined spots in the selection that follows. From the box below, choose the letter that describes each mistake and write it in the space provided. (The same kind of mistake may appear more than once.) Then, in the spaces provided between the lines, correct each mistake.

a. fragment	d. missing capital letter
b. run-on	e. missing comma
c. dropped verb ending	f. homonym mistake

The best advice I ever got was from a minister. I went to see him. After an episode in which I betrayed my wife. I had been married for a little over a year and felt closed in by my marriage. Somehow, seeing my unmarried friends play the field made me feel left out, I loved my wife but want freedom to have an affair on the side. I thought I had found it with the owner of a beauty parlor. Whom I met in my job selling supplies to beauty shops. One day, we arrange to meet at her shop after hours, when I supposedly was to drop off supplies. But we both knew the real purpose of that meeting. I spent an hour with her that afternoon. When I left, feeling guilty and dirty. I went home and took a shower but I still felt like a traitor. I decided I could cleanse myself only by confessing to my wife. But first I went to talk to my minister the next day. "don't tell your wife," he said. "Their's no reason to give her pain. You must carry your pain alone and learn from it." I never did tell my wife, I have never betrayed her again either.

1. _____   2. _____   3. _____   4. _____   5. _____
6. _____   7. _____   8. _____   9. _____   10. _____

■ Combined Editing Test 5

Identify the sentence-skills mistakes at the underlined spots in the selection that follows. From the box below, choose the letter that describes each mistake and write it in the space provided. (The same kind of mistake may appear more than once.) Then, in the space provided between the lines, correct each mistake.

a. fragment	d. faulty parallelism
b. run-on	e. mistake in pronoun agreement
c. mistake in subject-verb agreement	f. apostrophe mistake
	g. missing comma

<u>Although living alone can sometimes be lonely.</u> It is very convenient. When you live
1
by yourself, no one ever gives you a hard time for being a slob. You can do <u>Mondays</u>
2
breakfast dishes on Tuesday afternoon. <u>Or even wait until Friday if you have enough</u>
3
<u>spare dishes.</u> The same is true with the vacuuming and dusting. If you choose to wait until

things start growing out of the carpet or the knickknacks are knee-deep in dust before

<u>cleaning nobody</u> will care in the least. Also, you get to watch whichever television shows
4
you want whenever you want. The same is true for the radio and the <u>stereo, you</u> can play
5
whatever music you wish at any volume and never have to listen to <u>complaints'.</u> Another
6
nice thing about living alone is that there <u>are</u> never an argument about money. You always
7
know exactly who made every phone call, ate everything in the refrigerator, and <u>was</u>
<u>running</u> up the electric bill. And when you do get lonely, you can always call someone up
8
and invite <u>them</u> over without being stuck with company for too long. <u>Its</u> a lot harder to get
9   10
rid of somebody who lives with you.

1. _____   2. _____   3. _____   4. _____   5. _____

6. _____   7. _____   8. _____   9. _____   10. _____

■ Combined Editing Test 6

Identify the sentence-skills mistakes at the underlined spots in the selection that follows. From the box below, choose the letter that describes each mistake and write it in the space provided. (The same kind of mistake may appear more than once.) Then, in the space provided between the lines, correct each mistake.

a. fragment	d. mistake in pronoun agreement
b. run-on	e. missing comma
c. dangling modifier	f. cliché

When I worked behind an old-fashioned soda fountain in the amusement park. I loved
                                                                        1
to make ice cream sodas. Whenever someone ordered one I'd grab a tall, heavy soda glass
                                             2
by its base. Then move over to where the syrups were kept. Poising my left hand above the
            3   4
syrup dispenser, two inches of thick chocolate or vanilla flavoring would squirt into the

bottom of the glass. Next, I'd scoop two neat round balls of ice cream and drop it into the
                                                                                5
glass over the syrup. As the ice cream sank slowly into the syrup, causing curls of color to

swirl around I would insert a long-handled spoon with a small ladle. I'd briefly stir this
      6
mixture with the spoon, then I would squirt seltzer into the glass. Taking care to aim
               7   8
directly onto the ice cream. Last but by no means least, I'd add a scarlet cherry and serve
                             9
the soda on a paper place mat. Often, the customer would smile, I'd be given a good tip for
                                                           10
my creation.

1. _____   2. _____   3. _____   4. _____   5. _____
6. _____   7. _____   8. _____   9. _____   10. _____

■ Combined Editing Test 7

Identify the sentence-skills mistakes at the underlined spots in the selection that follows. From the box below, choose the letter that describes each mistake and write it in the space provided. (The same kind of mistake may appear more than once.) Then, in the space provided between the lines, correct each mistake.

a. fragment	d. mistake in pronoun reference
b. run-on	e. apostrophe mistake
c. inconsistent verb tense	f. missing comma

Children of the Night, founded and directed by Lois Lee, is helping many young runaways in Hollywood California. According to a segment on *Sixty Minutes* presented by
<u> </u>
1   2
Ed Bradley. Lee, a sociologist, has a twofold job. First, she spent time on the crime-ridden
<u> </u>
3
streets of Hollywood. She looks for missing girls between the ages of twelve and seventeen. And passes out a twenty-four-hour hot line number. The girls who seek her
<u> </u>
4
assistance are helped back into mainstream society, Lee said that 80 percent of first-time
<u> </u>
5
runaways who get help do not return to the streets'. The second aspect of Lees work is
<u> </u>   <u> </u>
6   7
fund-raising. Since she refuses government funds because of the restrictions they make Lee
<u> </u> <u> </u>
8   9
solicits money from various civic groups her goal is to establish a shelter for girls who
<u> </u>
10
cannot or will not go home to their families.

1. _____   2. _____   3. _____   4. _____   5. _____

6. _____   7. _____   8. _____   9. _____   10. _____

■ Combined Editing Test 8

Identify the sentence-skills mistakes at the underlined spots in the selection that follows. From the box below, choose the letter that describes each mistake and write it in the space provided. (Two mistakes appear more than once.) Then, in the space provided between the lines, correct each mistake.

a. fragment	e. irregular verb mistake
b. run-on	f. faulty parallelism
c. apostrophe mistake	g. missing comma
d. misplaced modifier	h. incorrect end mark

After suffering a heart attack, doctors rushed a middle-aged woman into surgery. On
                1
the operating table, she had a near-death experience, she saw herself moving swiftly through
                                                    2
a tunnel of light. At the end was God. She asked, "Has my time come?"

God answered, "You will live another 23 years, 7 months, and 5 days."

The woman made a miraculous recovery. With so much more time to live. She figured
                                                    3
she should make the most of it. She had her doctor's give her a face-lift a tummy tuck, and
                                         4   5
a job on her nose. She even bringed in a hairdresser to change her hair color.
        6   7
After her last operation, she left the hospital. Crossing the street on her way home. She
                                                8
was hit and killed by an ambulance. Appearing before God once again, she simply had to
ask, "You said I'd live another 23 years. Why didn't you pull me out of the path of that
ambulance."
    9
God replied "I didn't recognize you."
        10

1. _____   2. _____   3. _____   4. _____   5. _____

6. _____   7. _____   8. _____   9. _____   10. _____

■ Combined Editing Test 9

Identify the sentence-skills mistakes at the underlined spots in the selection that follows. From the box below, choose the letter that describes each mistake and write it in the space provided. (The same kind of mistake may appear more than once.) Then, in the space provided between the lines, correct each mistake.

a. fragment	e. run-on
b. misplaced modifier	f. missing apostrophe
c. homonym mistake	g. missing comma
d. inconsistent verb tense	h. mistake in subject-verb agreement

What started out as a camping trip turned into a nightmare for Eric Fortier and his three friends. The ordeal began when Eric felt something large press against the wall of his tent. He was sure it <u>were</u> a dog.

1

"My first thought was to push it <u>away</u>" he said. "A few seconds later my girlfriend saw

2

the shadow of a <u>bears</u> paw." <u>A large grizzly bear.</u>

3   4

The two screamed to warn others in a nearby tent, but it was <u>to</u> late. The bear ripped

5

into the neighboring tent and <u>attacks.</u>

6

Hearing his friends scream, Eric went after the bear. He <u>through</u> a large rock at the

7

animal, distracting it long enough for his friend Allen to escape. But then the bear caught Allen's girlfriend and began clawing her back.

<u>Desperate to save her, a pocket knife was the only weapon he could find.</u> He charged

8

the bear. <u>Stabbing it several times below the jaw.</u>

9

The bear tossed its victim aside and ran off. <u>Eric's friends survived because of his</u>

10

<u>bravery, their scars linger to this day.</u>

1. _____   2. _____   3. _____   4. _____   5. _____

6. _____   7. _____   8. _____   9. _____   10. _____

■ Combined Editing Test 10

Identify the sentence-skills mistakes at the underlined spots in the selection that follows. From the box below, choose the letter that describes each mistake and write it in the space provided. (The same kind of mistake may appear more than once.) Then, in the space provided between the lines, correct each mistake.

a. homonym mistake	e. mistake in subject-verb agreement
b. missing capital letter	f. dangling modifier
c. fragment	g. missing comma
d. run-on	h. apostrophe mistake

One of the most destructive diseases in the world today <u>are</u> also the most common: the
1

flu. Each year, this virus <u>effects</u> about 35 million <u>americans</u>, resulting in 115,000 hospital
2   3

visits and 30,000 deaths. In some <u>years'</u>, flu outbreaks can be even more severe. In 1918,
4

for example, a strain of the flu spread around the world. Over 20 million people died.

<u>Including 600,000 in the United States.</u>
5

One reason the virus is so destructive is that it spreads easily. A handshake or a hug

with an infected person can quickly spread the flu. In addition, the disease can pass to

others through the air when a flu victim coughs or sneezes. <u>Once exposed to the virus,</u>
6

<u>symptoms</u> such as fever, headache, <u>body aches chills</u>, cough, sore throat, stuffy nose, and
7

exhaustion appear in less than 24 hours.

Currently there is no cure of the flu, but there is good news. <u>For most people, the flu</u>

<u>goes away in about a week, vaccines are now available that can prevent the flu and reduce</u>
8

<u>its severity.</u> <u>Doctors'</u> recommend the "flu shot" to everyone. <u>Especially people over 65.</u>
9   10

1. _____ 2. _____ 3. _____ 4. _____ 5. _____

6. _____ 7. _____ 8. _____ 9. _____ 10. _____

■ Combined Editing Test 11

See if you can locate the ten sentence-skills mistakes in the following passage. The mistakes are listed below. As you find each mistake, write the number of the word group containing it in the space provided. Then, in the space between the lines, correct each mistake.

1 fragment _____

1 run-on _____

1 irregular verb mistake _____

1 mistake in subject-verb agreement

_____

1 apostrophe mistake _____

1 missing comma after introductory words _____

2 missing commas in a series _____

_____

2 missing commas around an interrupter _____ _____

¹The Race Across America an annual bicycle race starts in Huntington Beach, California, and ends 3,107 miles later in Atlantic City, New Jersey. ²One man always trains for this race by pedaling a stationary bike five hours at a time in a totally dark basement. ³Once the race begins, there are no time-outs. ⁴The cyclists' go for days without sleeping. ⁵Eventually, they grab sixty- or ninety-minute catnaps every day or so. ⁶But it is a time test, each of the bikers know that every minute of sleep gives someone else the chance to get ahead. ⁷In one of these races, the leader rode for 54 hours and 940 miles without sleep. ⁸When he got off his bike his muscles were so cramped that the flesh on his thighs hopped. ⁹As if Mexican jumping beans were under his skin. ¹⁰The winner of a recent race crossed the continent in eight days nine hours and forty-seven minutes.

■ Combined Editing Test 12

See if you can locate the ten sentence-skills mistakes in the following passage. The mistakes are listed below. As you find each mistake, write the number of the word group containing it in the space provided. Then, in the space between the lines, correct each mistake.

1 fragment _____

2 run-ons _____ _____

1 dangling modifier _____

2 mistakes in parallelism _____

_____

2 missing quotation marks _____

_____

1 missing comma around an

interrupter _____

1 homonym mistake _____

[1]The world seems to be divided into two kinds of people: the patient and the impatient. [2]People reveal which they are by their behavior in certain situations. [3]While waiting in line, patient people do constructive activities, such as reading a paperback and taking notes on a memo pad. [4]Impatient people treat waiting in line as torture. [5]Glaring at the helpless cashier, their fists are clenched. [6]They tap their feet and sighing loudly. [7]The way people drive is also revealing. [8]Patient people pass other cars only when necessary. [9]While waiting at stoplights, they hum along with the radio and relax. [10]Impatient people on the other hand, pass other cars at every opportunity and are racing their engines while waiting at stoplights. [11]These two types can also be spotted quickly in restaurants, the patient ones wait politely for the hostess to seat them and for their waitress to arrive. [12]Than, while waiting for their food, they converse. [13]Impatient people, however, are outraged if they aren't seated immediately. [14]And mumble such remarks as "I'm never coming here again" and If I had known it would be this crowded. . . . [15]They eat quickly and want the check immediately, a good meal for them is a fast one.

■ Combined Editing Test 13

See if you can locate the ten sentence-skills mistakes in the following passage. The mistakes are listed below. As you find each mistake, write the number of the word group containing it in the space provided. Then, in the space between the lines, correct each mistake.

1 fragment _____

1 run-on _____

1 dropped verb ending _____

1 irregular verb mistake _____

1 dangling modifier _____

1 missing capital letter _____

1 apostrophe mistake _____

2 missing quotation marks _____

_____

1 missing comma between complete thoughts _____

¹I have just register for my first college math class. ²The prospect of attending that class must have stirred up my old fears of math. ³Because I had a nightmare the other night. ⁴I was in a math class where the instructor was explaining a complicated theorem. ⁵For all I understood, he could have been speaking greek but the other students hung on his every word. ⁶Then he asked for volunteers to put their homework on the board. ⁷The other students demonstrated their desire for that privilege by waving their hands wildly. ⁸I slithered down in my seat, hoping the instructor would forget I was even there. ⁹He called on three other students, and then I heard my name—You too, Mr. Oliver. ¹⁰Feeling like a kindergartner, my weak legs somehow brang me to the board. ¹¹I began to doodle on it, the room suddenly became silent. ¹²I turned around to discover every pair of eye's in that room staring at me as if I were insane. ¹³Then the school bell rang, but no one budged—until I reached over to turn off my alarm.

■ Combined Editing Test 14

See if you can locate the ten sentence-skills mistakes in the following passage. The mistakes are listed below. As you find each mistake, write the number of the word group containing it in the space provided. Then, in the space between the lines, correct each mistake.

1 fragment _____

1 run-on _____

2 mistakes in subject-verb agreement

_____ _____

1 apostrophe mistake _____

1 mistake in pronoun agreement

_____

1 missing comma after introductory words _____

2 missing commas around an interrupter _____ _____

1 missing comma between complete thoughts _____

¹The numerous ads for cat and dog products shows that Americans are concerned about the well-being of its pets. ²The relationship between people and animals, however, is of as much value to humans as it is to animals. ³Our pets show us they have feelings and help create in us a respect for all living creatures. ⁴Pets are also important as companions. ⁵According to one study, they can be especially helpful at special times in peoples lives. ⁶Including during childhood and periods of depression and illness. ⁷Pets can also revitalize people. ⁸When they are brought into nursing homes depressed and bored elderly patients gain a new optimism. ⁹Pets can even reduce anxiety. ¹⁰One study demonstrated for example that gazing at a fish tank can reduce fear among patients about to undergo medical or dental surgery. ¹¹Yet another of the benefits of animals are that they provide important special services for humans. ¹²Seeing-eye dogs offer mobility—and companionship—to many blind people, trained monkeys do chores for the paralyzed. ¹³Dogs and horses are used in police work and cats are valued for their ability to limit the mouse population. ¹⁴Clearly, animals do as much for people as people do for them.

■ Combined Editing Test 15

See if you can locate the ten sentence-skills mistakes in the following passage. The mistakes are listed below. As you find each mistake, write the number of the word group containing it in the space provided. Then, in the space between the lines, correct each mistake.

2 fragments _____ _____   1 missing apostrophe _____

2 run-ons _____ _____   1 missing comma after introductory

1 irregular verb mistake _____   words _____

2 mistakes in subject-verb agreement 1 missing comma around an interrupter

_____ _____   _____

¹More young people are living with their parents than ever before. ²According to the United States Census Bureau about 50 percent of people aged eighteen to twenty-four live either at home or in college dorms. ³There appears to be several reasons for this situation, in the past, children often left home when they got married. ⁴Today, however people tend to get married at an older age. ⁵Than they once did. ⁶Also, the high divorce rate among Americans have brought many of them back home to their parents. ⁷In addition, the high cost of college keeps many students from moving into their own apartments. ⁸However, even entering the job market does not guarantee that young people will finally leave home, many simply do not earn incomes that allow them to support themselves. ⁹Children from well-off families are even more likely to stay home longer. ¹⁰Waiting to be able to support themselves in the lifestyle they growed up with. ¹¹Of course, most eventually do leave home. ¹²The Census Bureaus statistics show that only 9 percent of men and 5 percent of women aged thirty to thirty-four are still living with their parents.

■ Combined Editing Test 16

Each numbered line in the résumé excerpt below contains a sentence-skills mistake. Identify the mistake and write its item number in the appropriate space in the box below. Then correct the mistake in the space above each error.

Missing capital letter _____	Missing comma _____
_____ _____	Inconsistent verb tense _____
Homonym mistake _____ _____	Missing -*s* ending _____ _____
Apostrophe error _____	

Wanda Otero

[1] 15 Cyprus street

[2] Philadelphia PA 19111

Phone: (215) 555-1515

[3] **Objective:** I wish too obtain a full-time position with an opportunity for advancement and growth.

Work History:

Cashier at Wal-Mart • Philadelphia, PA • 2003 to current

Responsibilities:

- Used a computerized cash register
[4] • Accepted money and count change
[5] • Answered customers' questions and addressed there concerns
[6] • Processed purchases and return
[7] • Assisted manager with training new cashier's

Education:

[8] Philadelphia Regional High school • Philadelphia, PA

- Graduated June 2002

Special Skills:

[9] • Skilled with PC and Mac computer
[10] • Fluent in spanish

■ Combined Editing Test 17

Each underlined area in the résumé excerpt below contains a sentence-skills mistake. Identify the mistake and write its item number in the appropriate space in the box below. Then correct the mistake in the space above each error.

Missing capital letter _____	Nonstandard abbreviation _____
_____	Inconsistent verb tense _____
Dangling modifier _____	Run-on _____
Faulty parallelism _____	Apostrophe mistake _____
Clichés _____	Fragment _____

Ray Jackson

210 South Vincent <u>street</u>
             ₁

Glenview, CA 91325

Home phone <u>numb.</u>: (555) 555-5555
           ₂

OBJECTIVE: To acquire a position that includes challenging work, good benefits, and

<u>a salary that is competitive.</u>
           ₃

QUALIFICATIONS: <u>Organized, efficient, and flexible, my employers</u> have always been
                                    ₄

impressed with my work. I am a creative problem-solver, a fast learner, and a skilled

manager. <u>Who can work well alone or in groups.</u> No matter what the task, I always <u>keep</u>
         ₅

<u>my nose to the grindstone and work like a horse.</u> <u>I am comfortable in high-stress</u>
              ₆   ₇

<u>situations, I like working with the public.</u>

EDUCATION:

1996–2000	Diploma, Glenview Heights High School
2002–2004	<u>Associates'</u> Degree, Mesa Community College
	₈

EMPLOYMENT:

Assistant Manager, The Olive <u>garden</u> (1/2003 to present)
                         ₉

Resolved employee disputes and trained staff

Created schedules, interviewed applicants, and <u>hire</u> workers
                                              ₁₀

■ Combined Editing Test 18

Each underlined area in the cover letter below contains a sentence-skills mistake. Identify the mistake and write its item number in the appropriate space in the box below. Then correct the mistake in the space above each error.

Missing period _____	Run-on _____
Missing apostrophe _____	Dropped verb ending _____
Homonym mistake _____	Faulty parallelism _____
Missing capital letter _____	Missing colon _____
Fragment _____	Spelling error _____

<u>Mr John Grasso</u>
   1
Security Concepts, Inc.

Reading, PA 19818

<u>Dear Mr. Grasso</u>
      2
   I saw your advertisement for a Security Guard in last <u>Sundays</u> edition of the
                                                            3
Reading <u>eagle</u>. I feel strongly that I possess the skills needed for the job.
            4
   First of all, I have experience working in the security industry. For the past two

years, I <u>work</u> as a security assistant at West Chester University. My duties included
         5
escorting students to <u>there</u> dorms at night, monitoring campus security cameras, and
                        6
<u>identification card checks in university parking lots.</u>
                      7
   <u>Besides having experience.</u> I am also a reliable worker. <u>I always arrive to work on</u>
            8   9
time, I never call in sick. My supervisors at West Chester have praised my work, and I

have <u>recieved</u> many outstanding evaluations.
         10
   Please call me so we can talk in person about the position you're offering. I look

forward to hearing from you.

Sincerely,

David Manion
David Manion

■ Combined Editing Test 19

Each underlined area in the cover letter below contains a sentence-skills mistake. Identify the mistake and write its item number in the appropriate space in the box below. Then correct the mistake in the space above each error.

Missing apostrophe _____	Missing commas _____ _____
Homonym mistake _____	Dangling modifier _____ _____
_____	Dropped verb ending _____
Missing capital letter _____	Missing word _____

Tawana Stokes

Personnel Director

Childrens Hospital of Atlanta
    1

Atlanta, GA 20202

Dear Ms. Stokes,

    I attended a job fare last week and discovered that you're currently searching for a
              2

part-time phone receptionist. Friendly, outgoing, and dependable, the job is a perfect
                      3

match for me.

    I have just complete a program at the Atlanta business Institute wear I learned all the
             4   5   6

skills necessary to be an effective receptionist. Besides being able to answer the phone
                          7

and deal with the public, my training also prepared me to use the latest computer

software and manage multiple tasks with speed and accuracy.

    In addition, I am comfortable working alone or as part of group. My schedule is
                  8

completely flexible, and I can work mornings evenings and weekends. I hope to speak
                9

with you about this position in the days ahead.

    Thank you for your time and consideration.

Sincerely
  10

Julia Morgan

Julia Morgan

- **Combined Editing Test 20**

Each numbered box in the application below contains a sentence-skills mistake. See if you can identify each of the ten mistakes. As you find each, write the type of mistake you found in the space provided. Then correct it next to your answer. The first one has been done for you.

1. *missing comma: December 10, 2004* _____

2. _____

3. _____

4. _____

5. _____

6. _____

7. _____

8. _____

9. _____

10. _____

Dress-Right Stores • Employment Application		Date of Application 1 *December 10 2004*

Social Security # 123-45-6789	Last Name *Madden*	First Name *John*	Middle Initial *R.*

Address (Street number and name) 2 *102 South Hawthorne Blvd.*	City, State, and Zip Code 3 *Boston, Ma 02129*	

Desired Position 4 *Sales' Associate*	Date Available to Start 5 *Tomorow*	Home Phone	Business Phone

EDUCATION

Schools	Name and Location	Dates Attended (mo/yr) From: To:	Grad?	Major/Minor Course Work	Type of Degree
High School	6 *Central High school*	*9/00 to 6/04*	YES X NO		
College or University	7 *Boston Community Coll*	*9/04 to present*	YES NO X		
Other Training or Education	8 *Coarse in Web Design*		YES X NO		

WORK HISTORY (include volunteer experience. Use additional sheets if necessary.)

Current or Last Employer: 9 *Acme markets*	Address: *123 Cooper Road*	

Job Title: *Grocery Clerk*	Supervisor's Name and Title *Hank Fraley, Manager*	Telephone Number

Dates Employed (mo/yr–mo/yr) *11/03 to present*	Starting Salary *$ 6.00/hour*	Ending or Current Salary *$ 6.50/hour*	Reason for Leaving *Store is closing*

List major duties in order of their importance in the job:

10 *I stocked item, cleaned aisles, and set up displays. I trained staff and assisted customers. On weekends, I also worked as a cashier.*

Part Four

Readings for Writing

Introduction

Part Four provides a series of reading selections that should both capture your interest and enlarge your understanding. This part of the book begins by explaining the format of each selection, the four kinds of comprehension questions that accompany each reading, and four hints that can make for effective reading. After you read each selection, work through the reading comprehension, technique, and discussion questions that follow. They will help you understand, appreciate, and think about the selection. Then write a paragraph or essay on one of the three writing assignments provided.

As you work on a paper, refer as needed to the guidelines for effective writing in Part One and the rules of grammar, punctuation, and usage in Part Two. Doing so will help make these basic rules an everyday part of your writing.

Introduction to the Readings

This part of the book will help you become a better reader as well as a stronger writer. Reading and writing are closely connected skills—so practicing one skill helps develop the other. Included here are ten high-interest reading selections that provide inspiration for a wide range of paragraph and essay writing assignments.

The Format of Each Selection

To help you read the selections effectively—and write about them effectively—the following features are included.

Preview

A short preview introduces you to each reading selection and to its author. These previews will help you start thinking about a selection even before you start to read it.

"Words to Watch"

For each selection, there is a list of difficult words in the selection, with their paragraph numbers and their meanings as they are used in the reading. You may find it helpful to read through "Words to Watch" to remind yourself of meanings or to learn new ones. Within the reading itself, each listed word is marked with a small color bullet (•). When you're reading, if you are not sure of the definition of a word marked with this bullet, go back and look it up in "Words to Watch."

Reading Comprehension Questions

Following each selection, a series of questions gives you practice in four reading skills widely recognized as important to comprehension. These skills have to do with (1) vocabulary, (2) main and central ideas, (3) key details, and (4) inferences.

1 Understanding Vocabulary in Context   The *context* of a word is the words that surround it. We learn many words by guessing their meanings from their context. For example, look at the sentence below. Can you figure out the meaning of the italicized word? After reading the sentence, try to answer the multiple-choice item.

> Karen was *euphoric* when the college that was her first choice accepted her.

The word *euphoric* in the above sentence means

a. puzzled.

b. angry.

c. overjoyed.

d. sad.

You can figure out the meaning of *euphoric* on the basis of its context. Since Karen was accepted by the college that was her first choice, we can assume that she was overjoyed (*c*) rather than puzzled, angry, or sad. Understanding vocabulary in context is a very useful skill to develop, since we often meet new words in our reading. If we pay attention to their context, we may not need a dictionary to figure out what they mean.

2 Determining Main Ideas and the Central Idea   As you learned in Part One of this book, a paragraph is about a point, or main idea, which is often expressed in a topic sentence; and in an essay, there is an overall main idea, often called the central idea. While the reading selections here are longer than the essays you write for your classes, they follow this same pattern. Sometimes the author of a selection states the central idea directly in one or more sentences; sometimes the reader must figure it out. In either case, to know what an author is really saying, readers must determine the central idea and the main ideas that support it.

3 Recognizing Key Supporting Details   Supporting details are reasons, examples, and other kinds of information that help explain or clarify main ideas and the central idea. Recognizing key supporting details is an important part of understanding an author's message.

4 Making Inferences   Often, an author does not state a point directly. Instead, he or she may only suggest the point, and the reader must *infer* it—in other words, figure it out. We make inferences every day, basing them on our understanding and experience. For example, suppose you take your seat in a lecture class in which the instructor always reads from notes in a boring tone of voice. A fellow student comments, "Well, this should be another thrilling lecture." You readily infer—you conclude from the circumstances—that your classmate is not saying what he or she means. The meaning is really the opposite of what was said.

Here is another example of inference. Consider the sentence below. What can you infer from it? Circle the letter of the most logical inference.

Two elderly men silently played chess on a park bench, ignoring both the hot July sun and a fortyish woman who held a red umbrella over her head while watching their game.

The sentence suggests that

a. the men disliked the woman.

b. the woman was related to one of the men.

c. it was raining heavily.

d. the woman wanted to protect herself from the sun.

If the men were concentrating on their game, they would be likely to ignore their surroundings, including the woman, so nothing in the sentence suggests that they disliked her, and *a* is therefore not a logical inference. Also, nothing in the sentence suggests that the men knew the woman, so *b* is not a logical inference either. And *c* is also incorrect, since the sentence mentions only the sun: if it were sunny and raining at the same time, the sentence would surely note such an unusual situation. That leaves only *d* as the correct inference—that the woman was using the umbrella to protect herself from the "hot July sun."

Making inferences like these is often necessary for a full understanding of an author's point.

Technique Questions

Questions about *technique* point to methods writers have used to present their material effectively. In particular, technique questions make you aware of directly stated central ideas, methods of organization, transition words, and vivid details that help writers make their ideas come alive for the reader. Focusing on such techniques will help you use them in your own writing.

Discussion Questions

The discussion questions help you think in detail about ideas raised by the selection and make connections between the selection and your own life. They will help you look closely at what you value, whom you respect, and how you react to people and situations.

Writing Assignments

The writing assignments following each selection are based specifically on that selection. Many assignments provide guidelines on how to proceed, including suggestions about prewriting, possible topic sentences and thesis statements, and methods of development.

Hints for Effective Reading

Effective reading, like effective writing, does not happen all at once. Rather, it is a process. Often you begin with a general impression of what something means, and then, by rereading, you move to a deeper level of understanding of the material.

  Here are some hints for becoming a better reader.

1   **Read in the right place.**   Ideally, you should get settled in a quiet spot that encourages concentration. If you can focus your attention while lying on a bed or curled up in a chair, that's fine. But if you find that being very comfortable leads to daydreaming or dozing off rather than reading, then avoid getting too relaxed. You might find that sitting in an upright chair promotes concentration and keeps your mind alert.

2   **Preview the selection.**   Begin by reading the overview that precedes the selection. Then think for a minute about the title. A good title often hints at a selection's central idea, giving you insight into the piece even before you read it. For example, you can deduce from the title of Alice Walker's essay, "My Daughter Smokes," that Walker is likely going to offer a negative commentary about her daughter's habit.

3   **Read the selection right through for pleasure.**   Allow yourself to be drawn into the world that the author has created. Don't slow down or turn back. Instead, just read to understand as much as you can the first time through. After this reading, sit back for a moment and think about what you enjoyed in the piece.

4   **Deepen your sense of the selection.**   Go back and reread it, or at least reread the passages that may not have been clear the first time through. Look up any words that you cannot figure out from context, and write their meanings in the margin. Now ask yourself the following questions:

- What is the central idea of the piece?
- What are the main supporting points for the central idea?
- How does the author explain and illustrate these main supporting points?

Reread carefully the parts of the selection that seem most relevant to answering these questions. By asking yourself the questions and by rereading, you will gradually deepen your understanding of the material.

The Importance of Regular Reading

Chances are that you are not as good a reader as you should be to do well in college. If so, it's not surprising. You live in a culture where people watch an average of *over seven hours of television every day!* All that passive viewing does not allow much time for reading. Reading is a skill that must be actively practiced. The simple fact is that people who do not read very often are not likely to be strong readers.

Another reason for not reading much is that you may have a lot of responsibilities. You may be going to school and working at the same time, and you may have many family duties as well. Given a hectic schedule, you're not going to have much opportunity to read. When you have free time, you may be exhausted and find it easier to turn on the TV than to open a book.

A third reason for not reading is that our public school system may have soured you on it. One government study after another has said that our schools have not done a good job of turning people on to the rewards of reading. If you had to read a lot of uninteresting and irrelevant material in grade school and high school, you may have decided (mistakenly) that reading in general is not for you.

These reasons may help explain why you are not in the habit of regular reading. For people who are unpracticed readers, there is one overall key to becoming a better reader. That key, simple as it may sound, is to do a great deal of reading. The truth of the matter is that *reading is like any other skill. The more you practice, the better you get.*

Regular reading is a habit with many rewards. Research has shown that frequent reading improves vocabulary, spelling, reading speed, and comprehension, as well as grammar and writing style. All of these language and thinking skills develop in an almost painless way for the person who becomes a habitual reader.

The question to ask, then, is "What steps can I take to become a regular reader?" The first step is to develop the right attitude. Recognize that a person who can read well has more potential and more power than a person who cannot. Reading is a source of extraordinary power. Consider the experience of Ben Carson as told on pages 563–569 of this book. After he started reading two books a week, at his mother's insistence, his entire world changed. He moved from the bottom of his class to the head of his class, and he went on to become a world-famous surgeon. And Grant Berry, on pages 552–556, describes how a commitment to reading was the key to his hopes for the future. Increasingly in today's world, jobs involve processing information. More than ever, words are the tools of our trades. The better your command of words, the more success you are likely to have. And nothing else will give you a command of words like regular reading.

A second step toward becoming a regular reader is to subscribe to a daily newspaper and, every day, read the sections that interest you. Remember that it is not what you read that matters—for example, you should not feel obliged to read the editorial section if opinion columns are not your interest. Instead, what matters is *the very fact that you read*. Your favorite section may be the comics, or fashion, or sports, or movie reviews, or the front page. Feel perfectly free to read whatever you decide you want to read.

A third step is to subscribe to one or more magazines. On many college bulletin boards, you'll see displays offering a wide variety of magazines at discount rates for college students. You may want to consider a weekly newsmagazine, such as *Newsweek* or *Time,* or a weekly general-interest magazine such as *People*. You will also be able to choose from a wide variety of monthly magazines, some of which will suit your interests. You may also want to look over the magazine section at any newsstand or bookstore. Most magazines contain postage-paid subscriber cards inside that you can send in to start a subscription. Finally, you may want to visit the magazine section of your library on a regular basis to just sit and read for an hour or so.

A fourth step to regular reading is to create a half hour of reading in your daily schedule. That time might be during your lunch hour, or late afternoon before dinner, or the half hour or so before you turn off your light at night. Find a time that is possible for you and make reading then a habit. The result will be both recreation and personal growth.

A fifth step is to read aloud to your children, which will benefit both them and you. Alternatively, have a family reading time when you and your children take turns reading. There are many books on the market that can be enjoyed by both parents and children. One outstanding choice is *Charlotte's Web,* by E. B. White—a classic story available in any bookstore or library. The children's librarian at your local library may be a good source for books. There are also many choices in the children's section at almost any paperback bookstore. An excellent mail-order source of books for children is the Chinaberry Book Service, 2780 Via Orange Way, Suite B, Spring Valley, California 91978. In its catalog, recommended books are grouped in five levels, from titles suitable for the very young to titles for young adults. Many of the books are pictured, and each book is helpfully described. To get a catalog, you can call a toll-free number: 1-800-776-2242.

The most important step on the road to becoming a regular reader is to read books on your own. Reading is most valuable and most enjoyable when you get drawn into the special world created by a book. You can travel in that world for hours or days, unmindful for a while of everyday concerns. In that timeless zone you will come to experience the joy of reading. You will also add depth to your life and make more sense out of the world. Too many people are addicted to smoking or drugs or television; you should try, instead, to get hooked on books.

The books to read are simply any books that interest you. They might be comic books, science fiction, adventure stories, romances, suspense or detective stories, horror novels, autobiographies, or any other type of book. To select your books, browse in a paperback bookstore, a library, a reading center, or any other place with a large number of books. Or read the short descriptions of the widely popular books in the list that follows. Find something you like and begin your reading journey. If you stick to it and become a regular reader, you may find that you have done nothing less than change your life.

A List of Interesting Books

Autobiographies and Other Nonfiction

I Know Why the Caged Bird Sings, Maya Angelou

The author writes with love, humor, and honesty about her childhood and what it is like to grow up black and female.

Alicia: My Story, Alicia Appleman-Jurman

Alicia was a Jewish girl living with her family in Poland when the Germans invaded in 1941. Her utterly compelling and heartbreaking story shows some of the best and worst of which human beings are capable.

Growing Up, Russell Baker

Russell Baker's mother, a giant presence in his life, insisted that he make something of himself. In his autobiography, the prizewinning journalist shows that he did with an engrossing account of his own family and growing up.

In Cold Blood, Truman Capote

This book, a frightening true story about the murder of a family, is also an examination of what made their killers tick. Many books today tell gripping stories of real-life crimes. *In Cold Blood* was the first book of this type and may still be the best.

Gifted Hands, Ben Carson

This is the inspiring story of an inner-city kid with poor grades and little motivation who turned his life around. Dr. Carson is now a world-famous neurosurgeon at one of the best hospitals in the world; his book tells how he got there. In *Think Big* and *The Big Picture,* two related books, Dr. Carson tells more of his story and presents the philosophy that helped him make the most of his life.

Move On, Linda Ellerbee

A well-known television journalist writes about the ups and downs of her life, including her stay at the Betty Ford Center for treatment of her alcoholism.

The Diary of a Young Girl, Anne Frank

To escape the Nazi death camps, Anne Frank and her family hid for years in an attic. Her journal tells a story of love, fear, and courage.

Man's Search for Meaning, Viktor Frankl

How do people go on when they have been stripped of everything, including human dignity? In this short but moving book, the author describes his time in a concentration camp and what he learned there about survival.

The Story of My Life, Helen Keller

How Miss Keller, a blind and deaf girl who lived in isolation and frustration, discovered a path to learning and knowledge.

The Autobiography of Malcolm X, Malcolm X and Alex Haley

Malcolm X, the controversial black leader who was assassinated by one of his followers, writes about the experiences that drove him to a leadership role in the Black Muslims.

Makes Me Wanna Holler, Nathan McCall

A dramatic first-person account of how a bright young black man went terribly wrong and was lured into a life of crime. McCall, now a reporter for the *Washington Post,* eventually found a basis for self-respect different from that of his peers, who are murdered, commit suicide, become drug zombies, or wind up in prison.

Angela's Ashes, Frank McCourt

This widely popular autobiography tells the story of an Irish boy whose father was a drunkard and whose mother tried desperately to hold her family together. The poverty described is heartbreaking, and yet the book is wonderfully moving and often funny. You'll shake your head in disbelief at all the hardships, but at other times you'll laugh out loud at the comic touches.

A Hole in the World, Richard Rhodes

Little more than a year old when his mother killed herself, Rhodes has ever since been conscious of "a hole in the world" where his mother's love should have been. In this true and terrifying account of his boyhood, he describes how he managed to survive.

Down These Mean Streets, Piri Thomas

Life in a Puerto Rican ghetto is shown vividly and with understanding by one who experienced it.

Fiction

Watership Down, Richard Adams

A wonderfully entertaining adventure story about rabbits who act a great deal like people. The plot may sound unlikely, but it will keep you on the edge of your seat.

Patriot Games, Tom Clancy

In a story of thrills and suspense, a government agent helps stop an act of terrorism. The terrorists then plot revenge on the agent and his family.

The Cradle Will Fall, Mary Higgins Clark

A county prosecutor uncovers evidence that a famous doctor is killing women, not realizing that she herself is becoming his next target. One typical comment by a reviewer about Clark's books is that they are "a ticket to ride the roller coaster . . . once on the track, we're there until the ride is over."

Note: If you like novels with terror and suspense, many of Mary Higgins Clark's books are good choices.

And Justice for One, John Clarkson

In this adventure-thriller, a former Secret Service agent seeks revenge after his brother is almost killed and his girlfriend is kidnapped. Because of corruption in the police force, the agent must take the law into his own hands.

Deliverance, James Dickey

Several men go rafting down a wild river in Georgia and encounter beauty, violence, and self-knowledge.

Eye of the Needle, Ken Follett

A thriller about a Nazi spy—"The Needle"—and a woman who is the only person who can stop him.

Lord of the Flies, William Golding

Could a group of children, none older than twelve, survive by themselves on a tropical island in the midst of World War Three? In this modern classic, Golding shows us that the real danger is not the war outside but "the beast" within each of us.

Snow Falling on Cedars, David Guterson

This is a unique murder mystery. The story is set in the 1950s in an island community where a fisherman is found dead on his boat and another fisherman is quickly blamed for the death. The accused man is so proud that he refuses to defend himself for a crime he says he did not commit. Like all great stories, this one is about more than itself. It becomes a celebration of the mystery of the human heart.

The Silence of the Lambs, Thomas Harris

A psychotic killer is on the loose, and to find him, the FBI must rely on clues provided by an evil genius. Like some other works on this list, *The Silence of the Lambs* was made into a movie that is not as good as the book.

Flowers for Algernon, Daniel Keyes

A scientific experiment turns a retarded man into a genius. But the results are a mixture of joy and heartbreak.

The Shining, Stephen King

A haunted hotel, a little boy with extrasensory perception, and an insane father—they're all together in a horror tale of isolation and insanity. One review says, "Be prepared to be scared out of your mind. . . . Don't read this book when you are home alone. If you dare—once you get past a certain point, there's no stopping."

Note: If you like novels with terror and suspense, many of Stephen King's books are good choices.

Watchers, Dean Koontz

An incredibly suspenseful story about two dogs that undergo lab experiments. One dog becomes a monster programmed to kill, and it seeks to track down the couple who know its secret.

Note: If you like novels with a great deal of action and suspense, many of Dean Koontz's books are good choices.

To Kill a Mockingbird, Harper Lee

A controversial trial, involving a black man accused of raping a white woman, is the centerpiece of this story about adolescence, bigotry, and justice. One review described the book as "a novel of great sweetness, humor, compassion, and mystery carefully sustained."

The Natural, Bernard Malamud

An aging player makes a comeback that stuns the baseball world.

Waiting to Exhale, Terry McMillan

Four thirty-something black women all hope that Mr. Right will appear, but this doesn't stop them from living their lives. One reviewer wrote that McMillan "has such a wonderful ear for story and dialogue. She gives us four women with raw, honest emotions that breathe off the page."

Gone with the Wind, Margaret Mitchell

The characters and places in this book—Scarlett O'Hara, Rhett Butler, Tara—have become part of our culture because they are unforgettable.

A Day No Pigs Would Die, Robert Peck

A boy raises a pig that is intelligent and affectionate. Will the boy follow orders and send the animal off to be slaughtered? Read this short novel to find out.

Harry Potter and the Sorcerer's Stone, J. K. Rowling

The first in a series of award-winning stories that have captured the hearts of young and old alike, around the world. These funny, action-packed, touching books are about a likable boy who is mistreated by the relatives who take him in after his parents are killed. Then Harry discovers that he is a wizard, and his extraordinary adventures begin.

The Catcher in the Rye, J. D. Salinger

The frustrations and turmoil of being an adolescent have never been captured so well as in this book. The main character, Holden Caulfield, is honest, funny, affectionate, obnoxious, and tormented at the same time.

The Lord of the Rings, J. R. R. Tolkien

Enter an amazing world of little creatures known as Hobbits; you, like thousands of other readers, may never want to leave.

Charlotte's Web, E. B. White

This best-loved story, for children and adults, is about a little pig named Wilbur and his best friend, a spider named Charlotte. Wilbur is being fattened in order to be killed for a holiday meal; Charlotte must come up with a plan to save him.

A Change of Attitude

Grant Berry

■ **Preview**

Every college has them: students the same age as some of their professors, students rushing into class after a full day at work, students carrying photographs—not of their boyfriends or girlfriends, but of the children they too seldom see. In many cases, these students are as surprised as anyone to find themselves in college, after an earlier educational experience that was anything but positive. In this essay, one such student describes his development from a bored high-schooler to a committed college student.

■ **Words to Watch**

decades (3): periods of ten years

striven (3): tried

suavely (4): in a sophisticated manner

immaculately (4): perfectly clean

tedious (6): boring

trudging (6): moving with great effort

nil (6): zero

smugly (8): in a way that demonstrates self-satisfaction

deprivation (16): state of being without possessions

battering (22): pounding

For me to be in college is highly improbable. That I am doing well in 1
school teeters on the illogical. Considering my upbringing, past educational performance, and current responsibilities, one might say, "This guy hasn't got a chance." If I were a racehorse and college were the track, there would be few who would pick me to win, place, or show.

When I told my dad that I was going back to school, the only encourage- 2
ment he offered was this: "Send me anywhere, but don't send me back to school." For my father, school was the worst kind of prison, so I was raised believing that school at its best was a drag. My dad thought that the purpose of graduating from high school was so you never had to go back to school again, and I adopted this working stiff's philosophy.

I followed my dad's example the way a man who double-crosses the mob 3
follows a cement block to the bottom of the river. My dad has been a union

factory worker for more than two decades,* and he has never striven* to be anything more than average. Nonetheless, he is a good man; I love him very much, and I respect him for being a responsible husband and father. He seldom, if ever, missed a day of work; he never left his paycheck at a bar, and none of our household appliances were ever carted off by a repo-man. He took his family to church each week, didn't light up or lift a glass, and has celebrated his silver anniversary with his first, and only, wife. However, if he ever had a dream of being more than just a shop rat, I never knew about it.

Grant Berry looks over a book before class.

On the other hand, my dreams were big, but my thoughts were small. I was not raised to be a go-getter. I knew I wanted to go to work each day in a suit and tie; unfortunately, I could not define what it was I wanted to do. I told a few people that I wanted to have a job where I could dress suavely* and carry a briefcase, and they laughed in my face. They said, "You'll never be anything," and I believed them. Even now I am envious of an immaculately* dressed businessman. It is not the angry type of jealousy; it is the "wish it were me" variety.   4

Since I knew I was not going to further my education, and I didn't know what I wanted to do except wear a suit, high school was a disaster. I do not know how my teachers can respect themselves after passing me. In every high school there are cliques and classifications. I worked just hard enough to stay above the bottom, but I did not want to work hard enough to get into the clique with the honor roll students.   5

Also, I had always had a problem with reading. When I was a kid, reading for me was slow and tedious.* My eyes walked over words like a snail trudging* through mud. I couldn't focus on what I was reading, and this allowed my young, active mind to wander far from my reading material. I would often finish a page and not remember a single word I had just read. Not only was reading a slow process, but my comprehension was nil.* I wasn't dumb; in fact, I was at a high English level. However, reading rated next to scraping dog poop from the tread of my sneakers. I didn't yet know that reading could be like playing the guitar: the more you do it, the better you get. As far as reading was concerned, I thought I was stuck in the same slow waltz forever.   6

In junior high and high school, I read only when it was absolutely essential.   7
For example, I had to find out who Spiderman was going to web, or how many children Superman was going to save each month. I also had to find out which girls were popular on the bathroom walls. I'm ashamed to say that my mother even did a book report for me, first reading the book. In high school, when I would choose my own classes, I took art and electronics rather than English.

Even though I was raised in a good Christian home, the only things I cared   8
about were partying and girls. I spent all of my minimum-wage paycheck on

beer, cigarettes, and young ladies. As a senior, I dated a girl who was twenty. She had no restrictions, and I tried to keep pace with her lifestyle. I would stay out drinking until 3:00 A.M. on school nights. The next morning I would sleep through class or just not show up. It became such a problem that the school sent letters to my parents telling them that I would not be joining my class- mates for commencement if I didn't show up for class once in a while. This put the fear of the establishment in me because I knew the importance of gradu- ating from high school. Nonetheless, I never once remember doing homework my senior year. Yet in June, they shook my hand and forked over a diploma as I smugly* marched across the stage in a blue gown and square hat.

Since I felt I didn't deserve the piece of paper with the principal's and super-   9 intendent's signatures on it, I passed up not only a graduation party but also a class ring and a yearbook. If it were not for my diploma and senior pictures, there would not be enough evidence to convince a jury that I am guilty of attending high school at all. I did, however, celebrate with my friends on grad- uation night. I got loaded, misjudged a turn, flattened a stop sign, and got my car stuck. When I pushed my car with my girlfriend behind the steering wheel, mud from the spinning tire sprayed all over my nice clothes. It was quite a night, and looking back, it was quite a fitting closure for the end of high school.

> **"For my father, school was the worst kind of prison, so I was raised believing that school at its best was a drag."**

After graduation I followed my father's example and went to work,   10 plunging into the lukewarm waters of mediocrity. All I was doing on my job bagging groceries was trading dollars for hours. I worked just hard enough to keep from getting fired, and I was paid just enough to keep from quitting.

Considering the way my father felt about school, college was a subject   11 that seldom came up at our dinner table. I was not discouraged, nor was I encouraged, to go to college; it was my choice. My first attempt at college came when I was nineteen. I had always dreamed of being a disk jockey, so I enrolled in a broadcasting class. However, my experience in college was as for- gettable as high school. My habit of not doing homework carried over, and the class was such a yawner that I often forgot to attend. Miraculously, I man- aged to pull a C, but my dream was weak and quickly died. I did not enroll for the next term. My girlfriend, the one who kept me out late in high school, became pregnant with my child. We were married two days after my final class, and this gave me another excuse not to continue my education.

My first job, and every job since, has involved working with my hands and   12 not my head. I enjoyed my work, but after the money ran out, the month would keep going. One evening my wife's cousin called and said he had a way that we could increase our income. I asked, "How soon can you get here?" He walked us through a six-step plan of selling and recruiting, and when he was finished, my wife and I wanted in. Fumbling around inside his large brief- case, he told us we needed the proper attitude first. Emerging with a small stack of books, he said, "Read these!" Then he flipped the books into my lap. I groaned at the thought of reading all those volumes. If this guy wanted me to develop a good attitude, giving me books was having the opposite effect. However, I wanted to make some extra cash, so I assured him I would try.

I started reading the books each night. They were self-help, positive-mental-attitude manuals. Reading those books opened up my world; they put me in touch with a me I didn't know existed. The books told me I had potential, possibly even greatness. I took their message in like an old Chevrolet being pumped full of premium no-lead gasoline. It felt so good I started reading more. Not only did I read at night; I read in the morning before I went to work. I read during my breaks and lunch hour, when waiting for signal lights to turn green, in between bites of food at supper, and while sitting on the toilet. One of the books I read said that there is no limit to the amount of information our brains will hold, so I began filling mine up.   13

The process of reading was slow at first, just as it had been when I was a kid, but it was just like playing the guitar. If I struck an unclear chord, I would try it again, and if I read something unclear, I would simply read it again. Something happened: the more I read, the better I got at it. It wasn't long before I could focus in and understand without reading things twice. I began feeling good about my reading skills, and because of the types of books I was reading, I started feeling good about myself at the same time.   14

The income from my day job blossomed while the selling and recruiting business grew demanding, disappointing, and fruitless. We stopped working that soil and our business died, but I was hooked on reading. I now laid aside the self-help books and began reading whatever I wanted. I got my first library card, and I subscribed to *Sports Illustrated*. I found a book of short stories, and I dived into poetry, as well as countless newspaper articles, cereal boxes, and oatmeal packages. Reading, which had been a problem for me, became a pleasure and then a passion.   15

Reading moved me. As I continued to read in a crowded lunchroom, sometimes I stumbled across an especially moving short story or magazine article. For example, a young Romanian girl was saved from starvation and deprivation° by an adoptive couple from the United States. I quickly jerked the reading material to my face to conceal tears when she entered her new home filled with toys and stuffed animals.   16

Not only did reading tug at my emotions; it inspired me to make a move. All those positive-mental-attitude books kept jabbing me in the ribs, so last fall, at age twenty-seven, I decided to give college another try. Now I am back in school, but it's a different road I travel from when I was a teenager. Mom and Dad paid the amount in the right-hand column of my tuition bill then, but now I am determined to pay for college myself, even though I must miss the sound of the pizza delivery man's tires on my blacktop driveway. I hope to work my way out of my blue collar by paying for school with blue-collar cash.   17

As a meat-cutter, I usually spend between 45 and 50 hours a week with a knife in my hand. Some weeks I have spent 72 hours beneath a butcher's cap. In one two-week period I spent 141 hours with a bloody apron on, but in that time I managed to show up for all of my classes and get all of my homework done (except being short a few bibliography cards for my research paper).   18

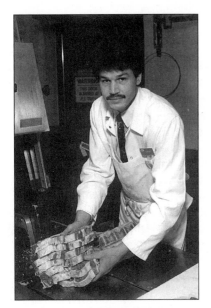

Grant continues to work as a
butcher full time.

Working full time and raising a family leave me lit- 19
tle free time. If I am not in class, I'm studying linking
verbs or trying to figure out the difference between
compound and complex sentences.

There are other obstacles and challenges staring me 20
in the face. The tallest hurdle is a lack of time for meeting all my obligations. For instance, my wife works two
nights a week, leaving me to care for my two daughters.
A twelve-hour day at work can lead to an evening coma
at home, so when Mom's punching little square buttons
on a cash register, I hardly have the energy to pour corn-
flakes for my kids, let alone outline a research paper.

Going to college means making choices, some of 21
which bring criticism. My neighbors, for example, hate my
sickly, brown lawn sandwiched between their lush, green,
spotless plots of earth, which would be the envy of any
football field. Just walking to my mailbox can be an awful
reminder of how pitiful my lawn looks when I receive an
unforgiving scowl from one of the groundskeepers who
live on either side of me. It is embarrassing to have such
a colorless lawn, but it will have to wait because I want
more out of life than a half-acre of green turf. Right now my time and money
are tied up in college courses instead of fertilizer and weed killer.

But the toughest obstacle is having to take away time from those I love 22
most. I am proud of the relationship I have with my wife and kids, so it tears
my guts out when I have to look into my daughter's sad face and explain that
I can't go to the Christmas program she's been practicing for weeks because I
have a final exam. It's not easy to tell my three-year-old that I can't push her
on the swings because I have a cause-and-effect paper to write, or tell my
seven-year-old that I can't build a snowman because I have an argument essay
to polish. As I tell my family that I can't go sledding with them, my wife lets

In the college computer lab, Grant works on a paper.

out a big sigh, and my kids yell,
"Puleeze, Daddy, can't you come
with us?" At these times I wonder if
my dream of a college education can
withstand such an emotional battering,* or if it is even worth it. But I
keep on keeping on because I must
set a good example for the four little eyes that are keeping watch over
their daddy's every move. I must succeed and pass on to them the right
attitude toward school. This time
when I graduate, because of the
hurdles I've overcome, there will be
a celebration—a proper one.

■ Reading Comprehension Questions

1. The word *clique* in "In every high school there are cliques and classifications. I worked just hard enough to stay above the bottom, but I did not want to work hard enough to get into the clique with the honor roll students" (paragraph 5) means
   a. grade.
   b. school.
   c. group.
   d. sports.

2. The word *scowl* in "Just walking to my mailbox can be an awful reminder of how pitiful my lawn looks when I receive an unforgiving scowl from one of the groundskeepers who live on either side of me" (paragraph 21) means
   a. sincere smile.
   b. favor.
   c. angry look.
   d. surprise.

3. Which sentence best expresses the central idea of the selection?
   a. The author was never encouraged to attend college or to challenge himself mentally on the job.
   b. After years of not caring about education, Berry was led by some self-help books to love reading, gain self-esteem, and attend college.
   c. The author's wife and children often do not understand why he is unable to take part in many family activities.
   d. The author was given a high school diploma despite the fact that he did little work and rarely attended class.

4. Which sentence best expresses the main idea of paragraph 13?
   a. Influenced by self-help books, the author developed a hunger for reading.
   b. People who really care about improving themselves will find the time to do it, such as during the early morning, at breaks, and during the lunch hour.
   c. Self-help books send the message that everyone is full of potential and even greatness.
   d. There is no limit to the amount of information the brain can hold.

5. Which sentence best expresses the main idea of paragraph 22?
   a. The author's decision to attend college is hurting his long-term relationship with his wife and daughters.
   b. The author has two children, one age three and the other age seven.
   c. The author enjoys family activities such as attending his children's plays and building snowmen.
   d. Although he misses spending time with his family, the author feels that graduating from college will make him a better role model for his children.

6. The author's reading skills
   a.   were strong even when he was a child.
   b.   improved as he read more.
   c.   were strengthened considerably in high school.
   d.   were sharpened by jobs he held after high school graduation.

7. The author's father
   a.   was rarely home while the author was growing up.
   b.   often missed work and stayed out late at bars.
   c.   was a college graduate.
   d.   disliked school.

8. In stating that his graduation night "was quite a fitting closure for the end of high school," Berry implies that
   a.   he was glad high school was finally over.
   b.   car troubles were a common problem for him throughout high school.
   c.   his behavior had ruined that night just as it had ruined his high school education.
   d.   despite the problems, the evening gave him good memories, just as high school had given him good memories.

9. We can infer from paragraph 21 that the author
   a.   does not tend his lawn because he enjoys annoying his neighbors.
   b.   receives a lot of mail.
   c.   is willing to make sacrifices for his college education.
   d.   has neighbors who care little about the appearance of their property.

10. We can infer that the author believes children
   a.   should be passed to the next grade when they reach a certain age, regardless of their test scores.
   b.   should not require a great deal of time from their parents.
   c.   fall into two categories: "born readers" and those who can never learn to read very well.
   d.   benefit from having role models who care about education.

■   Technique Questions

1. In explaining that he followed his father's example, the author compares himself to "a man who double-crosses the mob [and] follows a cement block to the bottom of the river." In this comparison, Berry strikingly makes the point that his own actions led him to an undesirable situation. Find two other places where the author uses a richly revealing comparison. Write those images below, and explain what Berry means by each one.

Image: _____

_____

Meaning: _____

Image: _____

_____

Meaning: _____

2. In most of his essay, Berry uses time order, but in some places he uses listing order. For example, what does Berry list in paragraphs 20–22?

_____

3. In closing his essay, Berry writes that at his college graduation, "there will be a celebration—a proper one." With what earlier event is he contrasting this graduation?

_____

■ Discussion Questions

1. The author looks back at this period of reading self-help books as one in which his attitude improved, eventually leading to his enrollment in college. Has a particular occurrence ever sharply changed your outlook on life? Was it something that you read, observed, or directly experienced? How did it happen? How did it change your point of view?

2. Berry writes that his father did not encourage him to go on to college. Nevertheless, he sees many positive things about his father. In what ways was his father a positive role model for him? In other words, is Berry's positive behavior as an adult partly a result of his father's influence? What do you see in your own adult behavior that you can attribute to your parents' influence?

3. Berry discusses some of the difficulties he faces as a result of being in college— struggling to find time to meet his obligations, giving up lawn care, spending less time with his family. What difficulties do you face as a result of fitting college into your life? What obligations must you struggle to fulfill? What activities remain undone?

■ Writing Assignments

1. Children are strongly influenced by the example of their parents (and other significant adults in their lives). For instance, the author of this essay followed his father's example of disliking school and getting a job that did not challenge him mentally.

Think about your growing-up years and about adults who influenced you, both positively and negatively. Then write a paragraph that describes one of these people and his or her influence on you. Supply plenty of vivid examples to help the reader understand how and why this person affected you.

The topic sentence of your paragraph should identify the person (either by name or by relationship to you) and briefly indicate the kind of influence he or she had on you. Here are some examples of topic sentences for this paper:

> My aunt's courage in difficult situations helped me to become a stronger person.
>
> My father's frequent trouble with the law made it necessary for me to grow up in a hurry.
>
> The pastor of our church helped me realize that I was a worthwhile, talented person.

2. Write a paragraph about one way that reading has been important in your life, either positively or negatively. To discover the approach you wish to take, think for a moment about the influence of reading throughout your life. When you were a child, was being read to at bedtime a highlight of your day? Did reading out loud in elementary school cause you embarrassment? Do you adore mysteries or true-crime books? Do you avoid reading whenever possible? Find an idea about the role of reading in your life that you can write about in the space of a paragraph. Your topic sentence will be a clear statement of that idea, such as:

> I first learned to read from watching *Sesame Street.*
>
> One key experience in second grade made me hate reading out loud in class.
>
> My parents' attitude toward reading rubbed off on me.
>
> Reading to my child at bedtime is an important time of day for both of us.
>
> Books have taught me some things I never would have learned from friends and family.
>
> There are several reasons why I am not a good reader.
>
> A wonderful self-help book has helped me build my self-esteem.

Develop your main idea with detailed explanations and descriptions. For example, if you decide to write about reading to your child at bedtime, you might describe the positions you and your child take (Is the child in bed? On the floor? On your lap?), one or two of the stories the child and you have loved, some of the child's reactions, and so on.

3. Berry's graduation-night celebration was a dramatic one and, he states, "a fitting closure for the end of high school." What was your high school graduation celebration like? Did you participate in any of the planning and preparation for

the events? Were finding a date and shopping for clothing for the prom fun or nerve-racking experiences? Was the event itself wonderful or disappointing? Write an essay telling the story of your graduation celebration from start to finish. Use many sharp descriptive details to help your readers envision events, decorations, clothing, cars, the weather, and so on. In addition, add meaning to your story by telling what you were thinking and feeling throughout the event.

You might try making a list as a way of collecting details for this paper. At first, don't worry about organizing your details. Just keep adding to your list, which might at one point look like this:

decorations committee

considered asking my cousin to go with me, if necessary

shopping for prom dress with Mom (and arguing)

afraid I'd be asked first by someone I didn't want to go with

talk of being up all night

pressed orchid corsage afterward

florist busy that week

working on centerpieces

feet hurt

Eventually, you will have enough information to begin thinking about the organization of your essay. Here's what the scratch outline for one such essay looks like:

<u>Central idea:</u> My high school prom was a mixture of fun and disappointment.

(1) Before the dance
 Work on the decorations com. (theme: sky's the limit)
 Anxiety over getting a date, finally relief
 Worn out shopping for a dress
 Last-minute preparations (getting flowers, having hair done, decorating ballroom)

(2) Night of the dance
 Picture-taking at home
 Squeezing gown into car, hem gets stuck in car door and grease rubs on it
 Beautiful ballroom
 Rotten meal
 Great band (even teachers yelling requests)
 After two dances had to take off heels
 Date kept dancing with others
 Danced with my brother, who came with my girlfriend
 Early breakfast served at hotel

(3) After the dance
Total exhaustion for two days
Extensive phone analysis of dance with girlfriends
Never went out with that date again
Several years later, prom dress, wrapped in a garbage bag, went to
Salvation Army

Perhaps you don't remember your graduation night celebration very well, or don't wish to. Feel free to write about another important social event instead, such as a high school reunion, a family reunion, or your own or someone else's wedding.

Do It Better!

Ben Carson, M.D., with Cecil Murphey

Preview

If you suspect that you are now as "smart" as you'll ever be, then read the following selection, taken from the book *Think Big*. It is about Dr. Ben Carson, who was sure he was "the dumbest kid in the class" in school. Carson tells how he turned his life around from what was a sure path to failure. Today he is a famous neurosurgeon at Johns Hopkins University Hospital in Baltimore, Maryland.

■ Words to Watch

inasmuch as (13): since

potential (18): capacity for development and progress

solely (20): alone

rebellious (46): resisting authority

indifferent (58): uninterested

startled (75): surprised

astonished (81): surprised

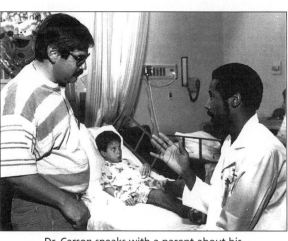

Dr. Carson speaks with a parent about his child's medical condition.

1 "Benjamin, is this your report card?" my mother asked as she picked up the folded white card from the table.

2 "Uh, yeah," I said, trying to sound casual. Too ashamed to hand it to her, I had dropped it on the table, hoping that she wouldn't notice until after I went to bed.

3 It was the first report card I had received from Higgins Elementary School since we had moved back from Boston to Detroit, only a few months earlier.

4 I had been in the fifth grade not even two weeks before everyone considered me the dumbest kid in the class and frequently made jokes about me. Before long I too began to feel as though I really was the most stupid kid in fifth grade. Despite Mother's frequently saying, "You're smart, Bennie. You can do anything you want to do," I did not believe her.

No one else in school thought I was smart, either.   5

Now, as Mother examined my report card, she asked, "What's this grade in   6
reading?" (Her tone of voice told me that I was in trouble.) Although I was
embarrassed, I did not think too much about it. Mother knew that I wasn't doing
well in math, but she did not know I was doing so poorly in every subject.

While she slowly read my report card, reading everything one word at a   7
time, I hurried into my room and started to get ready for bed. A few minutes
later, Mother came into my bedroom.

"Benjamin," she said, "are these your grades?" She held the card in front   8
of me as if I hadn't seen it before.

"Oh, yeah, but you know, it doesn't mean much."   9

"No, that's not true, Bennie. It means a lot."   10

"Just a report card."   11

"But it's more than that."   12

Knowing I was in for it now, I prepared to listen, yet I was not all that inter-   13
ested. I did not like school very much and there was no reason why I should.
Inasmuch as• I was the dumbest kid in the class, what did I have to look forward to? The others laughed at me and made jokes about me every day.

"Education is the only way you're ever going to escape poverty," she said.   14
"It's the only way you're ever going to get ahead in life and be successful. Do
you understand that?"

"Yes, Mother," I mumbled.   15

"If you keep on getting these kinds of grades you're going to spend the   16
rest of your life on skid row, or at best sweeping floors in a factory. That's not
the kind of life that I want for you. That's not the kind of life that God wants
for you."

I hung my head, genuinely ashamed. My mother had been raising me and   17
my older brother, Curtis, by herself. Having only a third-grade education herself, she knew the value of what she did not have. Daily she drummed into
Curtis and me that we had to do our best in school.

"You're just not living up to your potential•," she said. "I've got two   18
mighty smart boys and I know they can do better."

I had done my best—at least I had when I first started at Higgins   19
Elementary School. How could I do much when I did not understand anything
going on in our class?

In Boston we had attended a parochial school, but I hadn't learned much   20
because of a teacher• who seemed more interested in talking to another
female teacher than in teaching us. Possibly, this teacher was not solely• to
blame—perhaps I wasn't emotionally able to learn much. My parents had separated just before we went to Boston, when I was eight years old. I loved both
my mother and my father and went through considerable trauma over their
separating. For months afterward, I kept thinking that my parents would get
back together, that my daddy would come home again the way he used to,
and that we could be the same old family again—but he never came back.
Consequently, we moved to Boston and lived with Aunt Jean and Uncle

William Avery in a tenement building for two years until Mother had saved enough money to bring us back to Detroit.

Mother kept shaking the report card at me as she sat on the side of my bed. "You have to work harder. You have to use that good brain that God gave you, Bennie. Do you understand that?" 21

"Yes, Mother." Each time she paused, I would dutifully say those words. 22

"I work among rich people, people who are educated," she said. "I watch how they act, and I know they can do anything they want to do. And so can you." She put her arm on my shoulder. "Bennie, you can do anything they can do—only you can do it better!" 23

Mother had said those words before. Often. At the time, they did not mean much to me. Why should they? I really believed that I was the dumbest kid in fifth grade, but of course, I never told her that. 24

"I just don't know what to do about you boys," she said. "I'm going to talk to God about you and Curtis." She paused, stared into space, then said (more to herself than to me), "I need the Lord's guidance on what to do. You just can't bring in any more report cards like this." 25

As far as I was concerned, the report card matter was over. 26

The next day was like the previous ones—just another bad day in school, another day of being laughed at because I did not get a single problem right in arithmetic and couldn't get any words right on the spelling test. As soon as I came home from school, I changed into play clothes and ran outside. Most of the boys my age played softball, or the game I liked best, "Tip the Top." 27

We played Tip the Top by placing a bottle cap on one of the sidewalk cracks. Then taking a ball—any kind that bounced—we'd stand on a line and take turns throwing the ball at the bottle top, trying to flip it over. Whoever succeeded got two points. If anyone actually moved the cap more than a few inches, he won five points. Ten points came if he flipped it into the air and it landed on the other side. 28

When it grew dark or we got tired, Curtis and I would finally go inside and watch TV. The set stayed on until we went to bed. Because Mother worked long hours, she was never home until just before we went to bed. Sometimes I would awaken when I heard her unlocking the door. 29

Two evenings after the incident with the report card, Mother came home about an hour before our bedtime. Curtis and I were sprawled out, watching TV. She walked across the room, snapped off the set, and faced both of us. "Boys," she said, "you're wasting too much of your time in front of that television. You don't get an education from staring at television all the time." 30

Before either of us could make a protest, she told us that she had been praying for wisdom. "The Lord's told me what to do," she said. "So from now on, you will not watch television, except for two preselected programs each week." 31

"Just *two* programs?" I could hardly believe she would say such a terrible thing. "That's not—" 32

"And *only* after you've done your homework. Furthermore, you don't play outside after school, either, until you've done all your homework." 33

"Everybody else plays outside right after school," I said, unable to think 34 of anything except how bad it would be if I couldn't play with my friends. "I won't have any friends if I stay in the house all the time—"

"That may be," Mother said, "but everybody else is not going to be as 35 successful as you are—"

"But, Mother—"   36

"This is what we're going to do. I asked God for wisdom, and this is the 37 answer I got."

Dr. Carson and his wife, Candy, are photographed at home with their sons (from left to right) Murry, B.J., and Rhoeyce.

I tried to offer several other arguments, but Mother 38 was firm. I glanced at Curtis, expecting him to speak up, but he did not say anything. He lay on the floor, staring at his feet.

"Don't worry about everybody else. The whole 39 world is full of 'everybody else,' you know that? But only a few make a significant achievement."

The loss of TV and play time was bad enough. I got 40 up off the floor, feeling as if everything was against me. Mother wasn't going to let me play with my friends, and there would be no more television—almost none, anyway. She was stopping me from having any fun in life.

"And that isn't all," she said. "Come back, Bennie." 41

I turned around, wondering what else there 42 could be.

"In addition," she said, "to doing your homework, 43 you have to read two books from the library each week. Every single week."

"Two books? Two?" Even though I was in fifth 44 grade, I had never read a whole book in my life.

"Yes, two. When you finish reading them, you must 45 write me a book report just like you do at school. You're not living up to your potential, so I'm going to see that you do."

Usually Curtis, who was two years older, was the more rebellious*. But this 46 time he seemed to grasp the wisdom of what Mother said. He did not say one word.

She stared at Curtis. "You understand?"   47

He nodded.   48

"Bennie, is it clear?"   49

"Yes, Mother." I agreed to do what Mother told me—it wouldn't have 50 occurred to me not to obey—but I did not like it. Mother was being unfair and demanding more of us than other parents did.

The following day was Thursday. After school, Curtis and I walked to the 51 local branch of the library. I did not like it much, but then I had not spent that much time in any library.

We both wandered around a little in the children's section, not having any 52 idea about how to select books or which books we wanted to check out.

The librarian came over to us and asked if she could help. We explained 53 that both of us wanted to check out two books.

"What kind of books would you like to read?" the librarian asked. 54

"Animals," I said after thinking about it. "Something about animals." 55

"I'm sure we have several that you'd like." She led me over to a section 56 of books. She left me and guided Curtis to another section of the room. I flipped through the row of books until I found two that looked easy enough for me to read. One of them, *Chip, the Dam Builder*—about a beaver—was the first one I had ever checked out. As soon as I got home, I started to read it. It was the first book I ever read all the way through even though it took me two nights. Reluctantly I admitted afterward to Mother that I really had liked reading about Chip.

Within a month I could find my way around the children's section like some- 57 one who had gone there all his life. By then the library staff knew Curtis and me and the kind of books we chose. They often made suggestions. "Here's a delightful book about a squirrel," I remember one of them telling me.

As she told me part of the story, I tried to appear indifferent*, but as soon 58 as she handed it to me, I opened the book and started to read.

Best of all, we became favorites of the librarians. When new books came 59 in that they thought either of us would enjoy, they held them for us. Soon I became fascinated as I realized that the library had so many books—and about so many different subjects.

After the book about the beaver, I chose others about animals—all types 60 of animals. I read every animal story I could get my hands on. I read books about wolves, wild dogs, several about squirrels, and a variety of animals that lived in other countries. Once I had gone through the animal books, I started reading about plants, then minerals, and finally rocks.

My reading books about rocks was the first time the information ever 61 became practical to me. We lived near the railroad tracks, and when Curtis and I took the route to school that crossed by the tracks, I began paying atten- tion to the crushed rock that I noticed between the ties.

As I continued to read more about rocks, I would walk along the tracks, 62 searching for different kinds of stones, and then see if I could identify them.

Often I would take a book with me to make sure that I had labeled each 63 stone correctly.

"Agate," I said as I threw the stone. Curtis got tired of my picking up 64 stones and identifying them, but I did not care because I kept finding new stones all the time. Soon it became my favorite game to walk along the tracks and identify the varieties of stones. Although I did not realize it, within a very short period of time, I was actually becoming an expert on rocks.

"That day—for the first time—I realized that Mother had been right. Reading is the way out of ignorance, and the road to achievement. I did not have to be the class dummy anymore."

Two things happened in the second half of fifth grade that convinced me 65 of the importance of reading books.

First, our teacher, Mrs. Williamson, had a spelling bee every Friday after- 66
noon. We'd go through all the words we'd had so far that year. Sometimes
she also called out words that we were supposed to have learned in fourth
grade. Without fail, I always went down on the first word.

One Friday, though, Bobby Farmer, whom everyone acknowledged as the 67
smartest kid in our class, had to spell "agriculture" as his final word. As soon
as the teacher pronounced his word, I thought, I can spell that word. Just the
day before, I had learned it from reading one of my library books. I spelled
it under my breath, and it was just the way Bobby spelled it.

If I can spell "agriculture," I'll bet I can learn to spell any other word in 68
the world. I'll bet I can learn to spell better than Bobby Farmer.

Just that single word, "agriculture," was enough to give me hope.   69

The following week, a second thing happened that forever changed my 70
life. When Mr. Jaeck, the science teacher, was teaching us about volcanoes,
he held up an object that looked like a piece of black, glass-like rock. "Does
anybody know what this is? What does it have to do with volcanoes?"

Immediately, because of my reading, I recognized the stone. I waited, but 71
none of my classmates raised their hands. I thought, *This is strange. Not even
the smart kids are raising their hands.* I raised my hand.

"Yes, Benjamin," he said.   72

I heard snickers around me. The other kids probably thought it was a joke, 73
or that I was going to say something stupid.

"Obsidian," I said.   74

"That's right!" He tried not to look startled•, but it was obvious he hadn't 75
expected me to give the correct answer.

"That's obsidian," I said, "and it's formed by the supercooling of lava 76
when it hits the water." Once I had their attention and realized I knew information no other student had learned, I began to tell them everything I knew
about the subject of obsidian, lava, lava flow, supercooling, and compacting
of the elements.

When I finally paused, a voice behind me whispered, "Is that Bennie 77
Carson?"

"You're absolutely correct," Mr. Jaeck said, and he smiled at me. If he had 78
announced that I'd won a million-dollar lottery, I couldn't have been more
pleased and excited.

"Benjamin, that's absolutely, absolutely right," he repeated with enthu- 79
siasm in his voice. He turned to the others and said, "That is wonderful! Class,
this is a tremendous piece of information Benjamin has just given us. I'm very
proud to hear him say this."

For a few moments, I tasted the thrill of achievement. I recall thinking, 80
*Wow, look at them. They're all looking at me with admiration. Me, the
dummy! The one everybody thinks is stupid. They're looking at me to see if
this is really me speaking.*

Maybe, though, it was I who was the most astonished• one in the class. 81
Although I had been reading two books a week because Mother told me to,
I had not realized how much knowledge I was accumulating. True, I had

Dr. Carson finds time between surgical operations to deliver motivational talks to groups of schoolchildren.

learned to enjoy reading, but until then I hadn't realized how it connected with my schoolwork. That day—for the first time—I realized that Mother had been right. Reading is the way out of ignorance, and the road to achievement. I did not have to be the class dummy anymore.

82 For the next few days, I felt like a hero at school. The jokes about me stopped. The kids started to listen to me. *I'm starting to have fun with this stuff.*

83 As my grades improved in every subject, I asked myself, "Ben, is there any reason you can't be the smartest kid in the class? If you can learn about obsidian, you can learn about social studies and geography and math and science and everything."

84 That single moment of triumph pushed me to want to read more. From then on, it was as though I could not read enough books. Whenever anyone looked for me after school, they could usually find me in my bedroom—curled up, reading a library book—for a long time, the only thing I wanted to do. I had stopped caring about the TV programs I was missing; I no longer cared about playing Tip the Top or baseball anymore. I just wanted to read.

85 In a year and a half—by the middle of sixth grade—I had moved to the top of the class.

■ Reading Comprehension Questions

1. The word *trauma* in "I loved both my mother and my father and went through considerable trauma over their separating. For months afterward, I kept thinking that my parents would get back together, . . . but he never came back" (paragraph 20) means
   a. love.
   b. knowledge.
   c. distance.
   d. suffering.

2. The word *acknowledged* in "One Friday, though, Bobby Farmer, whom everyone acknowledged as the smartest kid in our class, had to spell 'agriculture' as his final word" (paragraph 67) means
   a. denied.
   b. recognized.
   c. forgot.
   d. interrupted.

3. Which sentence best expresses the central idea of the selection?
   a.   Children who grow up in single-parent homes may spend large amounts of time home alone.
   b.   Because of parental guidance that led to a love of reading, the author was able to go from academic failure to success.
   c.   Parents should stay committed to their marriage when their children are young.
   d.   Today's young people watch too much television day after day.

4. Which sentence best expresses the main idea of paragraph 56?
   a.   Bennie's first experience with a library book was positive.
   b.   The first book that Bennie ever checked out at a library was about a beaver.
   c.   The librarian was very helpful to Bennie and Curtis.
   d.   At first, Bennie could not read most of the animal books at the library.

5. Which sentence best expresses the main idea of paragraphs 61–64?
   a.   Books about rocks gave the author his first practical benefits from reading.
   b.   Curtis took little interest in what his brother had learned about rocks.
   c.   The author found a piece of agate by the railroad tracks.
   d.   Studying rocks can be a fascinating experience.

6. In Boston, Bennie
   a.   had an excellent teacher.
   b.   attended a public school.
   c.   longed for his parents to get together again.
   d.   lived with his father in a tenement building.

7. To get her sons to do better in school, Mrs. Carson insisted that they
   a.   watch educational TV.
   b.   finish their homework before playing.
   c.   read one library book every month.
   d.   all of the above.

8. We can conclude that Mrs. Carson believed
   a.   education leads to success.
   b.   her sons needed to be forced to live up to their potential.
   c.   socializing was less important to her sons than a good education.
   d.   all of the above.

9. We can infer that Bennie Carson believed he was dumb because
   a.   in Boston he had gotten behind in school.
   b.   other students laughed at him.
   c.   he had done his best when he first started at Higgins Elementary School, but still got poor grades.
   d.   all of the above.

10. From paragraphs 70–80, we can infer that
   a. Bennie thought his classmates were stupid because they did not know about obsidian.
   b. Mr. Jaeck knew less about rocks than Bennie did.
   c. this was the first time Bennie had answered a difficult question correctly in class.
   d. Mr. Jaeck thought that Bennie had taken too much class time explaining about obsidian.

■ Technique Questions

1. Instead of pausing to describe Bennie's mother, the author reveals her character through the specific details of her actions and words. For example, what does paragraph 25 tell us about Mrs. Carson?

   _____

   _____

   _____

   _____

2. What is the main order in which the details of this reading are organized—time order or listing order? Locate and write down three of the many transitions that are used as part of that order.

   _____

   _____

3. The author states in paragraph 65, "Two things happened in the second half of fifth grade that convinced me of the importance of reading books." In paragraph 66, the first of those two events is introduced with a listing transition. In paragraph 70, the second event is introduced with another listing transition. Write those two transitions on the lines below.

   _____   _____

■ Discussion Questions

1. The author recalls his failure in the classroom as an eight-year-old child by writing, "Perhaps I wasn't emotionally able to learn much." Why does he make this statement? In general, what things in a child's home or social life might interfere with his or her education?

2. Part of Mrs. Carson's plan for helping her sons do better in school was limiting them to two television shows a week. How much of a role do you think this limit played in the success of her plan? Do you agree with her that unrestricted television can be harmful to children? Explain.

3. Reading on a regular basis helped turn Carson's life around. Think about your daily schedule. If you were to do regular reading, where in your day could you find time to relax for half an hour and just read? What would you choose to read? How do you think you might benefit from becoming a regular reader?

■ Writing Assignments

1. The reading tells about some of Carson's key school experiences, both positive and negative. Write a paragraph about one of your key experiences in school. Use concrete details—actions, comments, reactions, and so on—to help your readers picture what happened. (To see how Carson used details to bring classroom scenes to life, look at paragraphs 65–82.)

To select an event to write about, try asking yourself the following questions:

- Which teachers or events in school influenced how I felt about myself?
- What specific incidents stand out in my mind as I think back to elementary school?

Once you know which experience you'll write about, use freewriting to help you remember and record the details. Here is one student's freewriting for this assignment.

> In second grade, Richard L. sat next to me. A really good artist. He would draw something, and it really looked like something. He was so good at choosing colors. Good at crayons, good at water paint. His pictures were always picked by teacher. They were shown on bulletin board. I remember his drawing of a circus and acrobats and animals and clowns. Many colors and details. I felt pretty bad in art. But I loved it and couldn't wait for art in class. One day the teacher read a story about a boy who looked at the mountains and wondered what was on the other side, the mountains were huge, dark. After the reading the teacher said "Paint something from the story." I painted those mountains, big purple brown mountains. Watercolor dripped to show slopes and a colored sunset, at the top of the picture a thin slice of blue sky. Next day I sat down in my desk in the morning. Then I saw my picture was on the bulletin board! Later teacher passed by me and put a hand on my shoulder and whispered good job, lovely picture. Made me feel really proud. The feeling lasted a long time.

After the details of the experience are on paper, you will be free to concentrate on a more carefully constructed version of the event. The author of the freewriting above, for instance, needed to think of a topic sentence. So when writing the first draft, she began with this sentence: "A seemingly small experience in elementary school encouraged me greatly." Writing drafts is also the time to add any persuasive details you may have missed at first. When working on her second draft, the author of the above added at the end: "I felt very proud, which gave me confidence to work harder in all my school subjects."

Before writing out your final version, remember to check for grammar, punctuation, and spelling errors.

2. Reading helped Bennie, and it can do a lot for adults too. Most of us, however, don't have someone around to insist that we do a certain amount of personal reading every week. In addition, many of us don't have the amount of free time that Bennie and Curtis had. How can adults find time to read more? Write a paragraph listing several ways adults can add more reading to their lives.

A good prewriting strategy for this assignment is making a list. Simply write out as many ways as you can think of. Don't worry about putting them in any special order. You will select and organize the strategies you wish to include in your paper after accumulating as many ideas as you can. Here is an example of a prewriting list for this paper:

> Ways adults can increase the amount of time they spend reading:
>
> on the bus to and from work/school
>
> while eating breakfast
>
> instead of watching some TV
>
> choose motivating materials (articles, books about hobbies, problems, etc.)

Feel free to use items from the above list, but add at least one or two of your own points to include in your paper.

3. "Do It Better!" suggests that television can interfere with children's academic progress. Write a paragraph on what you believe is another unfortunate effect of television. You may feel that television includes too much violence, that TV advertising encourages children to want to buy too much, or that TV sitcoms promote poor family values. After deciding what effect you wish to write about, make a list of possible points of support. You may find it helpful to spend a few sessions in front of the TV with a notebook. Following, for instance, is part of a list of notes that can be used to support the point "TV advertising promotes poor nutrition."

> During kids' cartoon show:
>
> A sugary chocolate cereal in which marshmallow ghosts appear once milk is added. Children are pictured enjoying these ghosts' appearances and loving the cereal.

Chocolate-dipped cookies are included in boxes of another chocolate cereal. Appealing cartoon characters invite children to look for these boxes.

<u>During talk show:</u>

Ad for soda (empty calories) shows symbols of Christmas, making the soda seem like a healthy holiday drink.

An ad for corn chips (high fat) shows happy, healthy faces finishing up a huge bowl of the chips.

Lost Years, Found Dreams

Regina Ruiz

■ Preview

Divorced, far from home, with three children, not very fluent in English—Regina Ruiz could easily have become a sad statistic, a woman sunk in despair after a failed marriage. But Ruiz decided she had given up enough years of her life; she would reclaim the rest. Her story is hardly a fairy tale with a magical happy ending. But it is perhaps even better; it is the story of a courageous, life-loving commitment to a new and meaningful future.

■ Words to Watch

regal (2): royal

haze (3): confused state of mind

intervened (7): came in to change a situation

bleak (8): not hopeful

bleary-eyed (18): with blurry vision

preoccupation (18): extreme concern with something

Morpheus (20): the god of dreams in Greek mythology

I feel funny. So very funny, telling you about my life, my feelings, my secrets. I do not know how to welcome you into my heart and soul. You see, nobody ever asked me what I thought or how I felt about life's challenges. Or, maybe, nobody ever really cared about what I thought. [1]

My journey to Burlington County College began many years ago in Caracas, Venezuela, where I was born and grew to be a young lady full of energy and life. My parents called me Regina because there was something regal° about the sound. They had high hopes of my marrying a local boy from a good, wealthy family. You know the kind—slick, black hair, long sideburns, driving a sports car. The kind who brings you flowers on every date and swears his undying love for you three days a week, and the other days he is sleeping with Maria, the local social worker. [2]

To get even, or because I was in a romantic haze,° I met and married a U.S. Marine from Des Moines, Iowa, who was stationed at our local embassy, where I also worked. [3]

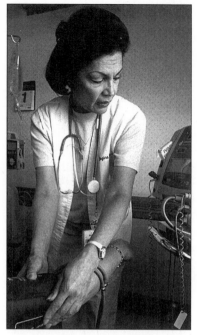

Regina Ruiz's nursing duties include taking a patient's blood pressure.

Marriage, a home in America, and three beautiful children occupied twenty-five years of my life.   4

Where did my life go? It went somewhere. But there is no lost-and-found department for lost years.   5

The marriage was bad. It was so bad that I cried every night for all those years. I would tell myself, "You are in a strange country—maybe the customs are different. The children need you, and you cannot admit failure to your parents back in Venezuela."   6

As luck would have it, fate intervened.* My ex-Marine husband found someone new and left me and the children with no money, very hurt and depressed.   7

I quickly took an inventory—foreign-born, with not a great command of the English language, no money, no job training, and two kids in college. The future looked bleak.*   8

But it did not stop. My father died. I loved him so much, and he was always my source of strength in need. Mother became ill.   9

I felt very hurt, lonely, angry, and very sorry for myself.   10

However, I remembered a saying my Dad would quote to me when things were going wrong and the future looked black. He may have gotten this quotation from the Spanish edition of *Reader's Digest*. He would say, "My dear, it is always the darkest when you are fresh out of matches."   11

"Dad, I am out of matches." Or so I thought.   12

I decided to make my life something worthwhile by helping people. I wanted to help and heal and maybe, at the same time, heal myself.   13

I appeared before the college doors with my knees shaking and full of doubt. I wanted to be a nurse.   14

I enrolled in college. I was proud of myself for not falling into the garbage pit waiting so close by.   15

Then the fun began—subjects which were very hard for me.   16

In order to survive, I managed to get two jobs to keep up with house payments and food. The kids found college money by working and by appealing to their father. I met my challenges on a daily basis.   17

Now, my days are very active and long. Before the sun makes its appearance, I stumble bleary-eyed* to the shower and afterward select the day's outfit. After a quick check in the mirror, I make my way downstairs to prepare a quick breakfast along with my lunch, feed the cat (who happens to be my alarm clock), and do what seem like a million other small chores. Then I drive for forty-five minutes to the Pemberton Campus, while studying my chemistry key notes on index cards before a test. I do this with tears in my eyes. You see, at the same time I am worrying about the situation with my water heater that slowly but surely is leaking and may not last until the new one can be   18

Regina continues to cut hair of her friends and family.

installed. In addition, I am anxious to schedule my exterminator's visit to treat the termites discovered in my basement. My preoccupation* with such household woes is due to a canceled appointment to have my furnace cleaned, which resulted in a periodic spray of soot.

After a hectic morning of classes, I rush to my car for a hurried thirty-minute ride to the office, where a desk piled high with import documents is waiting for me, along with innumerable phone calls from the brokers, customs officials, and suppliers. Meanwhile, an impatient boss wants to know the precise location of one of the fifty containers traveling between eastern Europe and Burlington, New Jersey. 19

As the clock winds toward 5 P.M., I get ready to travel back to the Cinnaminson Campus for another round of classes. As I arrive on campus, I waste another thirty minutes searching for that nonexistent parking spot. My class continues until ten o'clock in the evening, and I praise the Lord it doesn't last longer. By that time, I am beginning to see double. I slowly make my way to the car and begin the long commute home, counting in my mind how many customers I will see as a result of my second job—hairdressing. On evenings when I have no classes scheduled, I take appointments to cut hair or give permanents. As I arrive home, I find a hungry son and starving cat, both waiting to be fed. I usually cook something simple for us, then proceed to do the few dishes because I hate the thought of adding one more chore to my early-morning schedule. By the time I finish getting ready for bed, it is midnight; I look up and see the stairway leading to the bedroom, which by then seems longer than the one outside the Philadelphia Museum of Art, and proceed to crawl in bed and into the arms of Morpheus.* 20

> "I decided to make my life something worthwhile by helping people. I wanted to help and heal and maybe, at the same time, heal myself."

On many nights, I do not stay there long. At 3 A.M., maybe 4 A.M., my eyes pop open. The thought, "Am I ready for the test? Do I understand the material?" makes me sit upright in a panic. Rather than toss and turn uneasily for the rest of the night, I get out of bed and open my textbooks for a couple of hours. If fatigue finally wins, I may fall back into bed before getting up for the day. 21

Without long luxurious stretches of time to study, I must constantly search out such little windows of opportunity to prepare for class. When the laundry is washing, I study. While supper is simmering on the stove, I study. When a customer cancels her appointment for a haircut, I thank the Lord for a free hour, and I study. "Mom, if I studied half as hard as you, I'd be a straight-A student," says my son. But he understands that the life of a working mother 22 is not designed to make going to college easy. If I do not budget my time carefully, I will fail.

People question the wisdom of my studying to be a nurse. It may take four or five years. 23

"You will never last," they tell me. 24

"You will be too old to lift a bedpan," they mock. 25

But I am not discouraged. There are twenty more courses ahead of me before I get into the nursing area. While all these things challenge me, the greatest of all is to be able to hold my head high. 26

Somehow, just somehow, I think it might be all worth it—if I can hold the hand of someone dying all alone in a cold hospital ward and whisper in the patient's ear, "You are not alone, I am here, I am here, I will never leave you." 27

Maybe, just maybe, I will find that life that was lost. It is out there somewhere. 28

But I know one thing—I am in charge, and I will never let go again. Never. 29

An Update

Regina Ruiz successfully completed her registered nurse degree and is only a few credits away from earning her bachelor's degree at Jefferson University in Philadelphia. She is a nurse at Voorhees Pediatric Rehabilitation Hospital in New Jersey. 30

At the hospital, Regina's patients range in age from newborns to eighteen-year-olds. As she grows attached to particular patients, she requests that they be assigned to her daily shift, giving "extra love" to children battling illness, fear, and loneliness. "To see tiny preemies and children who are so sick grow and get better and be released to their families—it is wonderful to be part of that. School was very difficult, and nursing is a demanding profession, but when I am at work I am in heaven." 31

Regina enjoys reading to her two grandchildren, Rachel and Nicole.

When she is not working, she takes pride in keeping her home beautiful. "After my divorce and through all those long difficult years, I worried so much about not being able to keep up with things," she said. "The roof leaked so badly at one point I had trash cans sitting in the living room. So I had to learn to budget my money as well as my time. When I had three jobs, one was for tuition and food, and the others were for repairs—a roof, siding, new windows, everything. Now I can look at the house and feel so good. A little neighbor boy told me the other day, 'Mrs. Ruiz, you have the nicest house on the street.'" 32

She still does hair for a handful of longtime clients. "They were my friends 33
for so many years," she said. "When I'd come home from a test crying because
I was sure I'd failed, they'd be the ones to say, 'No, Regina! You're going to
make it.' Now, maybe I don't have to cut hair anymore to earn a living," she
says with a chuckle, "but how can I tell them to go jump in the lake?"

■ Reading Comprehension Questions

1. The words *took an inventory* in "I quickly took an inventory—foreign-born,
   with not a great command of the English language, no money, no job training, and two kids in college" (paragraph 8) mean
   a. fell asleep.
   b. made a detailed list.
   c. formed a plan of action.
   d. got a job.

2. The word *appealing* in "The kids found college money by working and by
   appealing to their father" (paragraph 17) means
   a. pretending.
   b. refusing.
   c. suggesting an alternative.
   d. making a request.

3. Which sentence best expresses the central idea of the selection?
   a. Ruiz could not tell her parents back in Venezuela that her marriage was
       unhappy.
   b. Ruiz should not have married the Marine and moved so far from home.
   c. After a bad marriage, Ruiz successfully took charge of her own life and
       future.
   d. Ruiz is often exhausted by her schedule of school and two jobs.

4. A main idea may cover more than one paragraph. Which sentence best
   expresses the main idea of paragraphs 11–13?
   a. Ruiz remembered a saying her father used to say.
   b. Ruiz at first saw no way out of a bad situation but then thought of a worth-
       while path.
   c. Ruiz's father may have gotten inspiration from the Spanish edition of
       Reader's Digest.
   d. Ruiz thought helping people was a worthwhile goal.

5. Which sentence best expresses the main idea of paragraphs 21–22?
   a. Ruiz never has time to study, so she goes to class unprepared.
   b. Ruiz always chooses to sleep an extra hour or two rather than study for
       class.
   c. Ruiz values studying and uses every spare minute for schoolwork.
   d. Because of her excess leisure time, Ruiz always has enough opportunity
       for study.

6. Ruiz's marriage ended when
   a. she left her husband for another man.
   b. she enrolled in college and her husband divorced her.
   c. her husband left her for another woman.
   d. Ruiz's parents demanded that she come back to Venezuela.

7. According to the "Update," Ruiz now works as a(n)
   a. office worker and baby-sitter.
   b. nurse and occasional hairdresser.
   c. translator and cleaning woman.
   d. parking lot attendant and veterinarian's assistant.

8. We can infer that Ruiz
   a. wishes she had married "a local boy from a good, wealthy family."
   b. believes she married the U.S. Marine too quickly.
   c. regrets having three children.
   d. believes enrolling in the nursing program was not wise.

9. We can infer that in the passage below, the author uses the word *matches* to refer to
   a. heat.
   b. solutions.
   c. the love between a child and a parent.
   d. something that will light a cigarette.

   He would say, "My dear, it is always the darkest when you are fresh out of matches." "Dad, I am out of matches." Or so I thought. (Paragraphs 11–12)

10. We can conclude one reason Ruiz wanted to become a nurse was that
    a. she believed that helping other people would help her too.
    b. Venezuela needed more nurses.
    c. her father always wanted her to be a nurse.
    d. nursing was the easiest course offered by the college she attended.

■ Technique Questions

1. In paragraph 5, Regina asks the question "Where did my life go?" Where in the essay does she return to the image of her "lost life"? Write here the number of the paragraph in which she returns to this image: _____ What is the difference between how she discusses her lost life in paragraph 5 and in the later paragraph?

_____

2. Ruiz begins her essay by describing a series of disappointments and her resulting depression. Later, she describes her decision to make something good out of her life and what her life has been like since then. In what paragraph of her essay does she make the transition between those two sections, and what word marks that transition?

_____

3. Who wrote paragraphs 1–29 of the reading? Was the update written by the same person? What evidence supports your answers to these questions?

_____

_____

_____

■ Discussion Questions

1. Ruiz stayed with an unhappy marriage for twenty-five years. During those years, she told herself, "You are in a strange country—maybe the customs are different. The children need you, and you cannot admit failure to your parents back in Venezuela." Judging from your own experience and observations of people around you, are these typical reasons for remaining in an unhappy relationship? Are these *good* reasons?

2. Like Ruiz, adults who return to college often have a difficult time balancing the demands of their work, family, and classes. What challenges do you face as a student? What ways have you found to deal with them?

3. Ruiz briefly explains her decision to become a nurse. Why have you chosen your own course of study? What about it interests you? What do you hope it will offer you after college?

■ Writing Assignments

1. Ruiz and her parents had very different ideas about whom she should marry. How well have your plans for your life conformed to your parents' hopes for you? Write a paragraph about a decision in your life on which you and your parents have either clashed or agreed. Include concrete details in your paragraph that show exactly what your parents had in mind and how they communicated their hopes to you. Also explain clearly your decision and the reasons for it. Here are some sample topic sentences for this assignment:

Although my parents urged me to become a teacher, I am studying to be a veterinary assistant.

My parents did not want me to marry my high school girlfriend, and I surprised them—and myself—by doing what they wanted.

2. In paragraph 18, Regina writes about her typical morning, from stumbling out of bed to getting to and through school. She includes various specific details about getting ready in the morning, studying for a test while driving to school, and thinking about the "household woes" that plague her all the while. Write a paragraph describing your typical morning. To prepare yourself with plenty of concrete details, do some freewriting or make a list. After accumulating enough information about a typical morning, think of a topic sentence that will cover all of the details you will write about. Here, for instance, is one possible topic sentence:

> A typical morning in my life starts slowly before developing into some very hectic, but productive hours.

Before writing your final draft, double-check your topic sentence to see if it still covers the details in your paragraph or if it needs adjusting. (Perhaps, for example, you realize that your morning doesn't start so slowly after all.) Also, use a few time transitions to make the sequence of events clear to your reader. You could write, for example, "First I hear my alarm go off at 6 A.M. Then I take a shower, ending with a few seconds of ice-cold water to wake up my body and my brain."

3. Ruiz was proud of herself for taking control of her life and enrolling in college, rather than getting stuck in depression and self-pity after her marriage ended. When have you taken an action that you are proud of? Write an essay about such a time.

In your first paragraph, state your central idea. Here are some possibilities:

I am proud of myself for quitting smoking.

I am proud of myself for leaving an abusive marriage and getting my life together afterward.

I am proud of myself for confronting a friend about her drinking problem.

I am proud of myself for earning my high school diploma.

Then continue by explaining the situation you faced, how you decided to take the course of action you did, and what the results have been.

Below is a sample scratch outline for this paper.

Central idea: I am proud of myself for confronting a friend about her drinking problem.

1. Lana's drinking and its effect on her family and job performance
2. The day I told Lana she was hurting herself and her children
3. Lana's decision to join a twelve-step program

A great deal of specific detail would be needed to support each general point in this outline. Freewriting or making a list, or both, would help generate the necessary specific details.

The introduction of the outlined essay might begin with an anecdote dramatizing Lana's problem. The conclusion could restate the central idea and include a brief explanation of how Lana is doing now.

Papa

Leo Buscaglia

■ **Preview**

Leo Buscaglia gained worldwide fame as a favorite lecturer on public radio and the author of inspirational books including *Living, Loving, and Learning* and *The Fall of Freddie the Leaf.* Here, Buscaglia writes of the man who laid the foundation for his own lively curiosity and love of learning—the uneducated Italian factory worker whom Buscaglia knew as Papa.

■ **Words to Watch**

fathom (1): understand

insular (3): isolated

credo (4): a belief

complacency (4): self-satisfaction

stagnation (4): failure to develop

forum (5): a time and place for discussion

inevitable (6): sure to happen, unavoidable

pungent (7): strong and sharp

animated (8): lively

analytical (8): carefully examining

potent (11): strong

affirming (23): maintaining the truth of

Papa had a natural wisdom. He wasn't educated in the formal sense. When he was growing up at the turn of the century in a very small village in rural northern Italy, education was for the rich. Papa was the son of a dirt-poor farmer. He used to tell us that he never remembered a single day of his life when he wasn't working. The concept of doing nothing was never a part of his life. In fact, he couldn't fathom° it. How could one do nothing? 1

He was taken from school when he was in the fifth grade, over the protests of his teacher and the village priest, both of whom saw him as a young person with great potential for formal learning. Papa went to work in a factory in a nearby village, the very same village where, years later, he met Mama. 2

For Papa, the world became his school. He was interested in everything. He read all the books, magazines, and newspapers he could lay his hands on. 3

He loved to gather with people and listen to the town elders and learn about "the world beyond" this tiny, insular° region that was home to generations of Buscaglias before him. Papa's great respect for learning and his sense of wonder about the outside world were carried across the sea with him and later passed on to his family. He was determined that none of his children would be denied an education if he could help it.

Papa believed that the greatest sin of which we were capable was to go to bed at night as ignorant as we had been when we awakened that day. The credo° was repeated so often that none of us could fail to be affected by it. "There is so much to learn," he'd remind us. "Though we're born stupid, only the stupid remain that way." To ensure that none of his children ever fell into the trap of complacency°, he insisted that we learn at least one new thing each day. He felt that there could be no fact too insignificant, that each bit of learning made us more of a person and insured us against boredom and stagnation°.   4

So Papa devised a ritual. Since dinnertime was family time and we all came to dinner unless we were dying of malaria, it seemed the perfect forum° for sharing what new things we had learned that day. Of course, as children we thought this was perfectly crazy. There was no doubt, when we compared such paternal concerns with other children's fathers, Papa was weird.   5

It would never have occurred to us to deny Papa a request. So when my brother and sisters and I congregated in the bathroom to clean up for dinner, the inevitable° question was, "What did you learn today?" If the answer was "Nothing," we didn't dare sit at the table without first finding a fact in our much-used encyclopedia. "The population of Nepal is . . . ," etc.   6

Now, thoroughly clean and armed with our fact for the day, we were ready for dinner. I can still see the table piled high with mountains of food. So large were the mounds of pasta that as a boy I was often unable to see my sister sitting across from me. (The pungent° aromas were such that, over a half century later, even in memory they cause me to salivate.)   7

Dinner was a noisy time of clattering dishes and endless activity. It was also a time to review the activities of the day. Our animated° conversations were always conducted in Piedmontese dialect, since Mama didn't speak English. The events we recounted, no matter how insignificant, were never taken lightly. Mama and Papa always listened carefully and were ready with some comment, often profound and analytical°, always right to the point.   8

"That was a smart thing to do." "*Stupido*, how could you be so dumb?" "*Cose sia*, you deserved it." "*E allora*, no one is perfect." "*Testa dura* ('hardhead'), you should have known better. Didn't we teach you anything?" "Oh, that's nice." One dialogue ended and immediately another began. Silent moments were rare at our table.   9

Then came the grand finale to every meal, the moment we dreaded most—the time to share the day's new learning. The mental imprint of those sessions still runs before me like a familiar film clip, vital and vivid.   10

"Without being aware of it, our family was growing together, sharing experiences, and participating in one another's education. Papa was, without knowing it, giving us an education in the most real sense."

Papa, at the head of the table, would push his chair back slightly, a 11
gesture that signified the end of the eating and suggested that there would
be a new activity. He would pour a small glass of red wine, light up a thin,
potent° Italian cigar, inhale deeply, exhale, then take stock of his family.

For some reason this always had a slightly unsettling effect on us as we 12
stared back at Papa, waiting for him to say something. Every so often he
would explain why he did this. He told us that if he didn't take the time to
look at us, we would soon be grown and he would have missed us. So he'd
stare at us, one after the other.

Finally, his attention would settle upon one of us. "Felice,"* he would say 13
to me, "tell me what you learned today."

"I learned the population of Nepal is . . ."   14

Silence.   15

It always amazed me, and reinforced my belief that Papa was a little crazy, 16
that nothing I ever said was considered too trivial for him. First, he'd think
about what was said as if the salvation of the world depended on it.

"The population of Nepal. Hmmm. Well."   17

He would look down the table at Mama, who would be ritualistically fix- 18
ing her favorite fruit in a bit of leftover wine. "Mama, did you know that?"

Mama's responses were always astonishing and seemed to lighten the 19
otherwise reverential atmosphere. "Nepal," she'd say. "Nepal? Not only don't
I know the population of Nepal, I don't know where in God's world it is!" Of
course, this was only playing into Papa's hands.

"Felice," he'd say. "Get the atlas so we can show Mama where Nepal is." 20
And the search began. The whole family went on a search for Nepal. This
same experience was repeated until each family member had a turn. No dinner at our house ever ended without having been enlightened by at least a
half dozen such facts.

As children, we thought very little about these educational wonders and 21
even less about how we were being enriched. We couldn't have cared less.
We were too impatient to have dinner end so we could join our less-educated
friends in a rip-roaring game of kick the can.

In retrospect, after years of studying how people learn, I realize what a 22
dynamic educational technique Papa was offering us, reinforcing the value
of continual learning. Without being aware of it, our family was growing
together, sharing experiences, and participating in one another's education.
Papa was, without knowing it, giving us an education in the most real sense.

By looking at us, listening to us, hearing us, respecting our opinions, 23
affirming° our value, giving us a sense of dignity, he was unquestionably our
most influential teacher.

*Buscaglia's real first name.

■ Reading Comprehension Questions

1. The word *reverential* in "Mama's responses were always astonishing and seemed to lighten the otherwise reverential atmosphere" (paragraph 19) means
   a. relaxed.
   b. respectful.
   c. confusing.
   d. humorous.

2. The word *congregated* in "So when my brother and sisters and I congregated in the bathroom to clean up for dinner" (paragraph 6) means
   a. gathered.
   b. searched.
   c. argued.
   d. listened.

3. The word *retrospect* in "As children, we thought very little about these educational wonders and even less about how we were being enriched. . . . In retrospect, after years of studying how people learn, I realize what a dynamic educational technique Papa was offering us" (paragraph 22) means
   a. looking back.
   b. truth.
   c. imagination.
   d. part.

4. Which sentence best expresses the central idea of this selection?
   a. Buscaglia's father was a natural teacher who encouraged his children to love learning.
   b. Buscaglia's father insisted that his children come to the dinner table with one new fact each day.
   c. Dinnertime at the Buscaglia household was always a lively affair.
   d. The Buscaglia children treated their father with the kind of respect that is rarely seen today.

5. Which statement best expresses the main idea of paragraph 4?
   a. Buscaglia's father was scornful of people of low intelligence.
   b. Buscaglia's father frequently repeated himself.
   c. Believing that ignorance is sinful, Papa insisted that each child should learn one new fact a day.
   d. Papa believed that his children were born stupid and faced a life of boredom and lack of development.

6. A main idea may cover more than one paragraph. Which sentence best expresses the main idea of paragraphs 8 and 9?
   a. Buscaglia's parents listened and responded carefully to their children's conversation.
   b. Over dinner, everyone in the Buscaglia family talked.
   c. Buscaglia's parents were sometimes critical of their children.
   d. Because Mrs. Buscaglia did not speak English, the dinnertime conversation was in Piedmontese dialect.

7. Buscaglia states that he and his brother and sisters would
   a. invent made-up "facts" to satisfy his father.
   b. look up facts in the encyclopedia before dinner.
   c. compete with each other to find the most interesting fact.
   d. refuse to cooperate with his father's request.

8. Paragraphs 1 and 2 suggest that Buscaglia's father left school at a young age because
   a. he was considered too stupid to learn very much.
   b. his village priest recommended it.
   c. he could learn a lot on his own without school.
   d. his family needed him to earn money.

9. *True or false?* _____ Paragraph 5 suggests that many of the neighborhood fathers played similar learning games with their children over dinner.

10. Buscaglia implies that his mother
    a. approved of her husband's methods and played along with them.
    b. did not understand why her husband thought learning was so important.
    c. thought her husband was making fun of her ignorance.
    d. was better educated than her husband.

■ Technique Questions

1. How does Buscaglia organize most of the material in his essay—through time order or listing order?

   _____

2. Paragraph 9 consists almost entirely of direct quotations from Buscaglia's parents. Why do you think the author chose to quote their exact words?

   _____

   _____

   _____

   _____

3. In paragraphs 11 and 12, the author provides vivid details. Which do you find most memorable?

_____

What do these details add to the essay?

_____

_____

_____

■ Discussion Questions

1. If Buscaglia is writing in praise of his father's educational techniques, why does he mention that he and his siblings didn't think much of them at the time (paragraphs 5 and 21)?

2. Buscaglia states that his father gave him "an education in the most real sense." What does he mean? What about his father's teaching style was so real? In what ways was it similar to or different from what happens in a typical classroom?

3. Was it especially important that the Buscaglia children knew, for example, the population of Nepal? What do you think was important to Mr. Buscaglia about the children's learning such facts?

■ Writing Assignments

1. Write a paragraph in which you describe a typical scene in your own family when you were a child. Make the paragraph as richly detailed as you can. In order to remember details vividly, you might ask yourself the following questions:

   What sights, smells, and sounds were usually part of our dinnertime?

   What were some foods that were frequently served?

   Who was typically present at dinner? Where did each person sit?

   What was the mood usually like at dinner? Rushed? Relaxed? Informal? Argumentative? Quiet?

   Were certain items always on the table—a particular coffee cup, for instance, or a sugar bowl?

2. Buscaglia writes of his father's outstanding characteristic—he was a natural teacher. Think of a person you know who also has one very strong characteristic. It could be a positive characteristic, such as generosity, humor, or

helpfulness. Or it could be a less positive trait, perhaps pessimism, bad temper, or laziness. Write a paragraph that begins with a topic sentence naming the person and stating his or her outstanding characteristic. Then support your topic sentence. Use several brief examples or one extended example of the person's behavior.

3. Buscaglia's essay is an affectionate tribute to a man who helped him realize that learning is a lifelong process. Write an essay about three adults in your life who have each helped you learn something. They may have taught you to *do* something practical—for example, tune up a car, make a dress, or cook. Or they might have taught you how to *be* something you value—kind, hardworking, assertive.

Your topic sentence should name the three adults you will write about. Here is such a topic sentence:

My uncle, my stepmother, and a family friend have each helped me learn something important to me.

The first sentence of each of your main paragraphs should then specify what each person taught you. For example:

My uncle taught me to fly-fish.

Such a main idea sentence would then be followed by a description of how you observed your uncle fly-fish, how you yourself learned from his example, and why you value what he taught you. Repeat this process for each of the three adults you are writing about.

Let's Get Specific

Beth Johnson

■ **Preview**

Some people are better writers than others. That's obvious to anyone who reads. There are writers whose material you just can't put down—and there are writers whose material you can't put down fast enough. One of the biggest differences between the skillful writer and the poor one is this: the successful writer uses specific, concrete language. The journalist and teacher Beth Johnson explains the power of specific language and demonstrates how any writer can become more skilled in its use.

■ **Words to Watch**

instinctive (2): natural

prospective (2): expected, or possible

vividly (2): clearly, in lifelike images

glaze (3): become glassy

blandly (7): dully

intuitively (8): naturally

parody (8): imitation meant to be amusing or mocking

crave (9): strongly desire

anecdote (12): story

sustain (17): support

Imagine that you've offered to fix up your sister with a blind date. "You'll 1
like him," you tell her. "He's really nice." Would that assurance be enough to
satisfy her? Would she contentedly wait for Saturday night, happily anticipat-
ing meeting this "nice" young man? Not likely! She would probably bombard
you with questions: "But what's he like? Is he tall or short? Funny? Serious?
Smart? Kind? Shy? Does he work? How do you know him?"

Such questions reveal the instinctive° hunger we all feel for specific detail. 2
Being told that her prospective° date is "nice" does very little to help your
sister picture him. She needs concrete details to help her vividly° imagine this
stranger.

The same principle applies to writing. Whether you are preparing a 3
research paper, a letter to a friend, or an article for the local newspaper, your
writing will be strengthened by the use of detailed, concrete language. Specific

language energizes and informs readers. General language, by contrast, makes their eyes glaze* over.

The following examples should prove the point.   4

Dear Sir or Madam:

Please consider my application for a job with your company. I am a college graduate with experience in business. Part-time jobs that I have held during the school year and my work over summer vacations make me well-qualified for employment. My former employers have always considered me a good, reliable worker. Thank you for considering my application.

Sincerely,

Bob Cole

Dear Sir or Madam:

I would like to be considered for an entry-level position in your purchasing department. I graduated in June from Bayside College with a 3.5 GPA and a bachelor's degree in business administration. While at Bayside, I held a part-time job in the college's business office, where I eventually had responsibility for coordinating food purchasing for the school cafeteria. By encouraging competitive bidding among food suppliers, I was able to save the school approximately $2,500 in the school year 1998–1999. During the last three summers (1997–1999), I worked at Bayside Textiles, where I was promoted from a job in the mailroom to the position of assistant purchasing agent, a position that taught me a good deal about controlling costs. Given my background, I'm confident I could make a real contribution to your company. I will telephone you next Tuesday morning to ask if we might arrange an interview.

Sincerely,

Julia Moore

Which of the preceding letters do you think makes a more convincing case   5
for these job seekers? If you're like most people, you would choose the second. Although both letters are polite and grammatically acceptable, the first one suffers badly in comparison with the second for one important reason. It is *general* and *abstract*, while the second is *specific* and *concrete*.

Let's look at the letters again. The differing styles of the two are evident   6
in the first sentence. Bob is looking for "a job with your company." He doesn't specify what kind of job—it's for the employer to figure out if Bob wants to work as a groundskeeper, on an assembly line, or as a salesperson. By contrast, Julia is immediately specific about the kind of job she is seeking—"an entry-level position in your purchasing department." Bob tells only that he is "a college graduate." But Julia tells where she went to college, what her grade point average was, and exactly what she studied.

The contrast continues as the two writers talk about their work experience.   7
Again, Bob talks in vague, general terms. He gives no concrete evidence to show how the general descriptions "well-qualified" and "good, reliable worker" apply to him. But Julia backs up her claims. She tells specifically what

positions she's held (buyer for cafeteria, assistant purchasing clerk for textile company), gives solid evidence that she performed her jobs well (saved the school $2,500, was promoted from mailroom), and explains what skills she has acquired (knows about controlling costs). Julia continues to be clear and concrete as she closes the letter. By saying, "I will telephone you next Tuesday morning," she leaves the reader with a helpful, specific piece of information. Chances are, her prospective employer will be glad to take her call. The chances are equally good that Bob will never hear from the company. His letter was so blandly* general that the employer will hardly remember receiving it.

> "Vague, general language is the written equivalent of baby food. It is adequate; it can sustain life. But it isn't very interesting."

Julia's letter demonstrates the power of specific detail—a power that we all appreciate intuitively.* Indeed, although we may not always be aware of it, our opinions and decisions are frequently swayed by concrete language. On a restaurant menu, are you more tempted by a "green salad" or "a colorful salad bowl filled with romaine and spinach leaves, red garden-fresh tomatoes, and crisp green pepper rings"? Would being told that a movie is "good" persuade you to see it as much as hearing that it is "a hilarious parody* of a rock documentary featuring a fictional heavy-metal band"? Does knowing that a classmate has "personal problems" help you understand her as well as hearing that "her parents are divorcing, her brother was just arrested for selling drugs, and she is scheduled for surgery to correct a back problem"? **8**

When we read, all of us want—even crave*—this kind of specificity. Concrete language grabs our attention and allows us to witness the writer's world almost firsthand. Abstract language, on the other hand, forces us to try to fill in the blanks left by the writer's lack of specific imagery. Usually we tire of the effort. Our attention wanders. We begin to wonder what's for lunch and whether it's going to rain, as our eyes scan the page, searching for some concrete detail to focus on. **9**

Once you understand the power of concrete details, you will gain considerable power as a writer. You will describe events so vividly that readers will feel they experienced them directly. You will sprinkle your essays with nuggets of detail that, like the salt on a pretzel, add interest and texture. **10**

Consider the following examples and decide for yourself which came from a writer who has mastered the art of the specific detail. **11**

Living at Home

Unlike many college students, I have chosen to live at home with my parents. Naturally, the arrangement has both good and bad points. The most difficult part is that, even though I am an adult, my parents sometimes still think of me as a child. Our worst disagreements occur when they expect me to report to them as though I were still twelve years old. Another drawback to living with my parents is that I don't feel free to have friends over to "my place." It's not that my parents don't welcome my friends in their home, but I can't tell my friends to drop in anytime as I would if I lived alone.

But in other ways, living at home works out well. The most obvious plus is that I am saving a lot of money. I pay room and board, but that doesn't compare to what renting an apartment would cost. There are less measurable advantages as well. Although we do sometimes fall into our old parent-child roles, my parents and I are getting to know each other in new ways. Generally, we relate as adults, and I think we're all gaining a lot of respect for one another.

The Pros and Cons of Living at Home

Most college students live in a dormitory or apartment. They spend their hours surrounded by their own stereos, blaring hip-hop or rock music; their own furnishings, be they leaking beanbag chairs or Salvation Army sofas; and their own choice of foods, from tofu-bean sprout casseroles to a basic diet of Cheetos. My life is different. I occupy the same room that has been mine since babyhood. My school pictures, from gap-toothed first-grader to cocky senior, adorn the walls. The music drifting through my door from the living room ranges from Lawrence Welk to . . . Lawrence Welk. The food runs heavily to Mid-American Traditional: meatloaf, mashed potatoes, frozen peas.

Yes, I live with my parents. And the arrangement is not always ideal. Although I am twenty-four years old, my parents sometimes slip into a time warp and mentally cut my age in half. "Where are you going, Lisa? Who will you be with?" my mother will occasionally ask. I'll answer patiently, "I'm going to have pizza with some people from my psych class." "But where?" she continues. "I'm not sure," I'll say, my voice rising just a hair. If the questioning continues, it will often lead to a blowup. "You don't need to know where I'm going, OK?" I'll say shrilly. "You don't have to yell at me," she'll answer in a hurt voice.

Living at home also makes it harder to entertain. I find myself envying classmates who can tell their friends, "Drop in anytime." If a friend of mine "drops in" unexpectedly, it throws everyone into a tizzy. Mom runs for the dustcloth while Dad ducks into the bedroom, embarrassed to be seen in his comfortable, ratty bathrobe.

On the other hand, I don't regret my decision to live at home for a few years. Naturally, I am saving money. The room and board I pay my parents wouldn't rent the tiniest, most roach-infested apartment in the city. And despite our occasional lapses, my parents and I generally enjoy each other's company. They are getting to know me as an adult, and I am learning to see them as people, not just my parents. I realized how true this was when I saw them getting dressed up to go out recently. Dad was putting on a tie, and Mom one of her best dresses. I opened my mouth to ask where they were going when it occurred to me that maybe they didn't care to be checked up on any more than I did. Swallowing my curiosity, I simply waved good-bye and said, "Have a good time!"

Both passages could have been written by the same person. Both make 12 the same basic points. But the second passage is far more interesting because it backs up the writer's points with concrete details. While the first passage merely *tells* that the writer's parents sometimes treat her like a child, the second passage follows this point up with an anecdote° that *shows* exactly what she means. Likewise with the point about inviting friends over: the first passage only states that there is a problem, but the second one describes in concrete terms what happens if a friend does drop in unexpectedly. The first writer simply says that her room and board costs wouldn't pay for an apartment, but the second is specific about just how inadequate the money would be. And while the first passage uses abstract language to say that the writer and her parents are "getting to know each other in new ways," the second shows what that means by describing a specific incident.

Every kind of writing can be improved by the addition of concrete detail. 13 Let's look at one final example: the love letter.

> Dear April,
>
> I can't wait any longer to tell you how I feel. I am crazy about you. You are the most wonderful woman I've ever met. Every time I'm near you I'm overcome with feelings of love. I would do anything in the world for you and am hoping you feel the same way about me.
>
> Love,
>
> *Paul*

Paul has written a sincere note, but it lacks a certain something. That 14 something is specific detail. Although the letter expresses a lot of positive feelings, it could have been written by practically any love-struck man about any woman. For this letter to be really special to April, it should be unmistakably about her and Paul. And that requires concrete details.

Here is what Paul might write instead. 15

> Dear April,
>
> Do you remember last Saturday, as we ate lunch in the park, when I spilled my soda in the grass? You quickly picked up a twig and made a tiny dam to keep the liquid from flooding a busy anthill. You probably didn't think I noticed, but I did. It was at that moment that I realized how totally I am in love with you and your passion for life. Before that I only thought you were the most beautiful woman in the world, with your eyes like sparkling pools of emerald water and your chestnut hair glinting in the sun. But now I recognize what it means when I hear your husky laugh and I feel a tight aching in my chest. It means I could stand on top of the Empire State Building and shout to the world, "I love April Snyder." Should I do it? I'll be waiting for your reply.
>
> *Paul*

There's no guarantee that April is going to return Paul's feelings, but 16 she certainly has a better idea now just what it is about her that Paul finds so lovable, as well as what kind of guy Paul is. Concrete details have made this letter far more compelling.

Vague, general language is the written equivalent of baby food. It is 17 adequate; it can sustain* life. But it isn't very interesting. For writing to have satisfying crunch, sizzle, and color, it must be generously supplied with specifics. Whether the piece is a job application, a student essay, or a love letter, it is concrete details that make it interesting, persuasive, and memorable.

■ Reading Comprehension Questions

1. The word *swayed* in "our opinions and decisions are frequently swayed by concrete language" (paragraph 8) means
   a. hidden.
   b. repeated.
   c. influenced.
   d. shown to be wrong.

2. The word *compelling* in "she certainly has a better idea now just what it is about her that Paul finds so lovable . . . . Concrete details have made this letter far more compelling" (paragraph 16) means
   a. forceful and interesting.
   b. long and boring.
   c. empty and vague.
   d. silly but amusing.

3. Which sentence best expresses the central idea of the selection?
   a. Communication skills of all types are useful throughout life.
   b. Always be specific when applying for a job.
   c. Specific language will strengthen your writing.
   d. Most people need help with their writing skills.

4. Main ideas may cover more than one paragraph. Which sentence best expresses the main idea of paragraphs 6–7?
   a. In letters of application for a job, Bob and Julia have included their background and job goals.
   b. Bob and Julia have written letters of application for a job.
   c. While Bob says only that he's a college graduate, Julia goes into detail about where and what she studied and her grades.
   d. While Bob's job-application letter is probably too vague to be successful, Julia's very specific one is likely to get a positive response.

5. Which sentence best expresses the main idea of paragraph 8?
   a. Julia's letter is a good example of the power of specific details.
   b. Our opinions and decisions are often influenced by specific language.
   c. We want to hear exactly what's in a salad or movie before spending money on it.
   d. When we know just what someone's "personal problems" are, we understand him or her better.

6. Johnson states that abstract language
   a. is rare.
   b. lets us clearly see what the writer's world is like.
   c. tends to lose our attention.
   d. makes us want to read more of the writer's piece.

7. Johnson feels that concrete language
   a.   is hard to follow.
   b.   makes readers' eyes glaze over.
   c.   helps readers picture what the author is writing about.
   d.   is not appropriate for a menu or a parody.

8. In paragraphs 6–7, the author suggests that Bob Cole
   a.   is not qualified to enter the business world.
   b.   is lying about his education and work experience.
   c.   should have written a less wordy letter.
   d.   should have written a more detailed letter.

9. Which of the following sentences can we assume Beth Johnson would most approve of?
   a.   Shore City is an amusing but expensive place.
   b.   Shore City is an interesting place to spend a bit of time.
   c.   Shore City has an amusement park and racetrack, but all the hotel rooms cost over $100 a day.
   d.   There is a city near the shore which has some interesting attractions, but its hotels are quite expensive.

10. We can infer from the reading that specific details would be very important in
    a.   a novel.
    b.   a history textbook.
    c.   a biography.
    d.   all of the above.

■ Technique Questions

1. Essays often begin with an introduction that prepares readers for the author's central idea. How does Johnson begin her essay? Why do you think she chose this kind of introduction?

   _____

   _____

   _____

2. The authors of the papers on "living at home" are essentially using listing order. What are they listing?

   _____

3. Johnson takes her own advice and uses many concrete details in her essay. Locate two particularly strong examples of specific details in the reading that are not in the three pairs of samples, and write them below:

_____

_____

_____

■ Discussion Questions

1. At some earlier point in school, did you learn the importance of writing specifically? If so, do you remember when? If not, when do you think you should have been taught about the power of specific details in writing?

2. Johnson provides three pairs of examples: two job-application letters, two passages about living at home, and two love letters. Which pair most effectively makes her point for you about the value of writing specifically?

3. What kinds of writing will you be doing over the next few weeks, either in or out of school? Will it be papers for other classes, answers to essay questions, reports at work, letters of application for jobs, letters to friends, or other types of writing? Name one kind of writing you will be doing, and give an example of one way you could make that writing more specific.

■ Writing Assignments

1. Using the same level of detail as Julia's application letter in the reading, write a one-paragraph letter of application for a part-time or a full-time job. Like Julia Moore, be sure to include the following in your paragraph:

What kind of job you are applying for

Where you have worked previously

What positions you have held

Evidence that you performed your job well

Which skills you have acquired

2. In this reading, "The Pros and Cons of Living at Home" is a strong example of a "pro and con" analysis—one that details the advantages and disadvantages of something. Think of a topic about which you have conflicting views. It could be a decision you are struggling with, such as changing jobs or moving to a larger (or smaller) house or apartment. Or it could be a situation in

which you already find yourself, such as attending school while holding a job or having an elderly parent living with you. Write a paragraph in which you explain in detail what the pros and cons of the issue are.

Once you've chosen a topic, do some prewriting. A good strategy is to make two lists; one of the advantages, the other of the disadvantages. Here is a sample:

<u>Advantages of moving to a smaller apartment</u>

Save money on rent ($325 a month instead of $400 a month)

Save money on utilities (smaller heating bill)

Less space to clean (one bedroom instead of two)

<u>Disadvantages of moving to a smaller apartment</u>

Less space for all my furniture (big chest of drawers, sofa bed)

No spare bedroom (can't have friends sleep over)

Will get more cluttered (little space to display all my trophies, souvenirs, and sports equipment)

If you are not sure about which issue to write about, make lists for two or three topics. Then you'll have a better idea of which one will result in a better paper.

Use the lists of advantages and disadvantages as an outline for your paragraph, adding other ideas as they occur to you. Begin with a topic sentence such as "_____ has both advantages and disadvantages" or "I'm having a hard time deciding whether or not to _____." Next, write the supporting sentences, discussing first one side of the issue and then the other.

Be sure to include plenty of specific details. For inspiration, reread "The Pros and Cons of Living at Home" before writing your essay.

3. Johnson uses sharp, concrete details to make a point she feels strongly about—that specific language gives writing real power. Write an essay persuading readers of the importance of something you believe in strongly. Be sure to include at least one or two concrete, convincing examples for every point that you make. You might write about the value of something, such as:

Regular exercise

Volunteer work

Reading for pleasure

Gardening

Spending time with young (or grown) children

Periodic intense housecleaning

Alternatively, you can write about the negative aspects of something, such as:

Excessive television watching
Compulsive shopping
Tabloid journalism
Procrastinating
Smoking

Following is an example of an informal outline for this assignment. As the writer developed this outline into paragraphs, she added, subtracted, and rearranged some of her examples.

Central idea: Cleaning out closets every now and then can be rewarding.

(1) I get rid of things I no longer need, or never needed:
Pair of ten-year-old hiking boots, which I kept because they were expensive but that are thoroughly worn out
Portable TV that no longer works
Yogurt maker given to me by my first husband on our anniversary

(2) I make room for things I do need:
All my shoes and pocketbooks, which can be arranged in neat rows on the shelves instead of crammed into cartons
Christmas presents I buy for my family in July and want to hide

(3) I find things that I thought were lost forever or that I forgot I ever had:
Box of photographs from our first family vacation
My bowling trophy
Presents I bought for last Christmas and forgot about

All the Good Things

Sister Helen Mrosla

■ Preview

Teachers must often wonder if their efforts on behalf of their students are appreciated—or even noticed. In this article, Sister Helen Mrosla, a Franciscan nun from Little Falls, Minnesota, tells the story of a moment when she learned the answer to that question in a most bittersweet way. This powerful account of a true incident in her life has been reprinted many times, as well as widely circulated on the Internet.

■ Words to Watch

mischievousness (1): minor misbehavior

accustomed (2): used to

novice (3): new

deliberately (5): slowly and on purpose

accomplished (12): been successful at

lull (13): brief silence

sheepishly (20): with embarrassment

frazzled (20): worn-out; ragged

He was in the first third-grade class I taught at Saint Mary's School in Morris, Minnesota. All thirty-four of my students were dear to me, but Mark Eklund was one in a million. He was very neat in appearance but had that happy-to-be-alive attitude that made even his occasional mischievousness° delightful. [1]

Mark talked incessantly. I had to remind him again and again that talking without permission was not acceptable. What impressed me so much, though, was his sincere response every time I had to correct him for misbehaving— "Thank you for correcting me, Sister!" I didn't know what to make of it at first, but before long I became accustomed° to hearing it many times a day. [2]

One morning my patience was growing thin when Mark talked once too often, and then I made a novice° teacher's mistake. I looked at him and said, "If you say one more word, I am going to tape your mouth shut!" [3]

It wasn't ten seconds later when Chuck blurted out, "Mark is talking again." I hadn't asked any of the students to help me watch Mark, but since I had stated the punishment in front of the class, I had to act on it. [4]

I remember the scene as if it had occurred this morning. I walked to my 5 desk, very deliberately° opened my drawer, and took out a roll of masking tape. Without saying a word, I proceeded to Mark's desk, tore off two pieces of tape, and made a big X with them over his mouth. I then returned to the front of the room. As I glanced at Mark to see how he was doing, he winked at me.

That did it! I started laughing. The class cheered as I walked back to 6 Mark's desk, removed the tape, and shrugged my shoulders. His first words were, "Thank you for correcting me, Sister."

At the end of the year I was asked to teach junior-high math. The years 7 flew by, and before I knew it Mark was in my classroom again. He was more handsome than ever and just as polite. Since he had to listen carefully to my instruction in the "new math," he did not talk as much in ninth grade as he had talked in the third.

One Friday, things just didn't feel right. We had worked hard on a new 8 concept all week, and I sensed that the students were frowning, frustrated with themselves—and edgy with one another. I had to stop this crankiness before it got out of hand. So I asked them to list the names of the other students in the room on two sheets of paper, leaving a space after each name. Then I told them to think of the nicest thing they could say about each of their classmates and write it down.

It took the remainder of the class period to finish the assignment, and as 9 the students left the room, each one handed me the papers. Charlie smiled. Mark said, "Thank you for teaching me, Sister. Have a good weekend."

That Saturday, I wrote down the name of each student on a separate sheet 10 of paper, and I listed what everyone else had said about that individual.

On Monday I gave each student his or her list. Before long, the entire class 11 was smiling. "Really?" I heard whispered. "I never knew that meant anything to anyone!" "I didn't know others liked me so much!"

> **"I knew without looking that the papers were the ones on which I had listed all the good things each of Mark's classmates had said about him."**

No one ever mentioned those papers in class again. I never knew if the 12 students discussed them after class or with their parents, but it didn't matter. The exercise had accomplished° its purpose. The students were happy with themselves and one another again.

That group of students moved on. Several years later, after I returned from 13 a vacation, my parents met me at the airport. As we were driving home, Mother asked me the usual questions about the trip—the weather, my experiences in general. There was a slight lull° in the conversation. Mother gave Dad a sideways glance and simply said, "Dad?" My father cleared his throat as he usually did before something important. "The Eklunds called last night," he began. "Really?" I said. "I haven't heard from them in years. I wonder how Mark is."

Dad responded quietly. "Mark was killed in Vietnam," he said. "The 14
funeral is tomorrow, and his parents would like it if you could attend." To this
day I can still point to the exact spot on I-494 where Dad told me about Mark.

I had never seen a serviceman in a military coffin before. Mark looked so 15
handsome, so mature. All I could think at that moment was, Mark, I would
give all the masking tape in the world if only you would talk to me.

The church was packed with Mark's friends. Chuck's sister sang "The Bat- 16
tle Hymn of the Republic." Why did it have to rain on the day of the funeral?
It was difficult enough at the graveside. The pastor said the usual prayers, and
the bugler played taps. One by one those who loved Mark took a last walk
by the coffin and sprinkled it with holy water.

I was the last one to bless the coffin. As I stood there, one of the soldiers 17
who had acted as pallbearer came up to me. "Were you Mark's math teacher?"
he asked. I nodded as I continued to stare at the coffin. "Mark talked about
you a lot," he said.

After the funeral, most of Mark's former classmates headed to Chuck's 18
farmhouse for lunch. Mark's mother and father were there, obviously waiting for me. "We want to show you something," his father said, taking a wallet out of his pocket. "They found this on Mark when he was killed. We
thought you might recognize it."

Opening the billfold, he carefully removed two worn pieces of notebook 19
paper that had obviously been taped, folded, and refolded many times. I knew
without looking that the papers were the ones on which I had listed all the
good things each of Mark's classmates had said about him. "Thank you so
much for doing that," Mark's mother said. "As you can see, Mark treasured it."

Mark's classmates started to gather around us. Charlie smiled rather 20
sheepishly* and said, "I still have my list. It's in the top drawer of my desk at
home." Chuck's wife said, "Chuck asked me to put his list in our wedding
album." "I have mine too," Marilyn said. "It's in my diary." Then Vicki, another
classmate, reached into her pocketbook, took out her wallet, and showed her
worn and frazzled* list to the group. "I carry this with me at all times," Vicki
said without batting an eyelash. "I think we all saved our lists."

That's when I finally sat down and cried. I cried for Mark and for all his 21
friends who would never see him again.

■ Reading Comprehension Questions

1. The word *incessantly* in "Mark talked incessantly. I had to remind him again
   and again that talking without permission was not acceptable" (paragraph 2)
   means
   a. slowly.
   b. quietly.
   c. constantly.
   d. pleasantly.

2. The words *blurted out* in "It wasn't ten seconds later when Chuck blurted out, 'Mark is talking again'" (paragraph 4) mean
   a.   said suddenly.
   b.   ran away.
   c.   watched for.
   d.   looked at.

3. Which sentence best expresses the central idea of the selection?
   a.   Mark Eklund was a charming, talkative student who appreciated Sister Helen's efforts to teach him.
   b.   Sister Helen found out that an assignment she had given years ago had been very important to a beloved former student and his classmates.
   c.   When Sister Helen was a young teacher, she had some unusual classroom techniques.
   d.   The Vietnam War was a historical tragedy which took the life of one of Sister Helen's former students.

4. Which sentence best expresses the main idea of paragraphs 1–2?
   a.   Mark Eklund was in the first third-grade class Sister Helen taught at Saint Mary's School.
   b.   Mark Eklund was the most talkative of all Sister Helen's students.
   c.   Despite misbehaving in class, Mark Eklund was a very likeable person.
   d.   Although Sister Helen kept reminding Mark that talking without permission was not permitted, she was unable to stop him from talking.

5. Which sentence best expresses the main idea of paragraphs 8–12?
   a.   A difficult math concept had made Sister Helen's students irritable.
   b.   The "good things" assignment made the students feel happy with themselves and others.
   c.   Sister Helen gave up part of her weekend to write out a list of good things about each student.
   d.   At the end of Friday's class, both Charlie and Mark seemed to be in good moods.

6. When the students didn't mention the lists after the day they received them, Sister Helen
   a.   assumed that the assignment had been a failure.
   b.   didn't mind, because the assignment had done what she hoped.
   c.   called a few students to ask what they thought of the lists.
   d.   felt angry that the students didn't appreciate what she had done.

7. Sister Helen learned of Mark's death
   a.   when her parents called her while she was on vacation.
   b.   from Chuck, Mark's old friend.
   c.   from her father as they drove home from the airport.
   d.   from a story in the local newspaper.

8. In paragraph 3, the author implies
   a. a more experienced teacher would not have threatened Mark with tape.
   b. her decision to tape Mark's mouth shut was a good one.
   c. Mark was trying to annoy her by talking more often than usual.
   d. in order to correct Mark's behavior, she should have been more strict.

9. The author implies that
   a. she had known all along how important the lists were to her students.
   b. she did not support the war in Vietnam.
   c. the lists meant more to the students than she had ever realized.
   d. Mark's parents were jealous of her relationship with him.

10. It is reasonable to conclude that Mark
    a. cared as much for Sister Helen as she cared for him.
    b. never talked much about his past.
    c. planned to become a math teacher himself.
    d. had not stayed in touch with his classmates.

■ Technique Questions

1. Although Mark is described as someone who talks a lot, the author chooses to include Mark's spoken words just three times in her essay. Look at these three instances. What do they share? Why do you think Sister Helen chose to include these quotes?

   _____

   _____

   _____

   _____

2. How does Sister Helen present most of the information in her essay—in listing order or in time order? Find three examples from the essay which support your answer.

   _____

   _____

   _____

   _____

3. In paragraph 20, the author introduces a number of people who had not appeared elsewhere in the essay. What does Sister Helen accomplish by including these people at the end of her story?

_____

_____

_____

_____

_____

■ Discussion Questions

1. In this story, we read of two classroom incidents involving Sister Helen and her students. In one, she briefly taped a third-grader's mouth closed. In another, she encouraged junior-high students to think of things they liked about one another. In your opinion, what do these two incidents tell about Sister Helen? What kind of teacher was she? What kind of person?

2. At the end of the story, Sister Helen tells us that she "cried for Mark and for all his friends who would never see him again." Do you think she might have been crying for other reasons, too? Explain what they might be.

3. "All the Good Things" has literally traveled around the world. Not only has it been reprinted in numerous publications, but many readers have sent it out over the Internet for others to read. Why do you think so many people love this story? Why do they want to share it with others?

■ Writing Assignments

1. Do you have any souvenir that, like Sister Helen's lists, you have kept for years? Write a paragraph about that souvenir. Start your paragraph with a topic sentence such as "_____ is one of my oldest and proudest possessions." Then describe just what the item is, how you originally obtained it, and where you keep it now. Most importantly, explain why the souvenir is precious to you.

2. Although Sister Helen didn't want to do it, she felt she had to tape Mark's mouth shut after announcing that she would do so. When have you done something you didn't really want to do because others expected it? Write a paragraph about that incident. Explain why you didn't want to do it, why you felt pressure to do it, and how you felt about yourself afterward. Here are sample topic sentences for such a paragraph:

Even though I knew it was wrong, I told my friend's parents a lie to keep my friend out of trouble.

Last year, I pretended I didn't like a girl that I really did like because my friends convinced me she wasn't cool enough.

3. Mark Eklund obviously stood out in Sister Helen's memory. She paints a vivid "word portrait" of Mark as a third-grader. Write an essay about three fellow students who, for positive or negative reasons, you have always remembered. The three may have been your classmates at any point in your life. Your essay should focus on your memories of those students in the classroom—not on the playground, in the cafeteria, or outside of school. As you describe your memories of those three classmates in that setting, include details that appeal to as many senses as possible—hearing, sight, touch, smell—to make your readers picture those individuals and that time and place in your history.

   Alternatively, you may write an essay about three teachers whom you will always remember.

Responsibility

M. Scott Peck

■ Preview

The Road Less Traveled, a well-known book by psychiatrist and author M. Scott Peck, begins with this famous line: "Life is difficult." Peck encourages people to embrace the messy difficulties that make up life, stressing that growth and development are achieved only through hard work. The following excerpt from *The Road Less Traveled* emphasizes one of Peck's favorite themes: personal responsibility.

■ Words to Watch

self-evident (1): not requiring any explanation

ludicrous (2): laughable because of being obviously ridiculous

inquired (11): asked

clarified (19): made clear

amenable (23): agreeable

glared (37): stared angrily

We cannot solve life's problems except by solving them. This statement   1
may seem idiotically self-evident°, yet it is seemingly beyond the comprehension of much of the human race. This is because we must accept responsibility for a problem before we can solve it. We cannot solve a problem by saying, "It's not my problem." We cannot solve a problem by hoping that someone else will solve it for us. I can solve a problem only when I say, "This is my problem and it's up to me to solve it." But many, so many, seek to avoid the pain of their problems by saying to themselves: "This problem was caused by other people, or by social circumstances beyond my control, and therefore it is up to other people or society to solve this problem for me. It is not really my personal problem."

The extent to which people will go psychologically to avoid assuming   2
responsibility for personal problems, while always sad, is sometimes almost ludicrous°. A career sergeant in the army, stationed in Okinawa and in serious trouble because of his excessive drinking, was referred for psychiatric evaluation and, if possible, assistance. He denied that he was an alcoholic, or even that his use of alcohol was a personal problem, saying, "There's nothing else to do in the evenings in Okinawa except drink."

"Do you like to read?" I asked.   3
"Oh yes, I like to read, sure."   4
"Then why don't you read in the evening instead of drinking?"   5

"It's too noisy to read in the barracks."   6

"Well, then, why don't you go to the library?"   7

"The library is too far away."   8

"Is the library farther away than the bar you go to?"   9

"Well, I'm not much of a reader. That's not where my interests lie."   10

"Do you like to fish?" I then inquired*.   11

"Sure, I love to fish."   12

"Why not go fishing instead of drinking?"   13

"Because I have to work all day long."   14

"Can't you go fishing at night?"   15

"No, there isn't any night fishing in Okinawa."   16

"But there is," I said. "I know several organizations that fish at night here.   17
Would you like me to put you in touch with them?"

"Well, I really don't like to fish."   18

"What I hear you saying," I clarified*, "is that there are other things to do   19
in Okinawa except drink, but the thing you like to do most in Okinawa is drink."

"Yeah, I guess so."   20

"But your drinking is getting you in trouble, so you're faced with a real   21
problem, aren't you?"

"This damn island would drive anyone to drink."   22

I kept trying for a while, but the sergeant was not the least bit interested   23
in seeing his drinking as a personal problem which he could solve either with
or without help, and I regretfully told his commander that he was not
amenable* to assistance. His drinking continued, and he was separated from
the service in mid-career.

**"I can solve a problem only when I say, 'This is my problem and it's up to me
to solve it.'"**

A young wife, also in Okinawa, cut her wrist lightly with a razor blade and   24
was brought to the emergency room, where I saw her. I asked her why she
had done this to herself.

"To kill myself, of course."   25

"Why do you want to kill yourself?"   26

"Because I can't stand it on this dumb island. You have to send me back   27
to the States. I'm going to kill myself if I have to stay here any longer."

"What is it about living on Okinawa that's so painful for you?" I asked.   28

She began to cry in a whining sort of way. "I don't have any friends here,   29
and I'm alone all the time."

"That's too bad. How come you haven't been able to make any friends?"   30

"Because I have to live in a stupid Okinawan housing area, and none of   31
my neighbors speak English."

"Why don't you drive over to the American housing area or to the wives'   32
club during the day so you can make some friends?"

"Because my husband has to drive the car to work."   33

"Can't you drive him to work, since you're alone and bored all day?" I asked.   34

"No. It's a stick-shift car, and I don't know how to drive a stick-shift car,   35
only an automatic."

"Why don't you learn how to drive a stick-shift car?"   36

She glared* at me. "On these roads? You must be crazy."   37

■ Reading Comprehension Questions

1. The word *comprehension* in "This statement . . . is seemingly beyond the comprehension of much of the human race" (paragraph 1) means
   a. definition.
   b. understanding.
   c. confusion.
   d. absence.

2. The word *excessive* in "A career sergeant . . . in serious trouble because of his excessive drinking" (paragraph 2) means
   a. good-natured.
   b. unwilling.
   c. moderate.
   d. beyond what is normal.

3. Which sentence best expresses the central point of the entire selection?
   a . In Okinawa, Peck met two people who refused to take responsibility for their own problems.
   b. People demonstrate healthy creativity in the excuses they make for their irresponsibility.
   c. Many people, like the sergeant and the young wife, don't solve their problems because they refuse to take responsibility for them.
   d. The sergeant and the young wife would rather see their careers and lives ruined than take responsibility for their problems.

4. Which sentence best expresses the main idea of paragraphs 2–22?
   a. A career sergeant was in trouble because of his drinking.
   b. The sergeant denied that he had a problem with alcohol.
   c. Peck was expected to evaluate the sergeant and, if possible, help him.
   d. People will go to ridiculous lengths to avoid responsibility for their problems.

5. Which sentence best expresses the main idea of paragraph 23?
   a. Peck tried for some time to help the sergeant.
   b. Drinking has destroyed the lives of many people.
   c. The sergeant had a number of different resources to help him with his drinking problem.
   d. Despite Peck's efforts, the sergeant refused to take responsibility for his drinking problem.

6. Which of the following activities did Peck suggest to the sergeant to stop him from drinking?
   a. writing
   b. driving
   c. walking
   d. reading

7. The young wife first saw Peck because she
   a. was drinking too much.
   b. had cut her wrist.
   c. had tried to return to the States.
   d. wanted to learn to drive.

8. The young wife said she could not drive to the wives' club because
   a. she and her husband did not own a car.
   b. she had to be away at work all day.
   c. none of the other wives spoke English.
   d. she could not drive a stick-shift car.

9. We can infer that the sergeant and the young wife
   a. wanted someone else to take responsibility for their problems.
   b. knew each other.
   c. were good at taking responsibility for themselves back in the States.
   d. became happier and better adjusted after their meetings with Peck.

10. We can infer that the author probably believes that
    a. the sergeant and the young wife had no difficulties when they lived in the United States.
    b. the United States should increase the amount of support it gives to military families forced to live abroad.
    c. he cannot provide much help to people until they first accept responsibility for their problems.
    d. Okinawa is to blame for the problems of the sergeant and the young wife.

■ Technique Questions

1. What kind of evidence does Peck use to support the main idea in his essay— that people cannot solve their problems unless they first accept responsibility for them?

_____

_____

_____

2. In trying to help the sergeant and the young wife, the author asks a series of questions. What does he accomplish by including all these questions in his essay?

_____

_____

_____

_____

3. How does the author conclude his essay? What about this particular ending makes it effective?

_____

_____

_____

_____

_____

_____

■ Discussion Questions

1. Peck refers to the "ludicrous"—that is, ridiculous—lengths people will go to to avoid taking responsibility for their problems. What do you think he finds ludicrous about the sergeant's behavior? The young wife's? Do you find their behavior ridiculous? Why or why not?

2. What do you think was Peck's goal in his conversation with the young wife and the sergeant? Why is his method of treatment effective, or why is it not effective?

3. Why do you think so many people find it difficult to take responsibility for their own problems? How might they be helped to do so?

■ Writing Assignments

1. Write a paragraph about a time you have seen someone avoiding responsibility for his or her own problem. Begin with this topic sentence:

> Just like M. Scott Peck, I have seen someone refuse to take responsibility for his (or her) own problem.

Then go on to develop your paper by explaining who the person is, what the person's problem was, how he or she helped to create it, and how he or she blamed others or circumstances rather than accepted responsibility. Be sure to include, as Peck does, specific details, such as direct quotes or vivid descriptions, so readers can see the person and the situation you've chosen to write about.

2. Peck draws examples of irresponsible behavior from his practice as a military psychiatrist. But you can find examples of people dodging responsibility everywhere. What kinds of responsibility do students often avoid? Write a paragraph giving details about two or three ways students try to escape their responsibilities. In your paragraph, explain what kind of excuses they frequently make for their behavior. Using Peck's essay as a model, you may even choose to present a series of questions and answers between a student and an instructor to illustrate your main point.

3. Peck explains that the only way to solve a problem is to solve it—in other words, to take responsibility for the problem and find a solution. Write an essay about a time in your own life when you had to accept responsibility for a problem and figure out a solution for it. As you decide on a topic, you might list areas in which you have experienced problems. Here is one imaginary student's list:

- Getting along with parents
- Breaking off with friends who were a bad influence
- Managing money
- Holding a job
- Keeping up with schoolwork

Once you have decided on a topic to write about, you might begin with a statement like this:

> After blaming my teachers for my problems in school, I finally accepted responsibility for my own poor grades.

Alternatively, write about two or three problems you've had to face and solve.

A Small Victory

Steve Lopez

■ **Preview**

There are a million small miseries in a big city, and most of them go unnoticed and unrepaired. But when Steve Lopez, a columnist for the *Philadelphia Inquirer,* wrote about Ruby Knight, a gracious woman caught in a nightmarish tangle of medical red tape, he touched a nerve in his readers. You may or may not be surprised to learn of the outpouring of response to Lopez's article.

■ **Words to Watch**

dog days (1): hot humid summer days between early July and early September

metropolis (2): big city

bureaucracy (6): system in which complex rules interfere with effective action

meager (15): very small

inventory (15): amount of goods on hand

recurrence (38): reappearance

exclusively (40): entirely

sprawling (44): spread out (and therefore hard to deal with)

cynical (53): distrustful of people's motives

First Column, Written on July 22

On the dog days° of summer, ten floors above Camden [New Jersey], Ruby   1
Knight sets the fan at the foot of her bed and aims it at Philadelphia. Then
she sits in the window, breeze at her back, and lets her thoughts carry her
across the river to the city where she grew up.

She is seventy-one and has lived—since her husband passed on—in a high-   2
rise near the Ben Franklin Bridge toll plaza. The neighborhood isn't the greatest, but from the tenth floor, Philadelphia is a gleaming metropolis.° The city
sprouts above the river, and the sun glances off skyscrapers that shimmer in
the July heat.

Mrs. Knight watches the boats and ships on the river, the cars on the bridge.   3
She looks to North Philly and thinks back on her eighteen proud years as a crossing guard at Seventeenth and Ridge. And she worries about tomorrow.

Mrs. Knight, in the quiet of her home, is slowly starving.   4

She beat cancer: Her doctor calls it a near miracle. But now she's wrestling   5
a worse kind of beast.

Bureaucracy*.   6

Joseph Spiegel, a Philadelphia surgeon, tells the story: 7

In 1986, a tumor filled Mrs. Knight's throat. Spiegel removed her voice box   8
and swallowing mechanism. Mrs. Knight was fed through a tube to her stomach. It was uncomfortable and painful, but she was happy to be alive.

Although she couldn't speak, she learned to write real fast and took to   9
carrying a notepad around. She gets help from an older sister, Elizabeth
Woods, who herself beat a form of lung cancer that's often a quick killer.

The doctor was impressed by Mrs. Knight's fight. "She said she was placing   10
her faith in my hands and the Lord's," he says.

**"She beat cancer: Her doctor calls it a near miracle. But now she's wrestling a
worse kind of beast. Bureaucracy."**

Mrs. Knight had several more operations. But over the years, no sign of   11
cancer. And five months ago—she smiles at the memory—Spiegel removed
the tube. She was able to swallow again. After four years.

Little did she know the end of one problem was the start of another.   12

Instead of pouring her liquid nutrition down the tube, Mrs. Knight now   13
drank it. The same exact liquid.

But Medicare, which paid when it went down the tube, refused to pay   14
when it went down her throat.

Mrs. Knight, who lives on a fixed and meager* income, kept the liquid   15
cans in the corner of her living room, an open inventory.* She would look at
those cans as if they represented the days left in her life. And she began
rationing.

Mrs. Knight says her fighting weight is close to one hundred pounds.   16
When it dropped noticeably, she went to the doctor but had trouble making
her point.

"I think she was a little embarrassed that she couldn't afford to buy the   17
stuff," Spiegel says.

She had lost about ten pounds since her last visit, down to the high eight-   18
ies. She was on her way, Spiegel says, to starving herself to death.

Spiegel got an emergency supply of the liquid—she goes through about   19
six cans a day at one dollar a can—and began calling Medicare. If she ends
up in the hospital, Spiegel argued, it'll cost Medicare a lot more than six dollars a day.

But Medicare, with built-in safeguards against intentional or accidental   20
use of common sense, wouldn't budge.

"This is a federally funded program and we have specific guidelines for   21
what we can pay for and can't pay for," Jan Shumate said in an interview.
She's director of "Medicare Part B Services" in the Columbia, South Carolina,
claims office.

But it's the same liquid.   22

"Yes, I understand that."   23

It costs less than hospitalization.   24

"Yes, I understand that, but we're mandated to go by the rules."   25

Even if it costs more money?   26

"My only solution I can suggest is if she files again and it gets denied, she   27
can request an informal review."

The reasoning is Medicare can't pay for every substance somebody claims   28
to need for survival.

Spiegel says Mrs. Knight needs this drink. She can't eat or drink much   29
of anything else. He has told her he may have to put the tube back in her
stomach, so Medicare will pay again.

At the mere suggestion, Mrs. Knight loses it. No way. Her sister is with her,   30
the two of them confused by it all. They've beaten cancer, cheated the days,
and now this.

Mrs. Knight hustles to the bathroom and returns with the scale. She puts   31
it by her bed, gets on. The needle hits eighty-three. She stands at the win-
dow, frail against the Philadelphia skyline, grace and dignity showing
through her despair.

The two sisters look at the cans in the corner. There's enough for one   32
month, but Mrs. Knight will try to stretch it. On her pad, she writes:

"My trial. God's got to do something."   33

(Dr. Spiegel is at 215-545-3322.)   34

Follow-Up Column, Written on July 29

It's the kind of thing I don't get around to often enough. But today, I think   35
some thanks are in order.

The problem is, I won't be able to get to everyone. I don't even know   36
where to begin.

Maybe with last week's column.   37

Those who looked in this corner last Sunday saw a story about Ruby   38
Knight, a retired crossing guard in North Philadelphia. She had throat cancer
real bad at one time, but Dr. Joseph Spiegel removed a tumor and Mrs. Knight
has gone nearly five years without a recurrence.•

It took four years for Mrs. Knight, now seventy-one, to learn how to swal-   39
low again. And it was a big day for her about six months ago when Spiegel
removed the feeding tube from her stomach. Finally, she could swallow.

Problem was, she couldn't eat or drink regular food because of discomfort.   40
Her diet was still, exclusively,• a nutritional supplement called Ensure Plus.

Now here's the deal.   41

When Mrs. Knight poured it down the tube, it was covered by Medicare.   42
When she drank the same stuff, Medicare refused to cover it.

Medicare reasons that if you don't need a tube, you don't need a special   43
diet. The rule exists to avoid abuse.

"The idea is a good one," Spiegel says. "But Medicare is the biggest, most sprawling* bureaucracy of all." He says its inability to make reasonable exceptions often hurts the elderly poor. 44

Spiegel tried to get Medicare to change its mind, arguing that it would cost the government a lot more if he had to surgically implant the tube back in Mrs. Knight's stomach. But he got nowhere. 45

"We're mandated to go by the rules," a Medicare spokeswoman told me when I asked for an explanation. 46

Meanwhile, Mrs. Knight, without anyone's knowledge, was working on her own solution. She had begun rationing her Ensure Plus. 47

She kept a careful count of the cans, figuring she needed at least four a day to survive. Mrs. Knight stacked the fifty-one cans in her Camden living room, measuring the supply each day against her fixed income. 48

As Spiegel puts it, "she was slowly starving herself." She went from nearly one hundred pounds to eighty-three. 49

When I went to visit, I found one of the sweetest, most unassuming people I have ever met. Mrs. Knight's sister, Elizabeth Woods, is the same way. She's seventy-six and also beat cancer. They live in the same high-rise apartment house with a fabulous view of Philadelphia, and they help each other through the days. 50

Mrs. Knight can't speak, but she gets her points across just fine. She writes almost as fast as you can talk and she has a world-class hug. 51

The day after the column, Spiegel and his staff got to their Pine Street office at 8:00 A.M. There were seventy-four messages on the machine. By noon, there were 150. By closing time Monday, more than four hundred people had called. 52

"You can get cynical* about things," Spiegel says, "but then there's this outpouring of help from people. It's just astounding." 53

People called for two reasons. Compassion and anger. Everyone knows somebody who's been seriously ill. Everyone has had trouble with bureaucracy. 54

Ruby Knight hit the daily double. 55

And I would like to begin now with the thank-yous. First to Dr. Spiegel for his sense of compassion and outrage. To his staff—Lori, Gina, Maria, Sally, Laura, Monica, and Mike—for patiently handling calls, letters, and donations. "It was kind of fun," Maria says. 56

And thanks to readers whose names fill thirteen typed pages compiled by Spiegel's staff. One person gave a year's supply of Ensure Plus. One donated twenty cases. Some sent prayers, holy cards, religious medals. 57

Some thanked Mrs. Knight for her years as a crossing guard at Seventeenth and Ridge. Some people sent as much as four hundred dollars. One sent three one-dollar bills and a note: "I wish I could send more." 58

One sent ten dollars and this note: "May God bless you. I lost my dear husband to leukemia two and a half years ago." 59

Some called Medicare to complain. Some called Ensure Plus, where 60
spokeswoman Sharon Veach said she thought the company could arrange to
provide a lifetime supply, if needed.

Friday at noon, Spiegel, Maria, and Mike drove to Camden and dropped 61
in on Mrs. Knight with thirty cases of Ensure Plus and a list of donors.

Mrs. Knight was beside herself, humble, gracious, overwhelmed. She and 62
her sister kept looking at each other, shaking their heads.

"I'm speechless," Mrs. Knight wrote on her pad, and then laughed.   63

She said she would pray for everyone. She kept scribbling that she wishes 64
there were some way she could express thanks and love for the kindness of
strangers.

And I told her that she had.   65

■ Reading Comprehension Questions

1. The word *mandated* in "'This is a federally funded program and we have
   specific guidelines for what we can pay for and can't pay for. . . . we're
   mandated to go by the rules'" (paragraphs 21 and 25) means
   a.   not allowed.
   b.   scared.
   c.   mistaken.
   d.   required.

2. The word *compiled* in "thanks to readers whose names fill thirteen typed
   pages compiled by Spiegel's staff" (paragraph 57) means
   a.   put together.
   b.   paid for.
   c.   delayed.
   d.   remembered.

3. Which sentence best expresses the central idea of the selection?
   a.   The elderly poor usually suffer unnecessarily.
   b.   Individuals solved an elderly woman's problem that bureaucracy failed
        to handle.
   c.   Mrs. Knight's diet is made up almost completely of a liquid supplement.
   d.   Ruby Knight lost her voice box to throat cancer.

4. Which sentence best expresses the main idea of paragraph 15?
   a.   Mrs. Knight lives on a fixed income.
   b.   Mrs. Knight kept her supply of Ensure Plus in her living room.
   c.   Mrs. Knight looked every day at the cans of Ensure Plus in her living
        room.
   d.   Since Mrs. Knight could not afford more Ensure Plus, she began rationing
        the cans she had.

5. Which sentence best expresses the main idea of paragraph 52?
   a. Many people read the author's column about Mrs. Knight.
   b. Dr. Spiegel and his staff begin their work day at 8:00 A.M.
   c. Dr. Spiegel's office is a busy one.
   d. Many people called Dr. Spiegel in response to the author's column.

6. *True or false?* _____ Both Ruby Knight and her sister have been cured of cancer.

7. Even though she could swallow after the tube was removed, Mrs. Knight
   a. could comfortably take in only Ensure Plus.
   b. lost her taste for regular food.
   c. preferred to feed herself through a tube.
   d. wanted to go to the hospital.

8. Dr. Spiegel's argument to Medicare was that
   a. the government should pay for whatever a person claims to need for survival.
   b. Mrs. Knight had suffered greatly because of her cancer.
   c. it would cost the government less if Mrs. Knight didn't have a tube in her stomach.
   d. keeping Mrs. Knight out of the hospital would be helpful because the hospitals are already too full.

9. We can assume that Lopez included Dr. Spiegel's phone number
   a. with Dr. Spiegel's permission.
   b. to encourage people to help Mrs. Knight.
   c. because he believed people would want to help Mrs. Knight.
   d. all of the above.

10. Lopez would probably agree that
    a. all of Medicare's rules are totally senseless.
    b. Ensure Plus is too expensive.
    c. the Medicare system should find a way to make reasonable exceptions.
    d. people helped Mrs. Knight because they knew they would be praised in the newspaper.

■ Technique Questions

1. Lopez doesn't get directly into Mrs. Knight's problem until the end of paragraph 3. What does he accomplish by providing us with background information about Mrs. Knight?

   _____

   _____

   _____

2. To emphasize some of his points, Lopez at times uses very short paragraphs. Paragraph 6, in fact, consists of only one word. Find two of Lopez's particularly meaningful one-sentence paragraphs and write them in the spaces below:

a. _____

_____

b. _____

_____

3. Lopez directly quotes various people in his articles. For example, look at the quotations from Jan Shumate (paragraphs 21, 23, 25, 27), Dr. Spiegel (paragraphs 44 and 49), two of the donors (paragraphs 58–59), and Ruby Knight (paragraphs 33 and 63). Why might Lopez have decided to include some of the exact words people spoke? Why didn't he simply tell Mrs. Knight's story in only his own words?

_____

_____

■ Discussion Questions

1. In paragraph 20, Lopez writes that Medicare has "built-in safeguards against intentional or accidental use of common sense." What does he mean by "intentional or accidental use of common sense"?

2. Lopez writes, "People called for two reasons. Compassion and anger" (paragraph 54). What does he mean by that comment? Why do you think so many people reacted with such depth of feeling?

3. Do you know any people who, like Mrs. Knight and her sister, have struggled to live with quiet dignity? How have they been helped or harmed during this time by government programs?

■ Writing Assignments

1. Lopez writes, "Everyone knows somebody who's been seriously ill. Everyone has had trouble with bureaucracy" (paragraph 54). Write a paragraph about either of these topics. In your paragraph, describe the illness or the trouble with a bureaucratic agency. Then explain what was done to cope with this problem. One useful prewriting strategy for this assignment may be to ask and then answer questions, such as the following questions about illness:

Who was seriously ill? With what? What were the symptoms?

What was the effect of this illness on the patient? On the family?

What was done to help the sick person and his or her family cope?

What finally happened? Why?

Your topic sentence for the paragraph might be a sentence like one of the following:

My mother's bout with lung cancer has been a very difficult time for both Mom and the family.

Applying for a grant to help pay for my education has taught me the true meaning of "red tape."

To make the sequence of events in your paragraph clear, remember to use some time transition words such as *first, next, after,* and *finally.*

2. Mrs. Knight wished "there were some way she could express thanks and love for the kindness of strangers." Write a paragraph describing another situation in which one or more people have gone out of their way to help a stranger. Perhaps you know a retired person who tutors children in a shelter for the homeless, a bystander who helped a mugging victim, or simply someone who gave someone else another chance.

In your paragraph, provide plenty of details about the situation in question and the people involved. (To see how Lopez helps readers "know" Mrs. Knight and her sister, look, for example, at paragraphs 1–3, 31, and 50.)

Making a list is one way for you to think of a topic for this paper. Following is one student's list:

Helpful reactions to woman who fainted in church
People who helped when I ran out of gas
Helping a neighborhood family whose house burned down
Kind bus driver when I lost my wallet
Local family sponsored new immigrants
Volunteers at soup kitchen

After making such a list, a writer could choose the topic for which the most interesting, convincing support can be found. The writer could then use freewriting to begin generating material for a paragraph. If it becomes apparent that the support for that topic is weak, he or she could try another topic.

3. In his first column, Steve Lopez wrote about a problem he hoped his readers would help solve. Write an essay for your school newspaper discussing solutions to a problem you hope readers—students, instructors, administrators—will do something about. You might begin by listing some campus problems. Then, to see which is the most promising topic, you could make a separate rough list of possible solutions for each of those problems.

Once you choose a topic, continue making lists or use freewriting to develop two or three concrete solutions you hope to persuade your readers to support. In your essay, describe the problem and solutions in detail, using examples wherever possible.

Your thesis statement will be a summary statement, such as "There are several ways in which our campus should be made much safer" or "Students should be given more opportunities to get help from instructors and tutors."

Before beginning your first draft, create a rough outline as a guide. Here's one that includes three general ways in which the campus can be made safer, along with specific ways to put them into effect.

> <u>Central idea</u>: There are several ways that our campus can be made significantly safer.
> (1) Better lighting
>   In parking lots
>   Along dark walkways
>   In all building entranceways
> (2) Better coverage by campus police
>   Outside in busy and less busy places
>   Checking empty hallways, dark doorways, etc.
> (3) Safety information to students
>   Booklets on safe behavior
>   Information on crimes that have happened on campus

The writer who developed this outline enriched her essay by adding examples to emphasize many of her points. For instance, she told how one student was recently raped at night in a closet off an empty hallway. She also told how another student's purse was snatched as she walked back to her car in the middle of the day. In telling these anecdotes, she included concrete details to help readers "see" and "hear" what happened.

Finally, if you prefer, write about solving a problem off campus, such as one in your neighborhood or at a local beach.

The Most Hateful Words

Amy Tan

■ **Preview**

For years, a painful exchange with her mother lay like a heavy stone on Amy Tan's heart. In the following essay, Tan, author of best-selling novels including *The Joy Luck Club* and *The Kitchen God's Wife,* tells the story of how that weight was finally lifted. This essay is from her memoir, *The Opposite of Fate.*

■ **Words to Watch**

tormented (3): hurt or tortured

forbade (3): would not allow

impenetrable (3): impossible to get inside

frantically (9): excitedly, with great worry

The most hateful words I have ever said to another human being were to my mother. I was sixteen at the time. They rose from the storm in my chest and I let them fall in a fury of hailstones: "I hate you. I wish I were dead. . . ." 1

I waited for her to collapse, stricken by what I had just said. She was still standing upright, her chin tilted, her lips stretched in a crazy smile. "Okay, maybe I die too," she said between huffs. "Then I no longer be your mother!" We had many similar exchanges. Sometimes she actually tried to kill herself by running into the street, holding a knife to her throat. She too had storms in her chest. And what she aimed at me was as fast and deadly as a lightning bolt. 2

For days after our arguments, she would not speak to me. She tormented° me, acted as if she had no feelings for me whatsoever. I was lost to her. And because of that, I lost, battle after battle, all of them: the times she criticized me, humiliated me in front of others, forbade° me to do this or that without even listening to one good reason why it should be the other way. I swore to myself I would never forget these injustices. I would store them, harden my heart, make myself as impenetrable° as she was. 3

I remember this now, because I am also remembering another time, just a few years ago. I was forty-seven, had become a different person by then, had become a fiction writer, someone who uses memory and imagination. In fact, I was writing a story about a girl and her mother, when the phone rang. 4

It was my mother, and this surprised me. Had someone helped her make the call? For a few years now, she had been losing her mind through Alzheimer's disease. Early on, she forgot to lock her door. Then she forgot where she lived. She forgot who many people were and what they had 5 meant to her. Lately, she could no longer remember many of her worries and sorrows.

"Amy-ah," she said, and she began to speak quickly in Chinese. "Some-   6
thing is wrong with my mind. I think I'm going crazy."

I caught my breath. Usually she could barely speak more than two words   7
at a time. "Don't worry," I started to say.

"It's true," she went on. "I feel like I can't remember many things. I can't   8
remember what I did yesterday. I can't remember what happened a long time ago, what I did to you. . . ." She spoke as a drowning person might if she had bobbed to the surface with the force of will to live, only to see how far she had already drifted, how impossibly far she was from the shore.

She spoke frantically*: "I know I did something to hurt you."   9

"You didn't," I said. "Don't worry."   10

"I did terrible things. But now I can't remember what. . . . And I just want   11
to tell you . . . I hope you can forget, just as I've forgotten."

I tried to laugh so she would not notice the cracks in my voice. "Really,   12
don't worry."

"Okay, I just wanted you to know."   13

After we hung up, I cried, both happy and sad. I was again that sixteen-   14
year-old, but the storm in my chest was gone.

My mother died six months later. By then she had bequeathed to me her   15
most healing words, as open and eternal as a clear blue sky. Together we knew in our hearts what we should remember, what we can forget.

■ Reading Comprehension Questions

1. The word *stricken* in "I waited for her to collapse, stricken by what I had just said" (paragraph 2) means
   a.   wounded.
   b.   amused.
   c.   annoyed.
   d.   bored.

2. The word *bequeathed* in "By then she had bequeathed to me her most heal- ing words, as open and eternal as a clear blue sky" (paragraph 15) means
   a.   denied.
   b.   sold.
   c.   given.
   d.   cursed.

3. Which sentence best expresses the central idea of the selection?
   a.   Because of Alzheimer's disease, the author's mother forgot harsh words the two of them had said to one another.

b.   Amy Tan had a difficult relationship with her mother that worsened over the years.

c.   Years after a painful childhood with her mother, Amy Tan was able to realize peace and forgiveness.

d.   Despite her Alzheimer's disease, Amy Tan's mother was able to apologize to her daughter for hurting her.

4. Which sentence best expresses the main idea of paragraphs 1–2?
    a.   Amy Tan's mother was sometimes suicidal.
    b.   Amy Tan wanted to use words to hurt her mother.
    c.   It is not unusual for teenagers and their parents to argue.
    d.   Amy Tan and her mother had a very hurtful relationship.

5. Which sentence best expresses the main idea of paragraphs 8–9?
    a.   The author's mother was deeply disturbed by the thought that she had hurt her daughter.
    b.   Alzheimer's disease causes people to become confused and unable to remember things clearly.
    c.   The author's mother could not even remember what she had done the day before.
    d.   The author's mother had changed very little from what she was like when Tan was a child.

6. After arguing with her daughter, the author's mother would
    a.   say nice things about her to others.
    b.   immediately forget they had argued.
    c.   refuse to speak to her.
    d.   apologize.

7. When she was a young girl, the author swore that she would
    a.   never forget her mother's harsh words.
    b.   never be like her mother.
    c.   publicly embarrass her mother by writing about her.
    d.   never have children.

8. The first sign that the author's mother had Alzheimer's disease was
    a.   she forgot where she lived.
    b.   she could speak only two or three words at a time.
    c.   she forgot people's identities.
    d.   she forgot to lock her door.

9. We can infer from paragraph 2 that
    a.   the author wished her mother was dead.
    b.   the author immediately felt guilty for the way she spoke to her mother.
    c.   the author's mother was emotionally unstable.
    d.   the author's mother was physically abusive.

10. The author implies, in paragraphs 9–15, that
    a. she was pleased her mother realized how badly she had hurt her.
    b. her love and pity for her mother was stronger than her anger.
    c. she did not recall what her mother was talking about.
    d. she was annoyed by her mother's confusion.

■ Technique Questions

1. Tan begins her essay from the perspective of a sixteen-year-old girl, but finishes it from the perspective of a woman in her late forties. Where in the essay does Tan make the transition between those two perspectives? What words does she use to signal the change?

    _____

    _____

    _____

2. In paragraph 2, the author quotes her mother speaking in English, her second language. What features stand out in her mother's speech? Why do you think Tan chose to include her mother's actual words rather than rewrite them into "standard" English?

    _____

    _____

    _____

    _____

3. Tan uses weather images throughout her essay. Find three instances in which Tan mentions weather and list them below. What does she accomplish with this technique?

    _____

    _____

    _____

    _____

    _____

    _____

    _____

■ Discussion Questions

1. At age sixteen, Tan recalls "the times [my mother] criticized me, humiliated me in front of others, forbade me to do this or that without even listening to one good reason why it should be the other way." Did you have a difficult relationship with one or both of your parents? Were problems the result of your teenage behavior or of their behavior?

2. This essay brings to mind the phrase, "Forgive and forget." But is this advice always fair or realistic? Are there times when it is better to hold someone accountable than to forgive and forget? Explain.

3. In their discussion at the end of the essay, Tan chooses to keep her emotions hidden from her mother. Why do you think she does this?

■ Writing Assignments

1. Despite being an adult, Tan recalls feeling like "the same sixteen-year-old" girl when she speaks to her mother. Think about something in your life that has the power to reconnect you to a vivid memory. Write a paragraph in which you describe your memory and the trigger that "takes you back" to it. Begin your paragraph with a topic sentence that makes it clear to readers what you are going to discuss. Then provide specific details so readers can understand your memory. Here are sample topic sentences.

   > Whenever I see swings, I remember the day in second grade when I got into my first fist fight.
   > The smell of cotton candy takes me back to the day my grandfather brought me to my first baseball game.
   > I can't pass St. Joseph's Hospital without remembering the day, ten years ago, when my brother was shot.

2. In this essay, we see that Tan's relationship with her mother was very complicated. Who is a person with whom you have a complex relationship—maybe one you'd describe as "love/hate" or "difficult"? Write a paragraph about that relationship. Be sure to give examples or details that show readers why you have such difficulties with that person.
   Your topic sentence should introduce who you plan to discuss, such as:

   > My mother-in-law and I have contrasting points of view on several issues.
   > While I respect my boss, he is simply a very difficult person.
   > Even though I love my sister, I can't stand to be around her.

Whoever you choose, be sure to provide specific examples or details to help your reader understand why the relationship is so difficult for you. For example, if you decided to write about your boss, you will want to describe things he does that show just why you consider him so "difficult."

3. Like Tan's mother, most of us have done something in our lives we wish we could undo. If you could have a chance to revisit your past and change one of your actions, what would it be? Write an essay in which you describe something you would like to undo.

In your first paragraph, introduce exactly what you did. Here are three thesis statements that students might have written:

> I wish I could undo the night I decided to drive my car while I was drunk.
> If I could undo any moment in my life, it would be the day I decided to drop out of high school.
> One moment from my life I would like to change is the time I picked on an unpopular kid in sixth grade.

Be sure to provide details and, if appropriate, actual words that were spoken, so that your readers can "see and hear" what happened. Once you've described the moment that you wish to take back, write three reasons why you feel the way you do. Below is a scratch outline for the first topic.

> I wish I could undo the night I decided to drive my car while I was drunk.
> 1. Caused an accident that hurt others.
> 2. Lost my license, my car, and my job.
> 3. Affected the way others treat me.

In order to write an effective essay, you will need to provide specific details to explain each of the reasons you identify. For instance, to support the third reason above, you might detail possible new feelings of guilt and anger you have about yourself as well as provide examples of how individual people now treat you differently. To end your essay, you might describe what you would do today if you could replay what happened.

My Daughter Smokes

Alice Walker

■ **Preview**

Alice Walker is a famous writer, probably best known for her novel *The Color Purple*. In "My Daughter Smokes," her daughter's habit is a stepping stone to a broader discussion of smoking than the title suggests. She goes on to also tell of her father's experience with tobacco and from there slips into a discussion of tobacco that moves through the centuries and across continents.

■ **Words to Watch**

consort (2): spouse

pungent (3): having a sharp, bitter taste

dapper (4): stylishly dressed

perennially (6): continually

ritual (12): activity done regularly

emaciated (13): thin

futility (16): uselessness

empathy (17): understanding

denatured (17): changed from its natural state

mono-cropping (17): growing of single crops apart from other crops

suppressed (18): kept down

redeem (18): restore the honor of

cajole (20): gently urge

My daughter smokes. While she is doing her homework, her feet on the bench in front of her and her calculator clicking out answers to her algebra problems, I am looking at the half-empty package of Camels tossed carelessly close at hand. Camels. I pick them up, take them into the kitchen, where the light is better, and study them—they're filtered, for which I am grateful. My heart feels terrible. I want to weep. In fact, I do weep a little, standing there by the stove holding one of the instruments, so white, so precisely rolled, that could cause my daughter's death. When she smoked Marlboros and Players I hardened myself against feeling so bad; nobody I knew ever smoked these brands. 1

She doesn't know this, but it was Camels that my father, her grandfather, 2
smoked. But before he smoked "ready-mades"—when he was very young and
very poor, with eyes like lanterns—he smoked Prince Albert tobacco in cigarettes he rolled himself. I remember the bright-red tobacco tin, with a picture
of Queen Victoria's consort,° Prince Albert, dressed in a black frock coat and
carrying a cane.

The tobacco was dark brown, pungent,° slightly bitter. I tasted it more 3
than once as a child, and the discarded tins could be used for a number of
things: to keep buttons and shoelaces in, to store seeds, and best of all, to
hold worms for the rare times my father took us fishing.

By the late forties and early fifties no one rolled his own anymore (and 4
few women smoked) in my hometown, Eatonton, Georgia. The tobacco industry, coupled with Hollywood movies in which both hero and heroine smoked
like chimneys, won over completely people like my father, who were hope-
lessly addicted to cigarettes. He never looked as dapper° as Prince Albert,
though; he continued to look like a poor, overweight, overworked colored
man with too large a family; black, with a very white cigarette stuck in his
mouth.

I do not remember when he started to cough. Perhaps it was unnotice- 5
able at first. A little hacking in the morning as he lit his first cigarette upon
getting out of bed. By the time I was my daughter's age, his breath was a
wheeze, embarrassing to hear; he could not climb stairs without resting every
third or fourth step. It was not unusual for him to cough for an hour.

It is hard to believe there was a time when people did not understand that 6
cigarette smoking is an addiction. I wondered aloud once to my sister—who
is perennially° trying to quit—whether our father realized this. I wonder how
she, a smoker since high school, viewed her own habit.

It was our father who gave her her first cigarette, one day when she had 7
taken water to him in the fields.

"I always wondered why he did that," she said, puzzled, and with some 8
bitterness.

"What did he say?" I asked. 9

"That he didn't want me to go to anyone else for them," she said, "which 10
never really crossed my mind."

So he was aware it was addictive, I thought, though as annoyed as she 11
that he assumed she would be interested.

I began smoking in eleventh grade, also the year I drank numerous bot- 12
tles of terrible sweet, very cheap wine. My friends and I, all boys for this ven-
ture, bought our supplies from a man who ran a segregated bar and liquor
store on the outskirts of town. Over the entrance there was a large sign that
said COLORED. We were not permitted to drink here, only to buy. I smoked
Kools, because my sister did. By then I thought her toxic darkened lips and
gums glamorous. However, my body simply would not tolerate smoke. After
six months I had a chronic sore throat. I gave up smoking, gladly. Because it
was a ritual° with my buddies—Murl, Leon, and "Dog" Farley—I continued to
drink wine.

My father died from "the poor man's friend," pneumonia, one hard win- 13
ter when his bronchitis and emphysema had left him low. I doubt he had
much lung left at all, after coughing for so many years. He had so little breath
that, during his last years, he was always leaning on something. I remembered
once, at a family reunion, when my daughter was two, that my father picked
her up for a minute—long enough for me to photograph them—but the
effort was obvious. Near the very end of his life, and largely because he had
no more lungs, he quit smoking. He gained a couple of pounds, but by then
he was so emaciated° no one noticed.

When I travel to Third World countries I see many people like my father 14
and daughter. There are large billboards directed at them both: the tough,
"take-charge," or dapper older man, the glamorous, "worldly" young
woman, both puffing away. In these poor countries, as in American ghettos
and on reservations, money that should be spent for food goes instead to the
tobacco companies; over time, people starve themselves of both food and air,
effectively weakening and addicting their children, eventually eradicating
themselves. I read in the newspaper and in my gardening magazine that cigarette butts are so toxic that if a baby swallows one, it is likely to die, and
that the boiled water from a bunch of them makes an effective insecticide.

**"It is hard to believe there was a time when people did not understand that
cigarette smoking is an addiction."**

My daughter would like to quit, she says. We both know the statistics are 15
against her; most people who try to quit smoking do not succeed.*

There is a deep hurt that I feel as a mother. Some days it is a feeling of 16
futility.° I remember how carefully I ate when I was pregnant, how patiently
I taught my daughter how to cross a street safely. For what, I sometimes wonder; so that she can wheeze through most of her life feeling half her strength,
and then die of self-poisoning, as her grandfather did?

But, finally, one must feel empathy° for the tobacco plant itself. For thou- 17
sands of years, it has been venerated by Native Americans as a sacred medicine.
They have used it extensively—its juices, its leaves, its roots, its (holy) smoke—
to heal wounds and cure diseases, and in ceremonies of prayer and peace.
And though the plant as most of us know it has been poisoned by chemicals
and denatured° by intensive mono-cropping° and is therefore hardly the plant
it was, still, to some modern Indians it remains a plant of positive power.
I learned this when my Native American friends, Bill Wahpepah and his family, visited with me for a few days and the first thing he did was sow a few
tobacco seeds in my garden.

Perhaps we can liberate tobacco from those who have captured and 18
abused it, enslaving the plant on large plantations, keeping it from freedom
and its kin, and forcing it to enslave the world. Its true nature suppressed,°
no wonder it has become deadly. Maybe by sowing a few seeds of tobacco

*Three months after reading this essay, my daughter stopped smoking.

in our gardens and treating the plant with the reverence it deserves, we can redeem° tobacco's soul and restore its self-respect.

Besides, how grim, if one is a smoker, to realize one is smoking a slave.   19

There is a slogan from a battered women's shelter that I especially like: 20 "Peace on earth begins at home." I believe everything does. I think of a slogan for people trying to stop smoking: "Every home a smoke-free zone." Smoking is a form of self-battering that also batters those who must sit by, occasionally cajole° or complain, and helplessly watch. I realize now that as a child I sat by, through the years, and literally watched my father kill himself; surely one such victory in my family, for the rich white men who own the tobacco companies, is enough.

■ Reading Comprehension Questions

1. The word *eradicating* in "over time, people starve themselves of both food and air, effectively weakening and addicting their children, eventually eradicating themselves" (paragraph 14) means
   a. curing.
   b. feeding.
   c. destroying.
   d. controlling.

2. The word *venerated* in "For thousands of years, it has been venerated by Native Americans as a sacred medicine. They have used it extensively" (paragraph 17) means
   a. honored.
   b. ignored.
   c. ridiculed.
   d. forgotten.

3. Which of the following sentences best expresses the central idea of the essay?
   a. Most people who try to quit smoking are not successful.
   b. Pained by her daughter's cigarette addiction and the misdeeds of the tobacco companies, Walker urges people to stop smoking.
   c. Native Americans have used the tobacco plant for thousands of years as a sacred medicine and in ceremonies of prayer and peace.
   d. Tobacco advertisements that show healthy, attractive people are misleading.

4. Which sentence best expresses the main idea of paragraph 4?
   a. For Walker's father and others, the reality of smoking was very different from the images shown in ads and movies.
   b. Walker's father smoked because he wanted to be as stylish as Prince Albert.
   c. No one rolled his or her own cigarettes by the 1950s.
   d. Walker's father was poor, overweight, and overworked.

5. Which sentence best expresses the main idea of paragraph 5?
   a. Walker does not know when her father began to cough.
   b. When Walker was her daughter's age, she was embarrassed to hear her father wheezing.
   c. Walker's father's cough began quietly but grew to become a major problem.
   d. Walker's father had great difficulty climbing stairs.

6. Walker is especially upset that her daughter smokes Camel cigarettes because
   a. she believes Camels to be especially bad for people's health.
   b. Camels are the brand that Walker herself smoked as a teenager.
   c. Walker's father, who died as a result of smoking, smoked Camels.
   d. Camels' advertisements are glamorous and misleading.

7. When Walker's father picked up his granddaughter at a family reunion, he
   a. burned the child with his cigarette.
   b. put her down quickly so he could have another cigarette.
   c. warned her against smoking.
   d. was too weak to hold her for long.

8. We can infer that Walker
   a. believes people who are poor, uneducated, and nonwhite have been especially victimized by the tobacco industry.
   b. believes that tobacco should be made illegal.
   c. blames her father for her daughter's decision to smoke.
   d. believes Native Americans were wrong to honor the tobacco plant.

9. We can infer that, for Walker, smoking as a teenager
   a. was strictly forbidden by her parents.
   b. was an exciting experiment.
   c. was quickly habit-forming.
   d. was the end of her friendship with Murl, Leon, and "Dog" Farley.

10. We can infer that Walker's daughter
    a. did not care that her mother was concerned about her smoking.
    b. may have been helped to quit smoking by her mother's essay.
    c. remembered her grandfather well.
    d. did not believe that smoking was harmful to people's health.

■ Technique Questions

1. In which parts of her essay does Walker use time order? _____
   _____

2. Write down what you think are two of the most vivid images in Walker's essay. Then explain how each helps to further her central idea.

_____

_____

_____

3. How does Walker enlarge the significance of her essay so that it becomes more than the story of her daughter's smoking?

_____

_____

_____

_____

_____

_____

■ Discussion Questions

1. How would you deal with a friend who engages in self-destructive behavior, such as smoking, excessive drinking, or taking drugs? Would you ignore the behavior or try to educate the friend about its dangers? Is letting a friend know you are concerned worth risking the friendship?

2. The dangers of smoking are well documented. Study after study shows that smoking leads to a variety of illnesses, including cancer, emphysema, and heart disease. Newer studies are proving that secondhand smoke—smoke that nonsmokers breathe when they are around smokers—is dangerous as well. If you had the power to do so, would you make smoking illegal? Or do you believe that smoking should continue to be an individual's right?

3. Imagine learning that your sixteen-year-old child has begun smoking or drinking, or has become sexually active. Which discovery would worry you most? Would it make a difference if the child were a girl or a boy? What fears would each of these discoveries raise in you? How would you respond to your child?

■ Writing Assignments

1. Write a paragraph in which you try to persuade a friend to quit smoking. Explain in detail three reasons you think he or she should quit. Use transitions such as *first of all, second, another,* and *finally* as you list the three reasons.

2. In her essay, Walker is critical of the glamorous, healthy image presented by cigarette advertisements. Write a paragraph in which you describe what you think an honest cigarette advertisement would look like. Who would appear in the ad? What would they be doing? What would they be saying? Use the following as a topic sentence, or write one of your own.

> The elements of an honest cigarette "advertisement" would tempt people not to smoke.

In preparation for this assignment, you might study two or three cigarette ads, using them as inspiration for this assignment. Use the name of a real cigarette or make up a name.

3. What bad habits do *you* have? Write an essay explaining how you believe you acquired one of those habits, how you think it harms you, and how you could rid yourself of it. You might begin by making a list or questioning to help you find a bad habit you wish to write about. (We all have plenty of bad habits, such as smoking, drinking too much, spending money impulsively, biting our nails, eating too much food, and so on.)

Remember to write an informal outline to guide you in your writing. Here, for example, is one possible outline for this assignment:

> <u>Central idea</u>: A bad habit I intend to change is studying for tests at the last minute.
> (1) I acquired the habit in high school, where studying at the last minute was often good enough.
> For example, I studied for spelling tests in the hallway on the way to class.
> Even history tests were easy to study for because our teacher demanded so little.
> (2) I've learned the hard way that last-minute studying doesn't work well in college.
> During my first quarter, I got the first D I've ever gotten.
> I thought memorizing a few names would get me through my first business class, but was I ever wrong.
> (3) I took a study skills course, and what I learned is helping me get on the right track.
> I learned the benefits of taking class notes, and I'm trying to get better at getting down a written record of each lecture.
> I also learned that keeping up with readings and taking notes on a regular basis are needed for some classes.

The writer of the above outline still has to come up with many more details to expand each of her points. For instance, why did she get the D, and how did that help motivate her to improve her study habits? Also, what techniques is she experimenting with in her effort to improve her note-taking? She could add such details to her outline, or she could begin working them into her essay when she starts writing.

APPENDIXES

Introduction

Six appendixes follow. Appendix A consists of Parts of Speech, and Appendix B is a series of ESL Pointers. Appendixes C and D consist of a diagnostic test and an achievement test that measure many of the skills in this book. The diagnostic test can be taken at the outset of your work; the achievement test can be used to measure your progress at the end of your work. Appendix E supplies answers to the introductory activities and the practice exercises in Part Two. The answers, which you should refer to only after you have worked carefully through each exercise, give you responsibility for testing yourself. (To ensure that the answer key is used as a learning tool only, answers are *not* given for the review tests in Part Two or for the reinforcement tests in Part Three. These answers appear only in the Instructor's Manual; they can be copied and handed out at the discretion of your instructor.) Finally, Appendix F provides handy progress charts that you can use to track your performance on all the tests in the book and the writing assignments as well.

Parts of Speech

14.1

Words—the building blocks of sentences—can be divided into eight parts of speech. *Parts of speech* are classifications of words according to their meaning and use in a sentence.

This appendix will explain the eight parts of speech:

nouns	prepositions	conjunctions
pronouns	adjectives	interjections
verbs	adverbs	

Nouns

A *noun* is a word that is used to name something: a person, a place, an object, or an idea. Here are some examples of nouns:

Nouns			
woman	city	pancake	freedom
Alice Walker	street	diamond	possibility
Steve Martin	Chicago	Corvette	mystery

Most nouns begin with a lowercase letter and are known as *common nouns*. These nouns name general things. Some nouns, however, begin with a capital letter. They are called *proper nouns*. While a common noun refers to a person or thing in general, a proper noun names someone or something specific. For example, *woman* is a common noun—it doesn't name a particular woman. On the other hand, *Alice Walker* is a proper noun because it names a specific woman.

Practice 1

Insert any appropriate noun into each of the following blanks.

1. The shoplifter stole a(n) _____ from the department store.

2. _____ threw the football to me.

3. Tiny messages were scrawled on the _____.

4. A _____ crashed through the window.

5. Give the _____ to Keiko.

Singular and Plural Nouns

A *singular noun* names one person, place, object, or idea. A *plural noun* refers to two or more persons, places, objects, or ideas. Most singular nouns can be made plural with the addition of an *s*.

Some nouns, like *box*, have irregular plurals. You can check the plural of nouns you think may be irregular by looking up the singular form in a dictionary.

Singular and Plural Nouns	
Singular	*Plural*
goat	goats
alley	alleys
friend	friends
truth	truths
box	boxes

- For more information on nouns, see "Subjects and Verbs," pages 87–95.

Practice 2

Underline the three nouns in each sentence. Some are singular, and some are plural.

1. Two bats swooped over the heads of the frightened children.

2. The artist has purple paint on her sleeve.

3. The lost dog has fleas and a broken leg.

4. Tiffany does her homework in green ink.

5. Some farmers plant seeds by moonlight.

Pronouns

A *pronoun* is a word that stands for a noun. Pronouns eliminate the need for constant repetition. Look at the following sentences:

> The phone rang, and Malik answered the phone.
>
> Lisa met Lisa's friends in the record store at the mall. Lisa meets Lisa's friends there every Saturday.
>
> The waiter rushed over to the new customers. The new customers asked the waiter for menus and coffee.

Now look at how much clearer and smoother these sentences sound with pronouns.

> The phone rang, and Malik answered *it.*
>
> (The pronoun *it* is used to replace the word *phone.*)

> Lisa met *her* friends in the record store at the mall. *She* meets *them* there every Saturday.
>
> (The pronoun *her* is used to replace the word *Lisa's.* The pronoun *she* replaces *Lisa.* The pronoun *them* replaces the words *Lisa's friends.*)

> The waiter rushed over to the new customers. *They* asked *him* for menus and coffee.
>
> (The pronoun *they* is used to replace the words *the new customers.* The pronoun *him* replaces the words *the waiter.*)

Following is a list of commonly used pronouns known as personal pronouns:

Personal Pronouns						
I	you	he	she	it	we	they
me	your	him	her	its	us	them
my	yours	his	hers		our	their

Practice 3

Fill in each blank with the appropriate personal pronoun.

1. André feeds his pet lizard every day before school. _____ also gives _____ flies in the afternoon.

2. The reporter interviewed the striking workers. _____ told _____ about their demand for higher wages and longer breaks.

3. Students should save all returned tests. _____ should also keep _____ review sheets.

4. The pilot announced that we would fly through some air pockets. _____ said that we should be past _____ soon.

5. Adolfo returned the calculator to Sheila last Friday. But Sheila insists that _____ never got _____ back.

There are several types of pronouns. For convenient reference, they are described briefly in the box below.

Types of Pronouns

Personal pronouns can act in a sentence as subjects, objects, or possessives.

    Singular: I, me, my, mine, you, your, yours, he, him, his, she, her, hers, it, its

    Plural: we, us, our, ours, you, your, yours, they, them, their, theirs

Relative pronouns refer to someone or something already mentioned in the sentence.

    who, whose, whom, which, that

Interrogative pronouns are used to ask questions.

    who, whose, whom, which, what

Demonstrative pronouns are used to point out particular persons or things.

    this, that, these, those

    Note: Do not use *them* (as in *them* shoes), *this here, that there, these here,* or *those there* to point out.

Continued

Reflexive pronouns are those that end in -*self* or -*selves*. A reflexive pronoun is used as the object of a verb (as in *Cary cut **herself***) or the object of a preposition (as in *Jack sent a birthday card to **himself***) when the subject of the verb is the same as the object.

> *Singular:*   myself, yourself, himself, herself, itself
>
> *Plural:*   ourselves, yourselves, themselves

Intensive pronouns have exactly the same forms as reflexive pronouns. The difference is in how they are used. Intensive pronouns are used to add emphasis. (*I **myself** will need to read the contract before I sign it.*)

Indefinite pronouns do not refer to a particular person or thing.

> each, either, everyone, nothing, both, several, all, any, most, none

Reciprocal pronouns express shared actions or feelings.

> each other, one another

- For more information on pronouns, see "Pronoun Types," pages 207–219.

Verbs

Every complete sentence must contain at least one verb. There are two types of verbs: action verbs and linking verbs.

Action Verbs

An *action verb* tells what is being done in a sentence. For example, look at the following sentences:

> Mr. Jensen *swatted* at the bee with his hand.
> Rainwater *poured* into the storm sewer.
> The children *chanted* the words to the song.

In these sentences, the verbs are *swatted, poured,* and *chanted.* These words are all action verbs; they tell what is happening in each sentence.

- For more about action verbs, see "Subjects and Verbs," pages 87–95.

Practice 4

Insert an appropriate word in each blank. That word will be an action verb; it will tell what is happening in the sentence.

1. The surgeon _____ through the first layer of skin.

2. The animals in the cage _____ all day.

3. An elderly woman on the street _____ me for directions.

4. The boy next door _____ our lawn every other week.

5. Our instructor _____ our papers over the weekend.

Linking Verbs

Some verbs are *linking verbs*. These verbs link (or join) a noun to something that is said about it. For example, look at the following sentence:

The clouds *are* steel gray.

In this sentence, *are* is a linking verb. It joins the noun *clouds* to words that describe it: *steel gray*.

Other common linking verbs include *am, is, was, were, look, feel, sound, appear, seem,* and *become.*

• For more about linking verbs, see "Subjects and Verbs," pages 87–95.

Practice 5

In each blank, insert one of the following linking verbs: *am, feel, is, look, were.* Use each linking verb once.

1. The important papers _____ in a desk drawer.

2. I _____ anxious to get my test back.

3. The bananas _____ ripe.

4. The grocery store _____ open until 11 P.M.

5. Whenever I _____ angry, I go off by myself to calm down.

Helping Verbs

Sometimes the verb of a sentence consists of more than one word. In these cases, the main verb will be joined by one or more *helping verbs*. Look at the following sentence:

The basketball team *will be leaving* for their game at six o'clock.

In this sentence, the main verb is *leaving*. The helping verbs are *will* and *be*.
    Other helping verbs include *do, has, have, may, would, can, must, could,* and *should.*

• For more information about helping verbs, see "Subjects and Verbs," pages 87–95, and "Irregular Verbs," pages 161–171.

Practice 6

In each blank, insert one of the following helping verbs: *does, must, should, could, has been.* Use each helping verb once.

1. You _____ start writing your paper this weekend.
2. The victim _____ describe her attacker in great detail.
3. You _____ rinse the dishes before putting them into the dishwasher.
4. My neighbor _____ arrested for drunk driving.
5. The bus driver _____ not make any extra stops.

Prepositions

A *preposition* is a word that connects a noun or a pronoun to another word in the sentence. For example, look at the following sentence:

A man *in* the bus was snoring loudly.

In is a preposition. It connects the noun *bus* to *man*. Here is a list of common prepositions:

Prepositions				
about	before	down	like	to
above	behind	during	of	toward
across	below	except	off	under
after	beneath	for	on	up
among	beside	from	over	with
around	between	in	since	without
at	by	into	through	

The noun or pronoun that a preposition connects to another word in the sentence is called the *object* of the preposition. A group of words beginning with a preposition and ending with its object is called a *prepositional phrase.* The words *in the bus,* for example, are a prepositional phrase.

Now read the following sentences and explanations.

An ant was crawling *up the teacher's leg*.

The noun *leg* is the object of the preposition *up*. *Up* connects *leg* with the word *crawling*. The prepositional phrase *up the teacher's leg* describes *crawling*. It tells just where the ant was crawling.

The man *with the black moustache* left the restaurant quickly.

The noun *moustache* is the object of the preposition *with*. The prepositional phrase *with the black moustache* describes the word *man*. It tells us exactly which man left the restaurant quickly.

The plant *on the windowsill* was a present *from my mother*.

The noun *windowsill* is the object of the preposition *on*. The prepositional phrase *on the windowsill* describes the word *plant*. It describes exactly which plant was a present.

There is a second prepositional phrase in this sentence. The preposition is *from,* and its object is *mother*. The prepositional phrase *from my mother* explains *present*. It tells who gave the present.

- For more about prepositions, see "Subjects and Verbs," pages 87–95, and "Sentence Variety II," pages 251–264.

Practice 7

In each blank, insert one of the following prepositions: *of, by, with, in, without.*
Use each preposition once.

1. The letter from his girlfriend had been sprayed _____ perfume.

2. The weedkiller quickly killed the dandelions _____ our lawn.

3. _____ giving any notice, the tenant moved out of the expensive apartment.

4. Donald hungrily ate three scoops _____ ice cream and an order of French fries.

5. The crates _____ the back door contain glass bottles and old newspapers.

Adjectives

An *adjective* is a word that describes a noun (the name of a person, place, or thing). Look at the following sentence.

> The dog lay down on a mat in front of the fireplace.

Now look at this sentence when adjectives have been inserted.

> The *shaggy* dog lay down on a *worn* mat in front of the fireplace.

The adjective *shaggy* describes the noun *dog;* the adjective *worn* describes the noun *mat*. Adjectives add spice to our writing. They also help us to identify particular people, places, or things.

Adjectives can be found in two places:

1 An adjective may come before the word it describes (a *damp* night, the *moldy* bread, a *striped* umbrella).

2 An adjective that describes the subject of a sentence may come after a linking verb. The linking verb may be a form of the verb *be* (he *is* **furious**, I *am* **exhausted**, they are **hungry**). Other linking verbs include *feel, look, sound, smell, taste, appear, seem,* and *become* (the soup *tastes* **salty**, your hands *feel* **dry**, the dog *seems* **lost**).

Note   The words *a, an,* and *the* (called *articles*) are generally classified as adjectives.

• For more information on adjectives, see "Adjectives and Adverbs," pages 221–227.

Practice 8

Write any appropriate adjective in each blank.

1. The _____ pizza was eaten greedily by the _____ teenagers.
2. Melissa gave away the sofa because it was _____ and _____.
3. Although the alley is _____ and _____, Jian often takes it as a shortcut home.
4. The restaurant throws away lettuce that is _____ and tomatoes that are _____.
5. When I woke up in the morning, I had a(n) _____ fever and a(n) _____ throat.

Adverbs

An *adverb* is a word that describes a verb, an adjective, or another adverb. Many adverbs end in the letters *-ly*. Look at the following sentence:

The canary sang in the pet store window as the shoppers greeted each other.

Now look at this sentence after adverbs have been inserted.

The canary sang *softly* in the pet store window as the shoppers *loudly* greeted each other.

The adverbs add details to the sentence. They also allow the reader to contrast the singing of the canary and the noise the shoppers are making.

Look at the following sentences and the explanations of how adverbs are used in each case.

The chef yelled **angrily** at the young waiter.
(The adverb *angrily* describes the verb *yelled*.)

My mother has an **extremely** busy schedule on Tuesdays.
(The adverb *extremely* describes the adjective *busy*.)

The sick man spoke **very** faintly to his loyal nurse.

(The adverb *very* describes the adverb *faintly*.)

Some adverbs do not end in *-ly*. Examples include *very, often, never, always,* and *well.*

- For more information on adverbs, see "Adjectives and Adverbs," pages 221–227.

Practice 9

Fill in each blank with any appropriate adverb.

1. The water in the pot boiled _____.

2. Carla _____ drove the car through _____ moving traffic.

3. The telephone operator spoke _____ to the young child.

4. The game show contestant waved _____ to his family in the audience.

5. Wes _____ studies, so it's no surprise that he did _____ poorly on his finals.

Conjunctions

A *conjunction* is a word that connects. There are two types of conjunctions: coordinating and subordinating.

Coordinating Conjunctions

Coordinating conjunctions join two equal ideas. Look at the following sentence:

Kevin *and* Steve interviewed for the job, *but* their friend Anne got it.

In this sentence, the coordinating conjunction *and* connects the proper nouns *Kevin* and *Steve*. The coordinating conjunction *but* connects the first part of the sentence, *Kevin and Steve interviewed for the job,* to the second part, *their friend Anne got it.*

Following is a list of all the coordinating conjunctions. In this book, they are simply called *joining words.*

Coordinating Conjunctions (Joining Words)

and	so	nor	yet
but	or	for	

- For more on coordinating conjunctions, see information on joining words in "Run-Ons," pages 117–134, and "Sentence Variety I," pages 135–149.

Practice 10

Write a coordinating conjunction in each blank. Choose from the following: *and, but, so, or, nor*. Use each conjunction once.

1. Either Jerome _____ Alex scored the winning touchdown.

2. I expected roses for my birthday, _____ I received a vase of plastic tulips from the discount store.

3. The cafeteria was serving liver and onions for lunch, _____ I bought a sandwich at the corner deli.

4. Marian brought a pack of playing cards _____ a pan of brownies to the company picnic.

5. Neither my sofa _____ my armchair matches the rug in my living room.

Subordinating Conjunctions

When a *subordinating conjunction* is added to a word group, the words can no longer stand alone as an independent sentence. They are no longer a complete thought. For example, look at the following sentence:

Karen fainted in class.

The word group *Karen fainted in class* is a complete thought. It can stand alone as a sentence. See what happens when a subordinating conjunction is added to a complete thought:

When Karen fainted in class

Now the words cannot stand alone as a sentence. They are dependent on other words to complete the thought:

When Karen fainted in class, we put her feet up on some books.

In this book, a word that begins a dependent word group is called a *dependent word*. Subordinating conjunctions are common dependent words. Below are some subordinating conjunctions.

Subordinating Conjunctions			
after	even if	unless	where
although	even though	until	wherever
as	if	when	whether
because	since	whenever	while
before	though		

Following are some more sentences with subordinating conjunctions:

After she finished her last exam, Irina said, "Now I can relax."
(*After she finished her last exam* is not a complete thought. It is dependent on the rest of the words to make up a complete sentence.)

Lamont listens to books on tape **while** he drives to work.
(*While he drives to work* cannot stand by itself as a sentence. It depends on the rest of the sentence to make up a complete thought.)

Since apples were on sale, we decided to make an apple pie for dessert.
(*Since apples were on sale* is not a complete sentence. It depends on *we decided to make an apple pie for dessert* to complete the thought.)

- For more information on subordinating conjunctions, see information on dependent words in "Fragments," pages 97–115; "Run-Ons," pages 117–134; "Sentence Variety I," pages 135–149; and "Sentence Variety II," pages 251–264.

Practice 11

Write a logical subordinating conjunction in each blank. Choose from the following: *even though, because, until, when, before*. Use each conjunction once.

1. The bank was closed down by federal regulators _____ it lost more money than it earned.

2. _____ Paula wants to look mysterious, she wears dark sunglasses and a scarf.

3. _____ the restaurant was closing in fifteen minutes, customers sipped their coffee slowly and continued to talk.

4. _____ anyone else could answer it, Leon rushed to the phone and whispered, "Is that you?"

5. The waiter was instructed not to serve any food _____ the guest of honor arrived.

Interjections

An *interjection* is a word that can stand independently and is used to express emotion. Examples are *oh, wow, ouch,* and *oops.* These words are usually not found in formal writing.

"*Hey!*" yelled Maggie. "That's my bike."

Oh, we're late for class.

A Final Note

A word may function as more than one part of speech. For example, the word *dust* can be a verb or a noun, depending on its role in the sentence.

I *dust* my bedroom once a month, whether it needs it or not. (verb)

The top of my refrigerator is covered with an inch of *dust.* (noun)

ESL Pointers

This section covers rules that most native speakers of English take for granted but that are useful for speakers of English as a second language (ESL).

Articles

Types of Articles

An *article* is a noun marker—it signals that a noun will follow. There are two kinds of articles: indefinite and definite. The indefinite articles are *a* and *an*. Use *a* before a word that begins with a consonant sound:

> **a d**esk, **a p**hotograph, **a u**nicycle
>
> *(A* is used before *unicycle* because the *u* in that word sounds like the consonant *y* plus *u,* not a vowel sound.)

Use *an* before a word beginning with a vowel sound:

> **an e**rror, **an o**bject, **an h**onest woman
>
> *(Honest* begins with a vowel sound because the *h* is silent.)

The definite article is *the.*

> **the** sofa, **the** cup

An article may come right before a noun:

> **a** magazine, **the** candle

Or an article may be separated from the noun by words that describe the noun:

> **a** popular magazine, **the** fat red candle

Note   There are various other noun markers, including quantity words (*a few, many, a lot of*), numerals (*one, thirteen, 710*), demonstrative adjectives (*this, these*), adjectives (*my, your, our*), and possessive nouns (*Raoul's, the school's*).

Articles with Count and Noncount Nouns

To know whether to use an article with a noun and which article to use, you must recognize count and noncount nouns. (A *noun* is a word used to name something—a person, place, thing, or idea.)

Count nouns name people, places, things, or ideas that can be counted and made into plurals, such as *pillow, heater,* and *mail carrier* (*one pillow, two heaters, three mail carriers*).

Noncount nouns refer to things or ideas that cannot be counted and therefore cannot be made into plurals, such as *sunshine, gold,* and *toast.* The box below lists and illustrates common types of noncount nouns.

Common Noncount Nouns

Abstractions and emotions: justice, tenderness, courage, knowledge, embarrassment

Activities: jogging, thinking, wondering, golf, hoping, sleep

Foods: oil, rice, pie, butter, spaghetti, broccoli

Gases and vapors: carbon dioxide, oxygen, smoke, steam, air

Languages and areas of study: Korean, Italian, geology, arithmetic, history

Liquids: coffee, kerosene, lemonade, tea, water, bleach

Materials that come in bulk or mass form: straw, firewood, sawdust, cat litter, cement

Natural occurrences: gravity, sleet, rain, lightning, rust

Other things that cannot be counted: clothing, experience, trash, luggage, room, furniture, homework, machinery, cash, news, transportation, work

---

The quantity of a noncount noun can be expressed with a word or words called a *qualifier,* such as *some, more, a unit of,* and so on. In the following two examples, the qualifiers are shown in *italic* type, and the noncount nouns are shown in **boldface** type.

How *much* **experience** have you had as a salesclerk?

Our tiny kitchen doesn't have *enough* **room** for a table and chairs.

Some words can be either count or noncount nouns depending on whether they refer to one or more individual items or to something in general:

Three **chickens** are running around our neighbor's yard.

(This sentence refers to particular chickens; *chicken* in this case is a count noun.)

Would you like some more **chicken**?

(This sentence refers to chicken in general; in this case, *chicken* is a noncount noun.)

Using *a* or *an* with Nonspecific Singular Count Nouns

Use *a* or *an* with singular nouns that are nonspecific. A noun is nonspecific when the reader doesn't know its specific identity.

A photograph can be almost magical. It saves a moment's image for many years.

(The sentence refers to any photograph, not a specific one.)

An article in the newspaper today made me laugh.

(The reader isn't familiar with the article. This is the first time it is mentioned.)

Using *the* with Specific Nouns

In general, use *the* with all specific nouns—specific singular, plural, and noncount nouns. A noun is specific—and therefore requires the article *the*—in the following cases:

- When it has already been mentioned once:

  An article in the newspaper today made me laugh. **The** article was about a talking parrot who frightened away a thief.

  (*The* is used with the second mention of *article*.)

- When it is identified by a word or phrase in the sentence:

  The CD that is playing now is a favorite of mine.

  (*CD* is identified by the words *that is playing now*.)

- When its identity is suggested by the general context:

  The service at Joe's Bar and Grill is never fast.

  (*Service* is identified by the words *at Joe's Bar and Grill*.)

- When it is unique:

    Some people see a man's face in **the** moon, while others see a rabbit.
    (Earth has only one moon.)

- When it comes after a superlative adjective (for example, *best, biggest,* or *wisest*):

    The funniest movie I've seen is *Young Frankenstein.*

Omitting Articles   Omit articles with nonspecific plurals and nonspecific noncount nouns. Plurals and noncount nouns are nonspecific when they refer to something in general.

    Stories are popular with most children.

    Service is almost as important as food to a restaurant's success.

    Movies can be rented from many supermarkets as well as video stores.

Using *the* with Proper Nouns

Proper nouns name particular people, places, things, or ideas and are always capitalized. Most proper nouns do not require articles; those that do, however, require *the*. Following are general guidelines about when not to use *the* and when to use *the*.

Do not use *the* for most singular proper nouns, including names of the following:

- *People and animals* (Tom Cruise, Fluffy)
- *Continents, states, cities, streets, and parks* (South America, Utah, Boston, Baker Street, People's Park)
- *Most countries* (Cuba, Indonesia, Ireland)
- *Individual bodies of water, islands, and mountains* (Lake Michigan, Captiva Island, Mount McKinley)

    Use *the* for the following types of proper nouns:

- *Plural proper nouns* (the Harlem Globetrotters, the Marshall Islands, the Netherlands, the Atlas Mountains)
- *Names of large geographic areas, deserts, oceans, seas, and rivers* (the Midwest, the Kalahari Desert, the Pacific Ocean, the Sargasso Sea, the Nile River)
- *Names with the format* "the _____ of _____" (the king of Morocco, the Strait of Gibraltar, the University of Illinois)

Practice

Underline the correct word or words in parentheses.

1. (Map, The map) on the wall is old and out of date.
2. To show (affection, the affection), a cat will rub against you and purr.
3. This morning my daughter sang (a song, the song) I had not heard before.
4. She had learned (a song, the song) in her kindergarten class.
5. When Javier takes a test, he always begins by answering (the easiest, easiest) questions.
6. (Nile River, The Nile River) has been used for irrigation in Egypt since 4,000 B.C.
7. Although (Sahara Desert, the Sahara Desert) is very hot during the day, it can get terribly cold at night.
8. The reason we don't fall off the Earth is the pull of (gravity, the gravity).
9. (Patience, The patience) is not always a virtue.
10. Don't forget to put the (garbage, garbages) out to be picked up Wednesday morning.

Subjects and Verbs

Avoiding Repeated Subjects

In English, a particular subject can be used only once in a word group with a subject and a verb (that is, a clause). Don't repeat a subject in the same word group by following a noun with a pronoun.

> Incorrect: My *parents they* live in Miami.
> Correct: My **parents** live in Miami.
> Correct: **They** live in Miami.

Even when the subject and verb are separated by several words, the subject cannot be repeated in the same word group.

> Incorrect: The *windstorm* that happened last night *it* damaged our roof.
> Correct: The **windstorm** that happened last night **damaged** our roof.

Including Pronoun Subjects and Linking Verbs

Some languages omit a subject that is a pronoun, but in English, every sentence other than a command must have a subject. In a command, the subject *you* is understood: (You) Hand in your papers now.

Incorrect: The soup tastes terrible. *Is* much too salty.
Correct: The soup tastes terrible. **It is** much too salty.

Every English sentence must also have a verb, even when the meaning of the sentence is clear without the verb.

Incorrect: The table covered with old newspapers.
Correct: The table **is** covered with old newspapers.

Including *There* and *Here* at the Beginning of Sentences

Some English sentences begin with *there* or *here* plus a linking verb (usually a form of *to be: is, are,* and so on). In such sentences, the verb comes before the subject.

There are ants all over the kitchen counter.
(The subject is the plural noun *ants,* so the plural verb *are* is used.)

Here is the bug spray.
(The subject is the singular noun *spray,* so the singular verb *is* is used.)

In sentences like those above, remember not to omit *there* or *here.*

Incorrect: *Are* several tests scheduled for Friday.
Correct: **There are** several tests scheduled for Friday.

Not Using the Progressive Tense of Certain Verbs

The progressive tenses are made up of forms of *be* plus the *-ing* form of the main verb. They express actions or conditions still in progress at a particular time.

The garden **will be blooming** when you visit me in June.

However, verbs for mental states, the senses, possession, and inclusion are normally not used in the progressive tense.

Incorrect: I **am knowing** a lot about auto mechanics.

Correct: I **know** a lot about auto mechanics.

Incorrect: Gerald **is having** a job as a supermarket cashier.

Correct: Gerald **has** a job as a supermarket cashier.

Common verbs not generally used in the progressive tense are listed in the following box.

Common Verbs Not Generally Used in the Progressive

Verbs relating to thoughts, attitudes, and desires: agree, believe, imagine, know, like, love, prefer, think, understand, want, wish

Verbs showing sense perceptions: hear, see, smell, taste

Verbs relating to appearances: appear, look, seem

Verbs showing possession: belong, have, own, possess

Verbs showing inclusion: contain, include

Using Gerunds and Infinitives after Verbs

Before learning the rules about gerunds and infinitives, you must understand what they are. A *gerund* is the *-ing* form of a verb that is used as a noun:

Reading is a good way to improve one's vocabulary.

(*Reading* is the subject of the sentence.)

An *infinitive* is *to* plus the basic form of the verb (the form in which the verb is listed in the dictionary), as in **to eat**. The infinitive can function as an adverb, an adjective, or a noun.

On weekends, Betsy works at a convenience store **to make** some extra money.

(*To make some extra money* functions as an adverb that describes the verb *works*.)

My advisor showed me a good way **to study** for a test.

(*To study for a test* functions as an adjective describing the noun *way*.)

To forgive can be a relief.

(*To forgive* functions as a noun—it is the subject of the verb *can be*.)

Some verbs can be followed by only a gerund or only an infinitive; other verbs can be followed by either. Examples are given in the following lists. There are many others; watch for them in your reading.

Verb + gerund (*enjoy* + *skiing*)
Verb + preposition + gerund (*think* + *about* + *coming*)

Some verbs can be followed by a gerund but not by an infinitive. In many cases, there is a preposition (such as *for, in,* or *of*) between the verb and the gerund. Following are some verbs and verb-preposition combinations that can be followed by gerunds but not by infinitives:

admit	deny	look forward to
apologize for	discuss	postpone
appreciate	dislike	practice
approve of	enjoy	suspect of
avoid	feel like	talk about
be used to	finish	thank for
believe in	insist on	think about

Incorrect: The governor *avoids to make* enemies.
Correct: The governor **avoids making** enemies.

Incorrect: I *enjoy to go* to movies alone.
Correct: I **enjoy going** to movies alone.

Verb + infinitive (*agree* + *to leave*)

Following are common verbs that can be followed by an infinitive but not by a gerund:

agree	decide	manage
arrange	expect	refuse
claim	have	wait

Incorrect: I *arranged paying* my uncle's bills while he was ill.

Correct: I **arranged to pay** my uncle's bills while he was ill.

Verb + noun or pronoun + infinitive (*cause + them + to flee*)

Below are common verbs that are first followed by a noun or pronoun and then by an infinitive, not a gerund.

cause	force	remind
command	persuade	warn

Incorrect: The flood *forced them leaving* their home.

Correct: The flood **forced them to leave** their home.

Following are common verbs that can be followed either by an infinitive alone or by a noun or pronoun and an infinitive:

ask	need	want
expect	promise	would like

Rita **expects to go** to college.

Rita's parents **expect her to go** to college.

Verb + gerund or infinitive (*begin + packing* or *begin + to pack*)

Following are verbs that can be followed by either a gerund or an infinitive:

begin	hate	prefer
continue	love	start

The meaning of each verb in the box above remains the same or almost the same whether a gerund or an infinitive is used.

I love **to sleep** late.

I love **sleeping** late.

With the verbs below, the gerunds and the infinitives have very different meanings.

forget	remember	stop

Yuri **forgot putting money** in the parking meter.

(He put money in the parking meter, but then he forgot that he had done so.)

Yuri **forgot to put money** in the parking meter.

(He neglected to put money in the parking meter.)

Practice

Underline the correct word or words in parentheses.

1. The coffee table (wobbles, it wobbles) because one leg is loose.
2. The firewood is very dry. (Is, It is) burning quickly.
3. (Are knives and forks, There are knives and forks) in that drawer.
4. Olivia (seems, is seeming) sad today.
5. Our instructor warned us (studying, to study) hard for the exam.
6. When the little boy saw his birthday presents, he (very excited, became very excited).
7. Do you (feel like walking, feel like to walk) home?
8. A vegetarian (refuses eating, refuses to eat) meat.
9. The alarm on my watch (it started beeping, started beeping) in the middle of the church service.
10. I like small parties, but my boyfriend (prefers, is preferring) large noisy ones.

Adjectives

Following the Order of Adjectives in English

Adjectives describe nouns and pronouns. In English, an adjective usually comes directly before the word it describes or after a linking verb (a form of *be* or a "sense" verb such as *look, seem,* or *taste*), in which case it modifies the subject of the sentence. In each of the following two sentences, the adjective is **boldfaced** and the noun it describes is *italicized.*

Marta has **beautiful** *eyes.*

Marta's *eyes* are **beautiful**.

When more than one adjective modifies the same noun, the adjectives are usually stated in a certain order, though there are often exceptions. Following is the typical order of English adjectives:

Typical Order of Adjectives in a Series

1 Article or other noun marker: a, an, the, Helen's, this, seven, your

2 Opinion adjective: rude, enjoyable, surprising, easy

3 Size: tall, huge, small, compact

4 Shape: triangular, oval, round, square

5 Age: ancient, new, old, young

6 Color: gray, blue, pink, green

7 Nationality: Greek, Thai, Korean, Ethiopian

8 Religion: Hindu, Methodist, Jewish, Islamic

9 Material: fur, copper, stone, velvet

10 Noun used as an adjective: book (as in *book report*), picture (as in *picture frame*), tea (as in *tea bag*)

Here are some examples of the order of adjectives:

an exciting new movie

the petite young Irish woman

my favorite Chinese restaurant

Greta's long brown leather coat

In general, use no more than two or three adjectives after the article or another noun marker. Numerous adjectives in a series can be awkward: **that comfortable big old green velvet** couch.

Using the Present and Past Participles as Adjectives

The present participle ends in *-ing*. Past participles of regular verbs end in *-ed* or *-d;* a list of the past participles of many common irregular verbs appears on pages 163–164. Both types of participles may be used as adjectives. A participle used as an adjective may come before the word it describes:

There was a **frowning** *security guard.*

A participle used as an adjective may also follow a linking verb and describe the subject of the sentence:

The *security guard* was **frowning**.

While both present and past participles of a particular verb may be used as adjectives, their meanings differ. Use the present participle to describe whoever or whatever causes a feeling:

a **disappointing** *date*
(The date *caused* the disappointment.)

Use the past participle to describe whoever or whatever experiences the feeling:

the **disappointed** *neighbor*
(The neighbor *is* disappointed.)

Here are two more sentences that illustrate the differing meanings of present and past participles.

The waiter was **irritating**.
The diners were **irritated**.
(The waiter caused the irritation; the diners experienced the irritation.)

The following box shows pairs of present and past participles with similar distinctions.

annoying / annoyed	exhausting / exhausted
boring / bored	fascinating / fascinated
confusing / confused	surprising / surprised
depressing / depressed	tiring / tired
exciting / excited	

Practice

Underline the correct word or wording in parentheses.

1. When my grandfather died, he left me his (big old oak, old big oak) seaman's chest.
2. The guest lecturer at today's class was a (young Vietnamese Buddhist, Vietnamese Buddhist young) nun.
3. Yolanda's family lives in a (gray huge stone, huge gray stone) farmhouse.
4. Doesn't working all day and studying at night make you very (tired, tiring)?
5. The (fascinated, fascinating) children begged the magician to tell them how he made a rabbit disappear.

Prepositions Used for Time and Place

The use of a preposition in English is often not based on its common meaning, and there are many exceptions to general rules. As a result, correct use of prepositions must be learned gradually through experience. Following is a chart showing how three of the most common prepositions are used in some customary references to time and place:

Use of *On, In,* and *At* to Refer to Time and Place

Time

On *a specific day:* on Wednesday, on January 11, on Halloween

In *a part of a day:* in the morning, in the daytime (but *at* night)

In *a month or a year:* in October, in 1776

Continued

> ***In*** *a period of time:* in a second, in a few days, in a little while
> ***At*** *a specific time:* at 11 P.M., at midnight, at sunset, at lunchtime
>
> ## Place
>
> ***On*** *a surface:* on the shelf, on the sidewalk, on the roof
> ***In*** *a place that is enclosed:* in the bathroom, in the closet, in the drawer
> ***At*** *a specific location:* at the restaurant, at the zoo, at the school

Practice

Underline the correct preposition in parentheses.

1. May I come see you (on, at) Saturday?
2. We will eat dinner (on, at) 7 P.M.
3. I found this book (on, in) the library.
4. Alex will be leaving for the army (in, at) a week.
5. David and Lisa met one another (on, at) the post office.

■ Review Test

Underline the correct word or words in parentheses.

1. I had to pull off the road because of the heavy (hail, hails).
2. (Are, There are) fresh cookies on the kitchen table.
3. Theresa does not like living alone—she becomes (frightening, frightened) at every little sound.
4. Have you gotten used to working (in, at) night?
5. Carla (practiced to give, practiced giving) her speech at least ten times.
6. What a (pretty red, red pretty) scarf you are wearing today!
7. That antique car (belongs to, is belonging to) my cousin.
8. Fireworks are set off (on, in) the Fourth of July to commemorate the American Revolution.
9. The newlyweds' apartment does not contain much (furnitures, furniture).
10. Paul's favorite pastime is going to (the rock concerts, rock concerts).

Sentence-Skills Diagnostic Test

Part 1

This diagnostic test will help check your knowledge of a number of sentence skills. In each item below, certain words are underlined. Write *X* in the answer space if you think a mistake appears at the underlined part. Write *C* in the answer space if you think the underlined part is correct.

The headings within the text ("Fragments," "Run-Ons," and so on) will give you clues to the mistakes to look for. However, you do not have to understand the heading to find a mistake. What you are checking is your own sense of effective written English.

Fragments

_____ 1. Because I didn't want to get wet. I waited for a break in the downpour. Then I ran for the car like an Olympic sprinter.

_____ 2. The baby birds chirped loudly, especially when their mother brought food to them. Their mouths gaped open hungrily.

_____ 3. Trying to avoid running into anyone. Cal wheeled his baby son around the crowded market. He wished that strollers came equipped with flashing hazard lights.

_____ 4. The old woman combed out her long, gray hair. She twisted it into two thick braids. And wrapped them around her head like a crown.

Run-Ons

_____ 5. Irene fixed fruits and healthy sandwiches for her son's lunch, he traded them for cupcakes, cookies, and chips.

_____ 6. Angie's dark eyes were the color of mink they matched her glowing complexion.

_____   7. My mother keeps sending me bottles of vitamins, but I keep forgetting to take them.

_____   8. The little boy watched the line of ants march across the ground, he made a wall of Popsicle sticks to halt the ants' advance.

Standard English Verbs

_____   9. When she's upset, Mary tells her troubles to her houseplants.

_____   10. The street musician counted the coins in his donations basket and pack his trumpet in its case.

_____   11. I tried to pull off my rings, but they was stuck on my swollen fingers.

_____   12. Belle's car have a horn that plays six different tunes.

Irregular Verbs

_____   13. I've swam in this lake for years, and I've never seen it so shallow.

_____   14. The phone rung once and then stopped.

_____   15. Five different people had brought huge bowls of potato salad to the barbecue.

_____   16. The metal ice cube trays froze to the bottom of the freezer.

Subject-Verb Agreement

_____   17. The records in my collection is arranged in alphabetical order.

_____   18. There was only one burner working on the old gas stove.

_____   19. My aunt and uncle gives a party every Groundhog Day.

_____   20. One of my sweaters have moth holes in the sleeves.

Consistent Verb Tense

_____   21. After I turned off the ignition, the engine continued to sputter for several minutes.

_____   22. Before cleaning the oven, I lined the kitchen floor with newspapers, open the windows, and shook the can of aerosol foam.

Pronoun Reference, Agreement, and Point of View

_____   23. All visitors should stay in their cars while driving through the wild animal park.

_____   24. At the library, they showed me how to use the microfilm machines.

_____   25. As I slowed down at the scene of the accident, you could see long black skid marks on the highway.

Pronoun Types

_____ 26. My husband is more sentimental than me.

_____ 27. Andy and I made ice cream in an old-fashioned wooden machine.

Adjectives and Adverbs

_____ 28. Brian drives so reckless that no one will join his carpool.

_____ 29. Miriam pulled impatiently at the rusty zipper.

_____ 30. I am more happier with myself now that I earn my own money.

_____ 31. The last screw on the license plate was the most corroded one of all.

Misplaced Modifiers

_____ 32. I stretched out on the lounge chair wearing my bikini bathing suit.

_____ 33. I replaced the shingle on the roof that was loose.

Dangling Modifiers

_____ 34. While doing the dishes, a glass shattered in the soapy water.

_____ 35. Pedaling as fast as possible, Todd tried to outrace the snapping dog.

Faulty Parallelism

_____ 36. Before I could take a bath, I had to pick up the damp towels on the floor, gather up the loose toys in the room, and the tub had to be scrubbed out.

_____ 37. I've tried several cures for my headaches, including drugs, meditation, exercise, and massaging my head.

Capital Letters

_____ 38. This fall we plan to visit Cape Cod.

_____ 39. Vern ordered a set of tools from the sears catalog.

_____ 40. When my aunt visits us, she insists on doing all the cooking.

_____ 41. Maureen asked, "will you split a piece of cheesecake with me?"

Numbers and Abbreviations

_____ 42. Before I could stop myself, I had eaten 6 glazed doughnuts.

_____ 43. At 10:45 A.M., a partial eclipse of the sun will begin.

_____ 44. Larry, who is now over six ft. tall, can no longer sleep comfortably in a twin bed.

End Marks

_____ 45. Jane wondered if her husband was telling the truth.

_____ 46. Does that stew need some salt?

Apostrophe

_____ 47. Elizabeths thick, curly hair is her best feature.

_____ 48. I tried to see through the interesting envelope sent to my sister but couldnt.

_____ 49. Pam's heart almost stopped beating when Roger jumped out of the closet.

_____ 50. The logs' in the fireplace crumbled in a shower of sparks.

Quotation Marks

_____ 51. Someone once said, "A lie has no legs and cannot stand."

_____ 52. "This repair job could be expensive, the mechanic warned."

_____ 53. "My greatest childhood fear," said Sheila, "was being sucked down the bathtub drain."

_____ 54. "I was always afraid of everybody's father, said Suzanne, except my own."

Comma

_____ 55. The restaurant's "sundae bar" featured bowls of whipped cream chopped nuts and chocolate sprinkles.

_____ 56. My sister, who studies karate, installed large practice mirrors in our basement.

_____ 57. When I remove my thick eyeglasses the world turns into an out-of-focus movie.

_____ 58. Gloria wrapped her son's presents in pages from the comics section, and she glued a small toy car atop each gift.

Spelling

_____ 59. When Terry practises scales on the piano, her whole family wears earplugs.

_____ 60. I wondered if it was alright to wear sneakers with my three-piece suit.

_____ 61. The essay test question asked us to describe two different theorys of evolution.

_____ 62. A theif stole several large hanging plants from Marlo's porch.

Omitted Words and Letters

_____ 63. After dark, I'm afraid to look in the closets or under the bed.

_____ 64. I turned on the television, but baseball game had been rained out.

_____ 65. Polar bear cubs stay with their mother for two year.

Commonly Confused Words

_____ 66. Before your about to start the car, press the gas pedal to the floor once.

_____ 67. The frog flicked it's tongue out and caught the fly.

_____ 68. I was to lonely to enjoy the party.

_____ 69. The bats folded their wings around them like leather overcoats.

Effective Word Choice

_____ 70. If the professor gives me a break, I might pass the final exam.

_____ 71. Harry worked like a dog all summer to save money for his tuition.

_____ 72. Because Monday is a holiday, sanitation engineers will pick up your trash on Tuesday.

_____ 73. Our family's softball game ended in an argument, as usual.

_____ 74. As for my own opinion, I feel that nuclear weapons should be banned.

_____ 75. This law is, for all intents and purposes, a failure.

Part 2 (Optional)

Do the following at your instructor's request. This second part of the test will provide more detailed information about skills you need to know. On separate paper, number and correct all the items you have marked with an X. For example, suppose you had marked the word groups below with an X. (Note that these examples are not taken from the actual test.)

4. When I picked up the tire. Something in my back snapped. I could not stand up straight.

7. The phone started ringing, then the doorbell sounded as well.

15. Marks goal is to save enough money to get married next year.

29. Without checking the rearview mirror the driver pulled out into the passing lane.

Here is how you should write your corrections on a separate sheet of paper:

4. When I picked up the tire, something in my back snapped.

7. The phone started ringing, and then the doorbell sounded as well.

15. Mark's

29. mirror, the driver

There are over forty corrections to make in all.

Sentence-Skills Achievement Test

Part I

This achievement test will help you check your mastery of a number of sentence skills. In each item below, certain words are underlined. Write *X* in the answer space if you think a mistake appears at the underlined part. Write *C* in the answer space if you think the underlined part is correct.

The headings within the test ("Fragments," "Run-Ons," and so on) will give you clues to the mistakes to look for.

Fragments

_____ 1. When the town's bully died. Hundreds of people came to his funeral. They wanted to make sure he was dead.

_____ 2. Suzanne adores junk foods, especially onion-flavored potato chips. She can eat an entire bag at one sitting.

_____ 3. My brother stayed up all night. Studying the rules in his driver's manual. He wanted to get his license on the first try.

_____ 4. Hector decided to take a study break. He picked up *TV Guide*. And flipped through the pages to find that night's listings.

Run-Ons

_____ 5. Ronnie leaned forward in his seat, he could not hear what the instructor was saying.

_____ 6. Our television set obviously needs repairs the color keeps fading from the picture.

_____ 7. Nick and Fran enjoyed their trip to Chicago, but they couldn't wait to get home.

_____ 8. I tuned in the weather forecast on the radio, I had to decide what to wear.

Standard English Verbs

——————— 9. My sister Louise <u>walks</u> a mile to the bus stop every day.

——————— 10. The play was ruined when the quarterback <u>fumble</u> the handoff.

——————— 11. When the last guests left our party, we <u>was</u> exhausted but happy.

——————— 12. I don't think my mother <u>have</u> gone out to a movie in years.

Irregular Verbs

——————— 13. My roommate and I <u>seen</u> a double feature this weekend.

——————— 14. My nephew must have <u>growed</u> six inches since last summer.

——————— 15. I should have <u>brought</u> a gift to the office Christmas party.

——————— 16. After playing touch football all afternoon, Al <u>drank</u> a quart of Gatorade.

Subject-Verb Agreement

——————— 17. The cost of those new tires <u>are</u> more than I can afford.

——————— 18. Nick and Fran <u>give</u> a New Year's Eve party every year.

——————— 19. There <u>was</u> only two slices of cake left on the plate.

——————— 20. Each of the fast-food restaurants <u>have</u> a breakfast special.

Consistent Verb Tense

——————— 21. After I folded the towels in the basket, I <u>remembered</u> that I hadn't washed them yet.

——————— 22. Before she decided to buy the wall calendar, Joanne <u>turns</u> its pages and looked at all the pictures.

Pronoun Reference, Agreement, and Point of View

——————— 23. All drivers should try <u>their</u> best to be courteous during rush hour.

——————— 24. When Bob went to the bank for a home improvement loan, <u>they</u> asked him for three credit references.

——————— 25. I like to shop at factory outlets because <u>you</u> can always get brand names at a discount.

Pronoun Types

——————— 26. My brother writes much more neatly than <u>me</u>.

——————— 27. Vonnie and <u>I</u> are both taking Introduction to Business this semester.

Adjectives and Adverbs

_____ 28. When the elevator doors closed <u>sudden</u>, three people were trapped inside.

_____ 29. The bag lady glared <u>angrily</u> at me when I offered her a dollar bill.

_____ 30. Frank couldn't decide which vacation he liked <u>best</u>, a bicycle trip or a week at the beach.

_____ 31. I find proofreading a paper much <u>more difficult</u> than writing one.

Misplaced Modifiers

_____ 32. The car was parked along the side of the road <u>with a flat tire</u>.

_____ 33. We bought a television set at our neighborhood discount store <u>that has stereo sound</u>.

Dangling Modifiers

_____ 34. <u>While looking for bargains at Sears</u>, an exercise bike caught my eye.

_____ 35. <u>Hurrying to catch the bus</u>, Donna fell and twisted her ankle.

Faulty Parallelism

_____ 36. Before she leaves for work, Agnes makes her lunch, does fifteen minutes of calisthenics, and <u>her two cats have to be fed</u>.

_____ 37. Three remedies for insomnia are warm milk, <u>taking a hot bath</u>, and sleeping pills.

Capital Letters

_____ 38. Every <u>Saturday</u> I get up early, even though I have the choice of sleeping late.

_____ 39. We stopped at the drugstore for some <u>crest</u> toothpaste.

_____ 40. Rows of crocuses appear in my front yard every <u>spring</u>.

_____ 41. The cashier said, "<u>sorry</u>, but children under three are not allowed in this theater."

Numbers and Abbreviations

_____ 42. Our train finally arrived—<u>2</u> hours late.

_____ 43. Answers to the chapter questions start on page <u>293</u>.

_____ 44. Three <u>yrs.</u> from now, my new car will finally be paid off.

End Marks

_____   45. I had no idea who was inside the gorilla suit at the Halloween party.

_____   46. Are you taking the makeup exam.

Apostrophe

_____   47. My fathers favorite old television program is *Star Trek*.

_____   48. I couldnt understand a word of that lecture.

_____   49. My dentist's recommendation was that I floss after brushing my teeth.

_____   50. Three house's on our street are up for sale.

Quotation Marks

_____   51. Garfield the cat is fond of saying, "I never met a carbohydrate I didn't like."

_____   52. "This restaurant does not accept credit cards, the waiter said."

_____   53. Two foods that may prevent cancer," said the scientist, "are those old stand-bys spinach and carrots."

_____   54. "I can't get anything done," Dad complained, if you two insist on making all that noise."

Comma

_____   55. The snack bar offered overdone hamburgers rubbery hot dogs and soggy pizza.

_____   56. My sister, who regards every living creature as a holy thing, cannot even swat a housefly.

_____   57. When I smelled something burning I realized I hadn't turned off the oven.

_____   58. Marge plays the musical saw at parties, and her husband does Dracula imitations.

Spelling

_____   59. No one will be admited without a valid student identification card.

_____   60. Pat carrys a full course load in addition to working as the night manager at a supermarket.

_____   61. Did you feel alright after eating Ralph's special chili?

_____   62. My parents were disappointed when I didn't enter the family busines.

Omitted Words and Letters

_____ 63. Both high schools in my hometown offer evening classes for adults.

_____ 64. I opened new bottle of ketchup and then couldn't find the cap.

_____ 65. Visiting hour for patients at this hospital are from noon to eight.

Commonly Confused Words

_____ 66. Shelley has always been to self-conscious to speak up in class.

_____ 67. Its not easy to return to college after raising a family.

_____ 68. "Thank you for you're generous contribution," the letter began.

_____ 69. Nobody knew whose body had been found floating in the swimming pool.

Effective Word Choice

_____ 70. My roommate keeps getting on my case about leaving clothing on the floor.

_____ 71. Karla decided to take the bull by the horns and ask her boss for a raise.

_____ 72. Although Lamont accelerated his vehicle, he was unable to pass the truck.

_____ 73. When the movie ended suddenly, I felt I had been cheated.

_____ 74. In light of the fact that I am on a diet, I have stopped eating between meals.

_____ 75. Personally, I do not think that everyone should be allowed to vote.

Part 2 (Optional)

Do the following at your instructor's request. This second part of the test will provide more detailed information about which skills you have mastered and which skills you still need to work on. On separate paper, number and correct all the items you have marked with an *X*. For example, suppose you had marked the word groups below with an *X*. (Note that these examples were not taken from the actual test.)

4. <u>When I picked up the tire</u>. Something in my back snapped. I could not stand up straight.

7. The phone started <u>ringing</u>, then the doorbell sounded as well.

15. <u>Marks</u> goal is to save enough money to get married next year.

29. Without checking the rearview <u>mirror the</u> driver pulled out into the passing lane.

Here is how you should write your corrections on a separate sheet of paper:

4. When I picked up the tire, something in my back snapped.

7. The phone started ringing, and then the doorbell sounded as well.

15. Mark's

29. mirror, the driver

There are over forty corrections to make in all.

Answers to Introductory Activities and Practice Exercises in Part Two

This answer key can help you teach yourself. Use it to find out why you got some answers wrong—you want to uncover any weak spot in your understanding of a given skill. By using the answer key in an honest and thoughtful way, you will master each skill and prepare yourself for many tests in this book that have no answer key.

SUBJECTS AND VERBS

Introductory Activity (page 87)

Answers will vary.

Practice 1 (89)

1. Carl spilled
2. ladybug landed
3. Nick eats
4. waitress brought
5. I found
6. Diane stapled
7. audience applauded
8. boss has
9. I tasted
10. paperboy threw

Practice 2 (90)

1. parents are
2. I am
3. Tri Lee was
4. dog becomes
5. Estelle seems
6. hot dog looks
7. people appear
8. students felt
9. cheeseburger has
10. telephone seemed

Practice 3 (90)

1. rabbits ate
2. father prefers
3. restaurant donated
4. Stanley looks
5. couple relaxed
6. Lightning brightened
7. council voted
8. throat kept
9. sister decided
10. I chose

Practice (91)

1. By accident, Anita dropped her folder into the mailbox.
2. Before the test, I glanced through my notes.
3. My car stalled on the bridge at rush hour.
4. I hung a photo of Whitney Houston above my bed.
5. On weekends, we visit my grandmother at a nursing home.
6. During the movie, some teenagers giggled at the love scenes.
7. A pedestrian tunnel runs beneath the street to the train station.
8. The parents hid their daughter's Christmas gifts in the garage.
9. All the teachers, except Mr. Blake, wear ties to school.
10. The strawberry jam in my brother's sandwich dripped onto his lap.

Practice (93)

1. Ellen has chosen
2. You should plan
3. Felix has been waiting
4. We should have invited
5. I would have preferred
6. Classes were interrupted
7. Sam can touch
8. I have been encouraging
9. Tony has agreed
10. students have been giving

Practice (94)

1. Boards and bricks make
2. We bought and finished
3. fly and bee hung
4. twins look, think, act, and dress
5. salmon and tuna contain
6. I waited and slipped
7. girl waved and smiled
8. bird dived and reappeared
9. Singers, dancers, and actors performed
10. magician and assistant bowed and disappeared

FRAGMENTS

Introductory Activity (97)

1. verb
2. subject
3. subject . . . verb
4. express a complete thought

Practice 1 (101)
Answers will vary.

Practice 2 (102)

Note   The underlined part shows the fragment (or that part of the original fragment not changed during correction).

1. When the waitress coughed in his food, Frank lost his appetite. He didn't even take home a doggy bag.
2. Our power went out during a thunderstorm.
3. Tony doesn't like going to the ballpark. If he misses an exciting play, there's no instant replay.
4. After the mail carrier comes, I run to our mailbox. I love to get mail even if it is only junk mail.
5. Even though she can't read, my little daughter likes to go to the library. She chooses books with pretty covers while I look at the latest magazines.

Practice 1 (104)

1. Vince sat nervously in the dentist's chair, waiting for his x-rays to be developed.
2. Looking through the movie ads for twenty minutes, Lew and Marian tried to find a film they both wanted to see.
3. As a result, it tipped over.

Practice 2 (104)
Rewritten versions may vary.

1. Some workers dug up the street near our house, causing frequent vibrations inside.
2. I therefore walked slowly into the darkened living room, preparing to look shocked.
   Or: I was preparing to look shocked.
3. Dribbling skillfully up the court, Luis looked for a teammate who was open.
4. Wanting to finish the dream, I pushed the snooze button.
5. To get back my term paper, I went to see my English instructor from last semester.

Practice 1 (106)

1. For example, she waits until the night before a test to begin studying.
2. My eleventh-grade English teacher picked on everybody except the athletes.
3. For example, he bought an air conditioner in December.

Practice 2 (107)
Rewritten versions may vary.

1. I find all sorts of things in my little boy's pockets, including crayons, stones, and melted chocolate.
2. There are certain chores I hate to do, especially cleaning windows.
3. The meat loaf, for instance, is as tender and tasty as shoe leather.
4. By midnight, the party looked like the scene of an accident, with people stretched out on the floor.
5. For example, the smiles of game show hosts look pasted on their faces.

Practice (108)
Rewritten versions may vary.

1. Artie tripped on his shoelace and then looked around to see if anyone had noticed.
   Or: Then he looked around to see if anyone had noticed.
2. I started the car and quickly turned down the blaring radio.
   Or: And I quickly turned down the blaring radio.
3. Its orange-red flames shot high in the air and made strange shadows all around the dark room.
4. She also forgot to take my name.
5. She places herself in front of a seated young man and stands on his feet until he gets up.
   Or: And she stands on his feet until he gets up.

RUN-ONS

Introductory Activity (117)

1. period
2. *but*
3. semicolon
4. *Although*

Practice 1 (120)

1. month. Its
2. porch. They
3. make. It
4. do. He
5. shirt. A
6. B.C. The
7. cheaply. She
8. desk. She
9. fireplace. The
10. traffic. Its

Practice 2 (121)

1. man. He
2. mailbox. Then
3. common. The
4. tiny. A
5. greyhound. It
6. Chinese. She
7. working. Its
8. lovely. It
9. drink. One
10. times. For

Practice 3 (121)

Answers will vary.

Practice 1 (123)

1. , but
2. , and
3. , and
4. , so
5. , but
6. , so
7. , for
8. , but
9. , so
10. , for

Practice 2 (124)

Answers will vary.

Practice (125)

1. dessert; I
2. ate; the
3. me; her
4. ground; old
5. queens; birth

Practice 1 (126)

Answers may vary.

1. drive; however, the
2. art; otherwise, it
3. gasoline; as a result, spectators (*or* thus *or* consequently *or* therefore)
4. started; however, all
5. feelers; consequently, they (*or* as a result *or* thus *or* therefore)

Practice 2 (127)

1. store; nevertheless, she
2. candy; as a result, he
3. strangers; however, he
4. schedule; otherwise, he
5. children; furthermore, she

Practice 1 (128)

1. since
2. Unless
3. because
4. After
5. although

Practice 2 (128)

Answers may vary.

1. Although I want to stop smoking, I don't want to gain weight.
2. Because it was too hot indoors to study, I decided to go down to the shopping center for ice cream.
3. While the puppy quickly ate, the baby watched with interest.
4. When the elderly woman smiled at me, her face broke into a thousand wrinkles.
5. Although this world map was published only three years ago, the names of some countries are already out of date.

SENTENCE VARIETY I

The Simple Sentence

Practice (136)

Answers will vary.

The Compound Sentence

Practice 1 (137)
Answers may vary; possible answers are given.
1. Cass tied the turkey carcass to a tree, and she watched the birds pick at bits of meat and skin.
2. I ran the hot water faucet for two minutes, but only cold water came out.
3. Nathan orders all his Christmas gifts through the Internet, for he dislikes shopping in crowded stores.
4. I need to buy a new set of tires, so I will read *Consumer Reports* to learn about various brands.
5. I asked Cecilia to go out with me on Saturday night, but she told me she'd rather stay home and watch TV.

Practice 2 (137)
Answers will vary.

The Complex Sentence

Practice 1 (139)
Answers may vary; possible answers are given.
1. When Cindy opened the cutlery drawer, a bee flew out.
2. Although I washed the windows thoroughly, they still looked dirty.
3. Because I never opened a book all semester, I guess I deserved to flunk.
4. When Manny gets up in the morning, he does stretching exercises for five minutes.
5. After my son spilled the pickle jar at dinner, I had to wash the kitchen floor.

Practice 2 (140)
Answers may vary; possible answers are given.
1. As Carlo set the table, his wife finished cooking dinner.
2. Although Maggie could have gotten good grades, she did not study enough.
3. After I watered my drooping African violets, they perked right up.
4. Though the little boy kept pushing the down button, the elevator didn't come any more quickly.
5. I never really knew what pain is until I had four impacted wisdom teeth pulled at once.

Practice 3 (141)
Answers may vary; possible answers are given.
1. Karen, who is an old friend of mine, just gave birth to twins.
2. The tea, which was hotter than I expected, burned the roof of my mouth.
3. I dropped the camera that my sister had just bought.
4. Ernie, who is visiting from California, brought us some enormous oranges.
5. Liz used a steam cleaner to shampoo her rugs, which were dirtier than she realized.

Practice 4 (142)

Answers will vary.

The Compound-Complex Sentence

Practice 1 (142)
Answers may vary.
1. After . . . for
2. When . . . but
3. when . . . and
4. Because . . . so
5. but . . . because

Practice 2 (142)
Answers will vary.

Review of Subordination and Coordination

Practice (143)
Answers will vary.
1. Though Sidney likes loud music, his parents can't stand it, so he wears earphones.
2. After the volcano erupted, the sky turned black with smoke. Nearby villagers were frightened, so they clogged the roads leading to safety.
3. After Glenda had a haircut today, she came home and looked in the mirror. Then she decided to wear a hat for a few days because she thought she looked like a bald eagle.
4. When I ran out of gas on the way to work, I discovered how helpful strangers can be. A passing driver saw I was stuck, so he drove me to the gas station and back to my car.

5. Our dog often rests on the floor in the sunshine while he waits for the children to get home from school. As the sunlight moves along the floor, he moves with it.

6. Because my father was going to be late from work, we planned to have a late dinner. But I was hungry before dinner, so I secretly ate a salami and cheese sandwich.

7. A baseball game was scheduled for early afternoon, but it looked like rain. So a crew rolled huge tarps to cover the field, and then the sun reappeared.

8. Cassy worries about the pesticides used on fruit, so she washes apples, pears, and plums in soap and water. Because she doesn't rinse them well, they have a soapy flavor.

9. Charlene needed to buy stamps, so she went to the post office during her lunch hour, when the line was long. After she waited there for half an hour, she had to go back to work without stamps.

10. After the weather suddenly became frigid, almost everyone at work caught a cold, so someone brought a big batch of chicken soup. She poured it into one of the office coffeepots, and the pot was empty by noon.

STANDARD ENGLISH VERBS

Introductory Activity (151)

played . . . plays
hoped . . . hopes
juggled . . . juggles

1. past time . . . -ed or -d
2. present time . . . -s

Practice 1 (153)

1. drives
2. gets
3. practices
4. makes
5. brushes
6. falls
7. C
8. comes
9. watches
10. buzzes

Practice 2 (153)

My little sister wants to be a singer when she grows up. She constantly hums and sings around the house. Sometimes she makes quite a racket. When she listens to music on the radio, for example, she sings very loudly in order to hear herself over the radio. And when she takes a shower, her voice rings through the whole house because she thinks nobody can hear her from there.

Practice 1 (154)

1. spilled
2. jailed
3. burned
4. tied
5. measured
6. C
7. smashed
8. constructed
9. leveled
10. realized

Practice 2 (155)

My cousin Joel completed a course in home repairs and offered one day to fix several things in my house. He repaired a screen door that squeaked, a dining room chair that wobbled a bit, and a faulty electrical outlet. That night when I opened the screen door, it loosened from its hinges. When I seated myself in the chair Joel had fixed, one of its legs cracked off. Remembering that Joel had also fooled around with the electrical outlet, I quickly called an electrician and asked him to stop by the next day. Then I prayed the house would not burn down before he arrived.

Practice 1 (157)

1. is
2. do
3. has
4. is
5. have
6. are
7. has
8. do
9. were
10. does

Practice 2 (158)

1. ~~does~~ do
2. ~~be~~ is
3. ~~be~~ are
4. ~~has~~ have
5. ~~were~~ was
6. ~~have~~ had
7. ~~was~~ were
8. ~~done~~ did
9. ~~do~~ does
10. ~~have~~ has

Practice 3 (158)

My cousin Rita has decided to lose thirty pounds, so she has put herself on a rigid diet that does not allow her to eat anything that she enjoys. Last weekend, while the family was at Aunt Jenny's house for dinner, all Rita had to eat was a can of Diet Delight peaches. We were convinced that Rita meant business when she joined an exercise club whose members have to work out on enormous machines and do twenty sit-ups just to get started. If Rita does reach her goal, we are all going to be very proud of her. But I would not be surprised if she does not succeed, because this is her fourth diet this year.

IRREGULAR VERBS

Introductory Activity (161)

1. *R* . . . screamed . . . screamed
2. *I* . . . wrote . . . written
3. *I* . . . stole . . . stolen
4. *R* . . . asked . . . asked
5. *R* . . . kissed . . . kissed
6. *I* . . . chose . . . chosen
7. *I* . . . rode . . . ridden
8. *R* . . . chewed . . . chewed
9. *I* . . . thought . . . thought
10. *R* . . . danced . . . danced

Practice 1 (165)

1.	came	6.	drove
2.	stood	7.	written
3.	built	8.	blew
4.	swum	9.	bought
5.	held	10.	knew

Practice 2 (165)

1.	(a) sleeps	6.	(a) buys
	(b) slept		(b) bought
	(c) slept		(c) bought
2.	(a) rings	7.	(a) choose
	(b) rang		(b) chose
	(c) rung		(c) chosen
3.	(a) write	8.	(a) eats
	(b) wrote		(b) ate
	(c) written		(c) eaten
4.	(a) stands	9.	(a) freezes
	(b) stood		(b) froze
	(c) stood		(c) frozen
5.	(a) swims	10.	(a) give
	(b) swam		(b) gave
	(c) swum		(c) given

Practice (168)

1.	lies	4.	laid
2.	Lying	5.	lay
3.	laid		

Practice (169)

1.	set	4.	Set
2.	sitting	5.	setting
3.	sat		

Practice (170)

1.	rises	4.	risen
2.	raised	5.	raise
3.	rose		

SUBJECT-VERB AGREEMENT

Introductory Activity (173)

Correct: The pictures in that magazine are very controversial.

Correct: There were many applicants for the job.

Correct: Everybody usually watches the lighted numbers in an elevator.

1. pictures . . . applicants   2. singular . . . singular

Practice (175)

1. trail ~~of bloodstains~~ leads
2. clothes ~~in the hall closet~~ take
3. basket ~~of fancy fruit and nuts~~ was
4. instructions ~~for assembling the bicycle~~ were
5. Smoke ~~from the distant forest fires~~ is
6. Workers ~~at that automobile plant~~ begin
7. date ~~on any of the cemetery gravestones~~ appears
8. line ~~of cars in the traffic jam~~ seems
9. boxes ~~in the corner of the attic~~ contain
10. bags ~~with the new insulation material~~ protect

Practice (176)

1.	is noise	6.	stands cutout
2.	are berries	7.	was shape
3.	were cans	8.	were sneakers
4.	sits cabin	9.	are magazines
5.	were students	10.	was row

Practice (177)

1.	keeps	6.	leans
2.	works	7.	expects
3.	pays	8.	was
4.	have	9.	stops
5.	slips	10.	has

Practice (178)

1.	sadden	4.	continue
2.	need	5.	tears
3.	have		

Practice (179)

1. has
2. goes
3. become
4. taste
5. are

CONSISTENT VERB TENSE

Introductory Activity (183)

Mistakes in verb tense: Alex discovers . . . calls . . . present . . . past

Practice (184)

1. rolled
2. purchased
3. stepped
4. crashed
5. snatched
6. covered
7. lifted
8. argues
9. swallowed
10. glowed

ADDITIONAL INFORMATION ABOUT VERBS

Tense

Practice (190)

1. had dried
2. had planned (*or* were planning)
3. is growing
4. had thrown
5. was carving (*or* had carved)
6. had opened
7. is caring
8. has watched
9. had walked
10. were trying

Verbals

Practice (191)

1. *P*
2. *G*
3. *I*
4. *G*
5. *P*
6. *I*
7. *G*
8. *I*
9. *P*
10. *P*

Active and Passive Verbs

Practice (193)

1. A man with a live parrot on his shoulder boarded the bus.
2. A large falling branch broke the stained-glass window.
3. The entire team autographed baseballs for hospitalized children.
4. A fire that started with a cigarette destroyed the hotel.
5. Doctors must face the pressures of dealing with life and death.
6. A sophisticated laser system directed the missile to its target.
7. A thick layer of yellowish grease covered the kitchen shelves.
8. A group of volunteers removed trash in the neighborhood park.
9. The state police captured most of the escaped convicts within a mile of the jail.
10. The judges awarded prizes for hog-calling and stone-skipping.

PRONOUN REFERENCE, AGREEMENT, AND POINT OF VIEW

Introductory Activity (195)

1. b
2. b
3. b

Practice (197)

Note   The practice sentences could be rewritten to have meanings other than the ones indicated below.

1. Fran removed the blanket from the sofa bed and folded the blanket up.
2. The defendant told the judge, "I am mentally ill."
3. Before the demonstration, the leaders passed out signs for us to carry.
4. Cindy complained to Rachel, "My (*or* Your) boyfriend is being dishonest."
5. Because I didn't rinse last night's dishes, my kitchen smells like a garbage can.
6. A film on endangered species really depressed the students.
   Or: Watching a film on endangered species really depressed the students.

7. The veterinarian said that if I find a tick on my dog, I should get rid of the tick immediately.

8. My sister removed the curtains from the windows so that she could wash the curtains.
   Or: So that she could wash the curtains, my sister removed them from the windows.
   Or: My sister removed the curtains from the windows so that she could wash the windows.
   Or: So that she could wash the windows, my sister removed the curtains from them.

9. Richard said his acupuncture therapist could help my sprained shoulder, but I don't believe in acupuncture.

10. I discovered when I went to sell my old textbooks that publishers have put out new editions, and nobody wants to buy my textbooks.
    Or: I discovered when I went to sell my old textbooks that nobody wants to buy them because publishers have put out new editions.

Practice (199)

1. they
2. their
3. it
4. them
5. their

Practice (201)

1. his
2. his
3. its
4. her
5. them
6. his or her
7. her
8. he
9. her
10. his or her

Practice (203)

1. my blood
2. they know
3. they have
4. they should receive
5. I can avoid
6. their hands
7. he can worry . . . his own
8. we could
9. she can still have . . . her day
10. our rights

PRONOUN TYPES

Introductory Activity (207)

Correct sentences:

Andy and I enrolled in a computer course.

The police officer pointed to my sister and me.

Lola prefers men who take pride in their bodies.

The players are confident that the league championship is theirs.

Those concert tickets are too expensive.

Our parents should spend some money on themselves for a change.

Practice 1 (210)

1. her (*O*)
2. She (*S*)
3. me (*O*)
4. her and me (*O*)
5. he (*S*)
6. I (*am* is understood) (*S*)
7. they (*S*)
8. me (*O*)
9. We (*S*)
10. I (*S*)

Practice 2 (211)
Answers will vary.
1. I
2. him *or* me
3. they
4. I *or* we
5. us
6. I *or* he *or* she *or* they *or* we
7. they *or* he *or* she
8. I *or* he *or* she *or* they *or* we
9. I *or* he *or* she *or* they *or* we
10. us *or* them

Practice 1 (213)

1. that
2. that
3. who
4. which
5. whom

Practice 2 (213)
Answers will vary.

Practice (214)

1. yours
2. his
3. theirs
4. your
5. mine

Practice 1 (216)

1.	This town	4. those candies
2.	those seats	5. those potholes
3.	That dress	

Practice 2 (216)
Answers will vary.

Practice (217)

1.	themselves	4. ourselves
2.	herself	5. themselves
3.	himself	

ADJECTIVES AND ADVERBS

Introductory Activity (221)
Answers will vary for 1–4.
Adjective . . . adverb . . . *ly . . . er . . . est*

Practice 1 (223)

tougher	toughest
more practical	most practical
quieter	quietest
more aggressive	most aggressive
clearer	clearest

Practice 2 (224)

1.	best	6. less
2.	dirtier	7. more stylish
3.	more considerate	8. sillier
4.	worse	9. slowest
5.	scariest	10. most fattening

Practice (225)

1.	badly	6. peacefully
2.	harshly	7. bright
3.	steep	8. loudly
4.	frequently	9. carefully
5.	truthfully	10. nicely

Practice (226)

1.	well	4. good
2.	good	5. well
3.	well	

MISPLACED MODIFIERS

Introductory Activity (229)

1. Intended: The farmers were wearing masks.
   Unintended: The apple trees were wearing masks.

2. Intended: The woman had a terminal disease.
   Unintended: The faith healer had a terminal disease.

Practice 1 (230)

Note   In each of the corrections below, the underlined part shows what was the misplaced modifier.

1. At the back of his cage, the tiger growled at a passerby.
2. Lee hung colorful scarves made of green and blue silk over her windows.
3. Standing on our front porch, we watched the fireworks.
4. Jason has almost two hundred baseball cards.
5. With a smile, the salesclerk exchanged the blue sweater for a yellow one.
6. We all stared at the man with curly purple hair in the front row of the theater.
7. I love the cookies with the chocolate frosting from the bakery.
8. During their last meeting, the faculty decided to strike.
9. Larry looked on with disbelief as his car burned.
10. My cousin sent me instructions in a letter on how to get to her house.

Practice 2 (232)

1. My mother sat lazily with a glass of lemonade in the hot sun, watching her grandchildren play.
2. My father agreed over the phone to pay for the car repairs.
   Or: Over the phone, my father agreed to pay for the car repairs.
3. I found a note from Jeff on the kitchen bulletin board.
4. The fires destroyed almost the entire forest.
5. During class, Jon read about how the American Revolution began.
   Or: Jon read during class about how the American Revolution began.

DANGLING MODIFIERS

Introductory Activity (235)

1. Intended: The giraffe was munching leaves from a tall tree.
    Unintended: The children were munching leaves.
2. Intended: Michael was arriving home after ten months in the army.
    Unintended: The neighbors were arriving home after ten months in the army.

Practice 1 (237)

Wording of answers may vary slightly.

1. A security guard pointed to the priceless painting that was hanging safely on a wall.
2. When I was five, my mother bought me a chemistry set.
3. C
4. Since the milk had turned sour, I would not drink it.
5. While I was talking on the phone, my hot tea turned cold.
6. Pete hated to look at the kitchen sink, which was piled high with dirty dishes.
7. Because I locked my keys in the car, the police had to open it for me.
8. Because the plants were drooping and looking all dried out, the children watered them.
9. After I sat through a long lecture, my foot was asleep.
10. Since I was late, stopping for coffee was out of the question.

Practice 2 (238)

Answers will vary.

FAULTY PARALLELISM

Introductory Activity (241)

Correct sentences:

I use my TV remote control to change channels, to adjust the volume, and to turn the set on and off.

One option the employees had was to take a cut in pay; the other was to work longer hours.

The refrigerator has a cracked vegetable drawer, a missing shelf, and a strange freezer smell.

Practice 1 (243)

2.	howling dogs	7.	having fun
3.	rude	8.	inexpensive desserts
4.	hiking	9.	on the closet floor
5.	poor security	10.	sings in the church choir
6.	cleaned the apartment		

Practice 2 (243)

1.	waited	6.	to suffocate
2.	cramming	7.	interrupted
3.	illness	8.	financial security
4.	late buses	9.	birds chirping
5.	attracting	10.	breathed fire

Practice 3 (244)

Answers will vary.

SENTENCE VARIETY II

-ing Word Groups

Practice 1 (251)

Answers will vary.

1. Picking up their cameras, the tourists began to leave the bus.
2. Jogging on the street, I was almost hit by a car.
3. Wincing with pain, Barbara untangled her snarled hair from the brush.
4. Waving her arms at the excited crowd, the singer ran to the front of the stage.
5. Losing by one point with thirty seconds left to play, the team braced itself for a last-ditch effort.

Practice 2 (252)

Answers will vary.

-ed Word Groups

Practice 1 (253)

Answers will vary.

1. Mary, startled by a thunderclap, sat up suddenly in bed.
2. Married for fifty years, my parents decided to have a second wedding.
3. Frightened by the large dog near the curb, Erica wouldn't leave her car.

4. Dotted with mold, the old orange felt like a marshmallow.

5. Ernie, determined to have plenty to eat during the movie, made a huge sandwich and popped popcorn.

Practice 2 (253)

Answers will vary.

-ly Openers

Practice 1 (254)

1. Noisily, we ate raw carrots and celery sticks.
2. Gently, Cliff spoke to his sobbing little brother.
3. Tenderly, the father picked up his baby daughter.
4. Anxiously, I paced up and down the hospital corridor.
5. Frantically, Anita repeatedly dived into the pool to find her engagement ring.

Practice 2 (255)

Answers will vary.

To Openers

Practice 1 (255)

1. To make the tub less slippery, Sally put a thick towel on the bottom.
2. To keep raccoons away, we now keep our garbage in the garage.
3. To count his pulse, Bill pressed two fingers against the large vein in his neck.
4. To steam her face, my aunt opens her dishwasher when it begins drying.
5. To help out the homeless, we looked through our closets for unused clothing.

Practice 2 (256)

Answers will vary.

Prepositional Phrase Openers

Practice 1 (257)

Answers will vary.

1. About once a week, we have dinner with my parents at a restaurant.
2. Before company came, I put the dirty cups away in the cupboard.

3. During my English exam, my eyes roamed around the room until they met the instructor's eye.
4. For twenty minutes, the little boy drew intently in a comic book without stopping once.
5. At the zoo, a playful young orangutan wriggled in a corner under a paper sack.

Practice 2 (258)

Answers will vary.

Series of Items: Adjectives

Practice 1 (259)

1. The old, peeling shingles blew off the roof during the blustery storm.
2. The lean, powerful dancer whirled across the stage with his graceful, elegant partner.
3. A large, furry rat scurried into the crowded kitchen of the restaurant.
4. The full, golden moon lit up the cloudy sky like a huge floating street lamp.
5. The oval plastic doorbell of the large, ornate house played a loud rock tune.

Practice 2 (260)

Answers will vary.

Series of Items: Verbs

Practice 1 (260)

1. The flea-ridden dog rubbed itself against the fence, bit its tail, and scratched its neck with its hind leg.
2. I put my homework on the table, made a cup of coffee, and turned the radio up full blast.
3. The driver stopped the school bus, walked to the back, and separated two children.
4. I rolled up my sleeve, glanced at the nurse nervously, shut my eyes, and waited for the worst to be over.
5. The parents applauded politely at the program's end, looked at their watches, exchanged looks of relief, and reached for their coats.

Practice 2 (261)

Answers will vary.

PAPER FORMAT

Introductory Activity (265)

In "A," the title is capitalized and has no quotation marks around it; there is a blank line between the title and the body of the paper; there are left and right margins around the body of the paper; no words are incorrectly hyphenated.

Practice 1 (267)

2. Do not use quotation marks around the title.
3. Capitalize the major words in the title ("Being a Younger Sister").
4. Skip a line between the title and first line of the paper.
5. Indent the first line of the paper.
6. Keep margins on both sides of the paper.

Practice 2 (267)

Answers may vary slightly.
1. Benefits of Pets
2. Learning How to Budget
3. The Value of a Study Group
4. A Special Relationship *or* Grandparents and Grandchildren
5. A Wise Decision

Practice 3 (268)

Answers may vary slightly.
1. The best children's television shows educate while they entertain, and they are not violent.
2. Women have made many gains in the workplace in the last decade.
3. The generation gap results from differing experiences of various age groups.
4. Correct
5. One of my important accomplishments was to finish high school despite my parents' divorce.

CAPITAL LETTERS

Introductory Activity (271)

1–13: Answers will vary, but all should be capitalized.
14–16: On . . . "Let's . . . I

Practice (274)

1. I . . . Boy Scouts
2. Friday . . . Thanksgiving . . . Target

3. Regal Cinema . . . If
4. New England . . . Republicans . . . Democrats
5. State Farm . . . Nationwide . . . Prudential Building
6. *Time . . . Newsweek* . . . California
7. Valentine's Day . . . Mother's Day
8. Pepsis . . . Fritos . . . Macintosh
9. Ford Taurus . . . Saturday
10. Broadway . . . *My Fair Lady*

Practice (277)

1. Hundred Years' War
2. Aunt Sophie . . . Polish
3. Independence Hall . . . Liberty Bell
4. World History . . . Middle Ages
5. Cuban . . . Spanish . . . Hispanic

Practice (277)

1. grandmother . . . spaghetti . . . meatballs
2. high school . . . basketball coach
3. shop . . . fashion magazines
4. parents' groups . . . ads . . . maniac
5. manager . . . restaurant . . . dessert

NUMBERS AND ABBREVIATIONS

Introductory Activity (283)

Correct choices:

First sentence: 8:55 . . . 65 percent
Second sentence: Nine . . . forty-five

Second sentence: brothers . . . mountain
Second sentence: hours . . . English

Practice (284)

1. 6:15
2. nine o'clock
3. July 28, 2004
4. six
5. 1600 Pennsylvania Avenue
6. Forty-three
7. $930.20
8. 60 . . . 64
9. 27 . . . 52
10. 50 percent

Practice (286)

1. newspaper . . . telephone
2. bushels . . . market . . . Route
3. Monday . . . September
4. psychology . . . England
5. chicken . . . macaroni
6. ounce . . . tablespoon
7. chemistry . . . Sunday . . . hours
8. January . . . company . . . year
9. license . . . medical
10. veteran . . . business . . . college

END MARKS

Introductory Activity (289)

1. depressed.
2. paper?
3. parked.
4. control!

Practice (291)

1. drown?
2. redhead.
3. me.
4. it!"
5. "vidiots."
6. accurate.
7. life?
8. truck!"
9. forward?"
10. married.

APOSTROPHE

Introductory Activity (293)

1. In each case, the *'s* indicates possession or ownership.
2. The apostrophes indicate omitted letters and shortened spellings.
3. In the first sentence, *s* indicates a plural noun; in the second sentence, *'s* indicates possession.

Apostrophe in Contractions

Practice 1 (294)

you've	we're	couldn't
haven't	you'll	they'll
he's	we'd	doesn't

Practice 2 (295)

1. didn't . . . wasn't
2. doesn't . . . she's
3. You're . . . can't
4. isn't . . . you've
5. We'd . . . don't

Practice 3 (295)

Answers will vary.

Practice (296)

1. It's . . . your
2. whose . . . who's
3. You're . . . your
4. There . . . their
5. It's . . . their

Apostrophe to Show Ownership or Possession

Practice 1 (297)

1. singer's voice
2. Dawn's garage
3. Murphy's law
4. computer's memory
5. my wife's mother
6. yesterday's meat loaf
7. My sister's promotion
8. Alexis's bratty little brother
9. the referee's call
10. the tanker's hull

Practice 2 (298)

1. horse's
2. brother's
3. son's
4. comedian's
5. landlord's
6. Ted's
7. teller's
8. people's
9. studio's
10. girl's

Practice 3 (299)

Sentences will vary.

2. teacher's
3. insect's
4. husband's
5. salesperson's

Practice (300)

1. parlors: parlor's, meaning "belonging to the parlor"
    aromas: simple plural meaning more than one aroma
    vents: simple plural meaning more than one vent
2. cars: car's, meaning "belonging to the car"
    streets: simple plural meaning more than one street
    buildings: simple plural meaning more than one building
3. Karens: Karen's, meaning "belonging to Karen"
    plants: simple plural meaning more than one plant
    stakes: simple plural meaning more than one stake
4. lakes: lake's, meaning "belonging to the lake"
    officials: simple plural meaning more than one official
5. positions: simple plural meaning more than one position
    exterminators: exterminator's, meaning "belonging to an exterminator"
6. candlelights: candlelight's, meaning "belonging to the candlelight"
    plates: simple plural meaning more than one plate
    goblets: simple plural meaning more than one goblet
7. Crackers: simple plural meaning more than one cracker
    slices: simple plural meaning more than one slice
    fathers: father's, meaning "belonging to my father"
8. insects: insect's, meaning "belonging to the insect"
    eggs: simple plural meaning more than one egg
    worms: simple plural meaning more than one worm
9. Seabirds: simple plural meaning more than one seabird
    oceans: ocean's, meaning "belonging to the ocean"
    surfers: simple plural meaning more than one surfer
10. daughters: daughter's, meaning "belonging to my daughter"
    prayers: simple plural meaning more than one prayer
    schools: simple plural meaning more than one school

Practice (302)

1. nurses' union
2. sisters' feet
3. lions' keeper
4. Tylers' new television set
5. parents' wedding pictures

QUOTATION MARKS

Introductory Activity (307)

1. Quotation marks set off the exact words of a speaker.
2. Commas and periods following quotations go inside quotation marks.

Practice 1 (309)

1. The chilling bumper sticker read, "You can't hug children with nuclear arms."
2. "One day we'll look back on this argument, and it will seem funny," Bruce assured Rosa.
3. "Hey, lady, this is an express line!" shouted the cashier to the woman with a full basket.
4. My grandfather was fond of saying, "Happiness is found along the way, not at the end of the road."
5. "When will I be old enough to pay the adult fare?" the child asked.
6. On his deathbed, Oscar Wilde is supposed to have said, "Either this wallpaper goes or I do."
7. The sign on my neighbor's front door reads, "Never mind the dog. Beware of owner."
8. "I'm not afraid to die," said Woody Allen. "I just don't want to be there when it happens."
9. My son once told me, "Sometimes I wish I were little again. Then I wouldn't have to make so many decisions."
10. "I don't feel like cooking tonight," Eve said to Adam. "Let's just have fruit."

Practice 2 (309)

1. Simon said, "Take three giant steps forward."
2. "Please don't hang up before leaving a message," stated the telephone recording.
3. Clark Kent asked a man on the street, "Where is the nearest phone booth?"
4. "You dirtied every pan in the kitchen just to scramble some eggs," Rico said in disgust.
5. "Nothing can be done for your broken little toe," the doctor said. "You have to wait for it to heal."

Practice 3 (310)

Answers will vary.

Practice 1 (311)

2. I said, "That's hard to believe, since Herb is a do-nothing."
3. Agnes replied, "Even so, he's gone up in the world."
4. I told her, "You must be kidding."
5. Agnes laughed and said, "Herb was moved from the first to the fourth floor today."

Practice 2 (312)

1. My doctor said that I need to lose weight.
2. Lola asked Tony if he ever washes his car.
3. The police officer asked if I knew how fast I was going.

4. Janie whispered that Harold's so boring he lights up a room when he leaves it.

5. The instructor said that movies are actually a series of still pictures.

Practice (313)

1. My sister just bought a VCR so she won't have to miss any more episodes of <u>General Hospital</u>.

2. Rita grabbed the <u>National Enquirer</u> and eagerly began to read the article "I Had a Space Alien's Baby."

3. Our exam will cover two chapters, "The Study of Heredity" and "The Origin of Diversity," in our biology textbook, <u>Life</u>.

4. The last song on the bluegrass program was called "I Ain't Broke but I'm Badly Bent."

5. The classic 1980s movie <u>Stand By Me</u> was actually based on "The Body," a short story written by Stephen King.

6. At last night's performance of <u>Annie Get Your Gun</u>, the audience joined the cast in singing "There's No Business Like Show Business."

7. A typical article in <u>Cosmopolitan</u> will have a title like "How to Hook a Man without Letting Him Know You're Fishing."

8. One way Joanne deals with depression is to get out her <u>Man of La Mancha</u> album and play the song "The Impossible Dream."

9. I read the article "How Good Is Your Breakfast?" in <u>Consumer Reports</u> while munching a doughnut this morning.

10. According to a <u>Psychology Today</u> article titled "Home on the Street," there are 36,000 people living on New York City's sidewalks.

COMMA

Introductory Activity (319)

1. a: card, . . . check, . . . ; ants, roaches,

2. b: car, . . . ; hiking,

3. c: leeches, . . . blood, . . . ; Derek, . . . arrested,

4. d: easy, . . . ; trees,

5. e: asked, . . . ; work, . . . said,

6. f: 1,500,000; Newark, New Jersey, . . . August 26, 2004,

Practice 1 (321)

1. work, food, or a place to live

2. Ice cream, crushed candy, Pepsi, and popcorn

3. eight hours, four hundred miles, and three rest stops

Practice 2 (321)

1. pennies, and a sock hidden under the seats

2. Squirrels, . . . and clouds of mosquitoes populate

3. spun to his left, . . . arms of the Panthers' center

Practice 1 (322)

1. done,   2. tape,   3. time,

Practice 2 (322)

1. presents, . . . ribbon and tied

2. aisle, I saw a bead of sweat roll from her forehead

3. For example, I wrote a note to remind me that

Practice 1 (323)

1. dancer, aided by members of the chorus,

2. Anderson, who were married on the Fourth of July,

3. repairman, unaware of the grease on his shoes,

Practice 2 (324)

1. gigantic, . . . the rest is deadwood

2. council, in a rare fit of wisdom

3. presidents of the United States,

4. aunt, a talkative woman,

Practice (325)

1. spacious, but
2. thunderstorm, so
3. C
4. space, for
5. C
6. supermarket, but
7. C
8. college, but
9. schoolwork, but
10. C

Practice 1 (326)

1. said,

2. temptation," Oscar Wilde advised,

3. family,"

Practice 2 (326)

1. poster in the subway station,

2. fine," . . . forgetting to kick."

3. think," the judge asked the defendant,

Practice (327)

1. me, madam,
2. 6,000 . . . 15,000
3. 15, 1912.
4. Teresa, . . . Love,
5. Washington, D.C., . . . 50,000 . . . 6,500

Practice (328)

1. We grew a pumpkin last year that weighed over one hundred pounds.
2. Anyone with a failing grade must report to the principal.
3. Last weekend a grizzly bear attacked a hiker who got too close to its cubs.
4. After watching my form on the high diving board, Mr. Riley, my instructor, asked me if I had insurance.
5. Rosa flew first to Los Angeles, and then she went to visit her parents in Mexico City.
6. The tall muscular man wearing the dark sunglasses is a professional wrestler.
7. Onions, radishes, and potatoes seem to grow better in cooler climates.
8. Whenever Vincent is in Las Vegas, you can find him at the blackjack table or the roulette wheel.
9. While I watched in disbelief, my car rolled down the hill and through the front window of a Chinese restaurant.
10. The question, sir, is not whether you committed the crime but when you committed the crime.

OTHER PUNCTUATION MARKS

Introductory Activity (333)

1. list:
2. life-size
3. (1856–1939)
4. track;
5. breathing—but alive

Practice (334)

1. diet:
2. summer:
3. columns:

Practice (335)

1. night; consequently,
2. raining; all
3. vegetarian; my . . . diabetic; and

Practice (336)

1. sea—shivering
2. —her third in three years—
3. time—eight

Practice (337)

1. slow-moving . . . no-passing
2. sugar-free . . . double-cheese
3. hard-hearted . . . teary-eyed

Practice (337)

1. Americans (80 percent) had
2. hours (3 to 4 P.M.) are
3. often (1) make a list and then (2) check off items I have done.

DICTIONARY USE

Introductory Activity (339)

1. fortutious (fortuitous)
2. hi/er/o/glyph/ics
3. be
4. oc/to/ge/nar'/i/an (primary accent is on *nar*)
5. (1) identifying mark on the ear of a domestic animal
   (2) identifying feature or characteristic

Answers to the practice activities are in your dictionary. Check with your instructor if you have any problems.

SPELLING IMPROVEMENT

Introductory Activity (349)

Misspellings:

akward . . . exercize . . . buisness . . . worried . . .
shamful . . . begining . . . partys . . . sandwichs . . .
heros

Practice (352)

1. hurried
2. admiring
3. denies
4. jabbing
5. magnified
6. committed
7. diving
8. hastily
9. propelling
10. nudges

Practice (353)

1. buses
2. groceries
3. potatoes
4. taxis
5. themselves
6. theories
7. passersby
8. alumni
9. sandwiches
10. mice

OMITTED WORDS AND LETTERS

Introductory Activity (359)

bottles . . . in the supermarket . . . like a wind-up toy . . .
his arms . . . an alert shopper . . . with the crying

Practice (360)

1. I grabbed a metal bar on the roof of the subway car as the train lurched into the station.

2. For most of our country's history, gold was the basis of the monetary system.

3. Maggie made about a quart of French-toast batter— enough to soak a few dozen slices.

4. Several pairs of sneakers tumbled around in the dryer and banged against the glass door.

5. To err is human and to forgive is divine, but never to make a mistake in the first place takes a lot of luck.

6. Raccoons like to wash their food in a stream with their nimble, glove-like hands before eating.

7. When I got to the grocery store, I realized I had left my shopping list in the glove compartment of my car.

8. Game shows are an inexpensive way for networks to make a high profit.

9. Soap operas, on the other hand, are very expensive to produce because of the high salaries of many cast members.

10. One memorable Friday the thirteenth, a friend of mine bought a black cat, broke a mirror, and walked under a ladder. He had a wonderful day!

Practice 1 (361)

1. sightseers . . . ghouls
2. sets . . . names
3. Dozens . . . beetles
4. dentists . . . restaurants . . . lines
5. workers . . . departments
6. lights . . . games . . . cars . . . persons
7. games . . . balls
8. shoes . . . jeans . . . months
9. stamps . . . pens
10. Workers . . . logs . . . chunks . . . chips

Practice 2 (362)

Answers will vary.

COMMONLY CONFUSED WORDS

Introductory Activity (365)

1. Incorrect: your   Correct: you're
2. Incorrect: who's   Correct: whose
3. Incorrect: there   Correct: their
4. Incorrect: to   Correct: too
5. Incorrect: Its   Correct: It's

Homonyms (366–374)

Sentences will vary.

all ready . . . already
break . . . brake
course . . . coarse
here . . . hear
whole . . . hole
its . . . it's
new . . . knew
know . . . no
pair . . . pear
passed . . . past
peace . . . piece
plain . . . plane
principal . . . principle
right . . . write
then . . . than
there . . . their . . . they're

through . . . threw

two . . . too . . . to

where . . . wear

weather . . . whether

who's . . . whose

you're . . . your

Other Words Frequently Confused (375–379)

Sentences will vary.

an . . . a

except . . . accept

advice . . . advise

affect . . . effect

Among . . . between

beside . . . besides

can . . . may

cloths . . . clothes

desert . . . dessert

dose . . . does

fewer . . . less

former . . . latter

learn . . . teach

loose . . . lose

quite . . . quiet

though . . . thought

Incorrect Word Forms (380–381)

being that (380)

1. Since (*or* Because) our stove doesn't work
2. since (*or* because) they don't speak to each other
3. since (*or* because) it's my birthday

can't hardly/couldn't hardly (380)

1. I can hardly
2. James could hardly
3. You could hardly

could of (381)

1. you could have
2. you could have
3. I could have

irregardless (381)

1. Regardless of your feelings
2. regardless of the weather
3. regardless of age

must of/should of/would of (381)

1. I must have
2. he would have
3. You should have

EFFECTIVE WORD CHOICE

Introductory Activity (385)

Correct sentences:
1. After a disappointing movie, we devoured a pizza.
2. Mourning the death of his best friend, Tennyson wrote the moving poem "In Memoriam."
3. Psychological tests will be given on Wednesday in the Student Center.
4. I think the referee made the right decision.
    1 . . . 2 . . . 3 . . . 4

Practice (387)

Answers may vary.
1. If you keep overeating, you're going to be fat.
2. My parents always refuse when I ask them for some money to buy new CDs.
3. The entire city was excited when the basketball team beat its opponent in the playoffs.
4. If Ellen would get less serious and stop talking about her troubles, a date with her wouldn't be so depressing.
5. I'm going to have to wait anxiously for the next couple of days, hoping the boss doesn't discover the mistake I made.

Practice 1 (389)

Answers will vary.
1. Substitute In brief for To make a long story short.
2. Substitute Very quickly for As quick as a wink.
3. Substitute is ignored for goes in one ear and out the other.
4. Substitute was delighted for felt like a million dollars.
5. Substitute rare for few and far between.

Practice 2 (389)

Answers will vary.

Practice (390)

1. Please ask one of our salespeople.
2. The weather is terrible today.
3. My parents want me to get a college degree.
4. Do not put your arm out of the car, or an accident might happen.
5. Many fires are caused by the careless use of portable heaters.

Practice (392)

1. There is no cure for the common cold.
2. My main point is that our state should legalize gambling.
3. Because Chen's car wouldn't start, he took a bus to work.
4. Even when I was a boy, my goal was to be a stockbroker.
5. Susan's daily exercises energize her.

Note   The above answers are examples of how the clichés could be corrected. Other answers are possible.

Progress Charts

Progress Charts for Mastery Tests

Enter Your Score for Each Test in the Space Provided

Individual Tests	1 Mastery	2 Mastery	3 Mastery	4 Mastery	5 IM	6 IM
Subjects and Verbs						▓
Fragments						
Run-Ons						
Sentence Variety I			▓	▓		
Standard English Verbs						
Irregular Verbs						
Subject-Verb Agreement						
Consistent Verb Tense			▓	▓		▓
Additional Information about Verbs	▓	▓	▓	▓		
Pronoun Reference, Agreement, and Point of View						▓
Pronoun Types			▓	▓		▓
Adjectives and Adverbs			▓	▓		▓
Misplaced Modifiers			▓	▓		▓
Dangling Modifiers			▓	▓		▓

Individual Tests Continued	1 Mastery	2 Mastery	3 Mastery	4 Mastery	5 IM	6 IM
Faulty Parallelism						
Sentence Variety II						
Capital Letters						
Numbers and Abbreviations						
End Marks						
Apostrophe						
Quotation Marks						
Comma						
Other Punctuation Marks						
Dictionary Use						
Spelling Improvement						
Omitted Words and Letters						
Commonly Confused Words						
Effective Word Choice						

Combined Tests	1 Mastery	2 Mastery	3 Mastery	4 Mastery	5 IM	6 IM
Fragments and Run-Ons						
Verbs						
Pronouns						
Faulty Modifiers and Parallelism						
Capital Letters and Punctuation						
Word Use						

Progress Chart for Editing and Proofreading Tests

Date	Step	Comments	To Do Next	Instructor's Initials
9/27	1A	Missed —ing frag; 3 copying mistakes	1B	JL
9/27	1B	No Mistakes—Good job!	2A	JL

Date	Step	Comments	To Do Next	Instructor's Initials

Progress Chart for Combined Editing Tests

Enter Your Score for Each Test in the Space Provided

Combined Test 1		Combined Test 11	
Combined Test 2		Combined Test 12	
Combined Test 3		Combined Test 13	
Combined Test 4		Combined Test 14	
Combined Test 5		Combined Test 15	
Combined Test 6		Combined Test 16	
Combined Test 7		Combined Test 17	
Combined Test 8		Combined Test 18	
Combined Test 9		Combined Test 19	
Combined Test 10		Combined Test 20	

Progress Chart for Writing Assignments

Date	Paper	Comments	To Do Next
10/15	Worst job	Promising but needs more support. Also, 2 frags and 2 run-ons.	Rewrite

Date	Paper	Comments	To Do Next

Credits

The American Heritage Dictionary, 4th edition, Copyright © 2001. The entry for *dictate* and the pronunciation key are reprinted with permission of Houghton Mifflin Company.

Berry, Grant, "A Change in Attitude." Copyright © 1995 by Townsend Press. Reprinted by permission.

Buscaglia, Leo, "Papa," from *Papa, My Father.* Copyright © 1980 by Leo F. Buscaglia, Inc. Reprinted by permission.

Carson, Ben, M.D., and Cecil Murphey, "Do It Better!" from *Think Big.* Copyright © 1996 by Zondervan Publishing House.

Johnson, Beth, "Let's Get Specific." Copyright © 1995 by Townsend Press. Reprinted with permission.

Kowal, Paul, of Cherry Hill, New Jersey. Photographs of Benjamin Carson on page 569 and Regina Ruiz on pages 576–578.

Lopez, Steve, "A Small Victory," from *The Philadelphia Inquirer.* Copyright © 1990 by The Philadelphia Inquirer. Reprinted with permission of The Philadelphia Inquirer.

Marcus, Larry, of Minneapolis, Minnesota. Photographs of Grant Berry on pages 553 and 556.

Mrosla, Sister Helen P., "All the Good Things." Originally published in Proteus, Spring 1991. Reprinted by permission as edited and published by *Reader's Digest* in October, 1991.

Office of Communications and Public Affairs, Johns Hopkins Children's Center, Baltimore, Maryland. Photographs of Benjamin Carson on pages 563 and 566.

Peck, Scott M., M.D., "Responsibility," from *The Road Less Traveled.* Copyright © 1978, Reprinted with permission of Simon and Schuster Adult Publishing Group.

Index

D

E

Editing and proofreading tests, 489–514
Editing tests, combined, 515–537
Effect, affect, 375–376
End marks:
   exclamation point, 291
   period, 290
   question mark, 290
Endings, dropped:
   on nouns, 361–362
   on verbs, 152–153
ESL pointers, 653–666
Essay, definition of, 26
Essays, writing, 26–36
   assignments, 80–84
   central idea of, 27
   with a computer, 34–36
   conclusion, 27, 31–32
   difference between paragraph and, 26–27
   introduction, 27, 28–31
   parts of, 27, 28–32, 73–75
     concluding paragraph, 27, 31–32,
       73–75
     introductory paragraph, 27, 28–31,
       73–75
     supporting paragraphs, 27, 31
   plan of development in, 65–66
   practice in, 65–75
   specific details in:
     providing, 68–70
     recognizing, 66–68
   support, 27, 31
   thesis statement in, 27, 29–30
   transitions in, 70–73
Evidence, specific, 12
Except, accept, 375
Exclamation point, 291

F

Fewer, less, 378
For as coordinating word, 119, 122, 136, 143,
   649–650
Format, paper, 265–269
Former, latter, 378

Fragments, sentence, 97–115
   added-detail, 105–107
   dependent-word, 98–102
   -ing and *to,* 102–105
   missing-subject, 108–115
Freewriting, 17
   activity in, 75
Fused sentences, 118

G

General versus specific, 39–44
Gerund, 191, 659–661
Goals of effective writing, 13–16
   how to reach, 16–26
Good, well, 225–226

H

Have verbs, 156
Hear, here, 367
Helping verbs, 188–190
Here at the beginning of clauses, 659
Here, hear, 367
Hole, whole, 368
Homonyms, 366
Hyphen, 336–337
Hyphenation, 336–337, 341

I

Incorrect word forms, 380–381
Indirect quotation, 311–312
Infinitive, 191, 255–256, 659–662
-ing and *to* fragments, 102–105
Interjections, 652
Interrupters, commas with, 322–324
Introduction, of an essay, 28–31
   activities in, 73–75
   four common methods of, 29–31
Introductory material, comma after, 321–322

T

U

V

W

Y